A Kodansha Comics Trade Paperback Original
Boys Run the Riot 3 copyright © 2020 Keito Gaku
English translation copyright © 2021 Keito Gaku

Published in the United States by Kodansha Comics, an imprint of Kodansha USA Publishing, LLC, New York.

Publication rights for this English edition arranged through Kodansha Ltd., Tokyo.

First published in Japan in 2020 by Kodansha Ltd., Tokyo as *Boys Run the Riot*, volume 3.

ISBN 978-1-64651-119-8

Printed in the United States of America.

www.kodansha.us

9 8 7 6 5 4 3 2 1
Translation: Leo McDonagh
Lettering: Ashley Caswell
Editing: Tiff Joshua TJ Ferentini
Kodansha Comics edition cover design by Phil Balsman

Publisher: Kiichiro Sugawara

Director of publishing services: Ben Applegate
Associate director of operations: Stephen Pakula
Publishing services managing editors: Alanna Ruse, Madison Salters
Assistant production managers: Emi Lotto, Angela Zurlo
Logo and character art ©Kodansha USA Publishing, LLC

THE SWEET SCENT OF LOVE IS IN THE AIR! FOR FANS OF OFFBEAT ROMANCES LIKE *WOTAKOI*

Sweat and Soap © Kintetsu Yamada / Kodansha Ltd.

In an office romance, there's a fine line between sexy and awkward... and that line is where Asako — a woman who sweats copiously — meets Koutarou — a perfume developer who can't get enough of Asako's, er, scent. Don't miss a romcom manga like no other!

One of CLAMP's biggest hits returns
in this definitive, premium, hardcover
20th anniversary collector's edition!

"A wonderfully
entertaining story
that would be a great
installment in anybody's
manga collection."
— Anime News Network

"CLAMP is an all-female
manga-creating
team whose feminine
touch shows in this
entertaining, sci-fi soap
opera."
— Publishers Weekly

Poor college student Hideki is down on his luck. All he wants is a
good job, a girlfriend, and his very own "persocom"—the latest
and greatest in humanoid computer technology. Hideki's luck
changes one night when he finds Chi—a persocom thrown out in
a pile of trash. But Hideki soon discovers that there's much more
to his cute new persocom than meets the eye.

KC
KODANSHA
COMICS

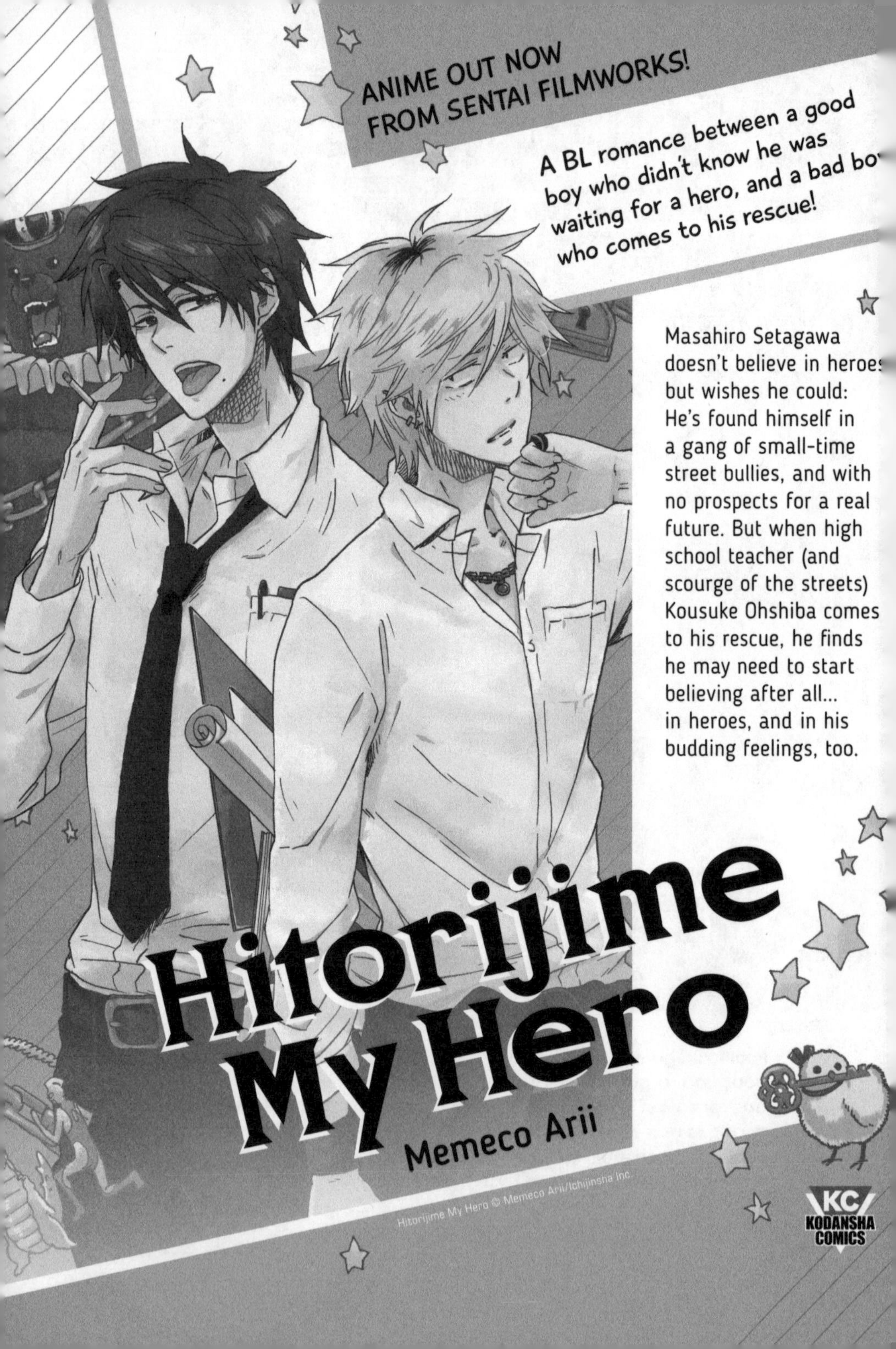
ANIME OUT NOW FROM SENTAI FILMWORKS!
A BL romance between a good boy who didn't know he was waiting for a hero, and a bad bo who comes to his rescue!
Masahiro Setagawa doesn't believe in heroes but wishes he could: He's found himself in a gang of small-time street bullies, and with no prospects for a real future. But when high school teacher (and scourge of the streets) Kousuke Ohshiba comes to his rescue, he finds he may need to start believing after all... in heroes, and in his budding feelings, too.
Hitorijime My Hero
Memeco Arii
Hitorijime My Hero © Memeco Arii/Ichijinsha Inc.
KC
KODANSHA COMICS

The slow-burn queer romance that'll sweep you off your feet!

10 DANCE

Inouesatoh presents

"A FANTASTIC DEBUT VOLUME... ONE OF MY FAVORITE BOOKS OF THE YEAR..."
— AiPT!

"10 DANCE IS A MUST-READ FOR ANYONE WHO'S ENJOYED MANGA AND ANIME ABOUT COMPETITIVE DANCE (ON OR OFF THE ICE!)."
—Anime UK News

Shinya Sugiki, the dashing lord of Standard Ballroom, and Shinya Suzuki, passionate king of Latin Dance: The two share more than just a first name and a love of the sport. They each want to become champion of the 10-Dance Competition, which means they'll need to learn the other's specialty dances, and who better to learn from than the best? But old rivalries die hard, and things get further complicated when they realize there might be more between them than an uneasy partnership...

KC KODANSHA COMICS

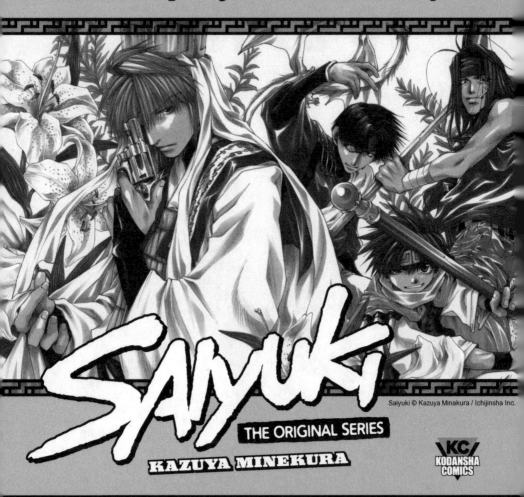

"Clever, sassy, and original....*xxxHOLiC* has the inherent hallmarks of a runaway hit."
—NewType magazine

Beautifully seductive artwork and uniquely Japanese depictions of the supernatural will hypnotize CLAMP fans!

Kimihiro Watanuki is haunted by visions of ghosts and spirits. He seeks help from a mysterious woman named Yuko, who claims she can help. However, Watanuki must work for Yuko in order to pay for her aid. Soon Watanuki finds himself employed in Yuko's shop, where he sees things and meets customers that are stranger than anything he could have ever imagined.

KC
KODANSHA COMICS

A SMART, NEW ROMANTIC COMEDY FOR FANS OF *SHORTCAKE CAKE* AND *TERRACE HOUSE!*

LIVING-ROOM

MATSUNAGA-SAN

Keiko Iwashita

KC KODANSHA COMICS

A romance manga starring high school girl Meeko, who learns to live on her own in a boarding house whose living room is home to the odd (but handsome) Matsunaga-san. She begins to adjust to her new life away from her parents, but Meeko soon learns that no matter how far away from home she is, she's still a young girl at heart — especially when she finds herself falling for Matsunaga-san.

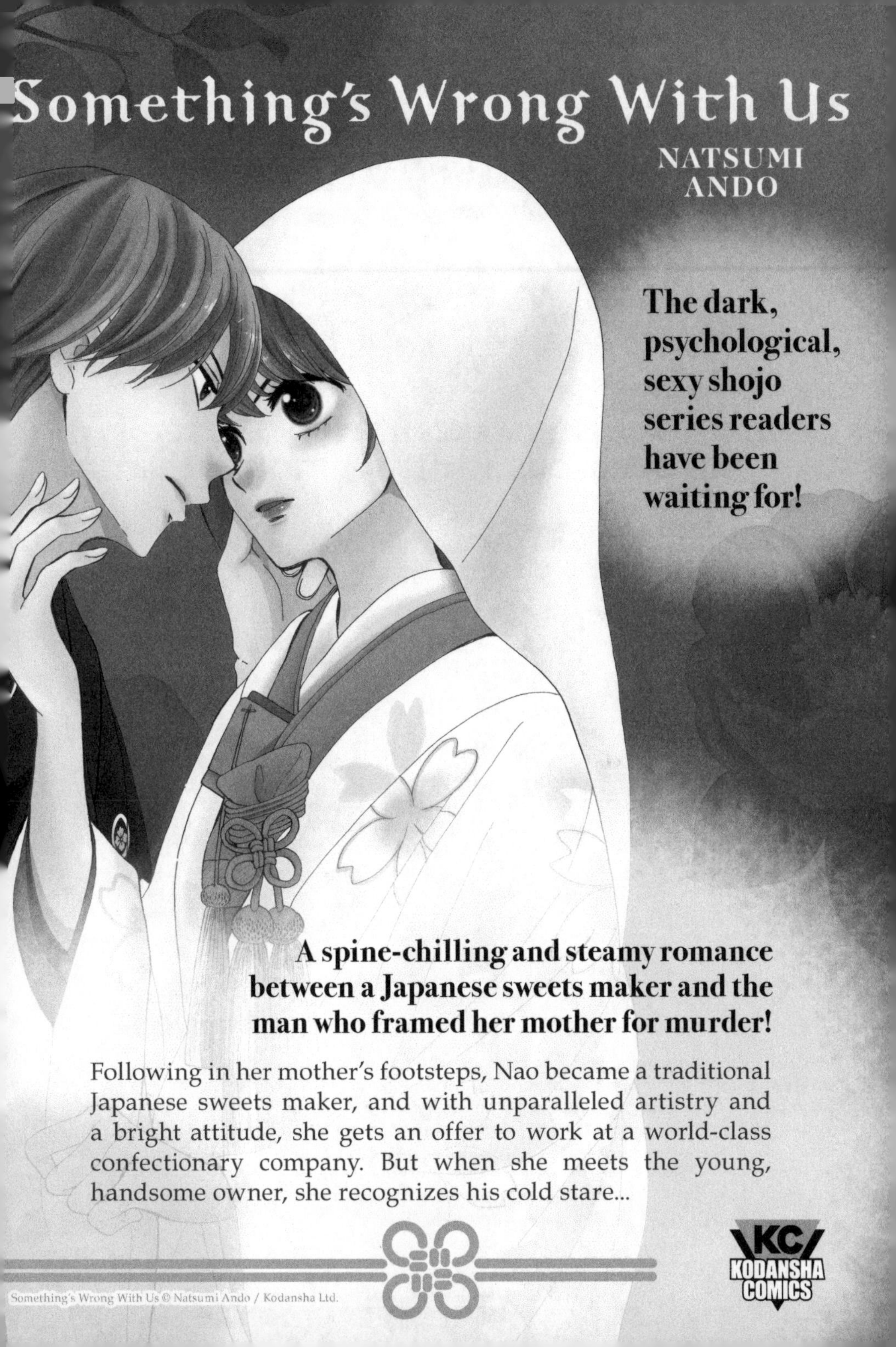
Something's Wrong With Us
NATSUMI ANDO
The dark, psychological, sexy shojo series readers have been waiting for!
A spine-chilling and steamy romance between a Japanese sweets maker and the man who framed her mother for murder!
Following in her mother's footsteps, Nao became a traditional Japanese sweets maker, and with unparalleled artistry and a bright attitude, she gets an offer to work at a world-class confectionary company. But when she meets the young, handsome owner, she recognizes his cold stare...
KC KODANSHA COMICS
Something's Wrong With Us © Natsumi Ando / Kodansha Ltd.

MAGIC ⬦ KNIGHT
RAYEARTH
25TH ANNIVERSARY EDITION
CLAMP

A BELOVED CLASSIC MAKES ITS STUNNING RETURN IN THIS GORGEOUS, LIMITED EDITION BOX SET!

This tale of three Tokyo teenagers who cross through a magical portal and become the champions of another world is a modern manga classic. The box set includes three volumes of manga covering the entire first series of *Magic Knight Rayearth*, plus the series's super-rare full-color art book companion, all printed at a larger size than ever before on premium paper, featuring a newly-revised translation and lettering, and exquisite foil-stamped covers.

A strictly limited edition, this will be gone in a flash!

The beloved characters from *Cardcaptor Sakura* return in a brand new, reimagined fantasy adventure!

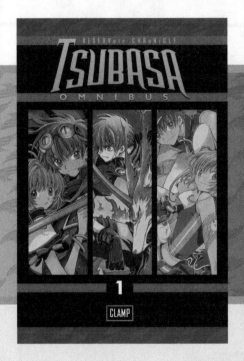

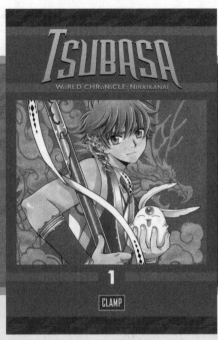

"[*Tsubasa*] takes readers on a fantastic ride that only gets more exhilarating with each successive chapter." —Anime News Network

In the Kingdom of Clow, an archaeological dig unleashes an incredible power, causing Princess Sakura to lose her memories. To save her, her childhood friend Syaoran must follow the orders of the Dimension Witch and travel alongside Kurogane, an unrivaled warrior; Fai, a powerful magician; and Mokona, a curiously strange creature, to retrieve Sakura's dispersed memories!

THE WORLD OF CLAMP!

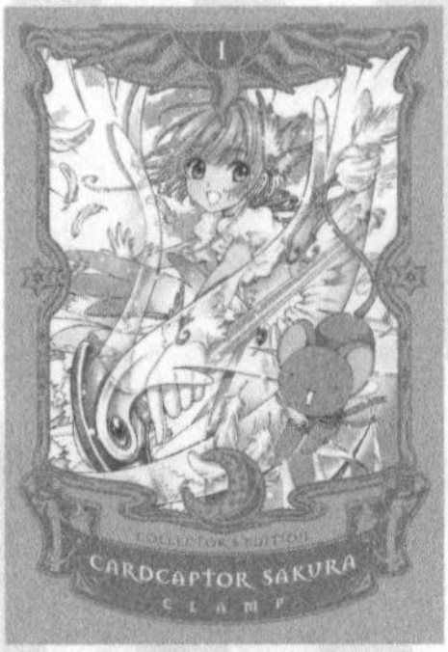
CARDCAPTOR SAKURA
CLAMP

Cardcaptor Sakura
Collector's Edition

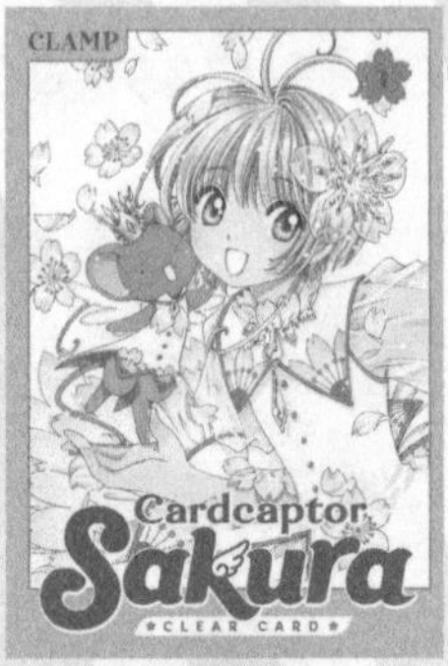
CLAMP
Cardcaptor
Sakura
CLEAR CARD

Cardcaptor Sakura:
Clear Card

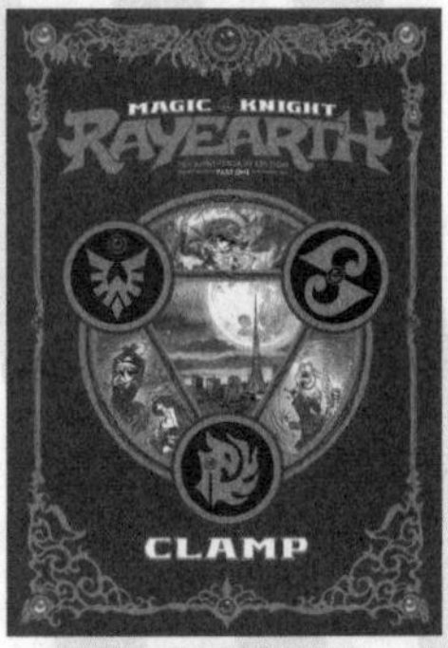
MAGIC KNIGHT
RAYEARTH
CLAMP

Magic Knight Rayearth
25th Anniversary Box Set

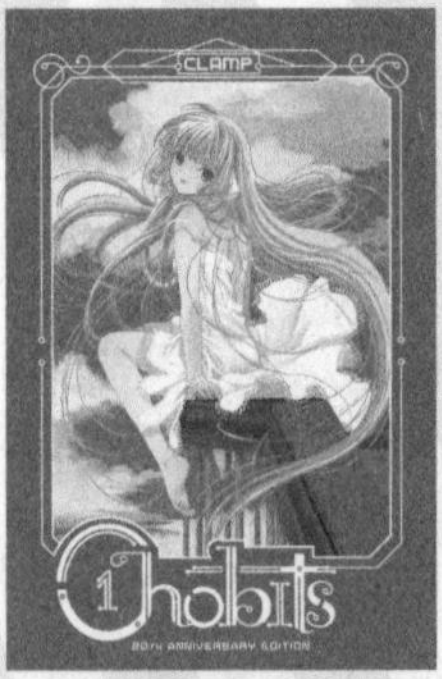
CLAMP
1
Chobits

Chobits

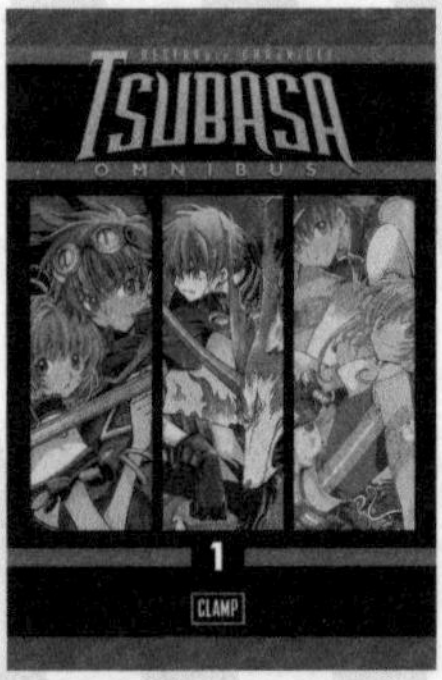
TSUBASA
OMNIBUS
1
CLAMP

TSUBASA Omnibus

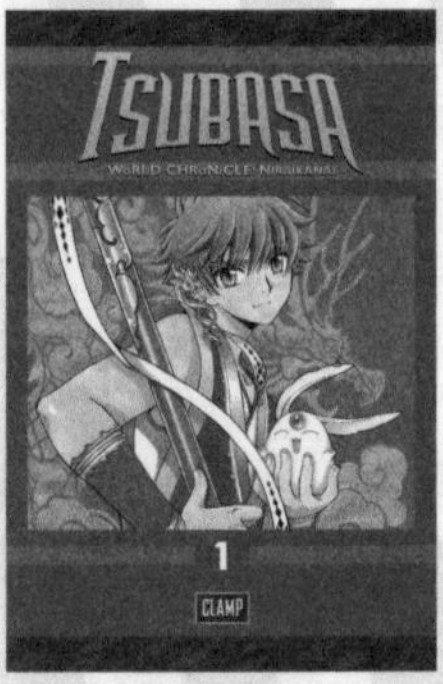
TSUBASA
1
CLAMP

TSUBASA WoRLD CHRoNiCLE

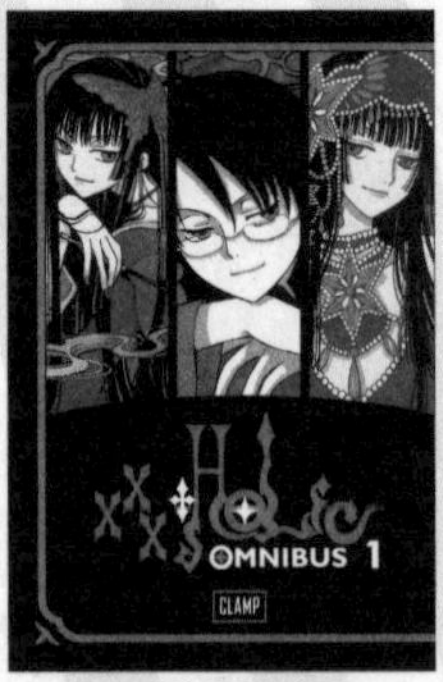
xxxHOLiC
OMNIBUS 1
CLAMP

xxxHOLiC Omnibus

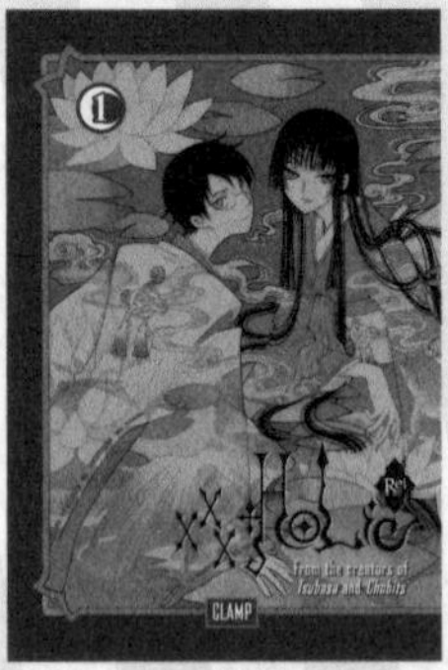
1
xxxHOLiC
CLAMP

xxxHOLiC Rei

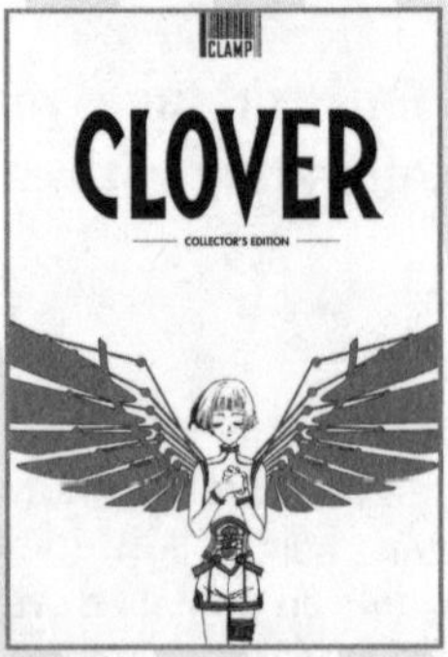
CLAMP
CLOVER
COLLECTOR'S EDITION

CLOVER Collector's Edition

KC KODANSHA COMICS

Kodansha Comics welcomes you to explore the expansive world of CLAMP, the all-female artist collective that has produced some of the most acclaimed manga of the century. Our growing catalog includes icons like *Cardcaptor Sakura* and *Magic Knight Rayearth*, each crafted with CLAMP's one-of-a-kind style and characters!

Young characters and steampunk setting, like *Howl's Moving Castle* and *Battle Angel Alita*

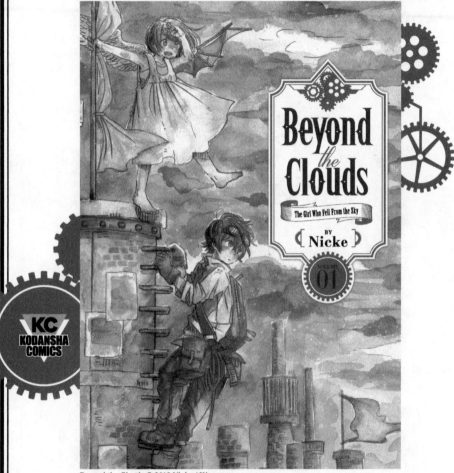

Beyond the Clouds © 2018 Nicke / Ki-oon

A boy with a talent for machines and a mysterious girl whose wings he's fixed will take you beyond the clouds! In the tradition of the high-flying, resonant adventure stories of Studio Ghibli comes a gorgeous tale about the longing of young hearts for adventure and friendship!

The adorable new odd-couple cat comedy manga from the creator of the beloved *Chi's Sweet Home*, in full color!

Praise for Chi's Sweet Home

"Nearly impossible to turn away... a true all-ages title that anyone, young or old, cat lover or not, will enjoy. The stories will bring a smile to your face and warm your heart."

—School Library Journal

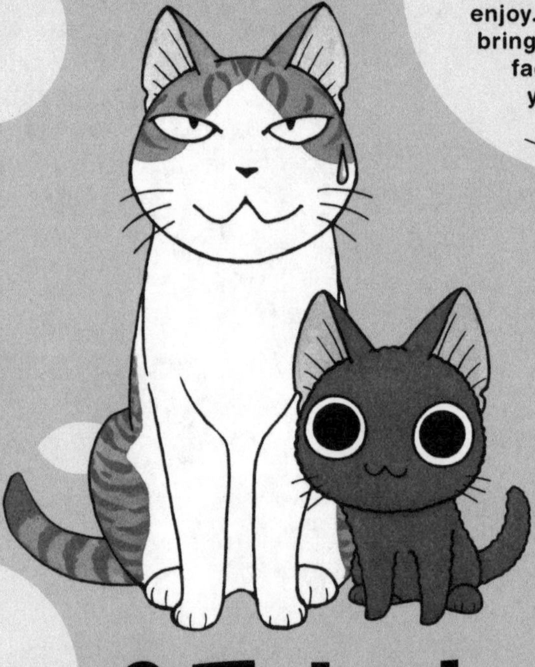

Sue & Tai-chan

Konami Kanata

Sue is an aging housecat who's looking forward to living out her life in peace... but her plans change when the mischievous black tomcat Tai-chan enters the picture! Hey! Sue never signed up to be a catsitter! *Sue & Tai-chan* is the latest from the reigning meow-narch of cute kitty comics, Konami Kanata.

Knight of the Ice ©Yayoi Ogawa/Kodansha Ltd.

SKATING THRILLS AND ICY CHILLS WITH THIS NEW TINGLY ROMANCE SERIES!

A rom-com on ice, perfect for fans of *Princess Jellyfish* and *Wotakoi*. Kokoro is the talk of the figure-skating world, winning trophies and hearts. But little do they know... he's actually a huge nerd! From the beloved creator of *You're My Pet* (*Tramps Like Us*).

Chitose is a serious young woman, working for the health magazine *SASSO*. Or at least, she would be, if she wasn't constantly getting distracted by her childhood friend, international figure skating star Kokoro Kijinami! In the public eye and on the ice, Kokoro is a gallant, flawless knight, but behind his glittery costumes and breathtaking spins lies a secret: He's actually a hopelessly romantic otaku, who can only land his quad jumps when Chitose is on hand to recite a spell from his favorite magical girl anime!

KC/
KODANSHA
COMICS

PERFECT WORLD

Rie Aruga

A TOUCHING NEW SERIES ABOUT LOVE AND COPING WITH DISABILITY

An office party reunites Tsugumi with her high school crush Itsuki. He's realized his dream of becoming an architect, but along the way, he experienced a spinal injury that put him in a wheelchair. Now Tsugumi's rekindled feelings will butt up against prejudices she never considered — and Itsuki will have to decide if he's ready to let someone into his heart...

"Depicts with great delicacy and courage the difficulties some with disabilities experience getting involved in romantic relationships... Rie Aruga refuses to romanticize, pushing her heroine to face the reality of disability. She invites her readers to the same tasks of empathy, knowledge and recognition."
—Slate.fr

"An important entry [in manga romance]... The emotional core of both plot and characters indicates thoughtfulness... [Aruga's] research is readily apparent in the text and artwork, making this feel like a real story."
—Anime News Network

KC KODANSHA COMICS

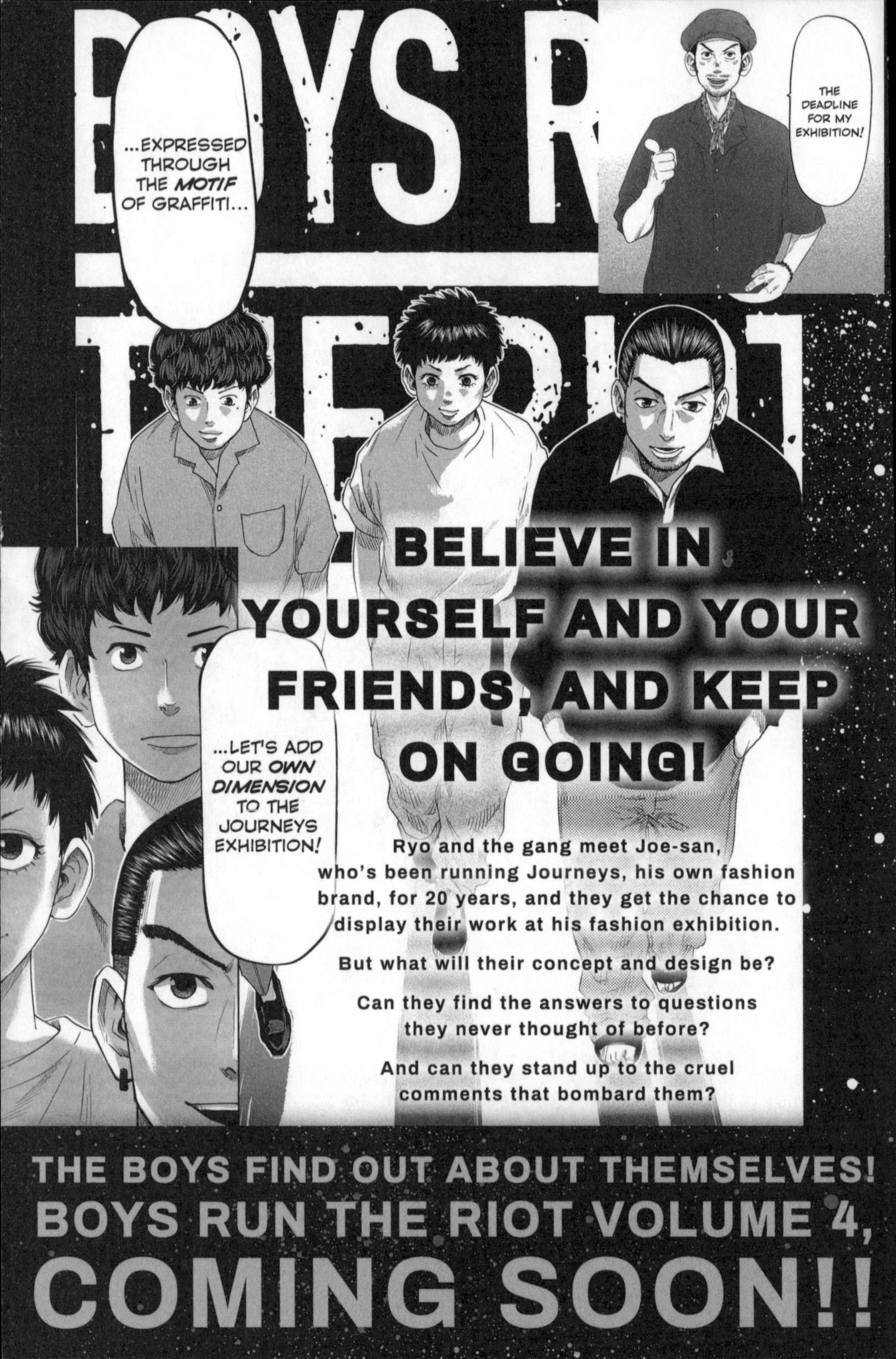
BOYS RUN THE RIOT
THE DEADLINE FOR MY EXHIBITION!
...EXPRESSED THROUGH THE *MOTIF* OF GRAFFITI...
...LET'S ADD OUR *OWN DIMENSION* TO THE JOURNEYS EXHIBITION!
BELIEVE IN YOURSELF AND YOUR FRIENDS, AND KEEP ON GOING!
Ryo and the gang meet Joe-san, who's been running Journeys, his own fashion brand, for 20 years, and they get the chance to display their work at his fashion exhibition.
But what will their concept and design be?
Can they find the answers to questions they never thought of before?
And can they stand up to the cruel comments that bombard them?
THE BOYS FIND OUT ABOUT THEMSELVES!
BOYS RUN THE RIOT VOLUME 4, COMING SOON!!

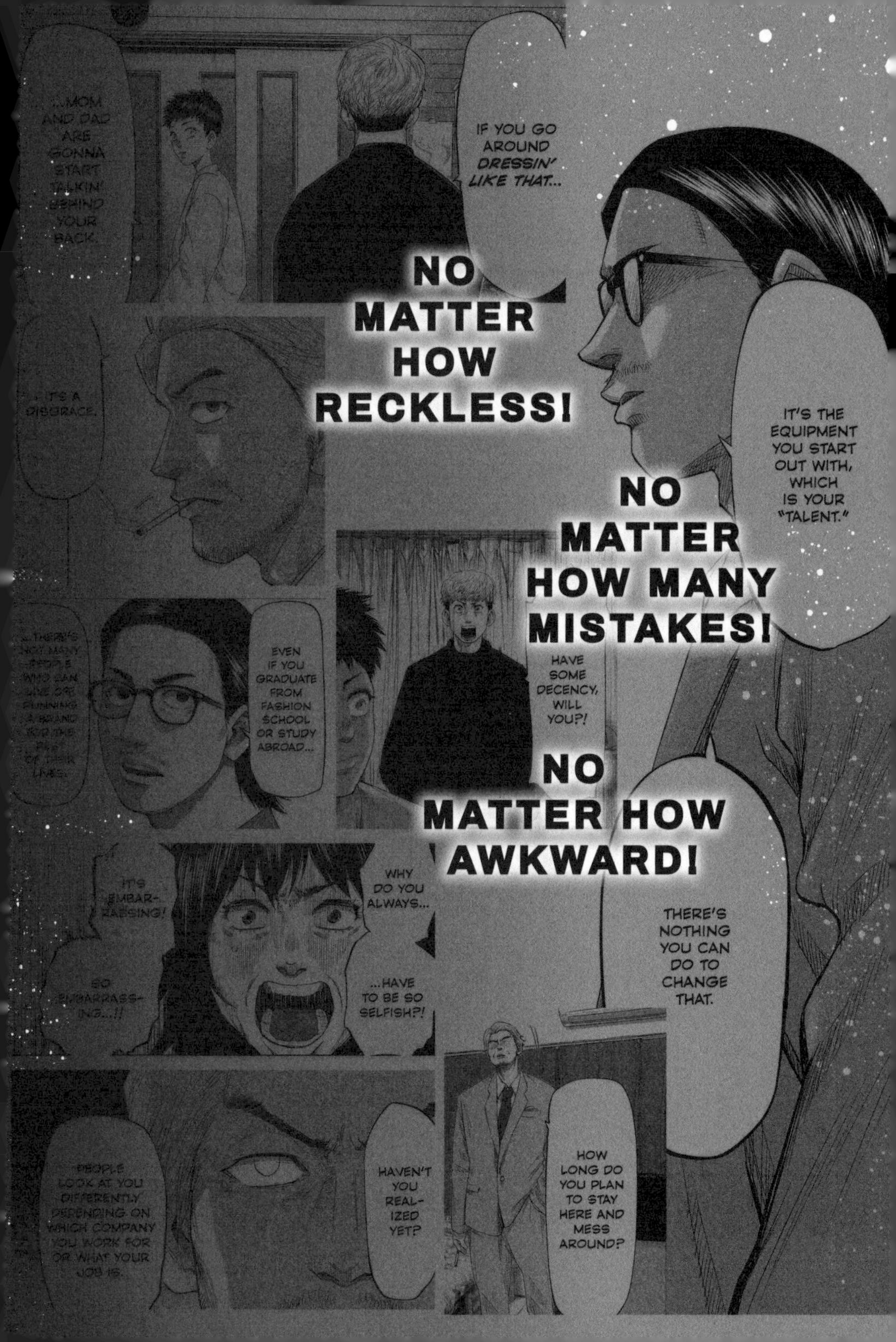

IF YOU GO AROUND *DRESSIN'* *LIKE THAT*...
...MOM AND DAD ARE GONNA START TALKIN' BEHIND YOUR BACK.
NO MATTER HOW RECKLESS!
...IT'S A DISGRACE.
IT'S THE EQUIPMENT YOU START OUT WITH, WHICH IS YOUR "TALENT."
NO MATTER HOW MANY MISTAKES!
HAVE SOME DECENCY, WILL YOU?!
EVEN IF YOU GRADUATE FROM FASHION SCHOOL OR STUDY ABROAD...
...THERE'S NOT MANY PEOPLE WHO CAN LIVE OFF RUNNING A BRAND FOR THE REST OF THEIR LIVES.
NO MATTER HOW AWKWARD!
WHY DO YOU ALWAYS...
...HAVE TO BE SO SELFISH?!
IT'S EMBARRASSING!
SO EMBARRASSING...!!
THERE'S NOTHING YOU CAN DO TO CHANGE THAT.
HOW LONG DO YOU PLAN TO STAY HERE AND MESS AROUND?
HAVEN'T YOU REALIZED YET?
PEOPLE LOOK AT YOU DIFFERENTLY DEPENDING ON WHICH COMPANY YOU WORK FOR OR WHAT YOUR JOB IS.

BOYS RUN THE RIOT VOLUME 3
ORIGINAL U.S. COVER SKETCH
BY AUTHOR KEITO GAKU

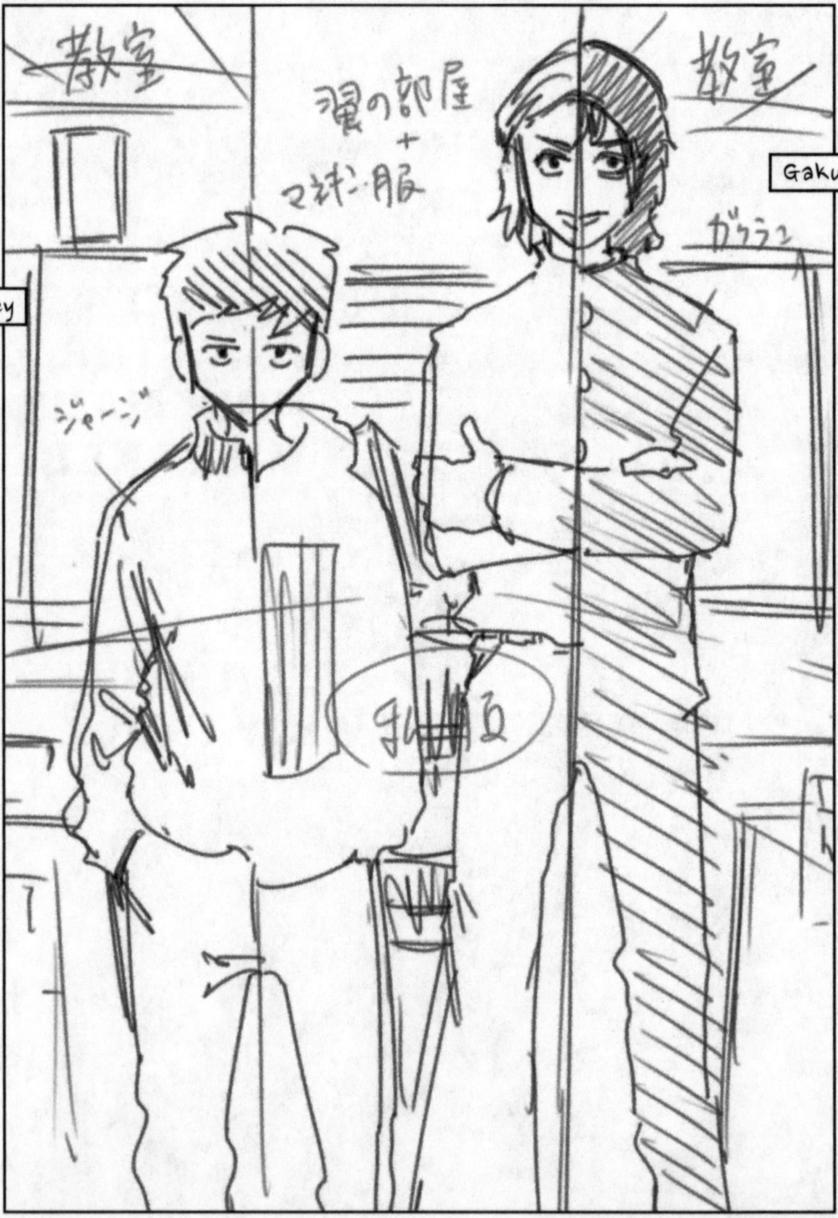
Classroom
Tsubasa's studio and mannequins
Classroom
Gakuran
Jersey

TRANSLATION NOTES

GYARU, page 32

Gyaru, though initially borrowed from the English term "girl" and "gal", has since become a subculture of Japanese street fashion. *Gyaru* typically bleach and dye their hair lighter, wear a lot of make-up and gaudy accessories, and often tan their skin. *Gyaru* are considered to be cheerful, sociable, and trendy, but, because of their appearance, are also sometimes thought of as vain, shallow, or airheaded.

CROSSDRESSER, page 159

In the original Japanese, this character is asking if Tsubasa is an *onee*. *Onee* literally means "big sister." It can be used for anyone assigned male at birth who acts or looks effeminate, so it can encompass effeminate gay men, crossdressers, drag queens, transgender women, and transfeminine people. Some people do not like being called *onee*, but some people do, and even self-identify as *onee*.

X-GENDER, page 175

X-gender is a Japanese term for a gender identity that is neither male nor female, and is similar to the terms "nonbinary" and "genderqueer" in English. The term x-gender is often used both on its own as its own gender identity and as an umbrella term for various nonbinary genders (See translation note below).

NONBINARY, GENDER NEUTRAL, BIGENDER, AGENDER, GENDERFLUID, page 176

The gender identities Kashiwabara lists here all fall under the nonbinary umbrella, and are gender identities that exist outside of the gender binary—meaning that they refer to genders that are neither male nor female. "Nonbinary" refers to a gender that is neither strictly male nor female, and can be used both on its own as its own gender identity, and as an umbrella term for various nonbinary genders; "Gender neutral" refers to someone with a neutral gender identity or expression; "Bigender" refers to someone who identifies as two different genders, either simultaneously or by fluctuating between the two; "Agender" refers to someone who does not identify as any particular gender; and "Genderfluid" refers to someone whose gender identity may shift between different genders at different times, or in different circumstances.

GAKURAN, page 191

Here, and more clearly on the cover image, we see Tsubasa wearing a *gakuran*, or a type of traditional Japanese male school uniform. *Gakuran* are typically worn by middle school and high school boys, and are normally all black or navy blue. A *gakuran* consists of a button-down top with a standing collar, and straight-leg slacks.

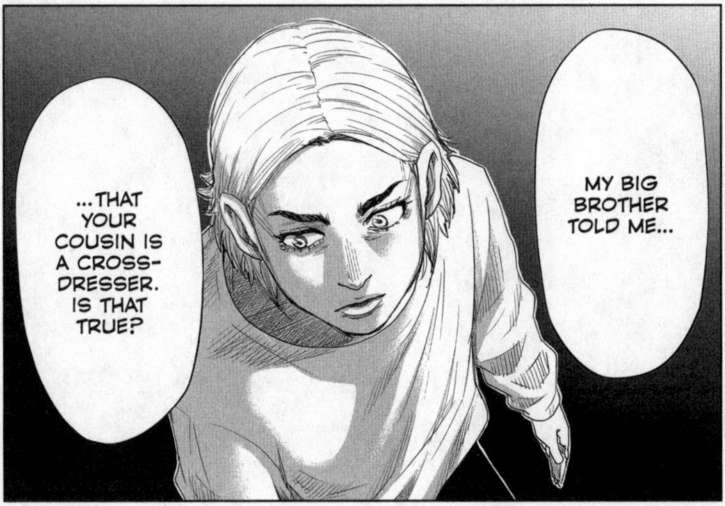
MY BIG BROTHER TOLD ME...
...THAT YOUR COUSIN IS A CROSS-DRESSER. IS THAT TRUE?

SPECIAL THANKS

CONTRIBUTORS

Artist: knott aka 2G INDAHOUSE (Instagram: knott2g)

Art director: SAYAKA (Twitter/Instagram: @SAYAKACHAN)
(Chap. 21 Border, from page 86)

STAFF

Igarashi
Ryuusei Terada
Taiga Miyahara

SPECIAL VOLUME DESIGN

fake graphics – Akito Sumiyoshi

EDITORS

Hidemi Shiraki
Haruhito Uwai

SPECIAL VOLUME EDITORS

Tomohiro Ebitani
The Young Magazine editorial team

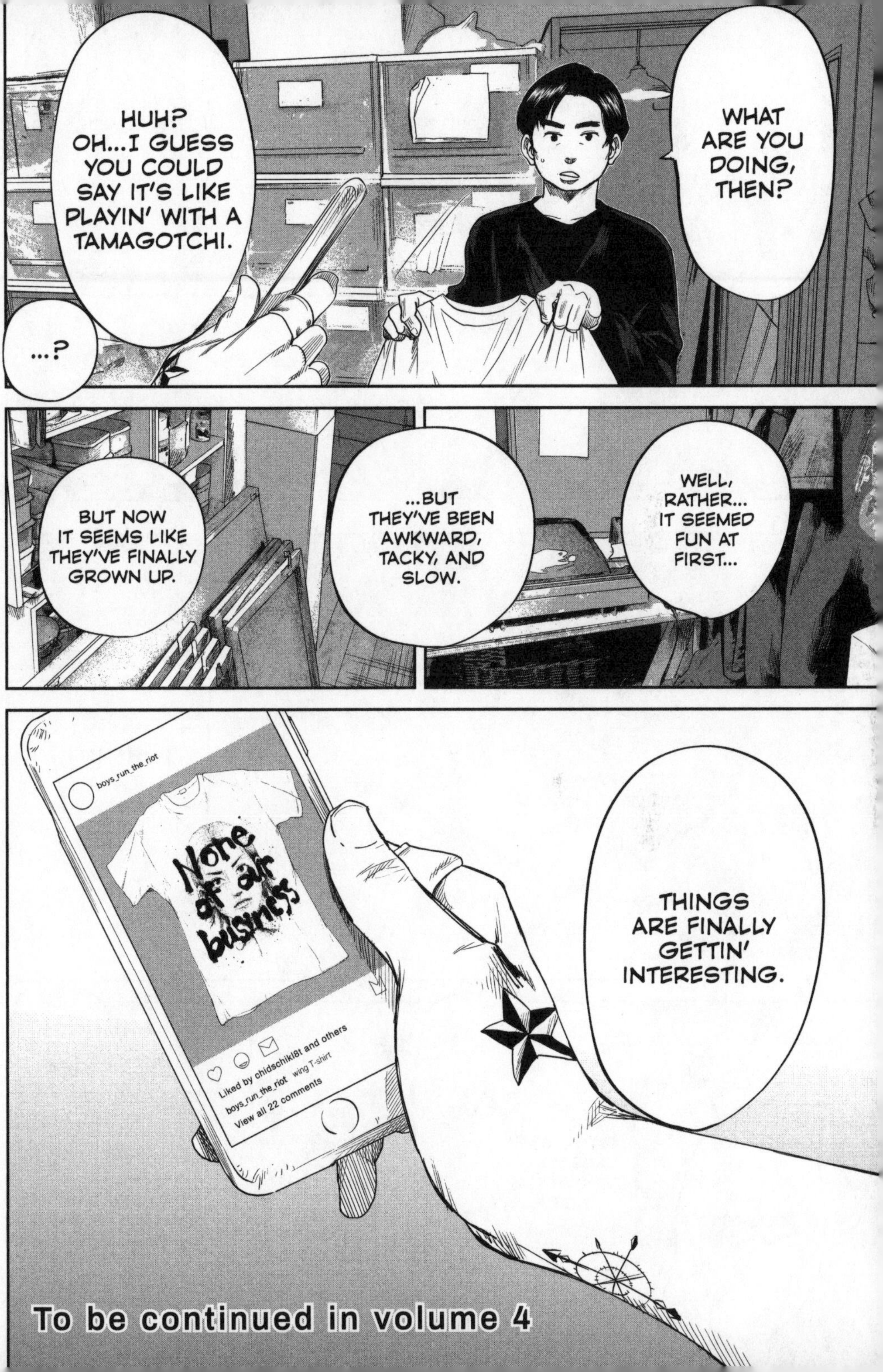
WHAT ARE YOU DOING, THEN?
HUH? OH...I GUESS YOU COULD SAY IT'S LIKE PLAYIN' WITH A TAMAGOTCHI.
...?
WELL, RATHER... IT SEEMED FUN AT FIRST...
...BUT THEY'VE BEEN AWKWARD, TACKY, AND SLOW.
BUT NOW IT SEEMS LIKE THEY'VE FINALLY GROWN UP.
THINGS ARE FINALLY GETTIN' INTERESTING.
boys_run_the_riot
Liked by chidschikl8t and others
boys_run_the_riot wing T-shirt
View all 22 comments
To be continued in volume 4

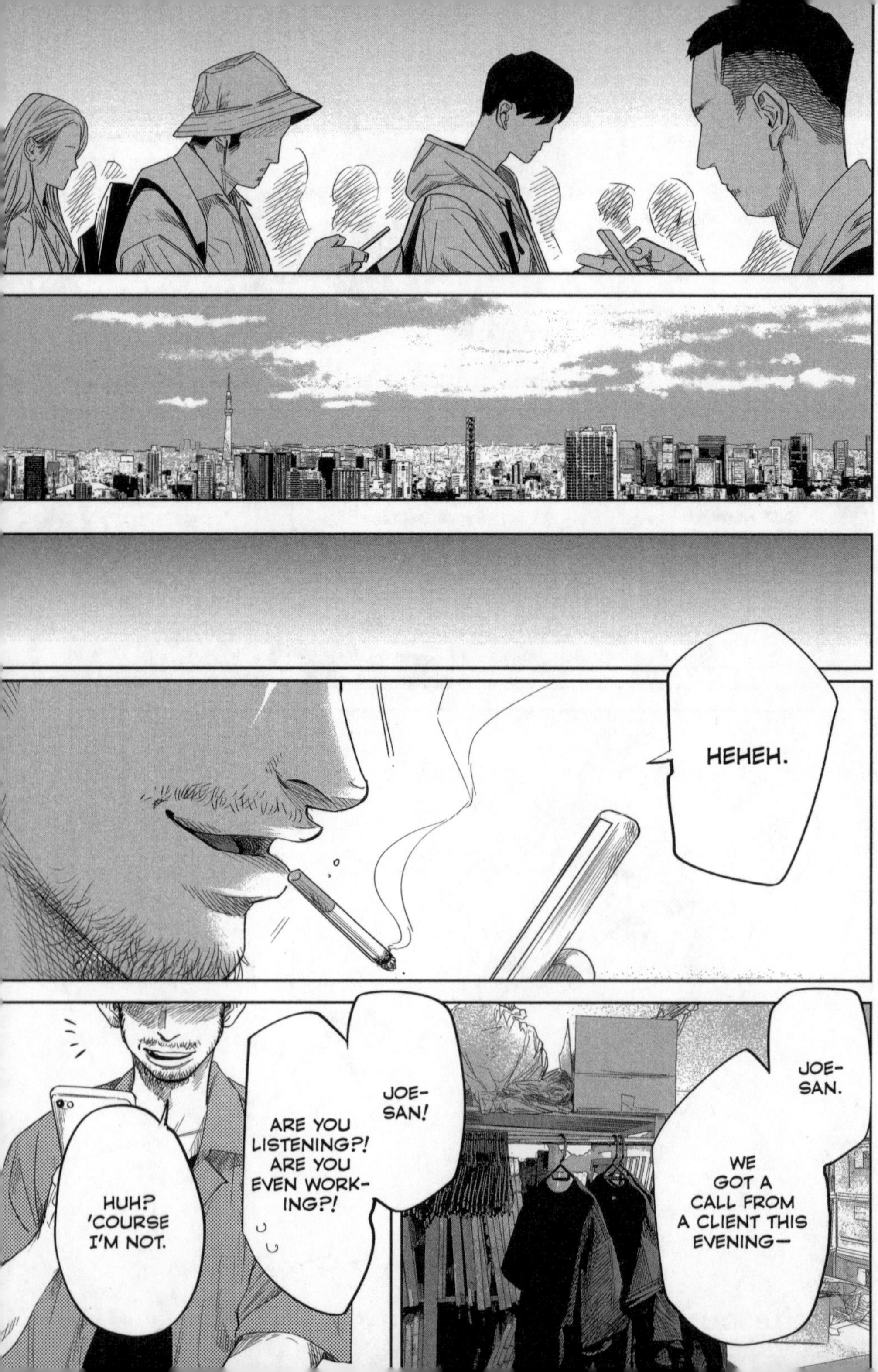
HEHEH.
JOE-SAN.
WE GOT A CALL FROM A CLIENT THIS EVENING—
JOE-SAN!
ARE YOU LISTENING?! ARE YOU EVEN WORKING?!
HUH? 'COURSE I'M NOT.

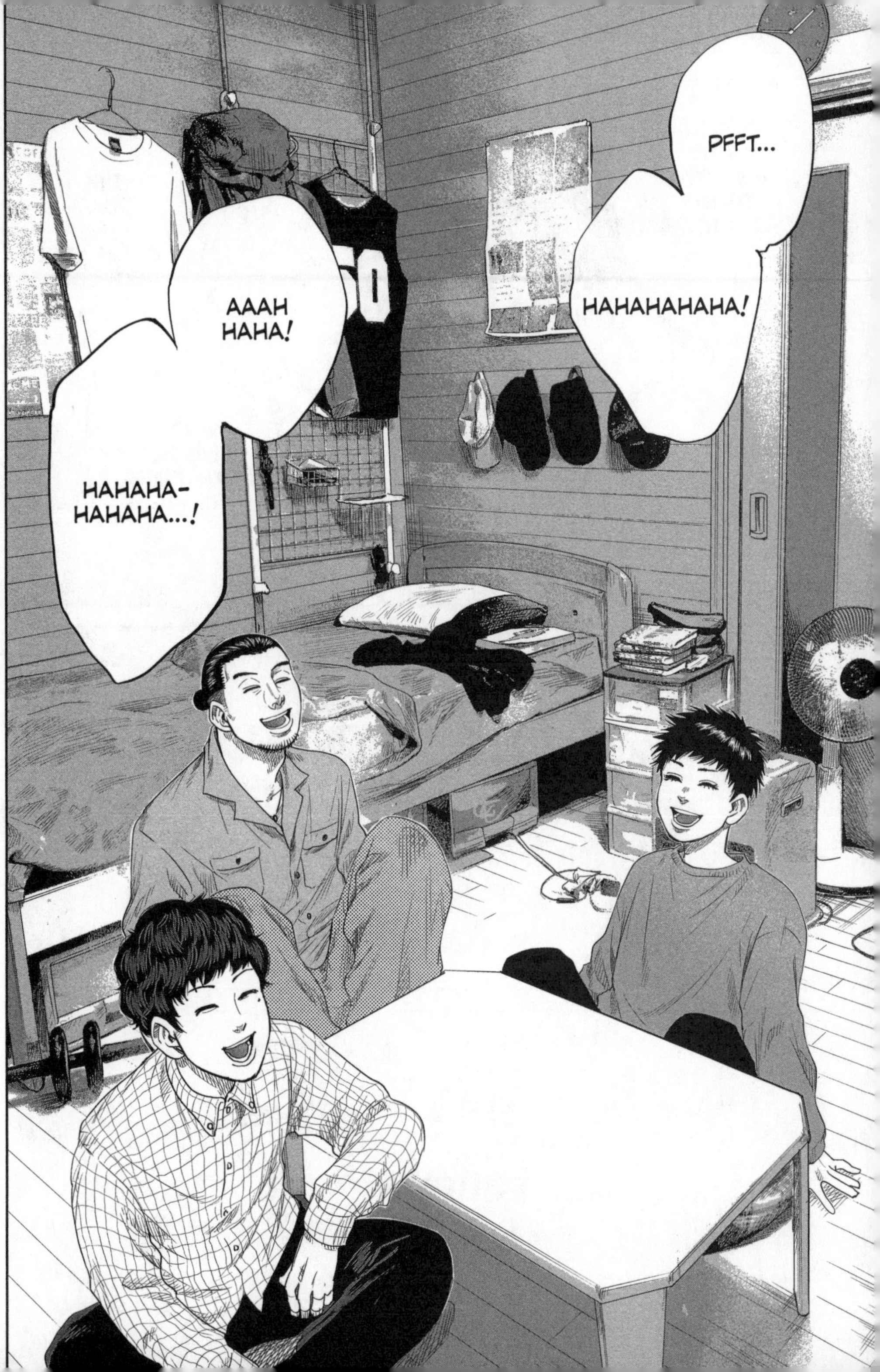
PFFT...
HAHAHAHAHA!
AAAH HAHA!
HAHAHA-HAHAHA...!

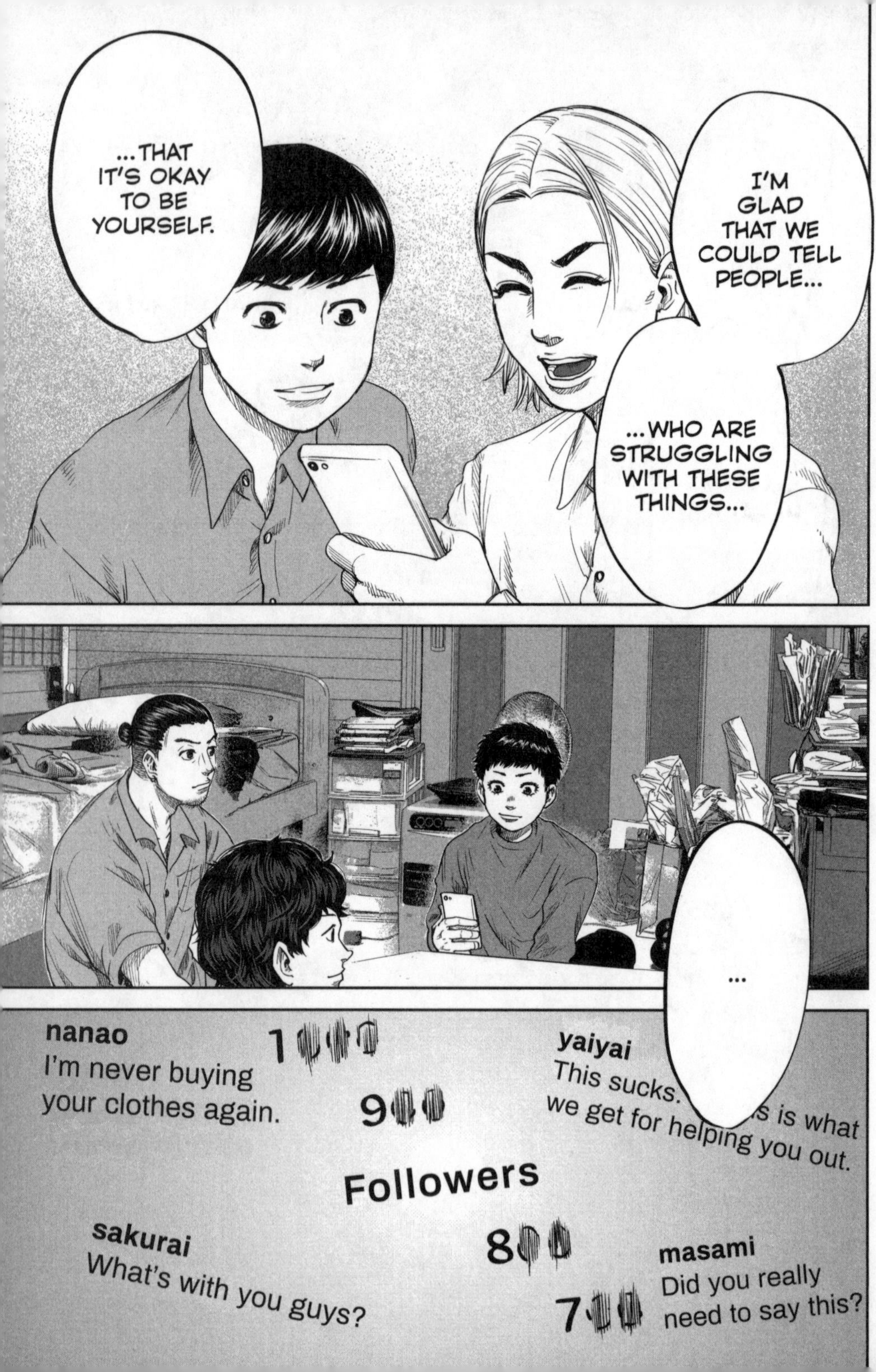
I'M GLAD THAT WE COULD TELL PEOPLE...
...WHO ARE STRUGGLING WITH THESE THINGS...
...THAT IT'S OKAY TO BE YOURSELF.
...
yaiyai
This sucks.
s is what we get for helping you out.
nanao
I'm never buying your clothes again.
Followers
masami
Did you really need to say this?
sakurai
What's with you guys?

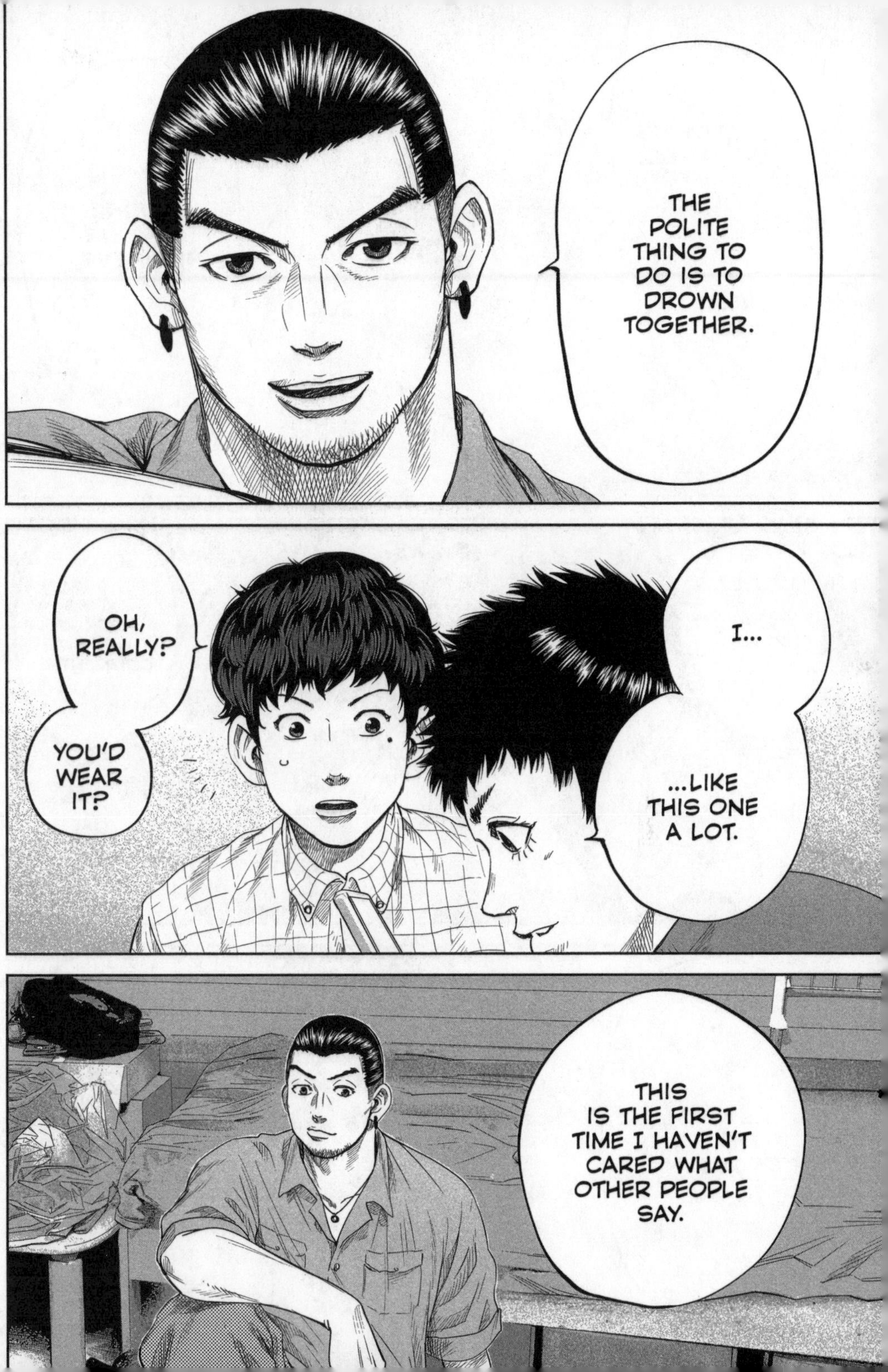
THE POLITE THING TO DO IS TO DROWN TOGETHER.
I...
...LIKE THIS ONE A LOT.
OH, REALLY?
YOU'D WEAR IT?
THIS IS THE FIRST TIME I HAVEN'T CARED WHAT OTHER PEOPLE SAY.

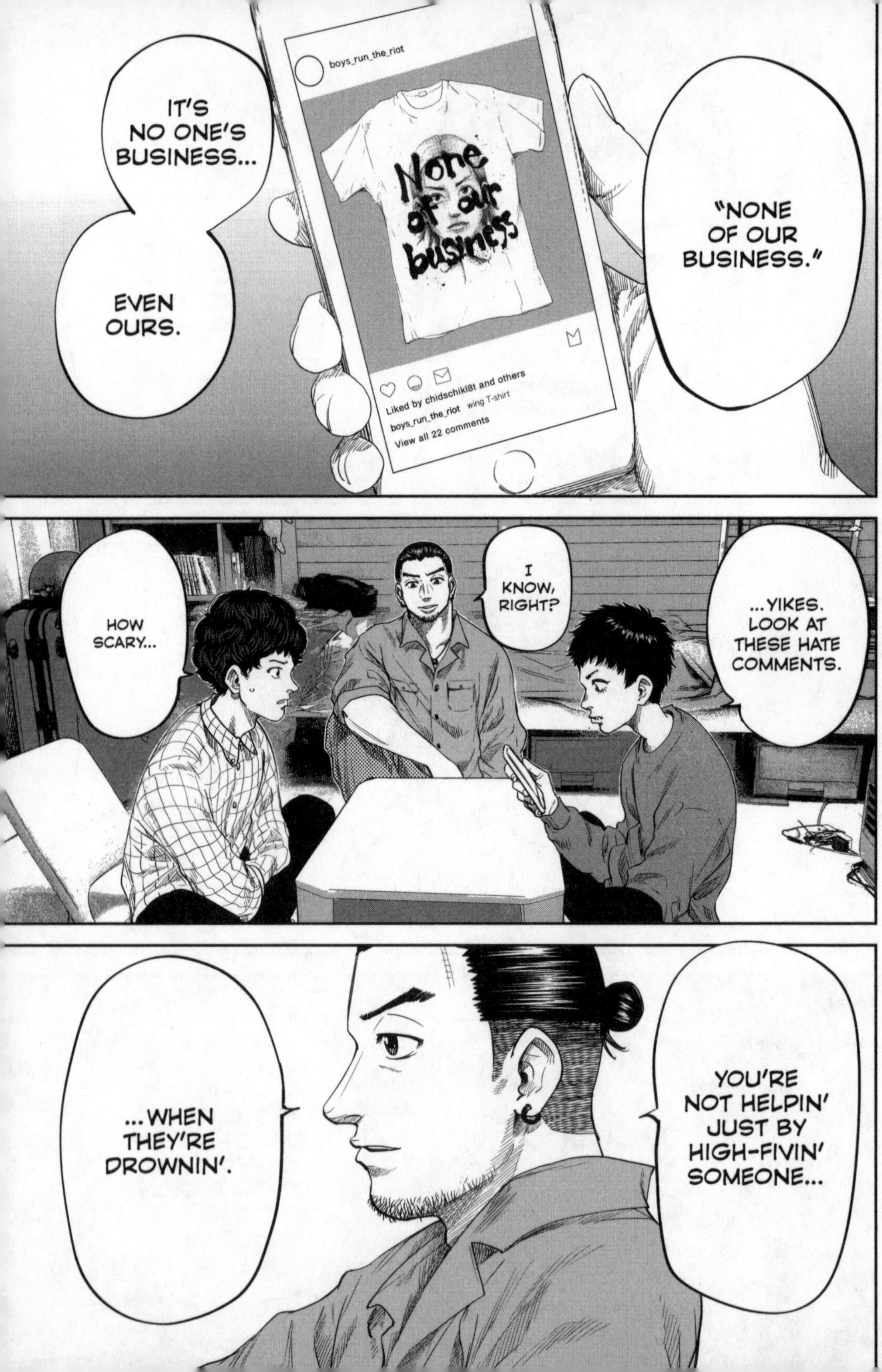
"NONE OF OUR BUSINESS."
IT'S NO ONE'S BUSINESS...
EVEN OURS.
boys_run_the_riot
None of our business
Liked by chidschikl8t and others
boys_run_the_riot wing T-shirt
View all 22 comments
...YIKES. LOOK AT THESE HATE COMMENTS.
I KNOW, RIGHT?
HOW SCARY...
YOU'RE NOT HELPIN' JUST BY HIGH-FIVIN' SOMEONE...
...WHEN THEY'RE DROWNIN'.

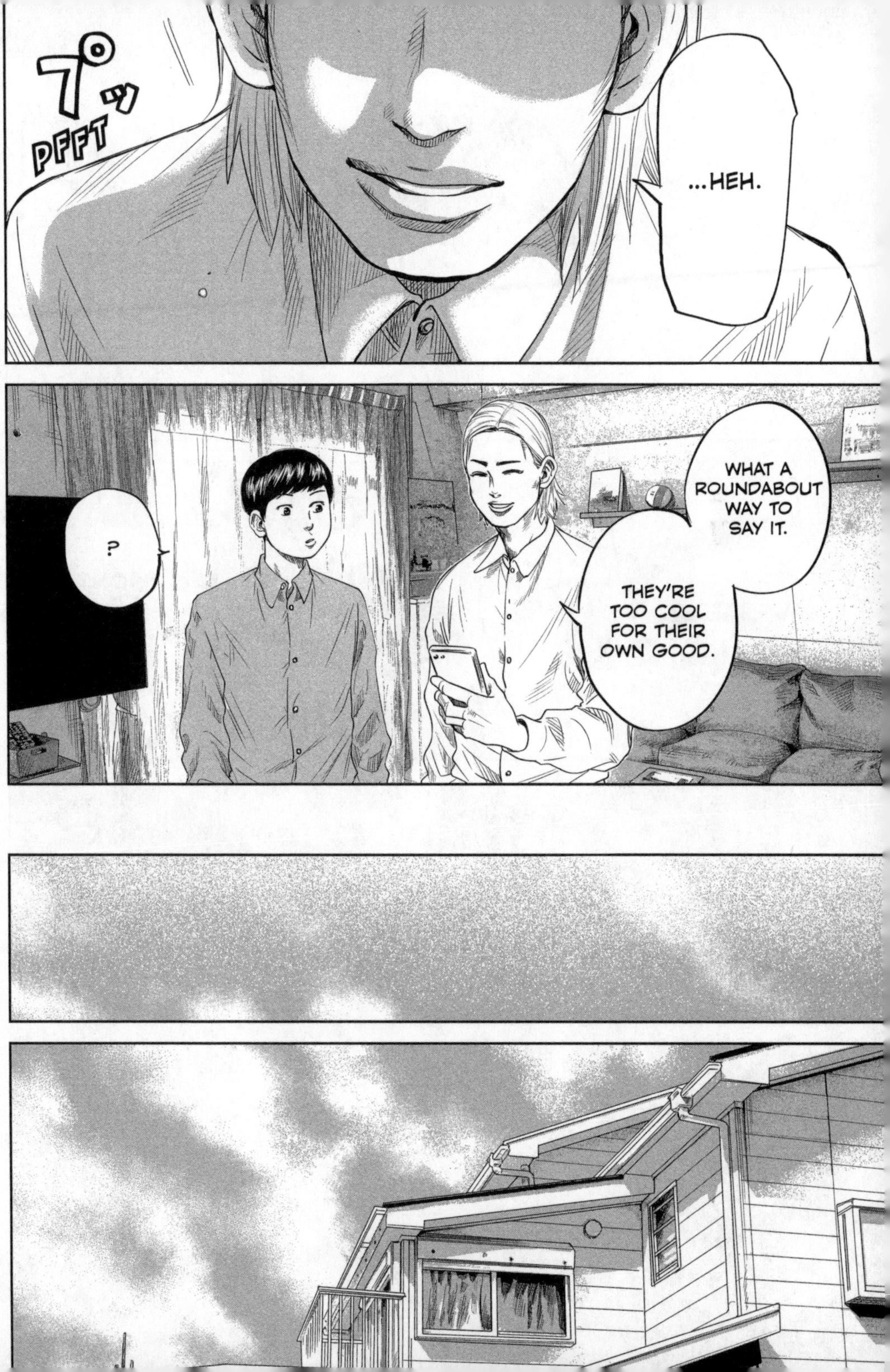
...HEH.
プッ
PFFT
WHAT A ROUNDABOUT WAY TO SAY IT.
THEY'RE TOO COOL FOR THEIR OWN GOOD.
?

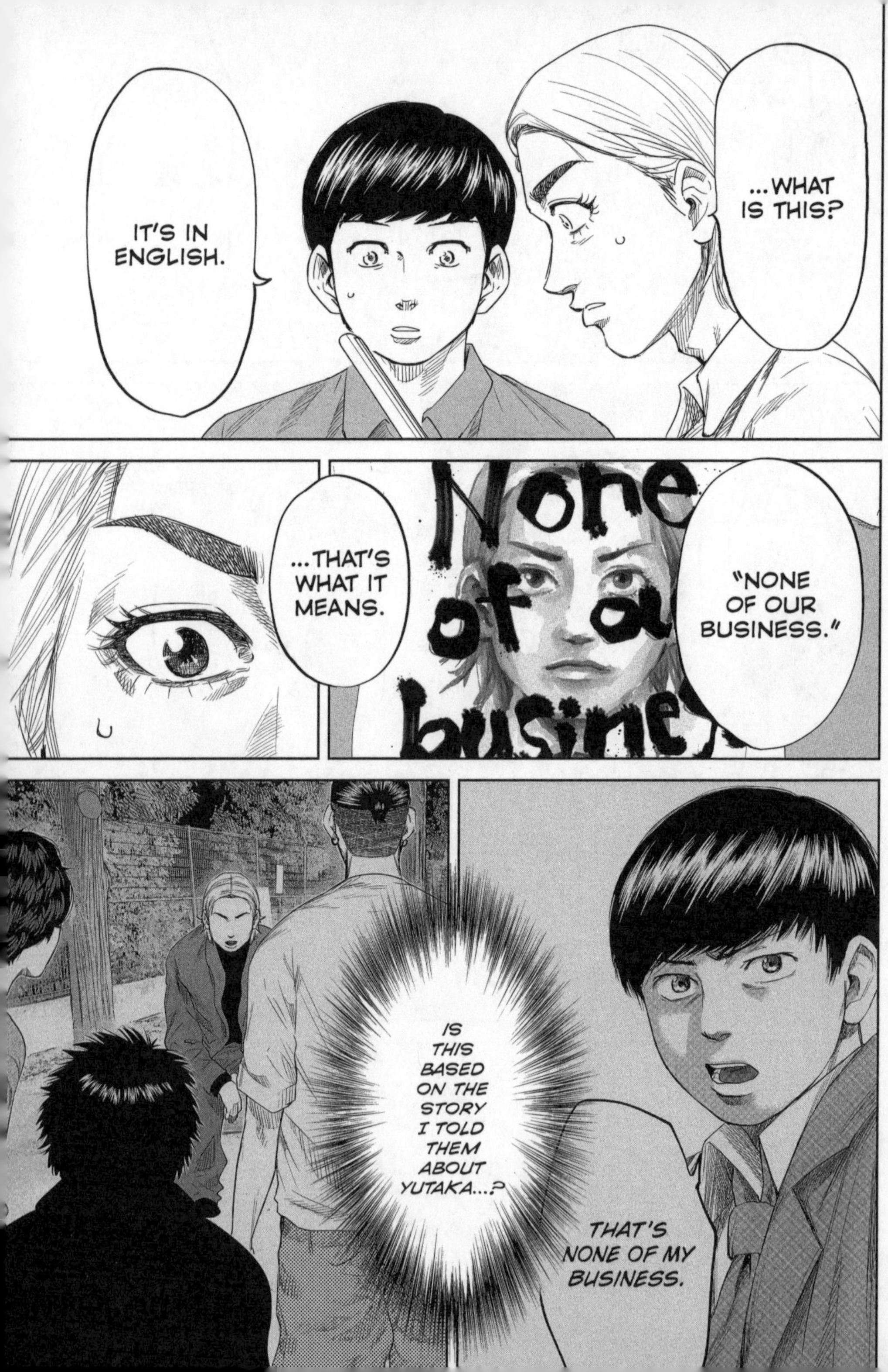
...WHAT IS THIS?
IT'S IN ENGLISH.
"NONE OF OUR BUSINESS."
...THAT'S WHAT IT MEANS.
THAT'S NONE OF MY BUSINESS.
IS THIS BASED ON THE STORY I TOLD THEM ABOUT YUTAKA...?

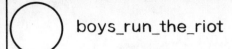

Liked by chidschikl8t and others

boys_run_the_riot wing T-shirt

View all 22 comments

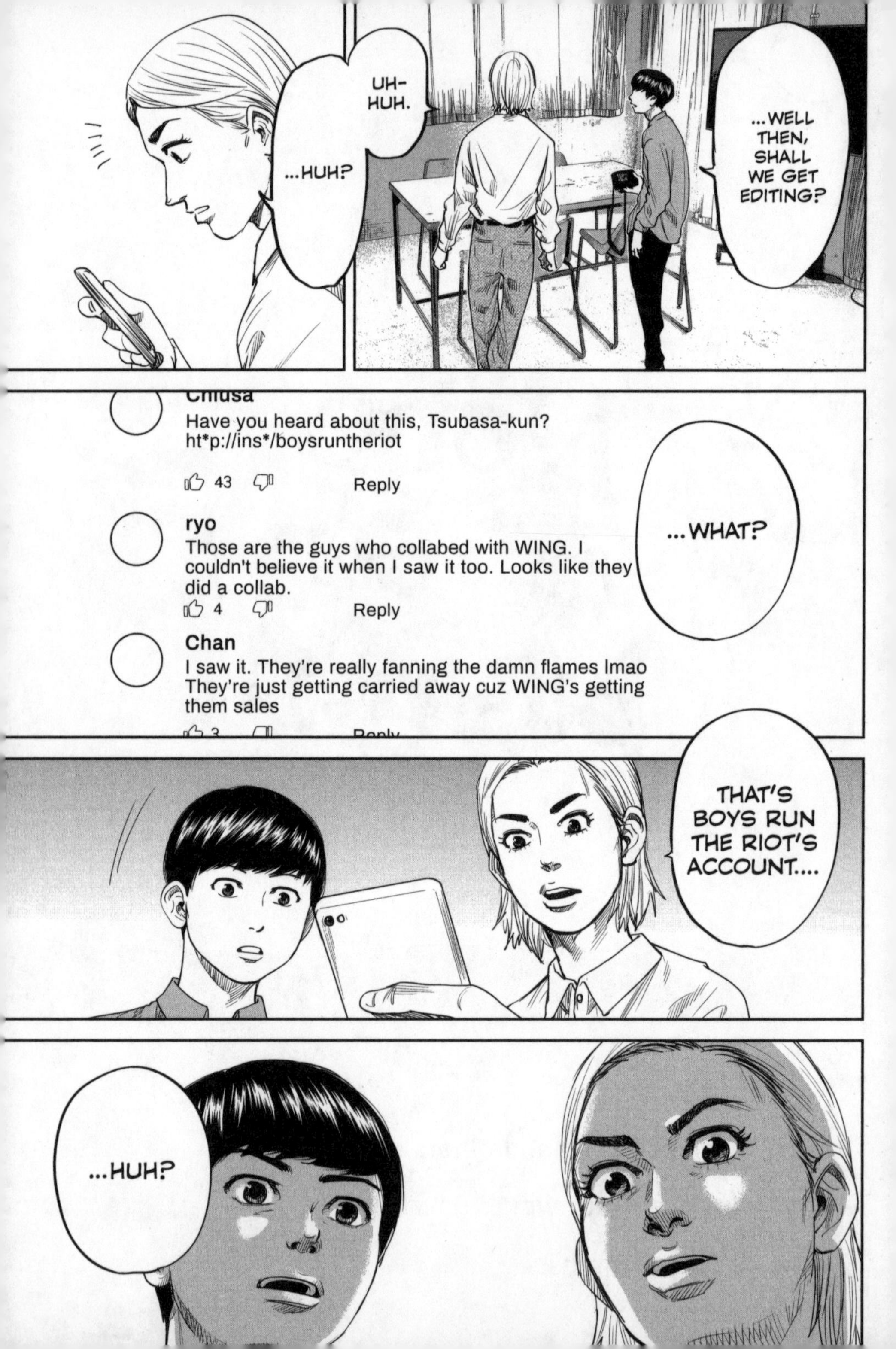
...WELL THEN, SHALL WE GET EDITING?
UH-HUH.
...HUH?
Chiusa
Have you heard about this, Tsubasa-kun?
ht*p://ins*/boysruntheriot
43 Reply
ryo
Those are the guys who collabed with WING. I couldn't believe it when I saw it too. Looks like they did a collab.
4 Reply
Chan
I saw it. They're really fanning the damn flames lmao They're just getting carried away cuz WING's getting them sales
...WHAT?
THAT'S BOYS RUN THE RIOT'S ACCOUNT....
...HUH?

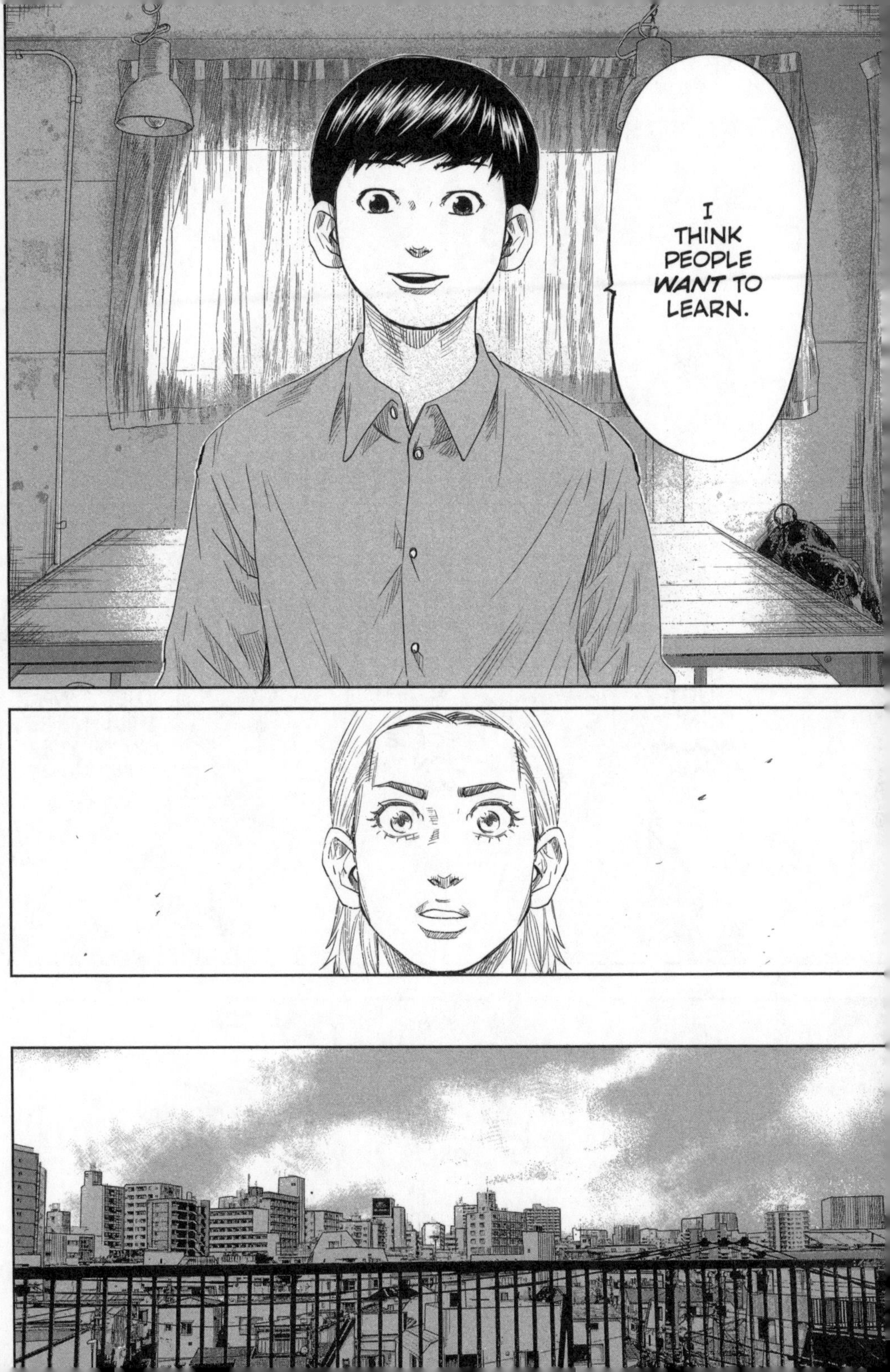
I THINK PEOPLE WANT TO LEARN.

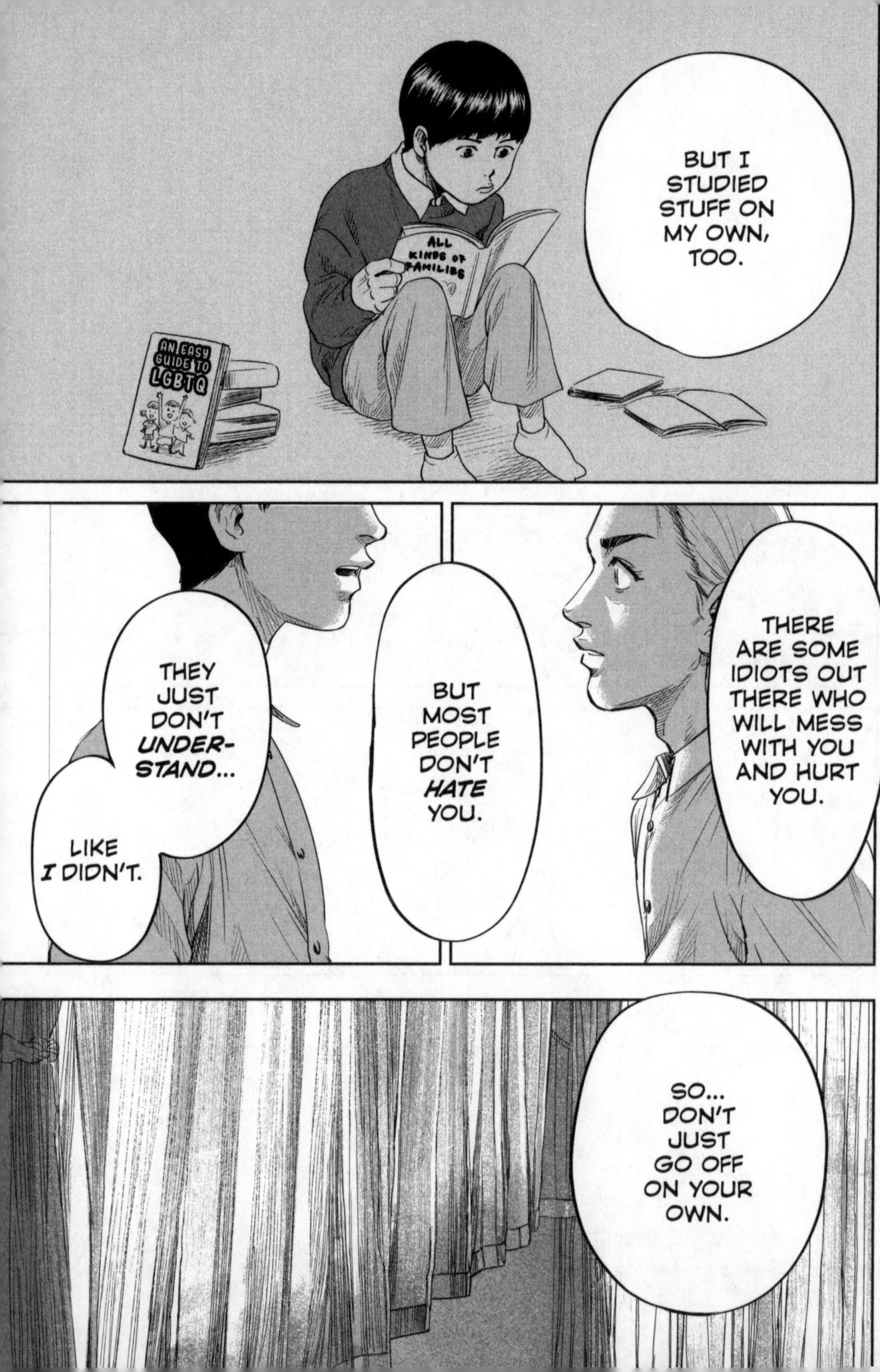
BUT I STUDIED STUFF ON MY OWN, TOO.
ALL KINDS OF FAMILIES
AN EASY GUIDE TO LGBTQ
THERE ARE SOME IDIOTS OUT THERE WHO WILL MESS WITH YOU AND HURT YOU.
BUT MOST PEOPLE DON'T *HATE* YOU.
THEY JUST DON'T *UNDER-STAND*...
LIKE *I* DIDN'T.
SO... DON'T JUST GO OFF ON YOUR OWN.

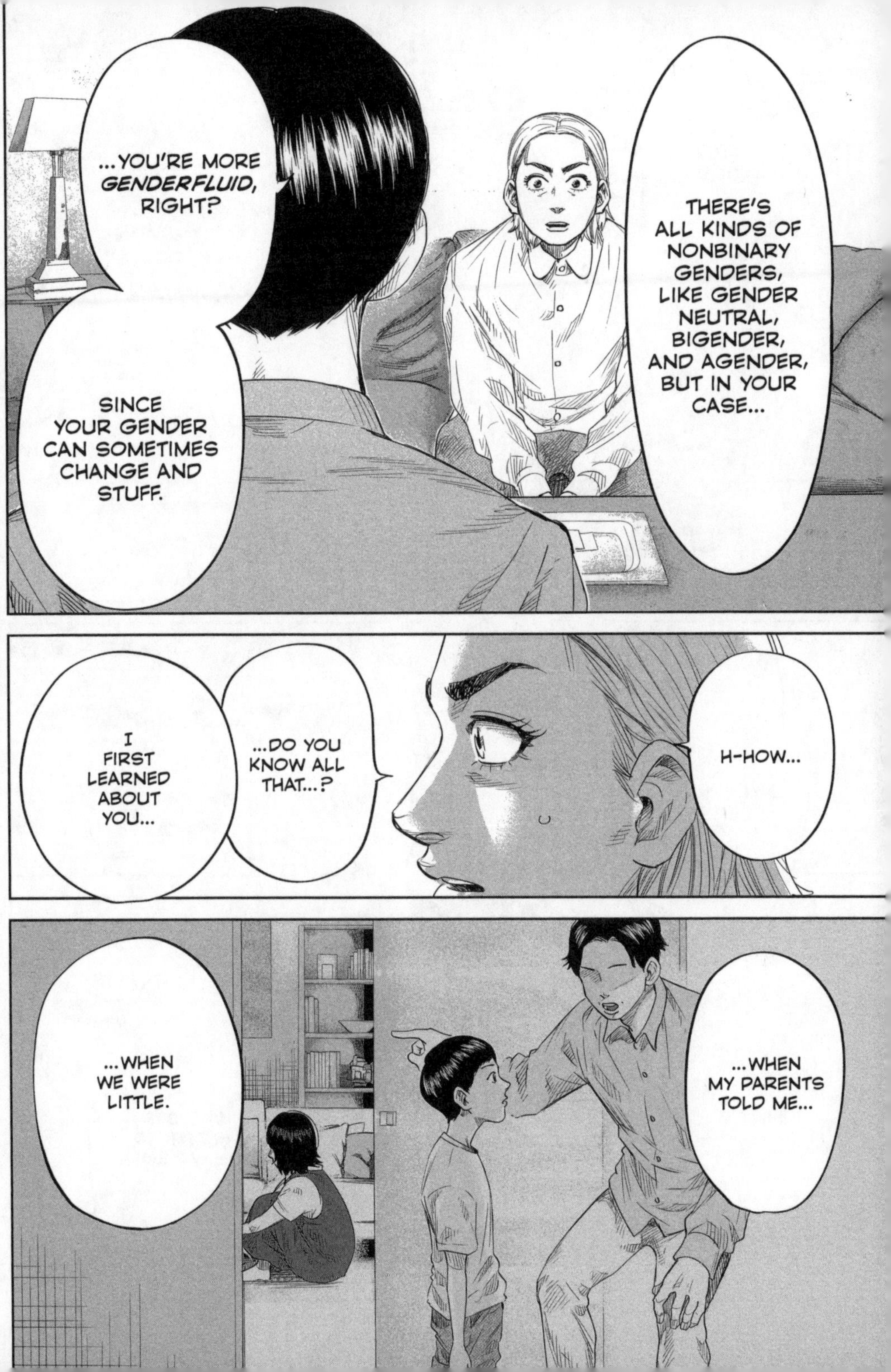
THERE'S ALL KINDS OF NONBINARY GENDERS, LIKE GENDER NEUTRAL, BIGENDER, AND AGENDER, BUT IN YOUR CASE...
...YOU'RE MORE *GENDERFLUID*, RIGHT?
SINCE YOUR GENDER CAN SOMETIMES CHANGE AND STUFF.
H-HOW...
...DO YOU KNOW ALL THAT...?
I FIRST LEARNED ABOUT YOU...
...WHEN MY PARENTS TOLD ME...
...WHEN WE WERE LITTLE.

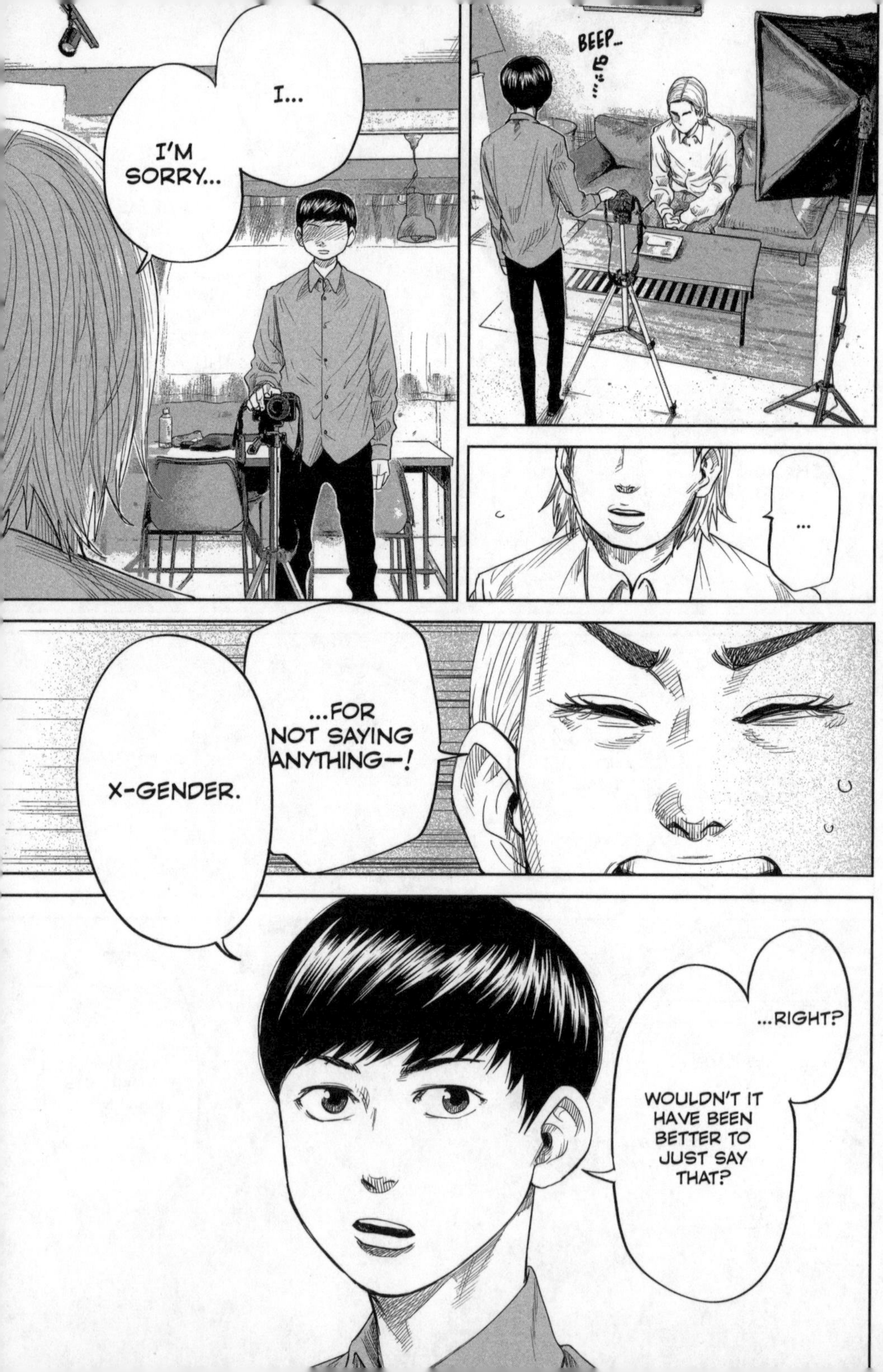
BEEP...
...
I...
I'M SORRY...
...FOR NOT SAYING ANYTHING—!
X-GENDER.
...RIGHT?
WOULDN'T IT HAVE BEEN BETTER TO JUST SAY THAT?

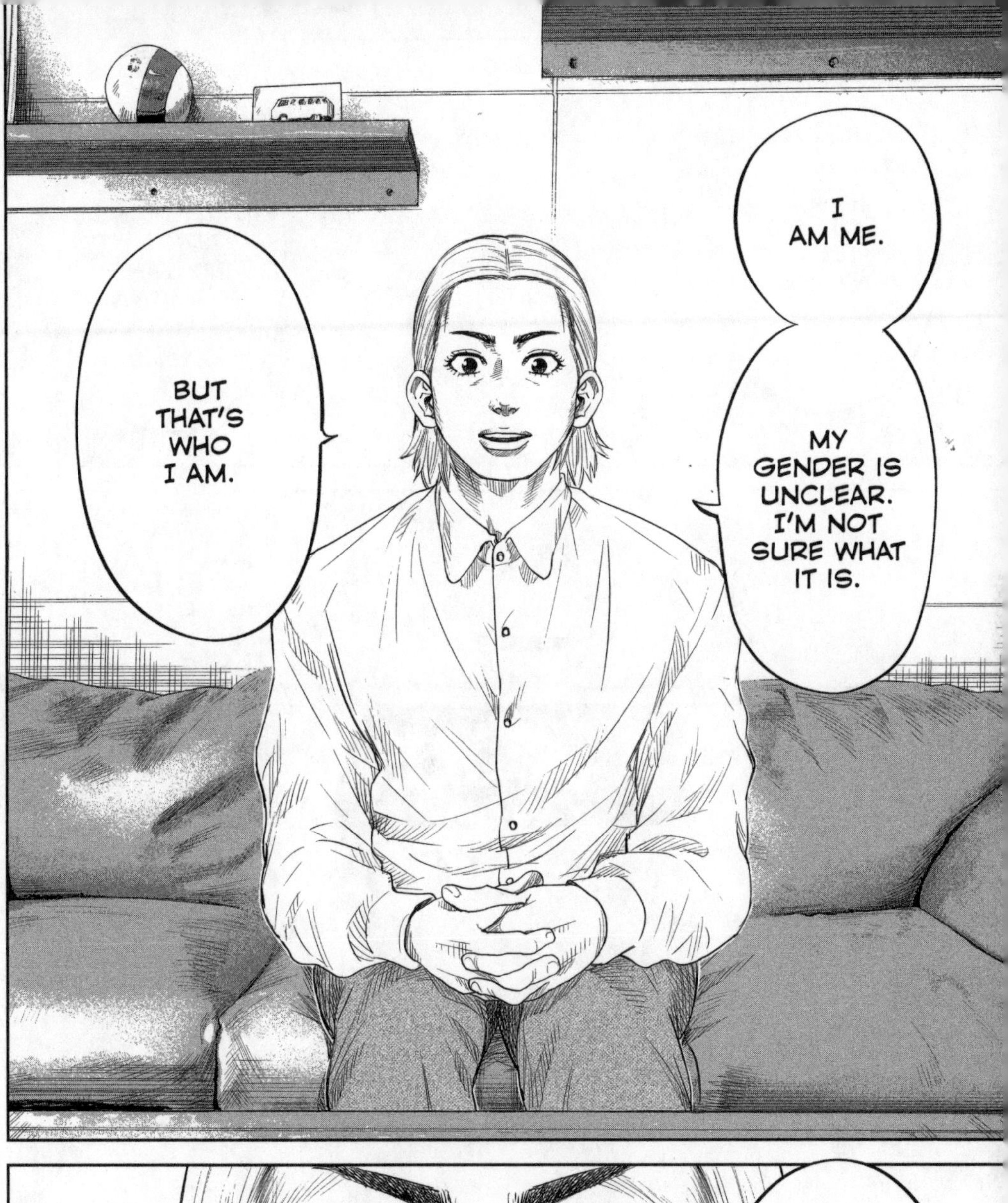
I AM ME.
MY GENDER IS UNCLEAR. I'M NOT SURE WHAT IT IS.
BUT THAT'S WHO I AM.
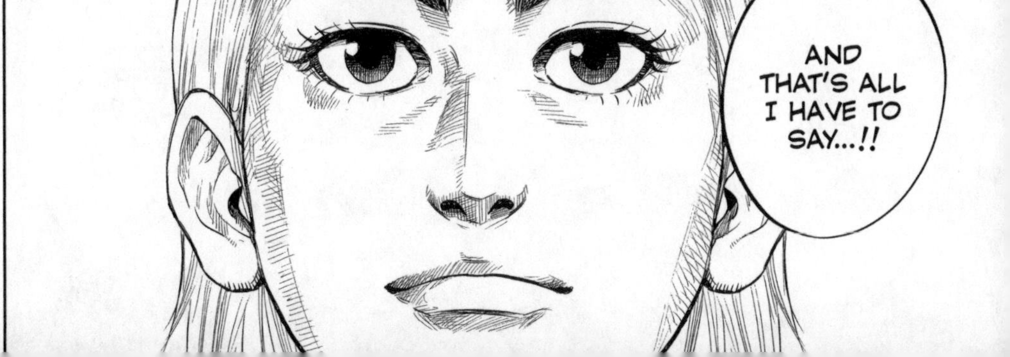
AND THAT'S ALL I HAVE TO SAY...!!

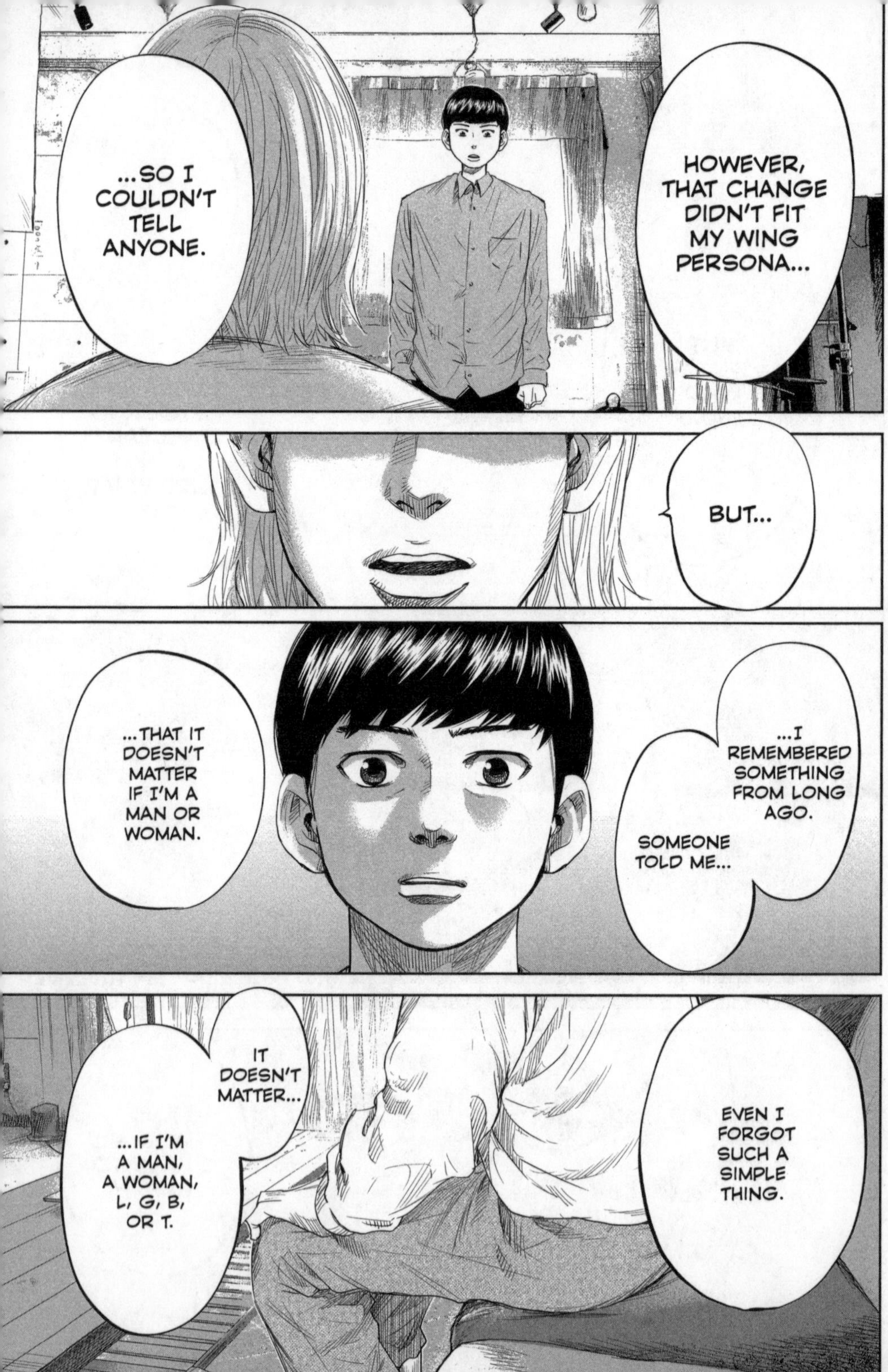
HOWEVER, THAT CHANGE DIDN'T FIT MY WING PERSONA...
...SO I COULDN'T TELL ANYONE.
BUT...
...I REMEMBERED SOMETHING FROM LONG AGO.
SOMEONE TOLD ME...
...THAT IT DOESN'T MATTER IF I'M A MAN OR WOMAN.
EVEN I FORGOT SUCH A SIMPLE THING.
IT DOESN'T MATTER...
...IF I'M A MAN, A WOMAN, L, G, B, OR T.

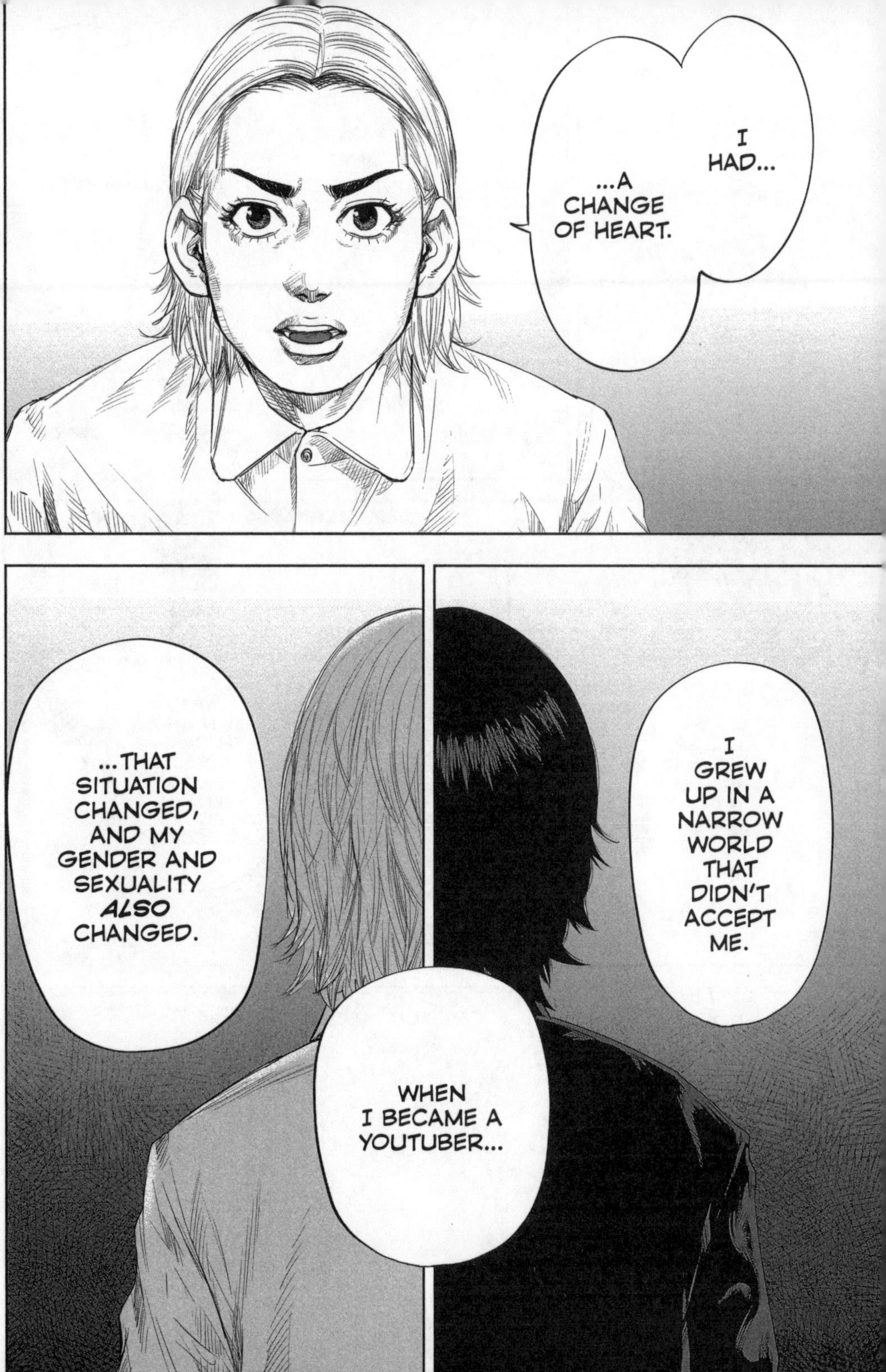
I HAD...
...A CHANGE OF HEART.
I GREW UP IN A NARROW WORLD THAT DIDN'T ACCEPT ME.
WHEN I BECAME A YOUTUBER...
...THAT SITUATION CHANGED, AND MY GENDER AND SEXUALITY *ALSO* CHANGED.

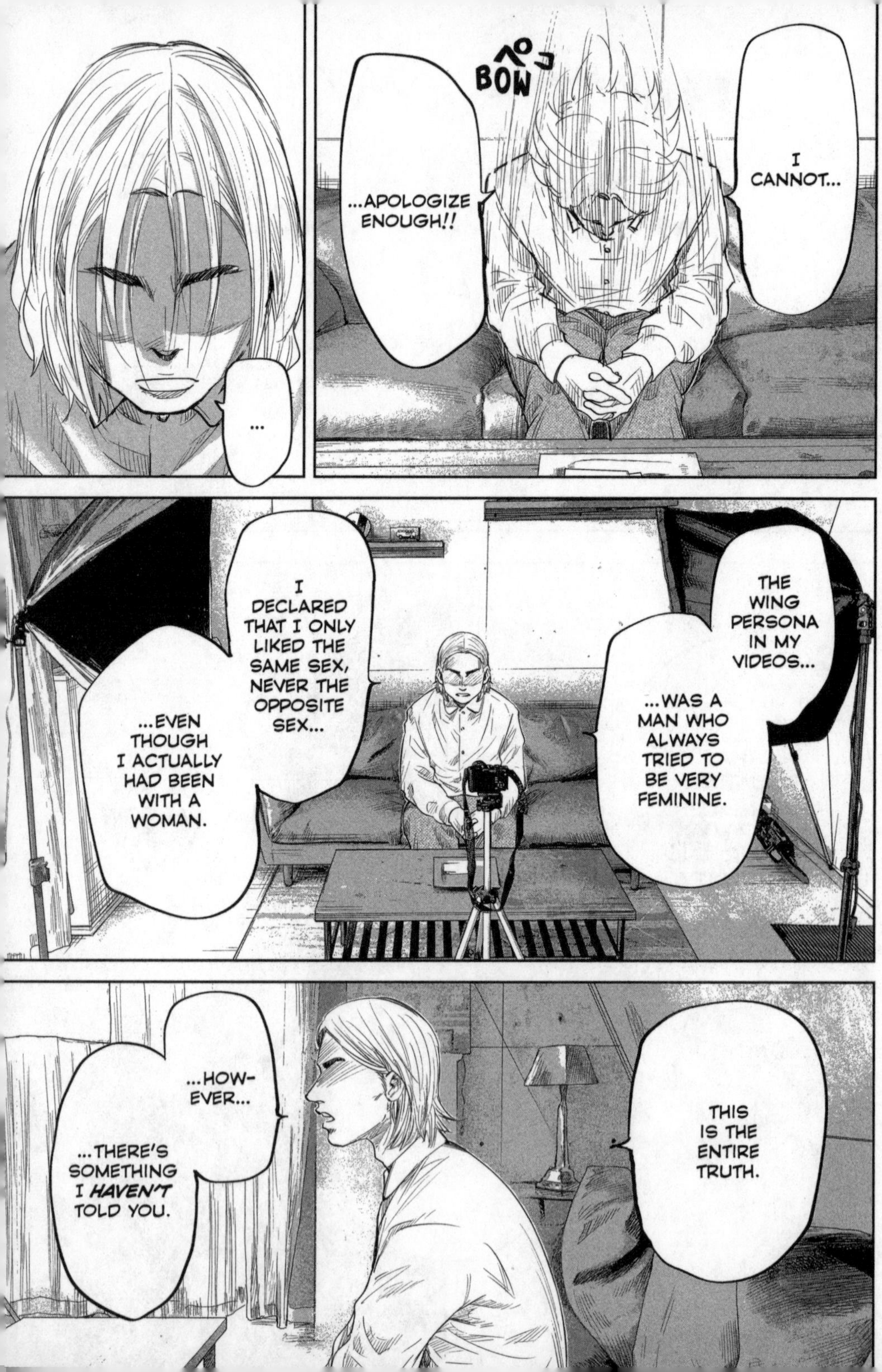
I CANNOT...
BOW
...APOLOGIZE ENOUGH!!
...
THE WING PERSONA IN MY VIDEOS...
...WAS A MAN WHO ALWAYS TRIED TO BE VERY FEMININE.
I DECLARED THAT I ONLY LIKED THE SAME SEX, NEVER THE OPPOSITE SEX...
...EVEN THOUGH I ACTUALLY HAD BEEN WITH A WOMAN.
THIS IS THE ENTIRE TRUTH.
...HOW-EVER...
...THERE'S SOMETHING I *HAVEN'T* TOLD YOU.

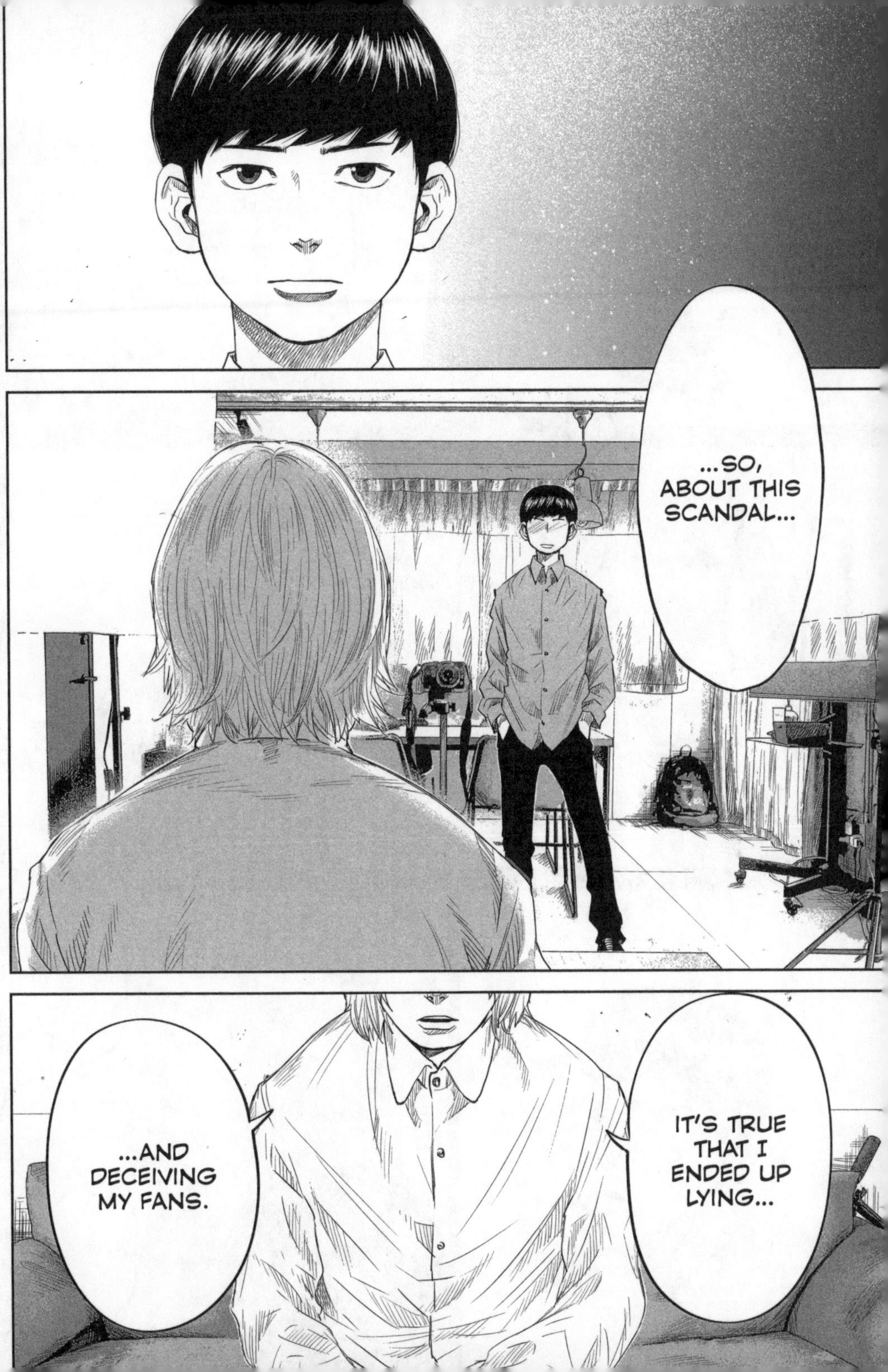
...SO, ABOUT THIS SCANDAL...
IT'S TRUE THAT I ENDED UP LYING...
...AND DECEIVING MY FANS.

Chap. 26 Character

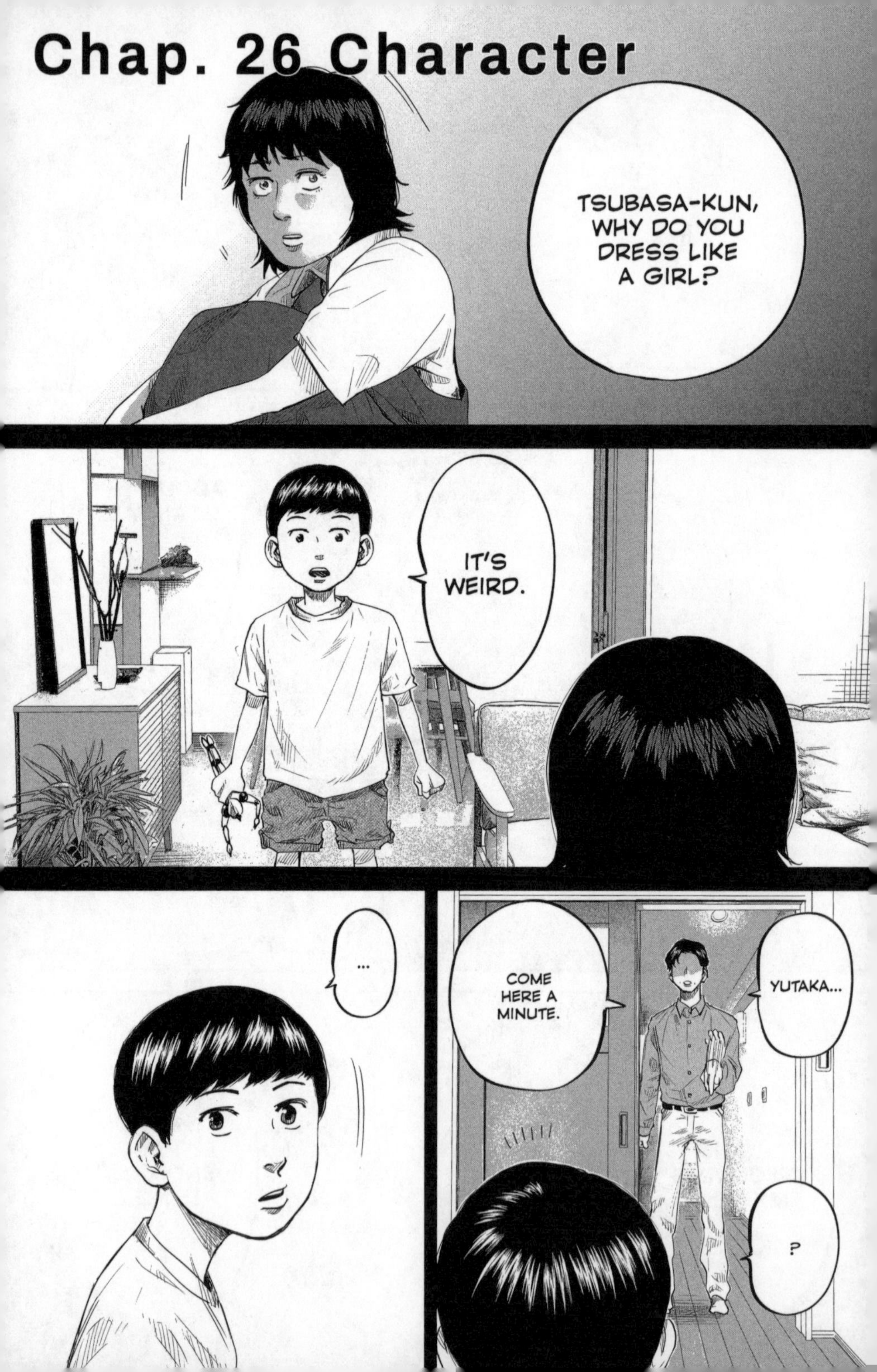
TSUBASA-KUN, WHY DO YOU DRESS LIKE A GIRL?
IT'S WEIRD.
YUTAKA...
COME HERE A MINUTE.
?
...

BOYS RUN

ボーイズ・ラン・ザ・ライオット

THE RIOT

BOYS RUN

ボーイズ・ラン・ザ・ライオット

THE RIOT

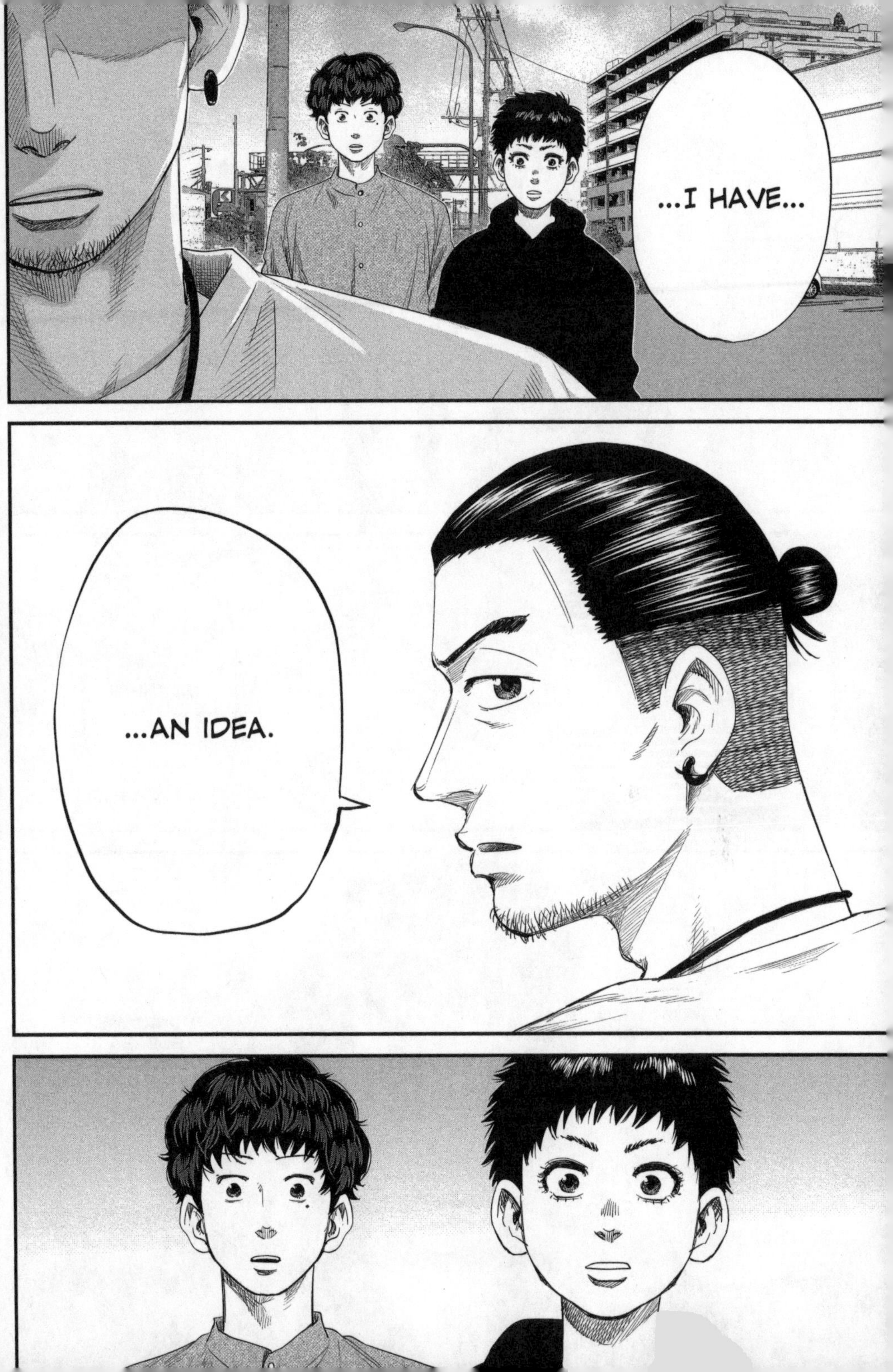
...I HAVE...
...AN IDEA.

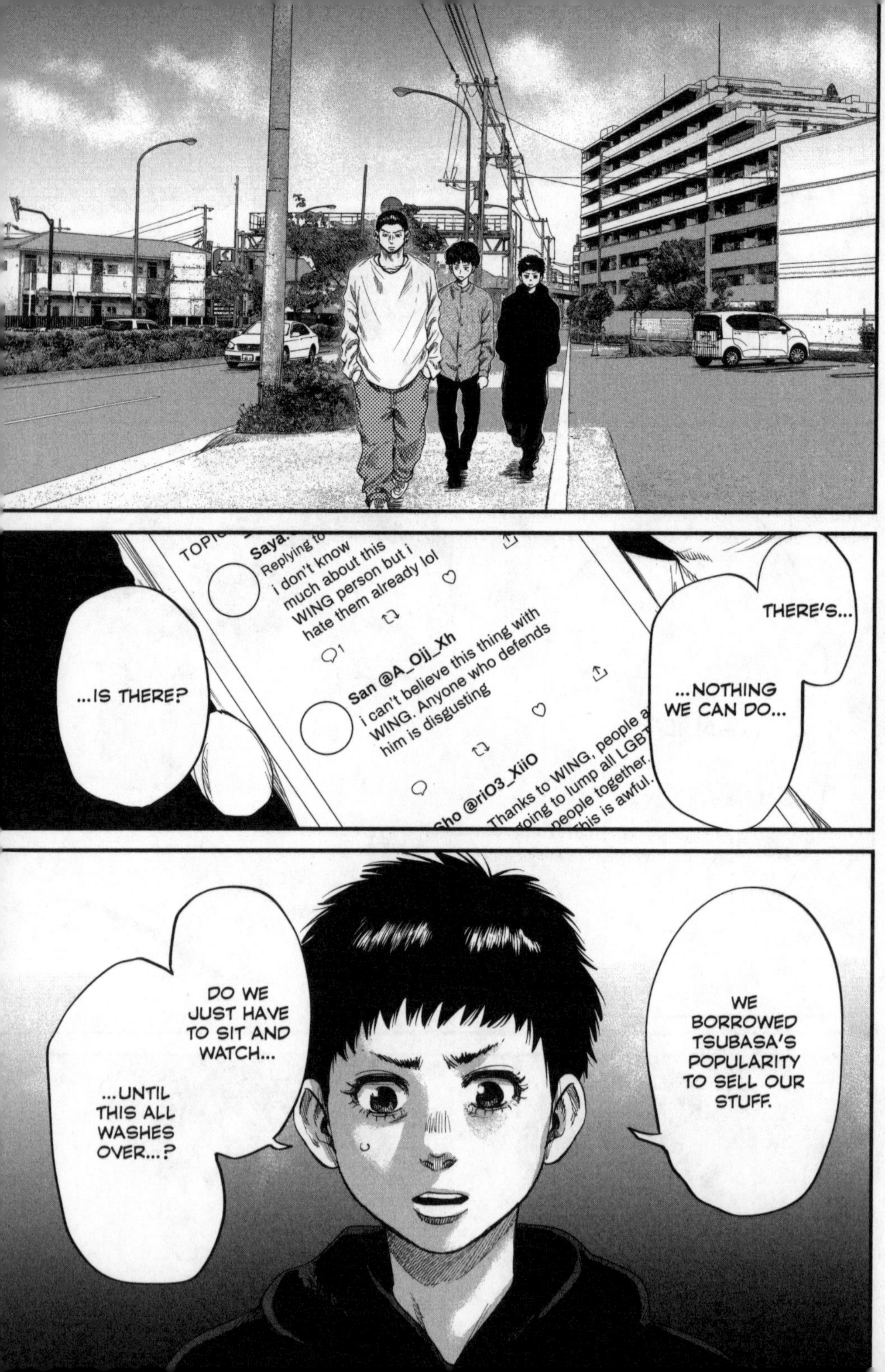
THERE'S...
...NOTHING WE CAN DO...
Saya.
Replying to
i don't know much about this WING person but i hate them already lol
San @A_Ojj_Xh
i can't believe this thing with WING. Anyone who defends him is disgusting
Cho @riO3_XiiO
...IS THERE?
WE BORROWED TSUBASA'S POPULARITY TO SELL OUR STUFF.
DO WE JUST HAVE TO SIT AND WATCH...
...UNTIL THIS ALL WASHES OVER...?

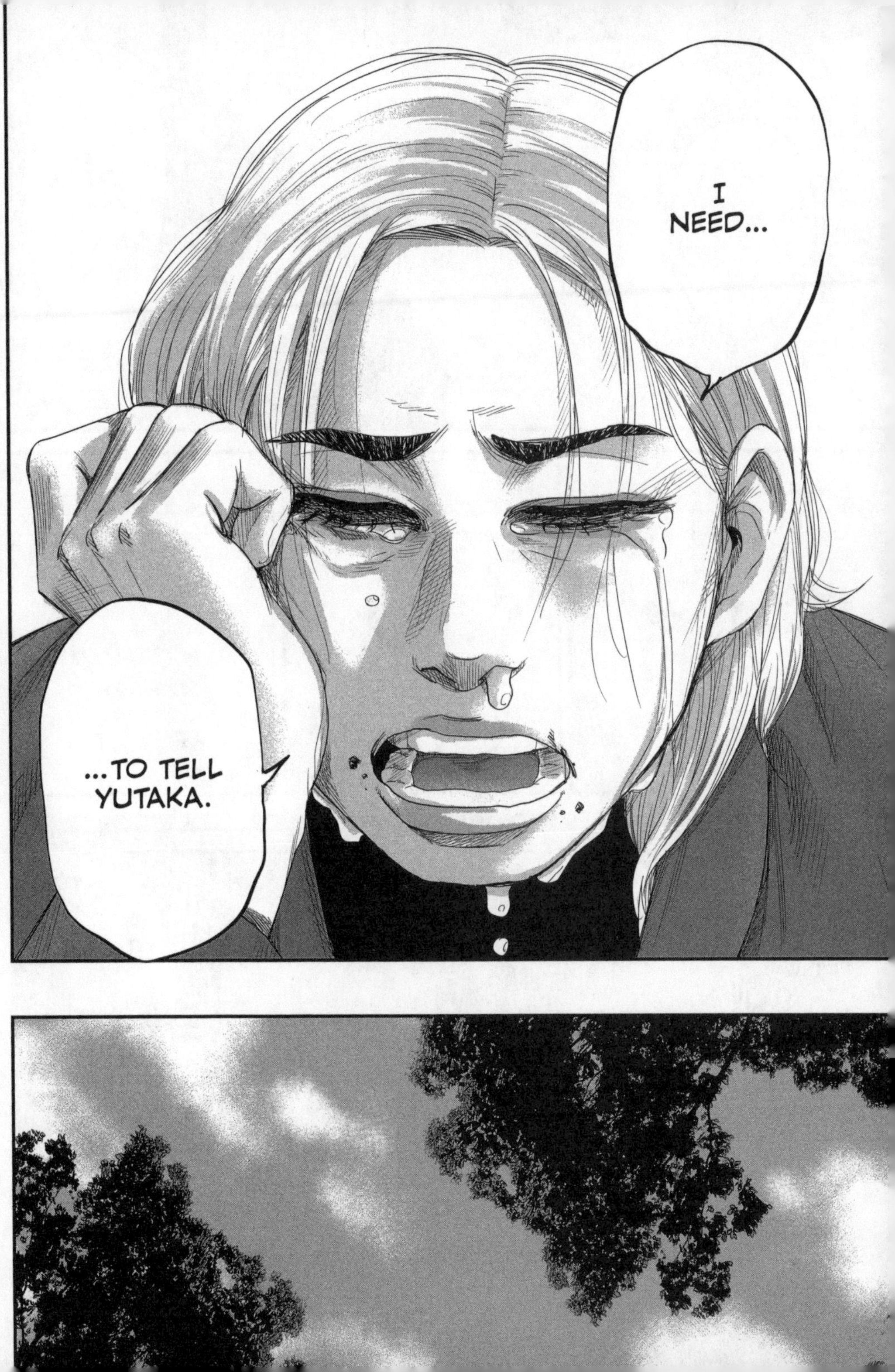
I NEED...
...TO TELL YUTAKA.

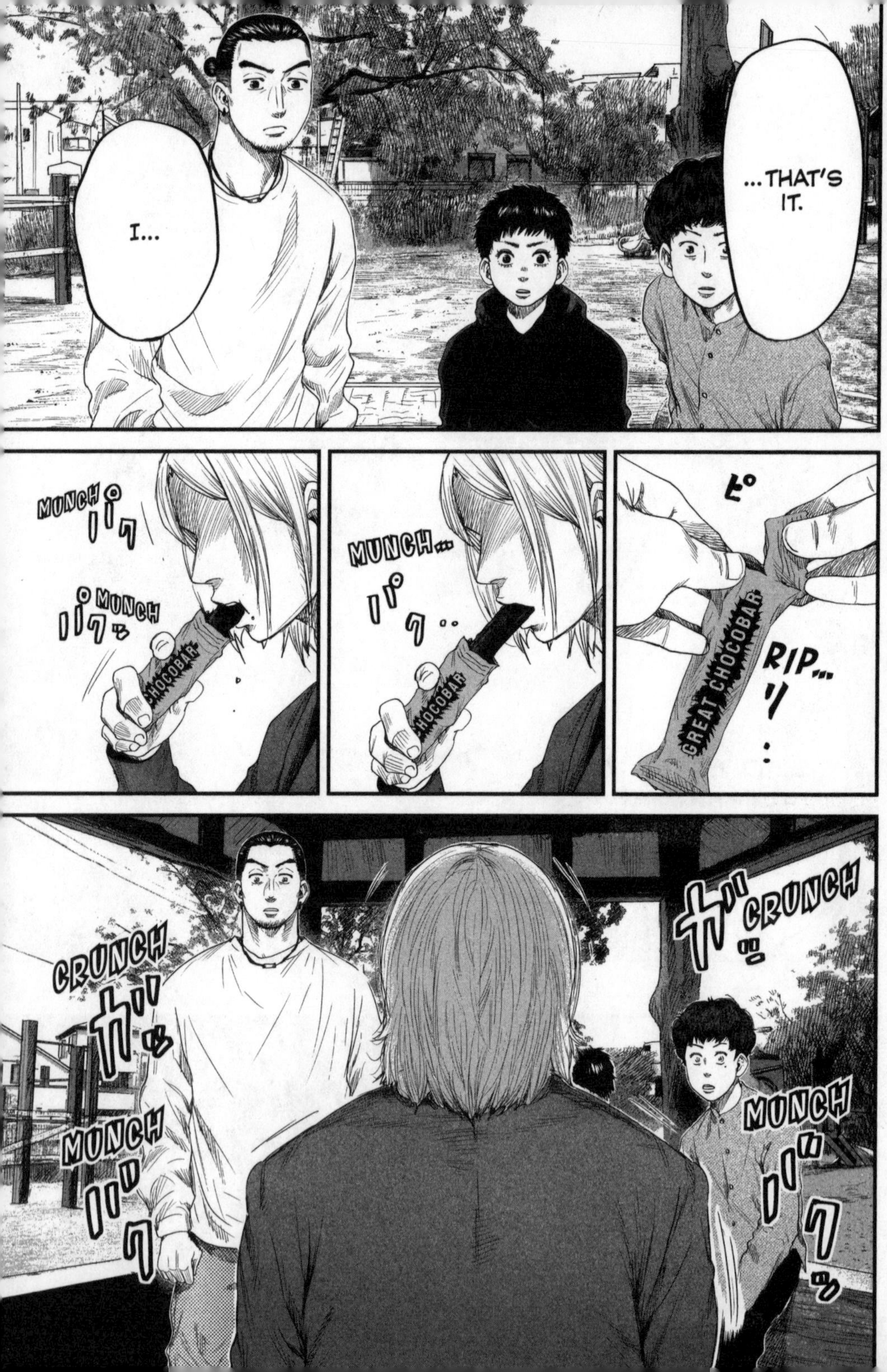

...THAT'S IT.
I...
ピ
GREAT CHOCOBAR
RIP...
リ
MUNCH...
パク..
CHOCOBAR
MUNCH
パク
MUNCH
パク
CHOCOBAR
CRUNCH
ガリ
MUNCH
バク
CRUNCH
ガリ
MUNCH
バク

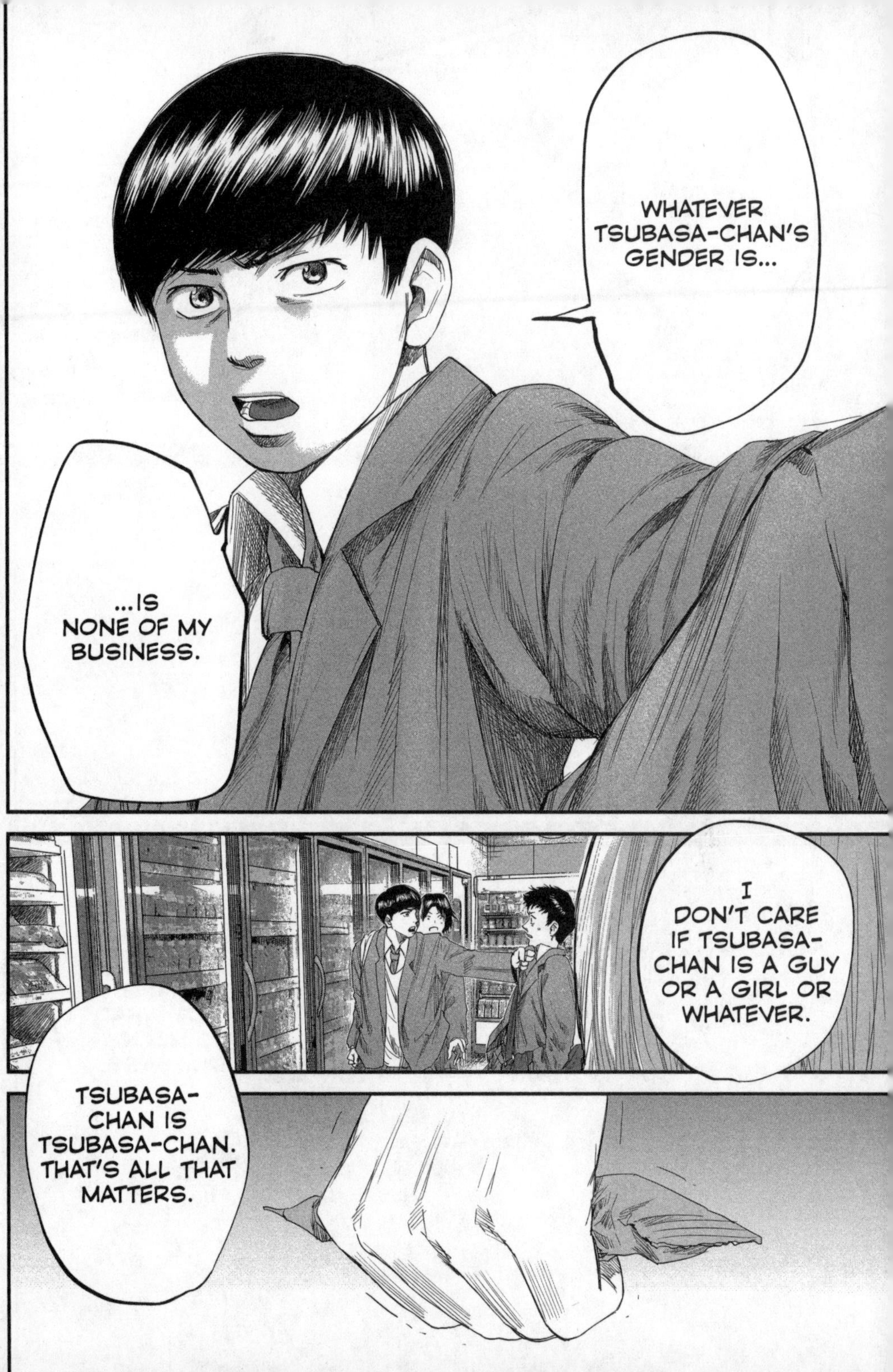
WHATEVER TSUBASA-CHAN'S GENDER IS...
...IS NONE OF MY BUSINESS.
I DON'T CARE IF TSUBASA-CHAN IS A GUY OR A GIRL OR WHATEVER.
TSUBASA-CHAN IS TSUBASA-CHAN. THAT'S ALL THAT MATTERS.

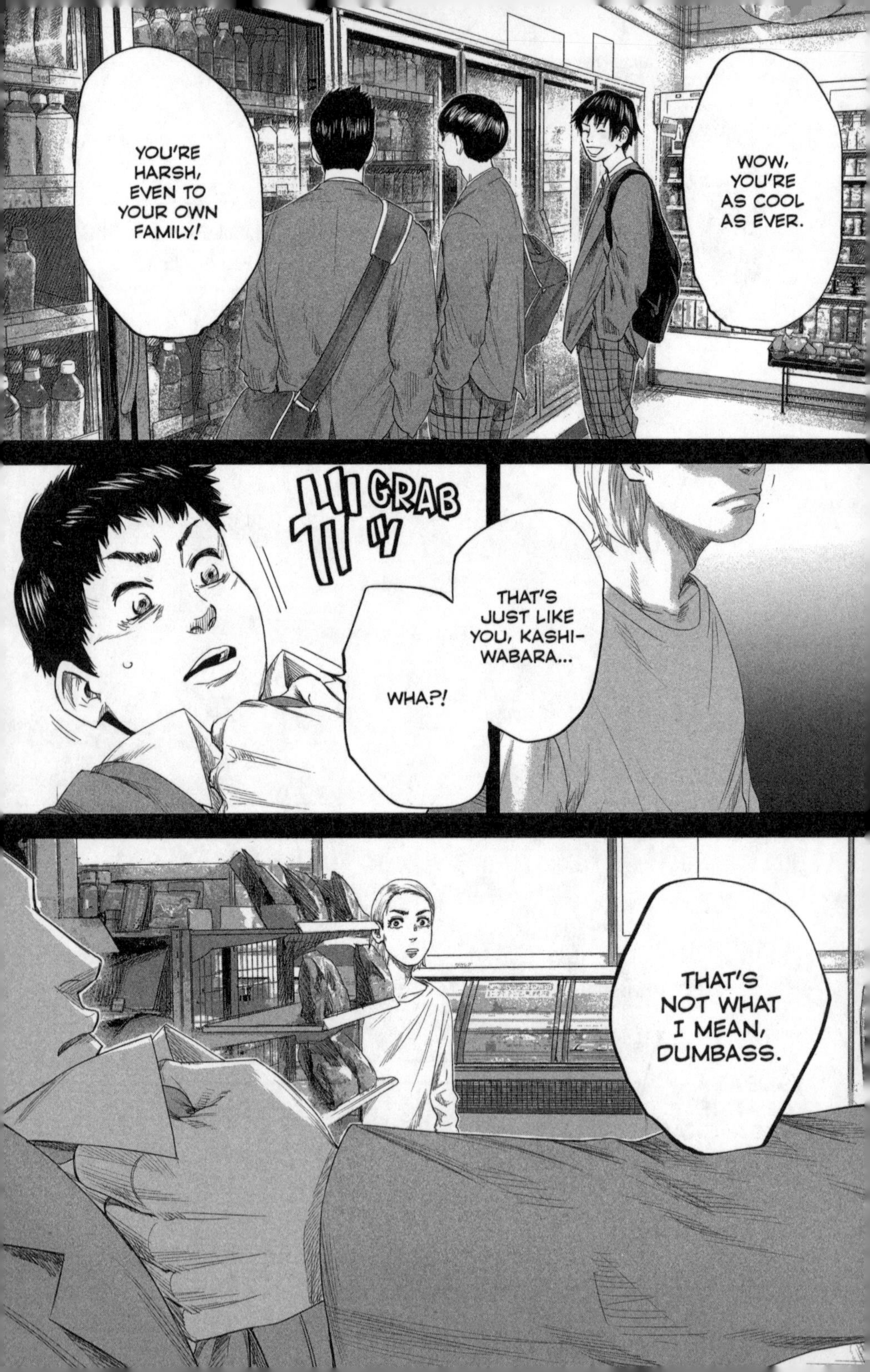
WOW, YOU'RE AS COOL AS EVER.
YOU'RE HARSH, EVEN TO YOUR OWN FAMILY!
THAT'S JUST LIKE YOU, KASHI-WABARA...
GRAB
WHA?!
THAT'S NOT WHAT I MEAN, DUMBASS.

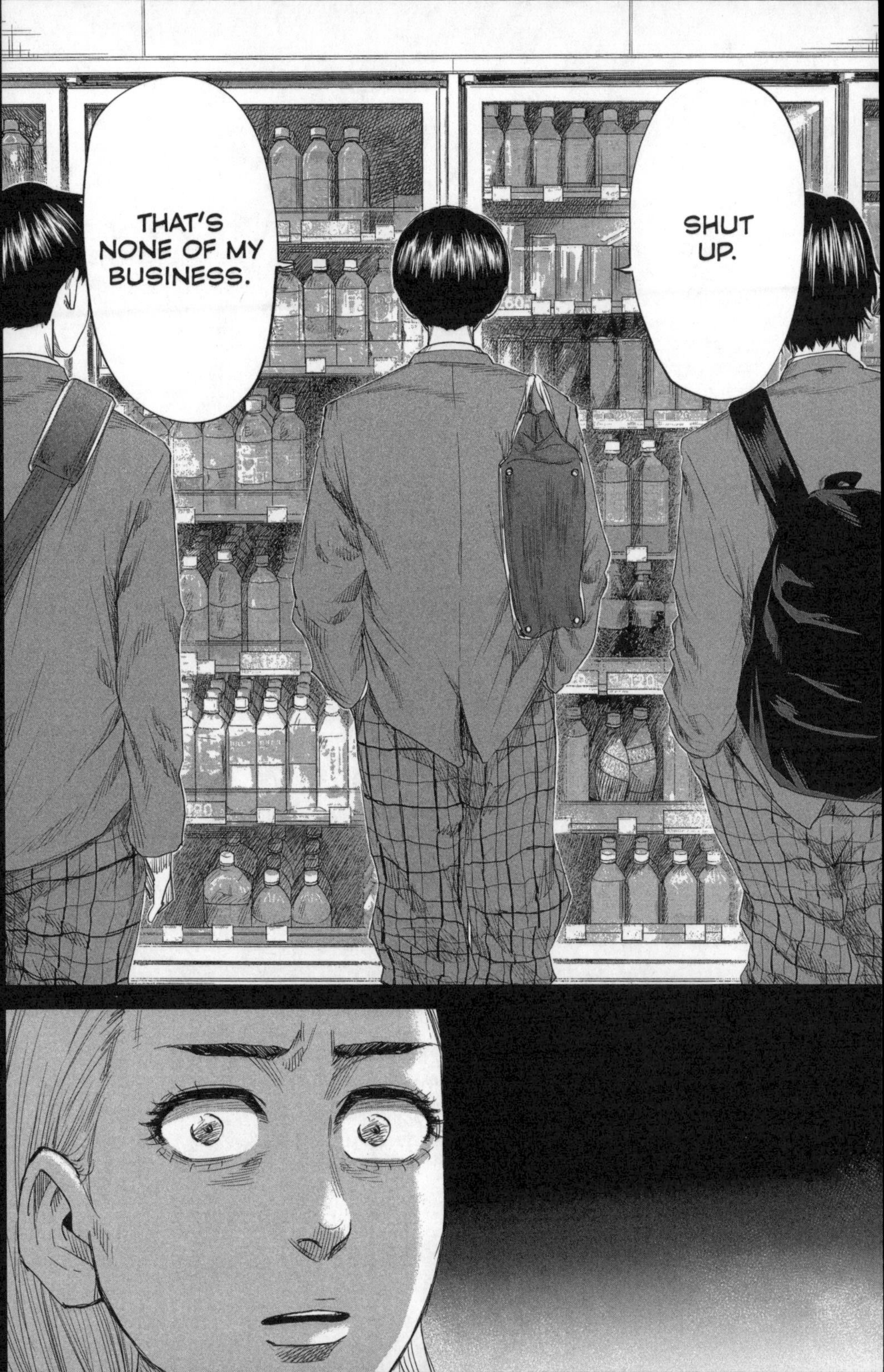
SHUT UP.
THAT'S NONE OF MY BUSINESS.

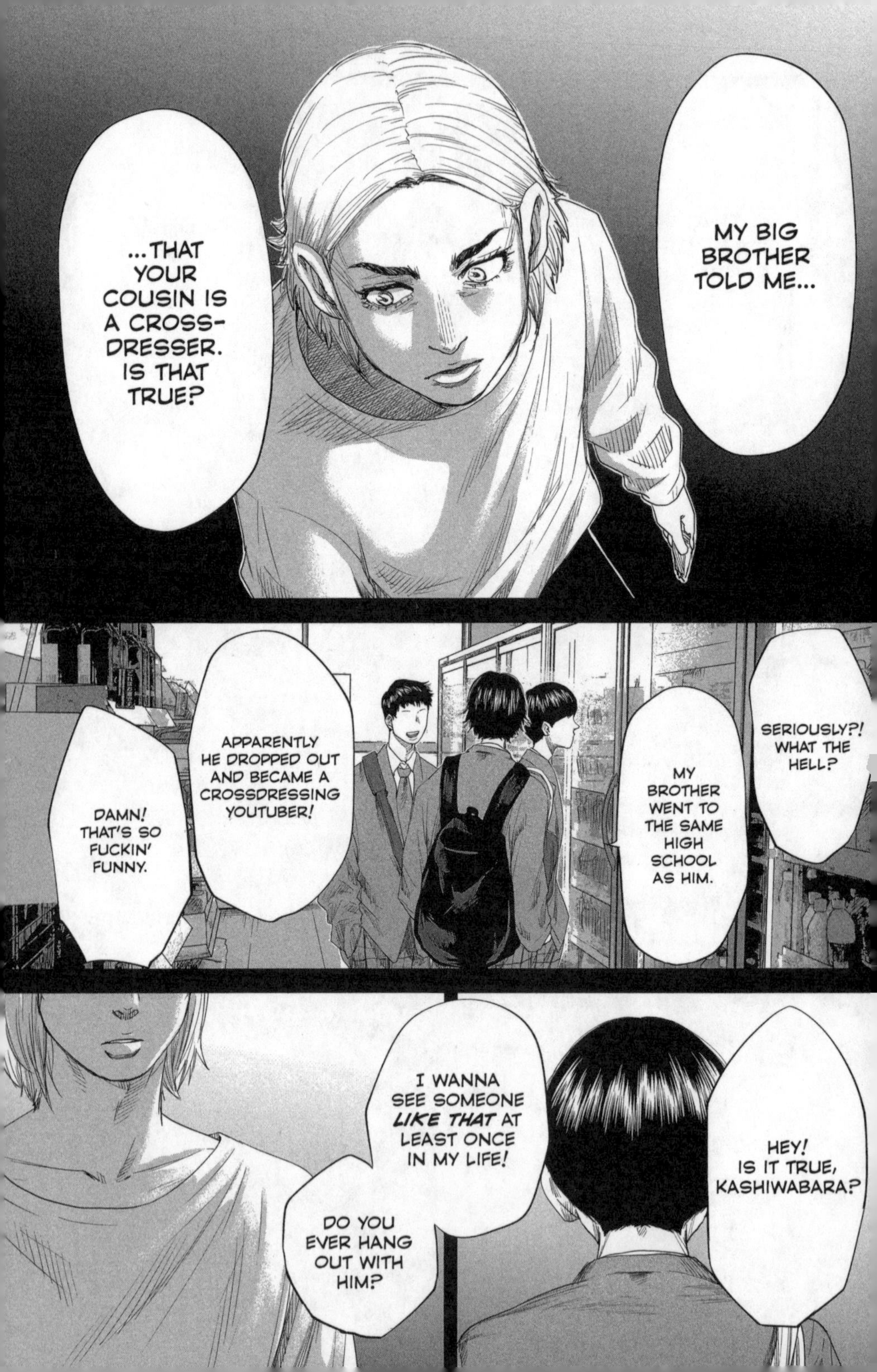
MY BIG BROTHER TOLD ME...
...THAT YOUR COUSIN IS A CROSS-DRESSER. IS THAT TRUE?
SERIOUSLY?! WHAT THE HELL?
MY BROTHER WENT TO THE SAME HIGH SCHOOL AS HIM.
APPARENTLY HE DROPPED OUT AND BECAME A CROSSDRESSING YOUTUBER!
DAMN! THAT'S SO FUCKIN' FUNNY.
HEY! IS IT TRUE, KASHIWABARA?
I WANNA SEE SOMEONE *LIKE THAT* AT LEAST ONCE IN MY LIFE!
DO YOU EVER HANG OUT WITH HIM?

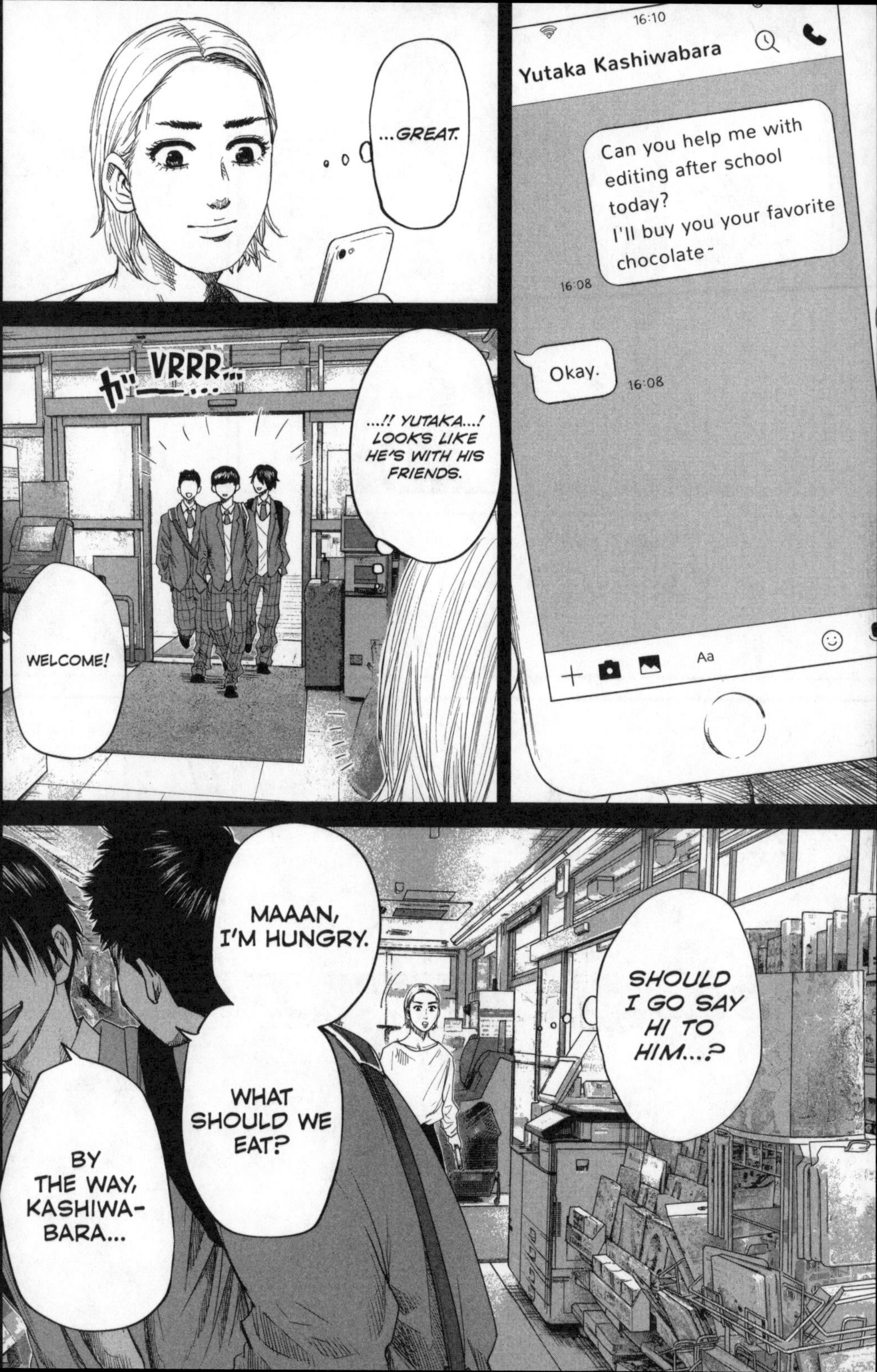
16:10
Yutaka Kashiwabara
Can you help me with editing after school today?
I'll buy you your favorite chocolate~
16:08
Okay.
16:08
Aa
...GREAT.
ガー VRRR...
...!! YUTAKA...! LOOKS LIKE HE'S WITH HIS FRIENDS.
WELCOME!
SHOULD I GO SAY HI TO HIM...?
MAAAN, I'M HUNGRY.
WHAT SHOULD WE EAT?
BY THE WAY, KASHIWA-BARA...

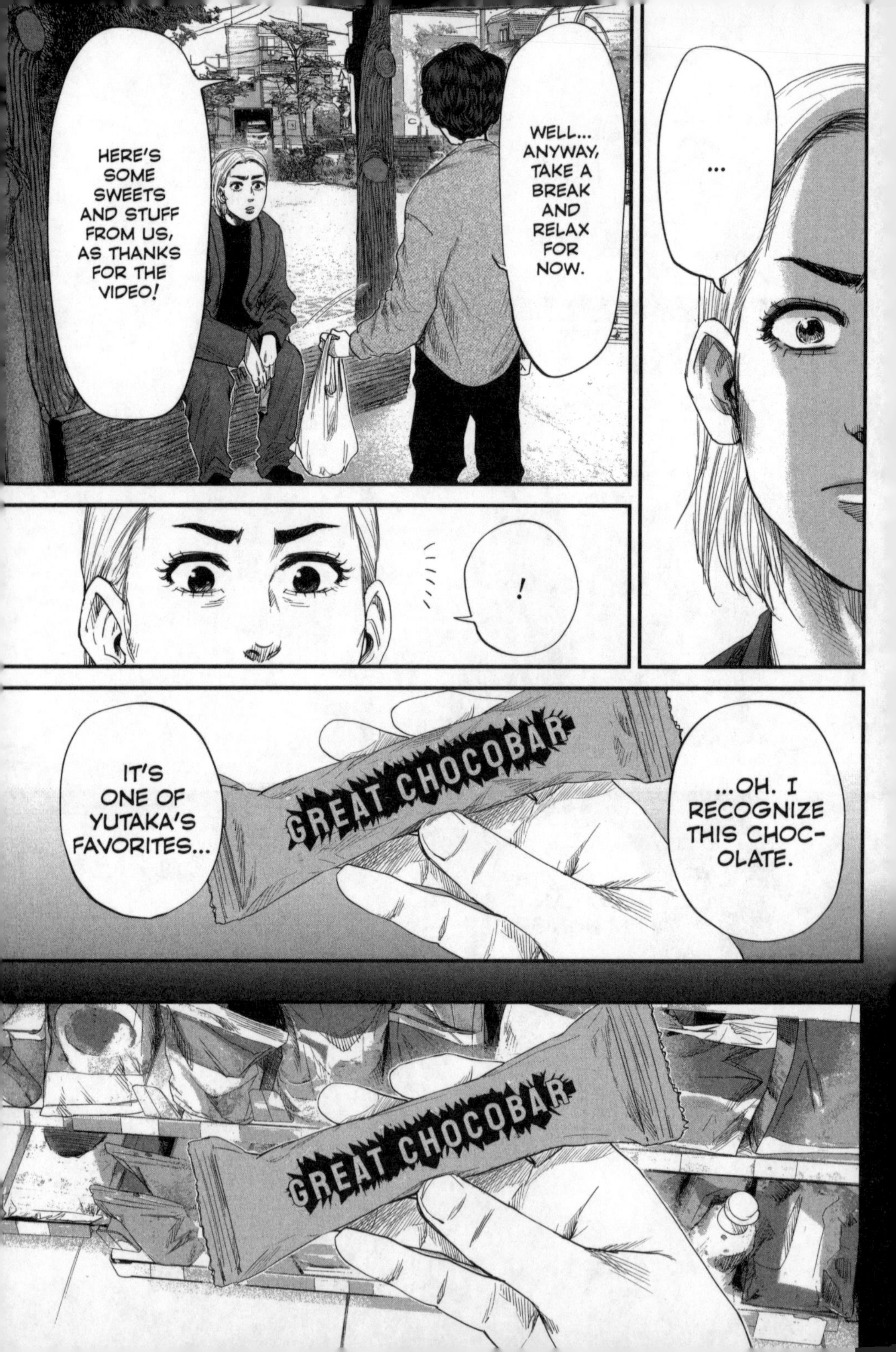
...
WELL... ANYWAY, TAKE A BREAK AND RELAX FOR NOW.
HERE'S SOME SWEETS AND STUFF FROM US, AS THANKS FOR THE VIDEO!
!
...OH. I RECOGNIZE THIS CHOC-OLATE.
GREAT CHOCOBAR
IT'S ONE OF YUTAKA'S FAVORITES...
GREAT CHOCOBAR

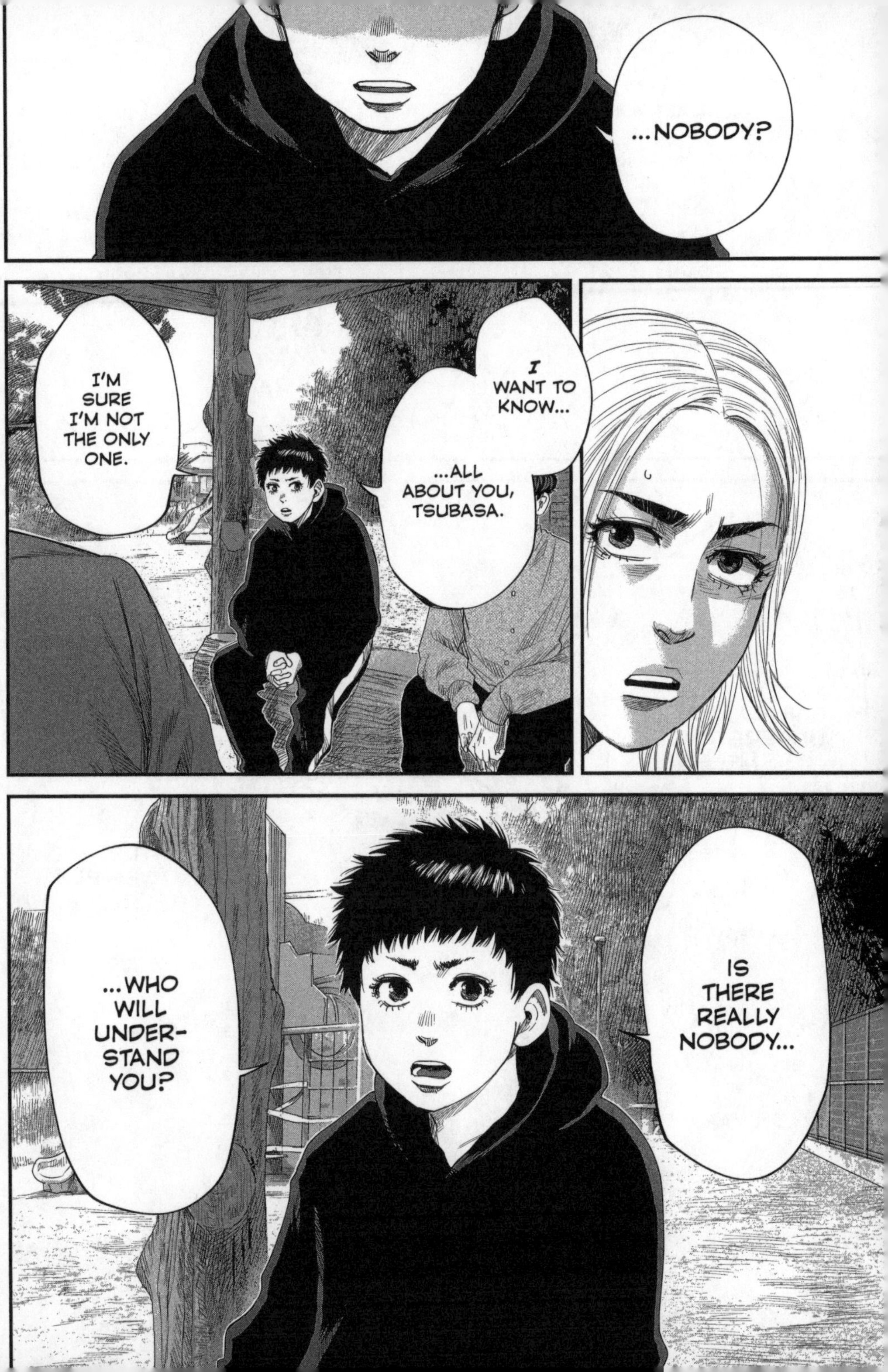
...NOBODY?
I WANT TO KNOW...
...ALL ABOUT YOU, TSUBASA.
I'M SURE I'M NOT THE ONLY ONE.
IS THERE REALLY NOBODY...
...WHO WILL UNDER-STAND YOU?

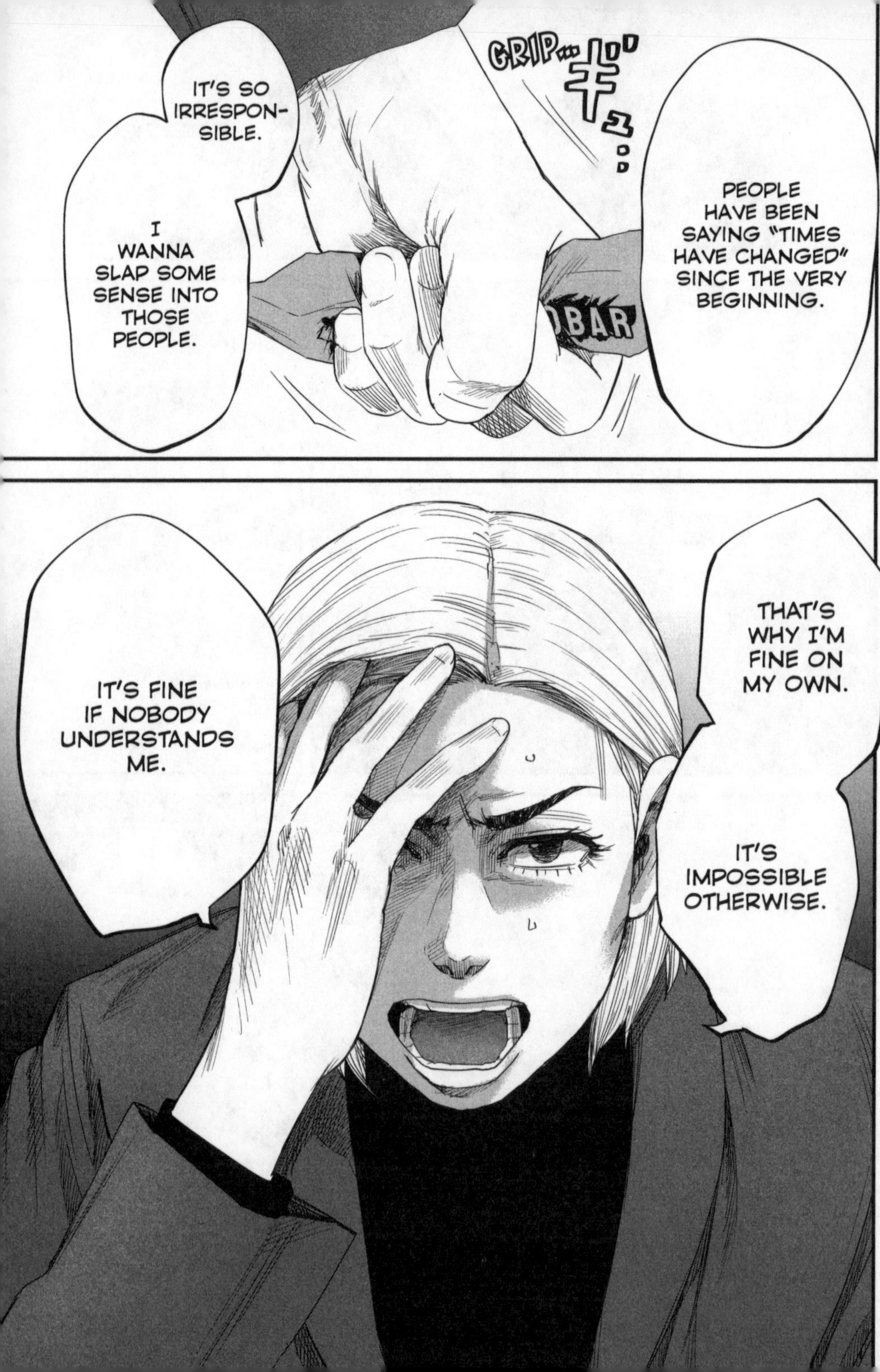
PEOPLE HAVE BEEN SAYING "TIMES HAVE CHANGED" SINCE THE VERY BEGINNING.
GRIP...
IT'S SO IRRESPON-SIBLE.
I WANNA SLAP SOME SENSE INTO THOSE PEOPLE.
THAT'S WHY I'M FINE ON MY OWN.
IT'S IMPOSSIBLE OTHERWISE.
IT'S FINE IF NOBODY UNDERSTANDS ME.

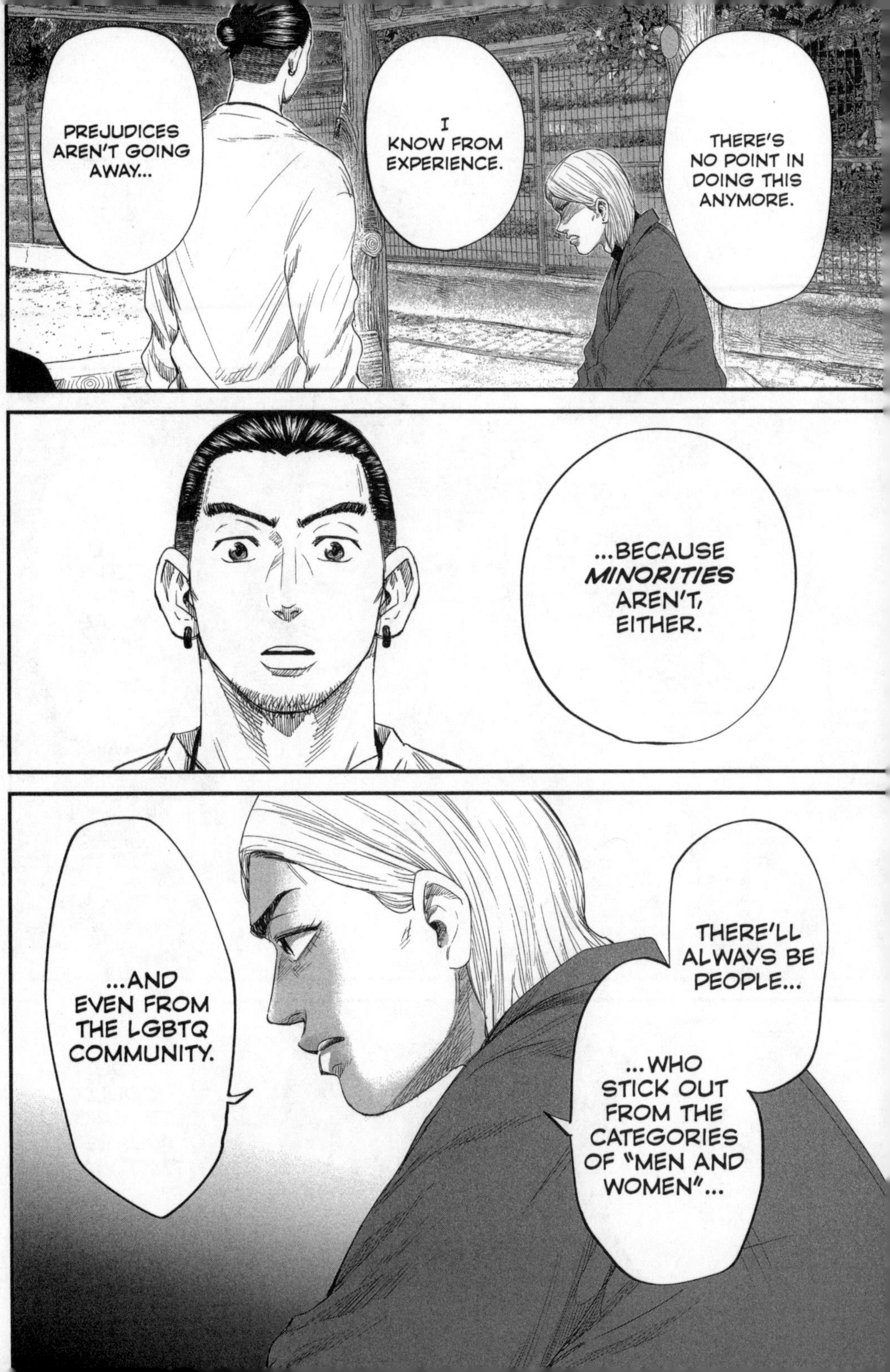
THERE'S NO POINT IN DOING THIS ANYMORE.
I KNOW FROM EXPERIENCE.
PREJUDICES AREN'T GOING AWAY...
...BECAUSE *MINORITIES* AREN'T, EITHER.
THERE'LL ALWAYS BE PEOPLE...
...WHO STICK OUT FROM THE CATEGORIES OF "MEN AND WOMEN"...
...AND EVEN FROM THE LGBTQ COMMUNITY.

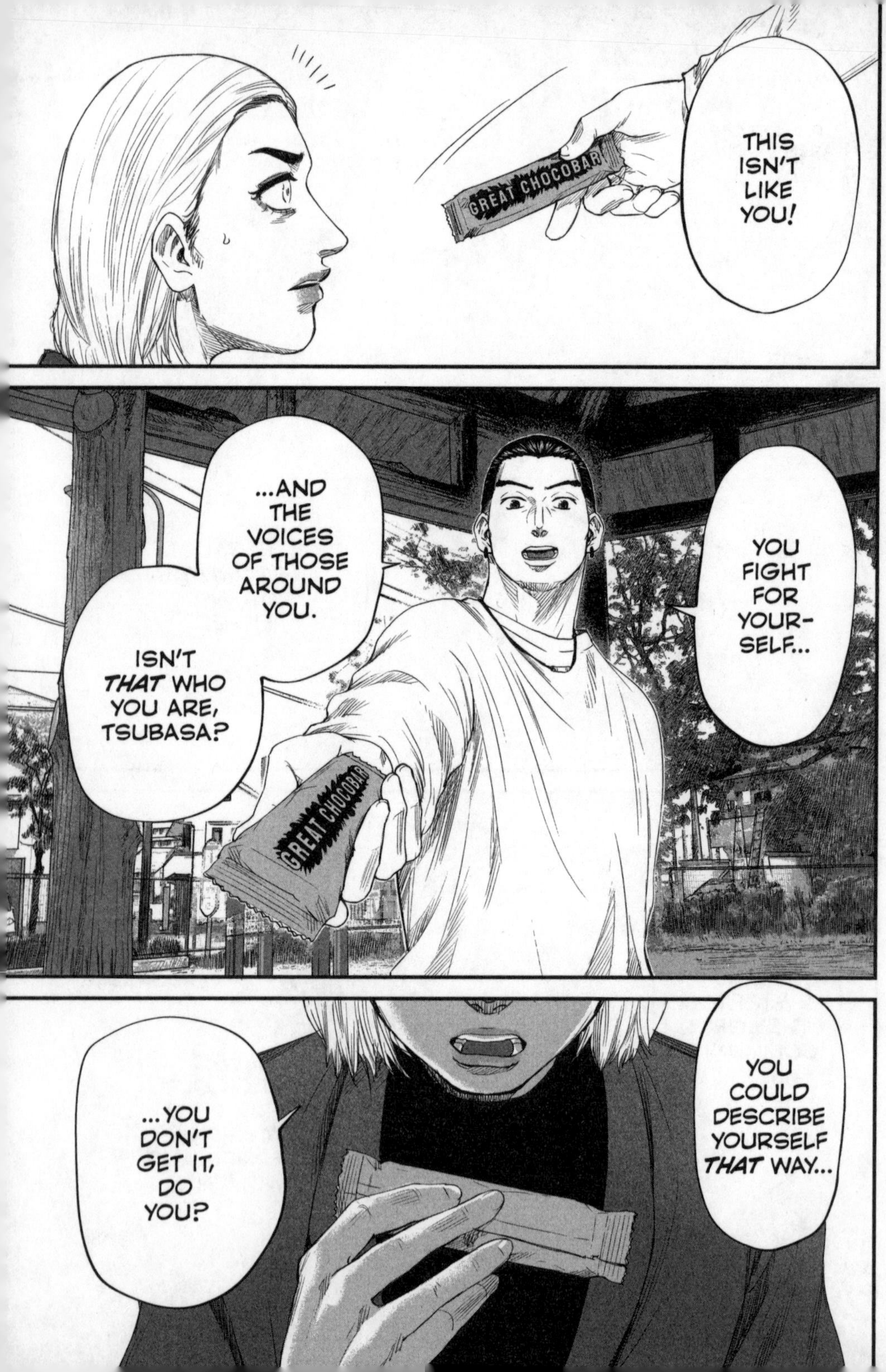
THIS ISN'T LIKE YOU!
GREAT CHOCOBAR
YOU FIGHT FOR YOUR-SELF...
...AND THE VOICES OF THOSE AROUND YOU.
ISN'T *THAT* WHO YOU ARE, TSUBASA?
GREAT CHOCOBAR
YOU COULD DESCRIBE YOURSELF *THAT* WAY...
...YOU DON'T GET IT, DO YOU?

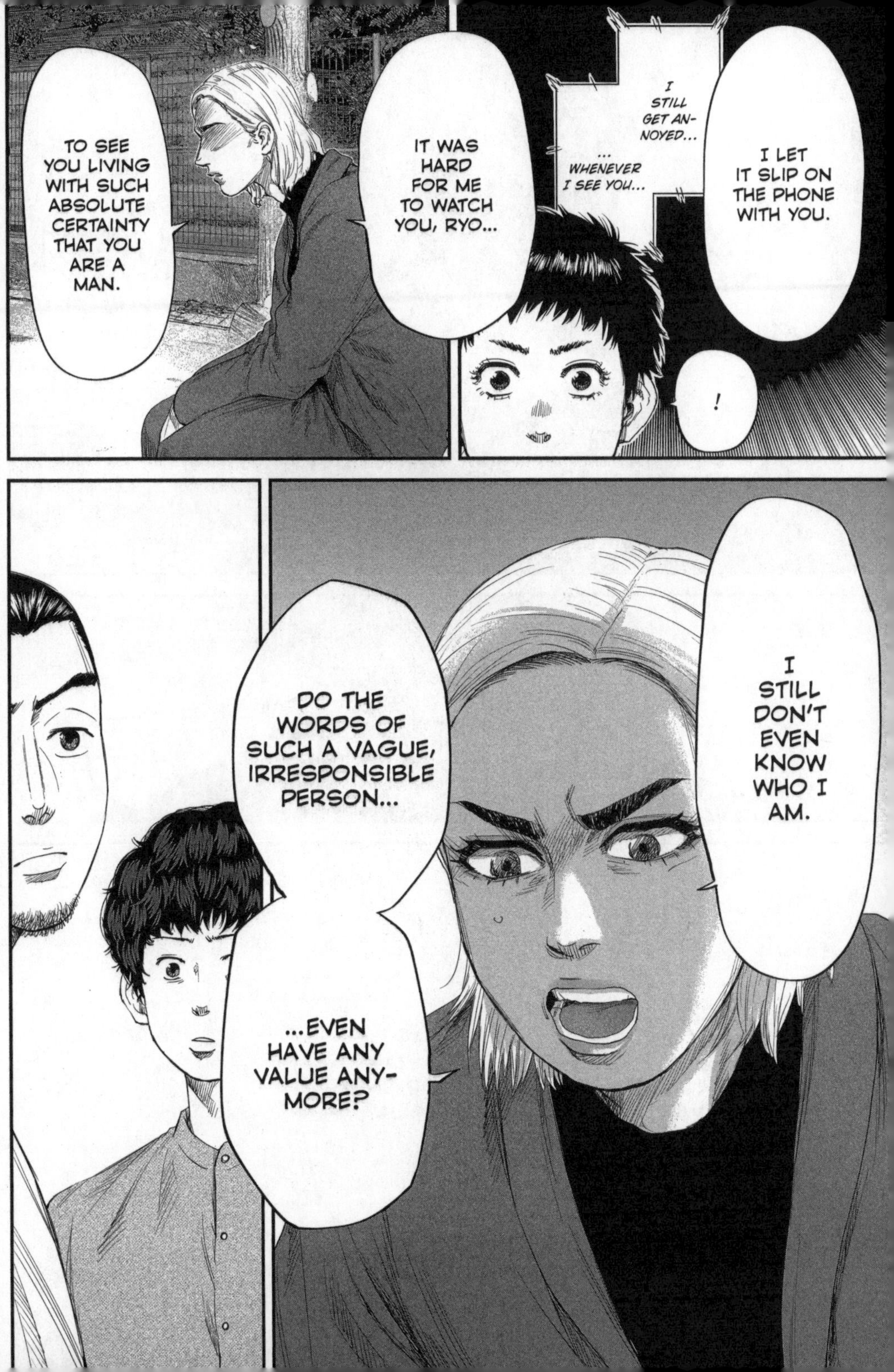
I LET IT SLIP ON THE PHONE WITH YOU.
I STILL GET AN-NOYED...
...WHENEVER I SEE YOU...
!
IT WAS HARD FOR ME TO WATCH YOU, RYO...
TO SEE YOU LIVING WITH SUCH ABSOLUTE CERTAINTY THAT YOU ARE A MAN.
I STILL DON'T EVEN KNOW WHO I AM.
DO THE WORDS OF SUCH A VAGUE, IRRESPONSIBLE PERSON...
...EVEN HAVE ANY VALUE ANY-MORE?

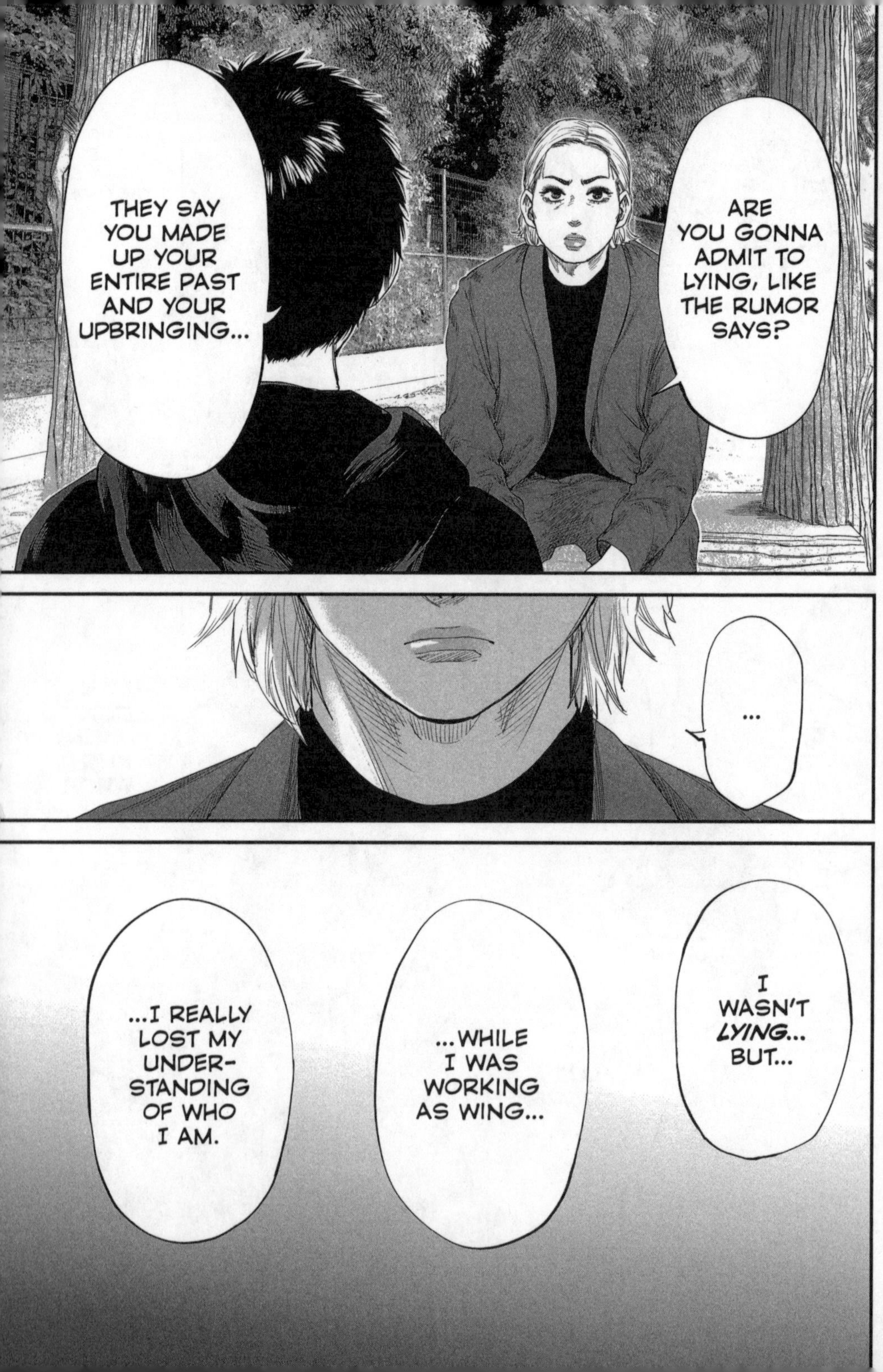
ARE YOU GONNA ADMIT TO LYING, LIKE THE RUMOR SAYS?
THEY SAY YOU MADE UP YOUR ENTIRE PAST AND YOUR UPBRINGING...
...
I WASN'T *LYING*... BUT...
...WHILE I WAS WORKING AS WING...
...I REALLY LOST MY UNDER-STANDING OF WHO I AM.

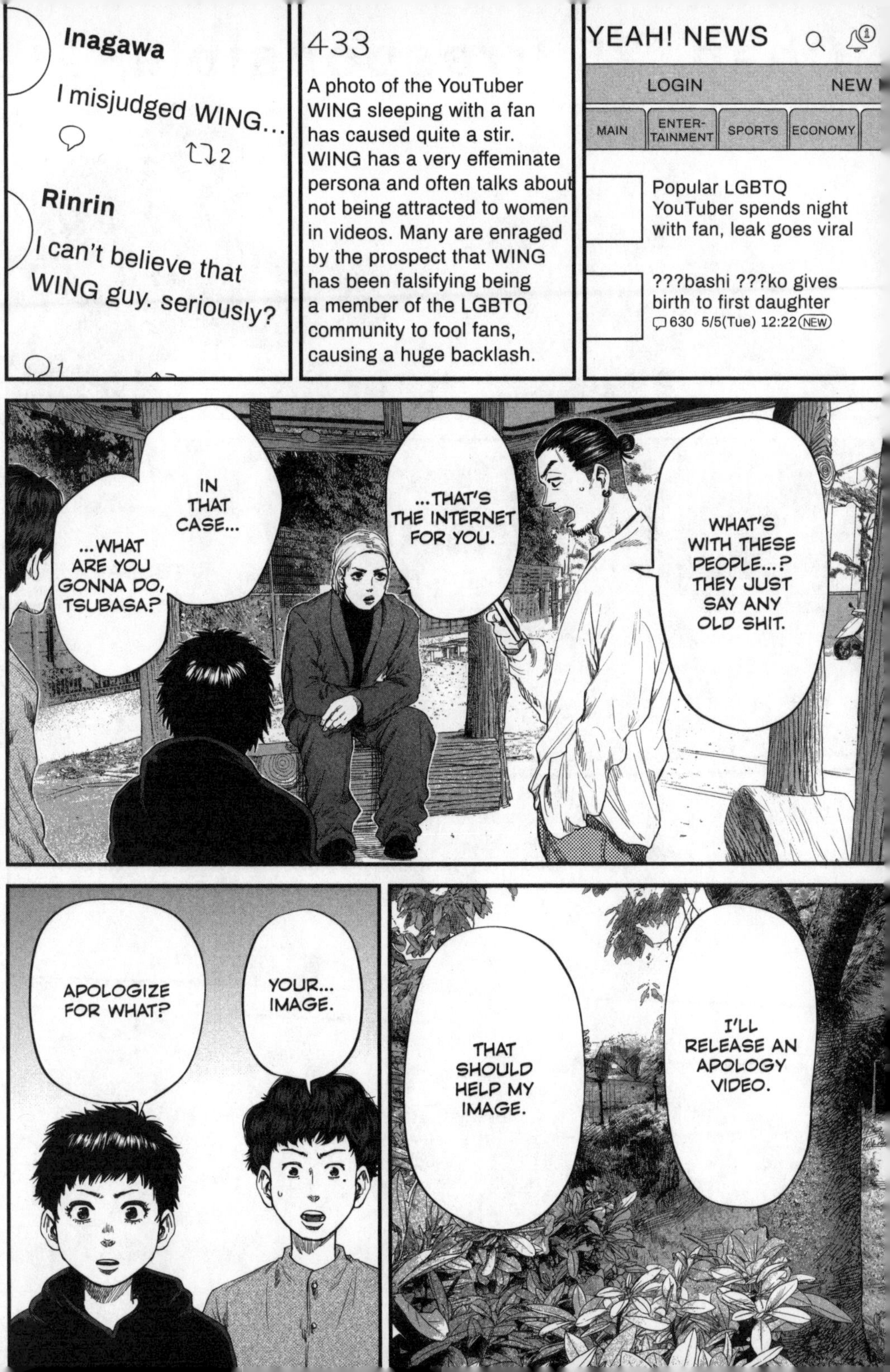
YEAH! NEWS
LOGIN
NEW
MAIN
ENTER-TAINMENT
SPORTS
ECONOMY
Popular LGBTQ YouTuber spends night with fan, leak goes viral
???bashi ???ko gives birth to first daughter
630 5/5(Tue) 12:22 NEW
433
A photo of the YouTuber WING sleeping with a fan has caused quite a stir. WING has a very effeminate persona and often talks about not being attracted to women in videos. Many are enraged by the prospect that WING has been falsifying being a member of the LGBTQ community to fool fans, causing a huge backlash.
Inagawa
I misjudged WING...
2
Rinrin
I can't believe that WING guy. seriously?
1
WHAT'S WITH THESE PEOPLE...? THEY JUST SAY ANY OLD SHIT.
...THAT'S THE INTERNET FOR YOU.
IN THAT CASE...
...WHAT ARE YOU GONNA DO, TSUBASA?
I'LL RELEASE AN APOLOGY VIDEO.
THAT SHOULD HELP MY IMAGE.
YOUR... IMAGE.
APOLOGIZE FOR WHAT?

Chap. 25 Irresponsible

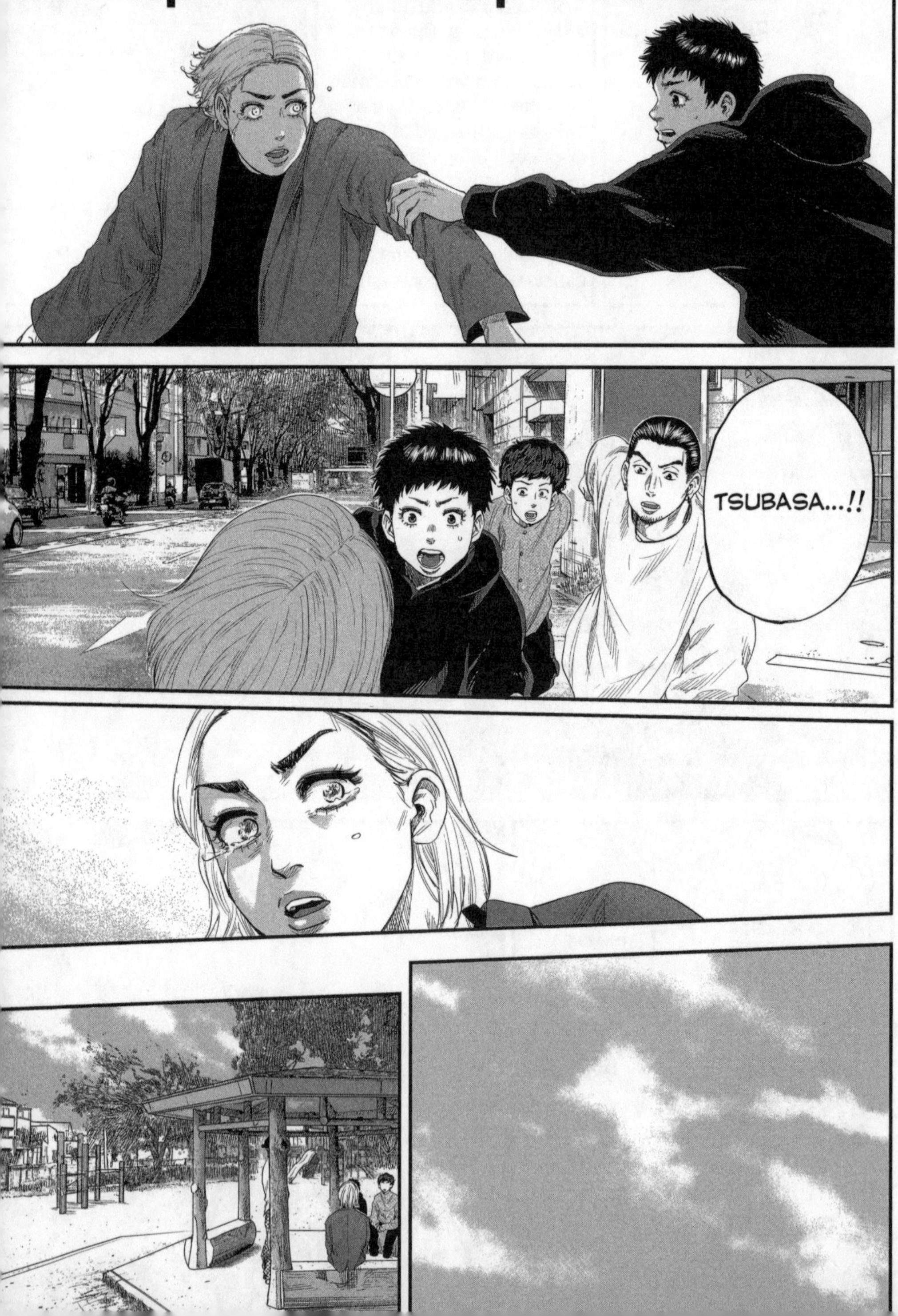
TSUBASA...!!

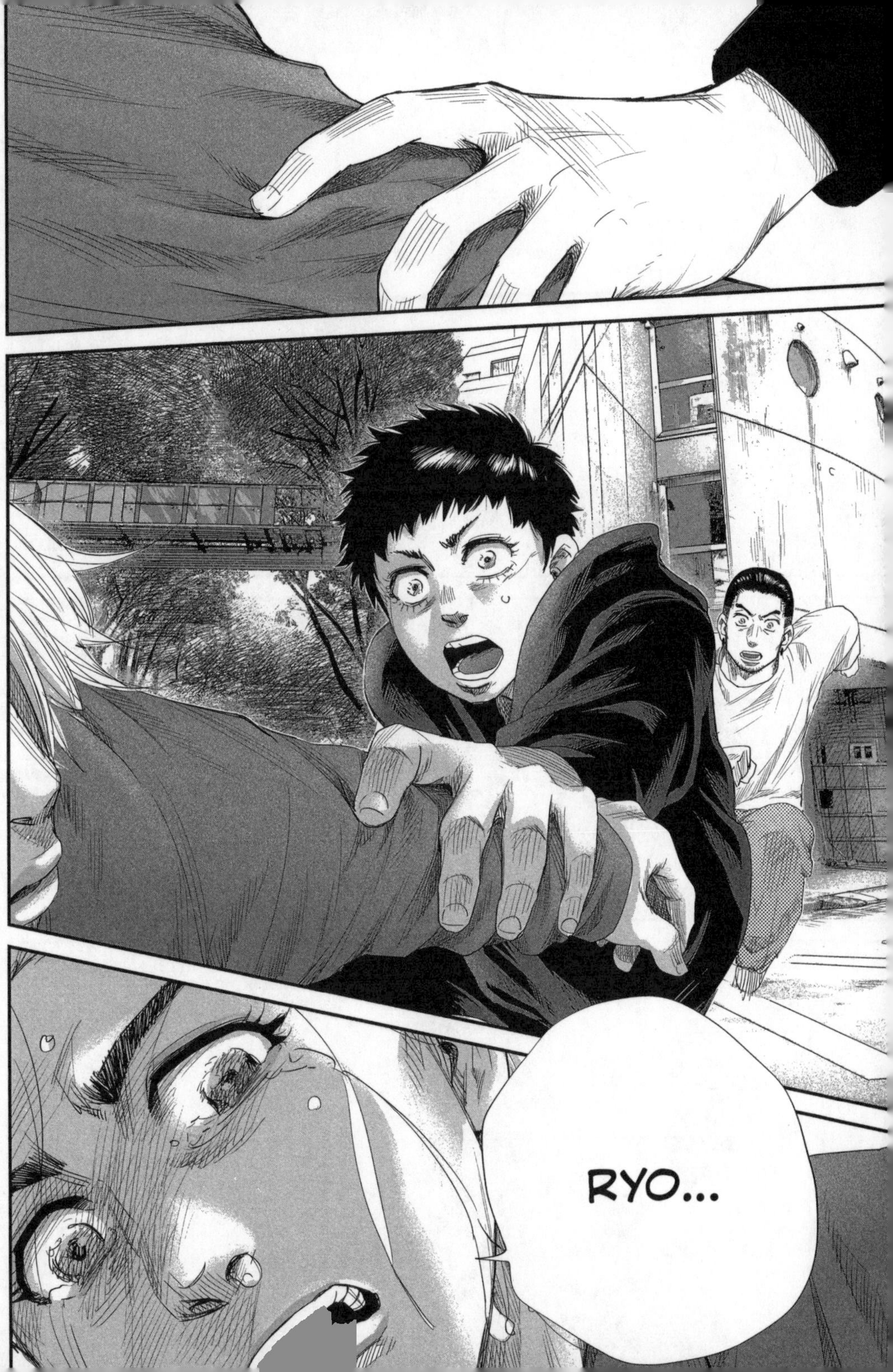
RYO...

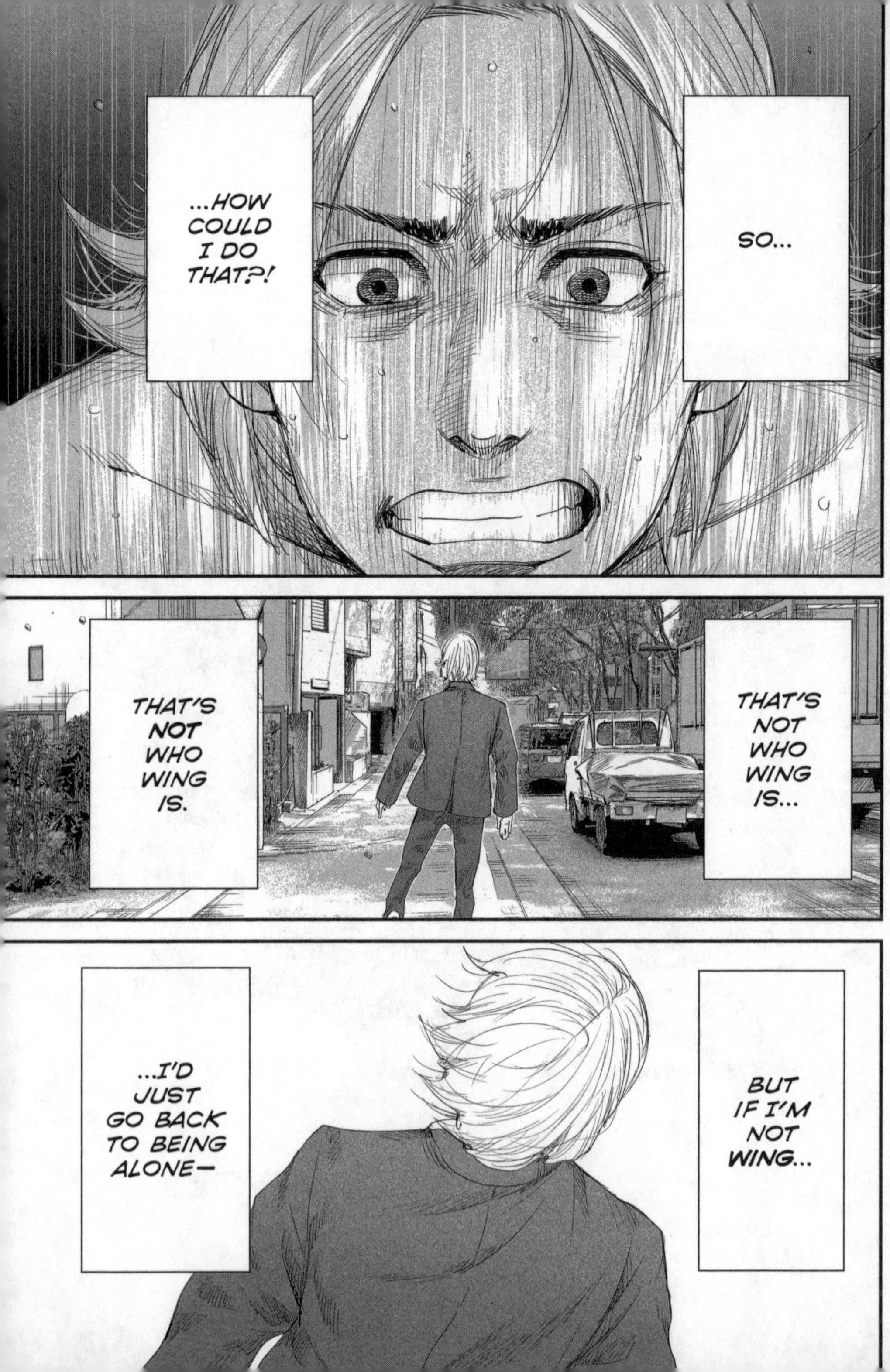
SO...
...HOW COULD I DO THAT?!
THAT'S NOT WHO WING IS...
THAT'S NOT WHO WING IS.
BUT IF I'M NOT WING...
...I'D JUST GO BACK TO BEING ALONE—

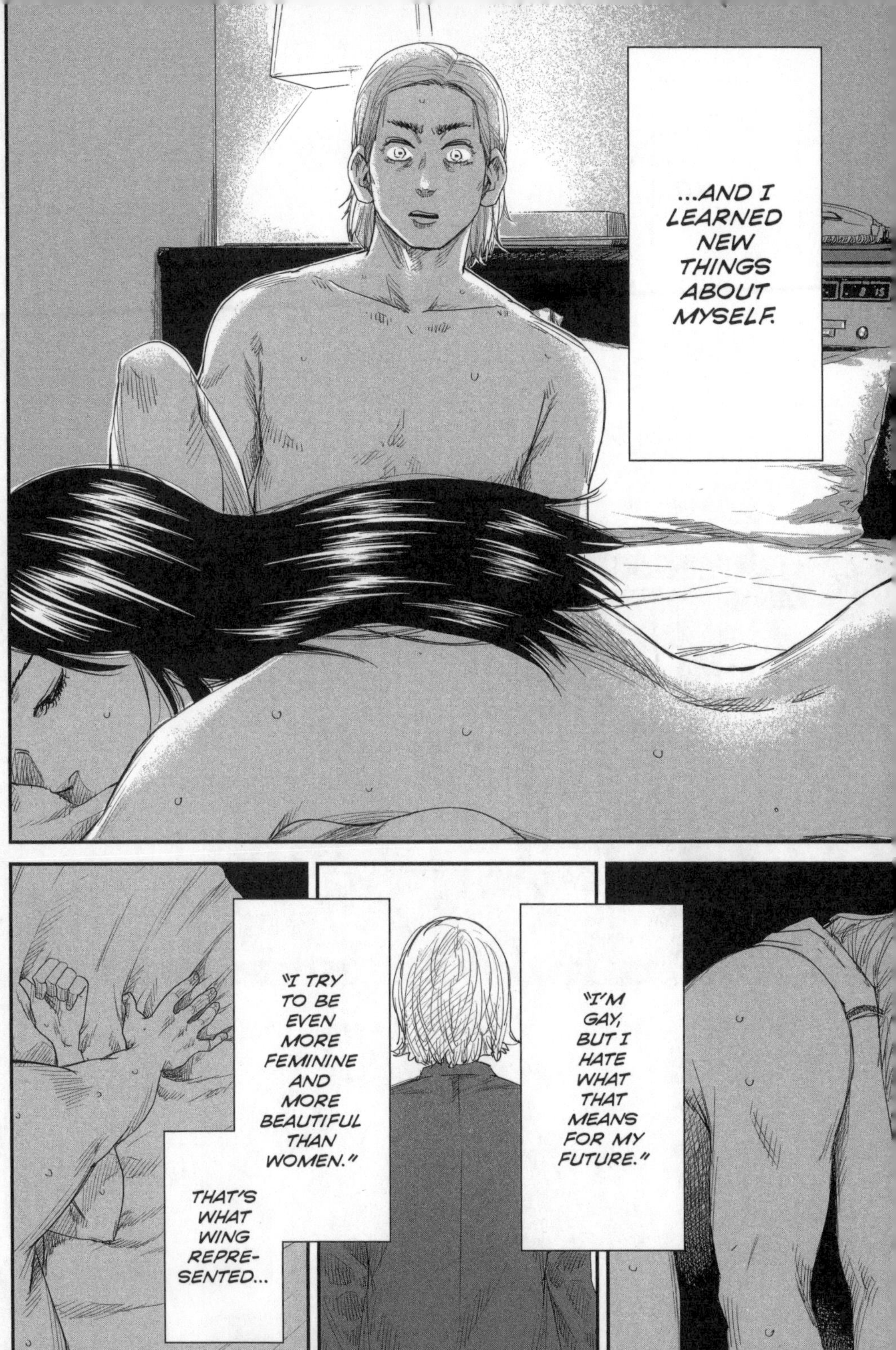
...AND I LEARNED NEW THINGS ABOUT MYSELF.
"I'M GAY, BUT I HATE WHAT THAT MEANS FOR MY FUTURE."
"I TRY TO BE EVEN MORE FEMININE AND MORE BEAUTIFUL THAN WOMEN."
THAT'S WHAT WING REPRE-SENTED...

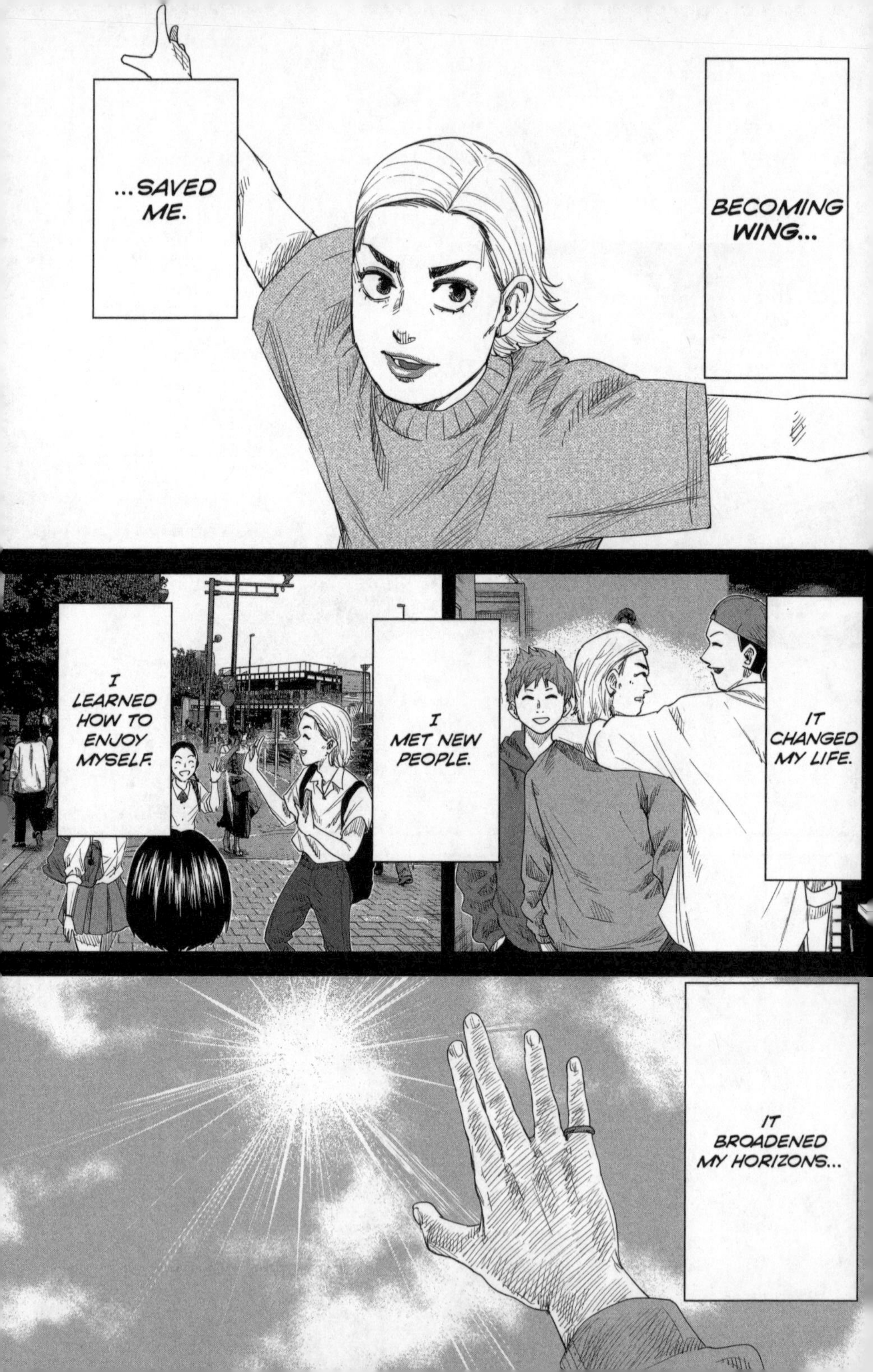
BECOMING WING...
...SAVED ME.
IT CHANGED MY LIFE.
I MET NEW PEOPLE.
I LEARNED HOW TO ENJOY MYSELF.
IT BROADENED MY HORIZONS...

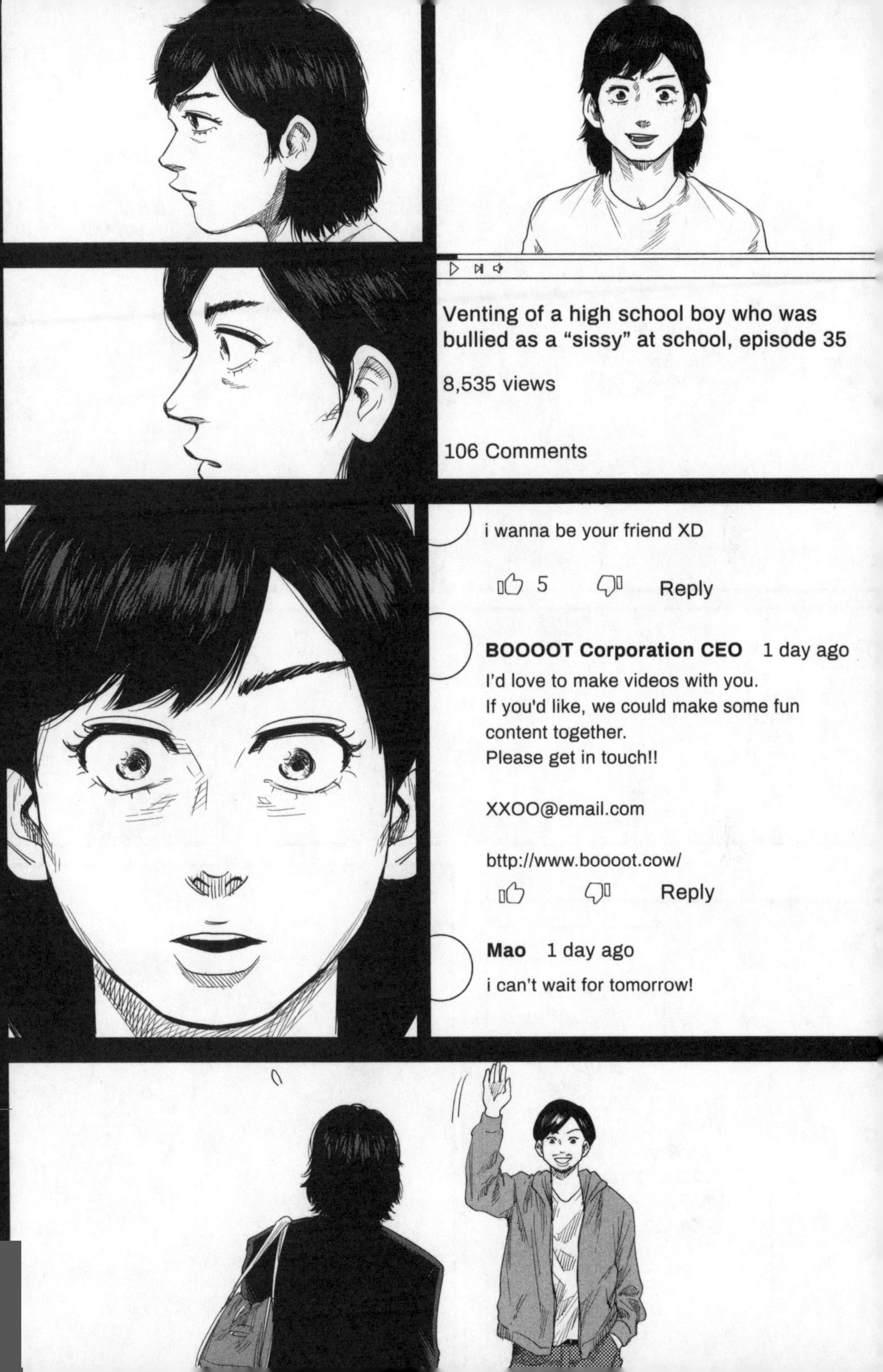
Venting of a high school boy who was bullied as a "sissy" at school, episode 35
8,535 views
106 Comments
i wanna be your friend XD
5
Reply
BOOOOT Corporation CEO 1 day ago
I'd love to make videos with you.
If you'd like, we could make some fun content together.
Please get in touch!!
XXOO@email.com
bttp://www.boooot.cow/
Reply
Mao 1 day ago
i can't wait for tomorrow!

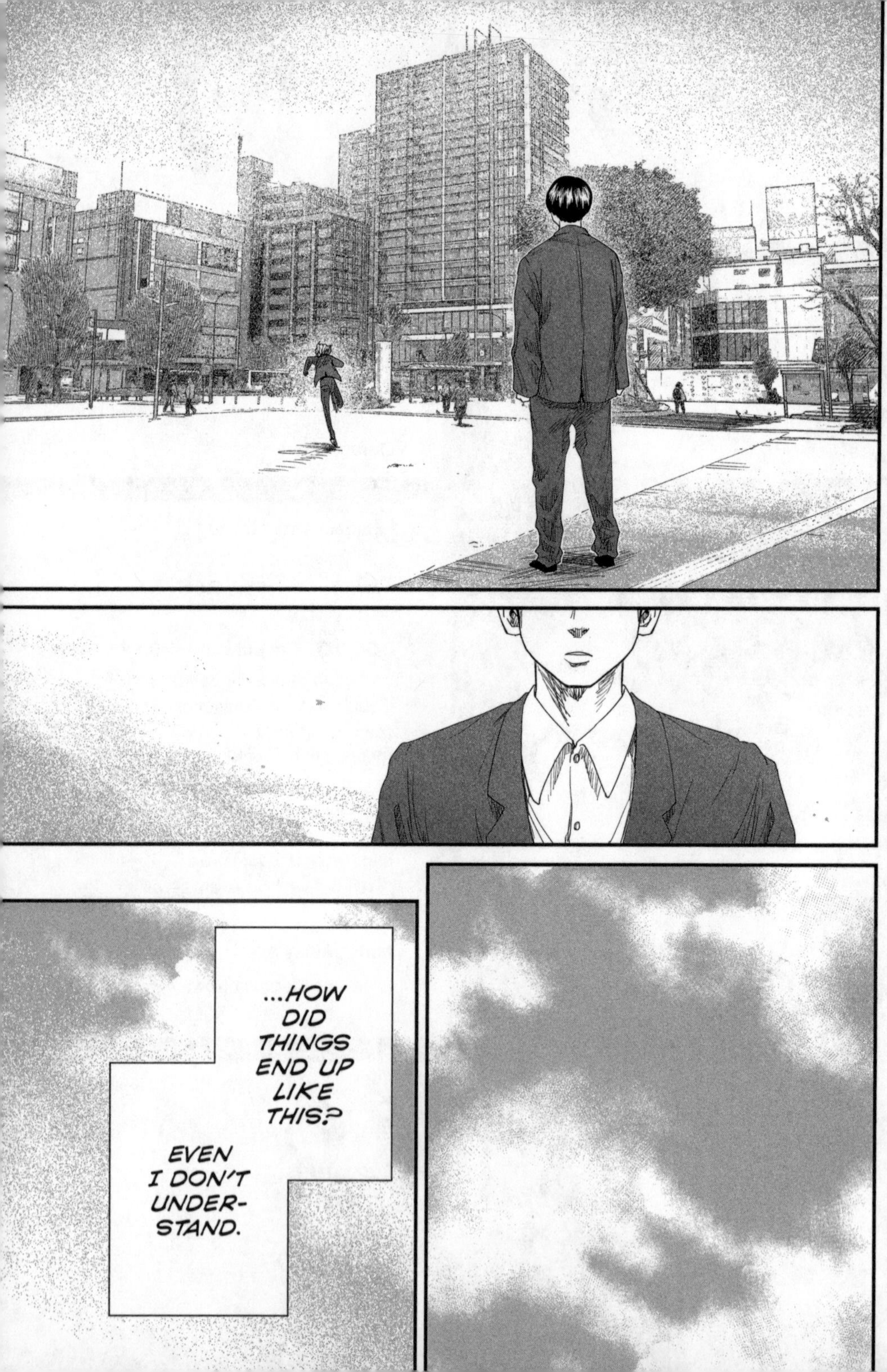
...HOW DID THINGS END UP LIKE THIS?
EVEN I DON'T UNDER-STAND.

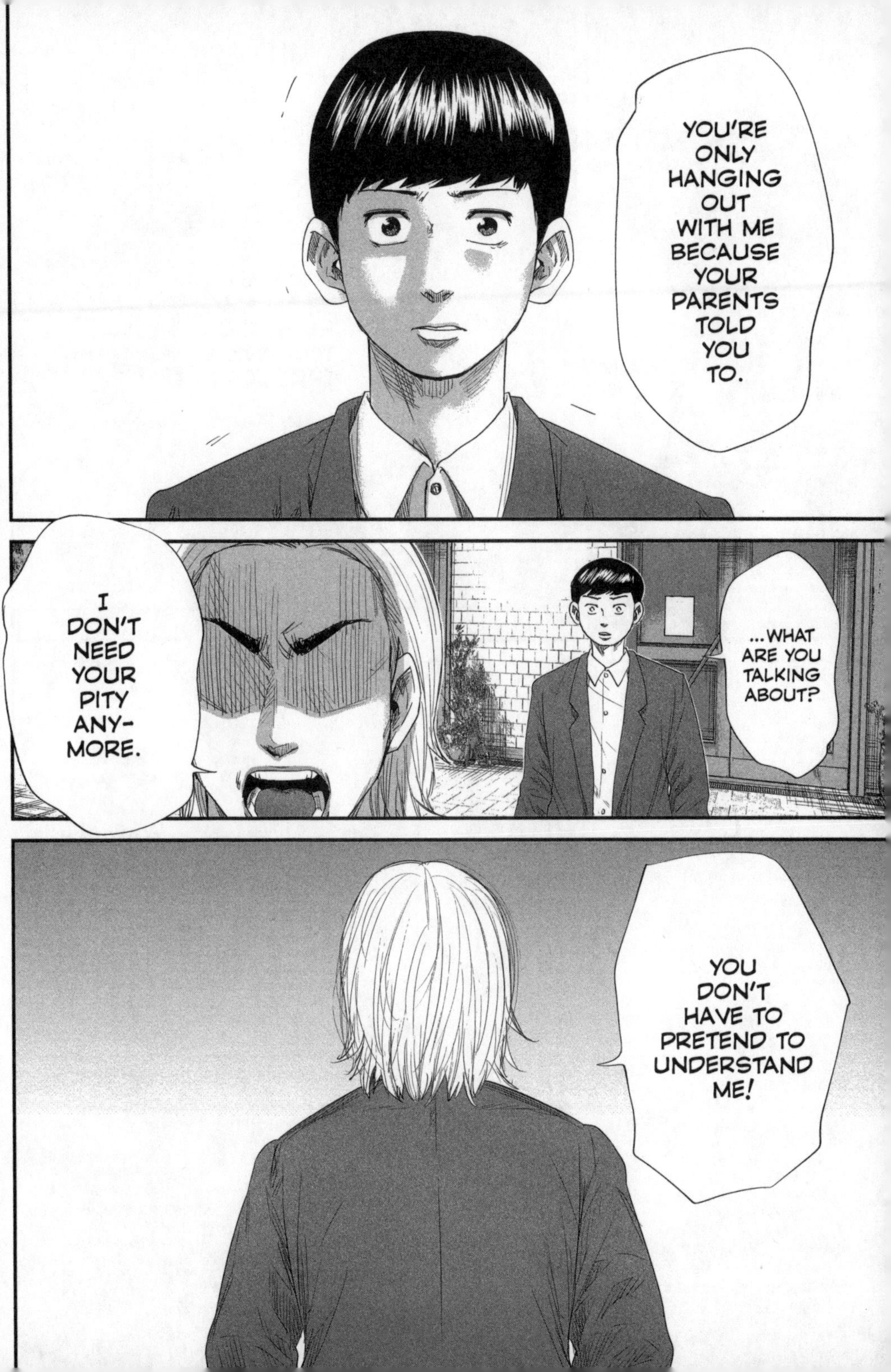
YOU'RE ONLY HANGING OUT WITH ME BECAUSE YOUR PARENTS TOLD YOU TO.
...WHAT ARE YOU TALKING ABOUT?
I DON'T NEED YOUR PITY ANY-MORE.
YOU DON'T HAVE TO PRETEND TO UNDERSTAND ME!

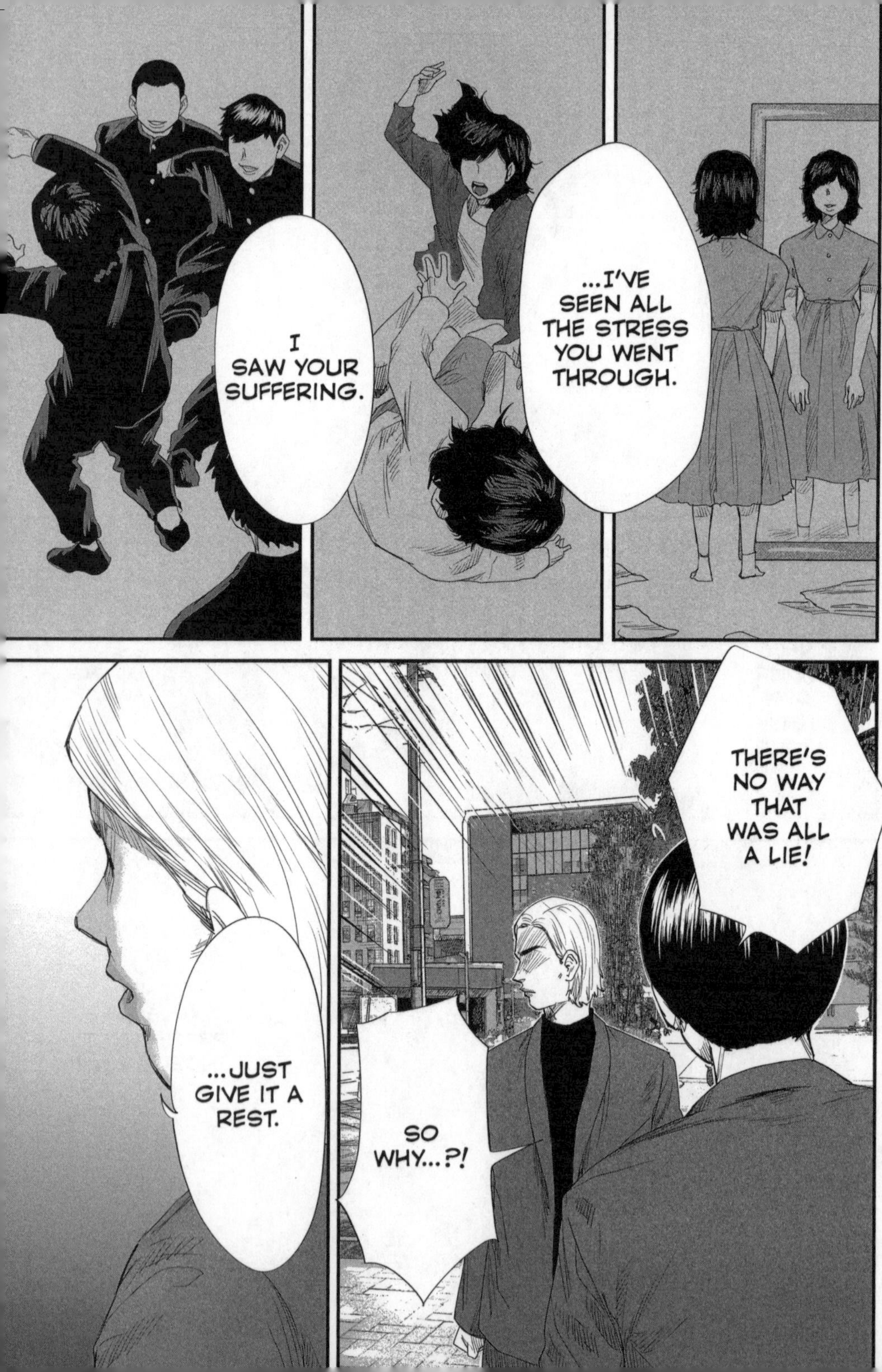
...I'VE SEEN ALL THE STRESS YOU WENT THROUGH.
I SAW YOUR SUFFERING.
THERE'S NO WAY THAT WAS ALL A LIE!
SO WHY...?!
...JUST GIVE IT A REST.

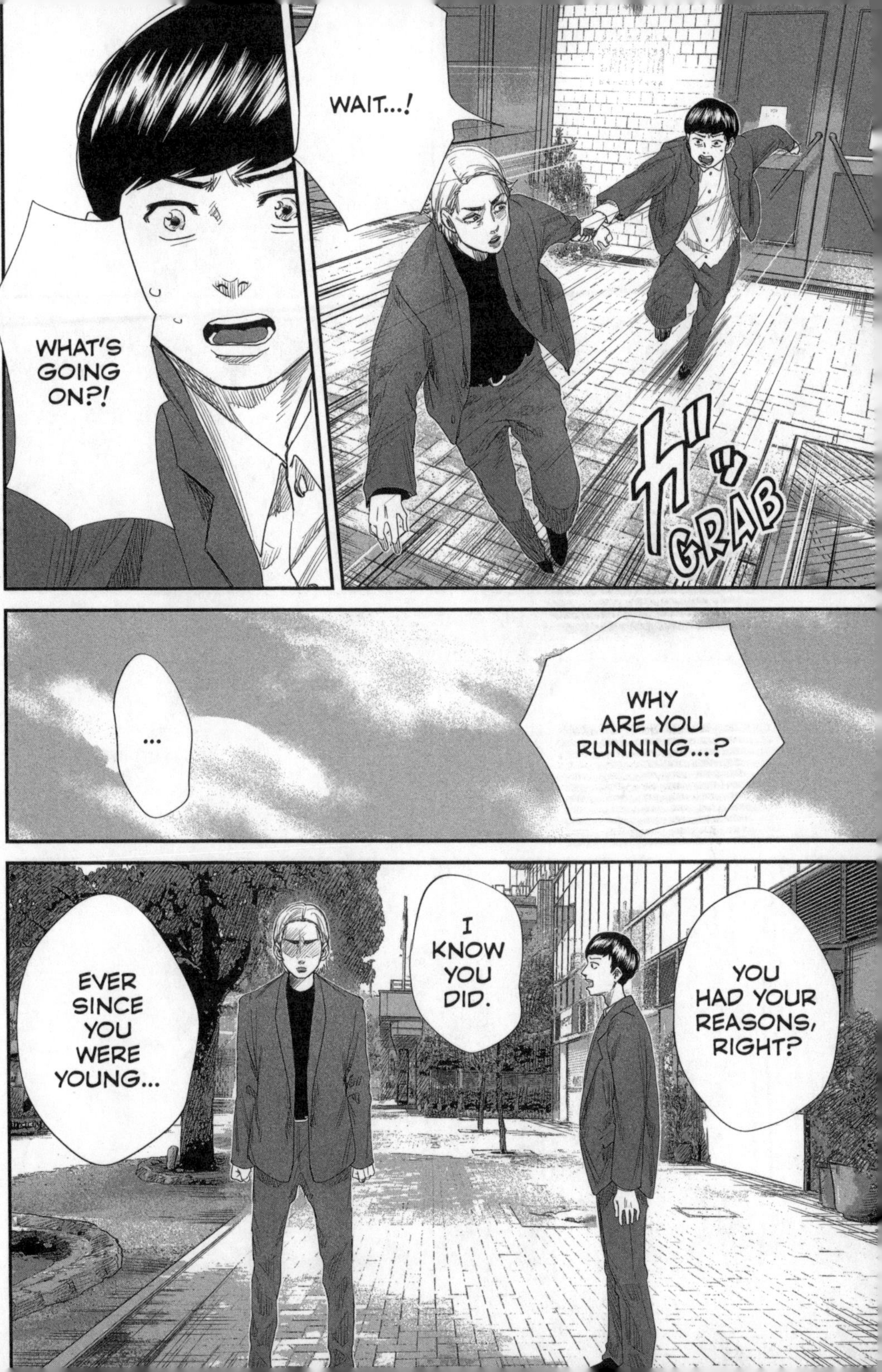
WAIT...!
ガッ
GRAB
WHAT'S GOING ON?!
WHY ARE YOU RUNNING...?
...
YOU HAD YOUR REASONS, RIGHT?
I KNOW YOU DID.
EVER SINCE YOU WERE YOUNG...

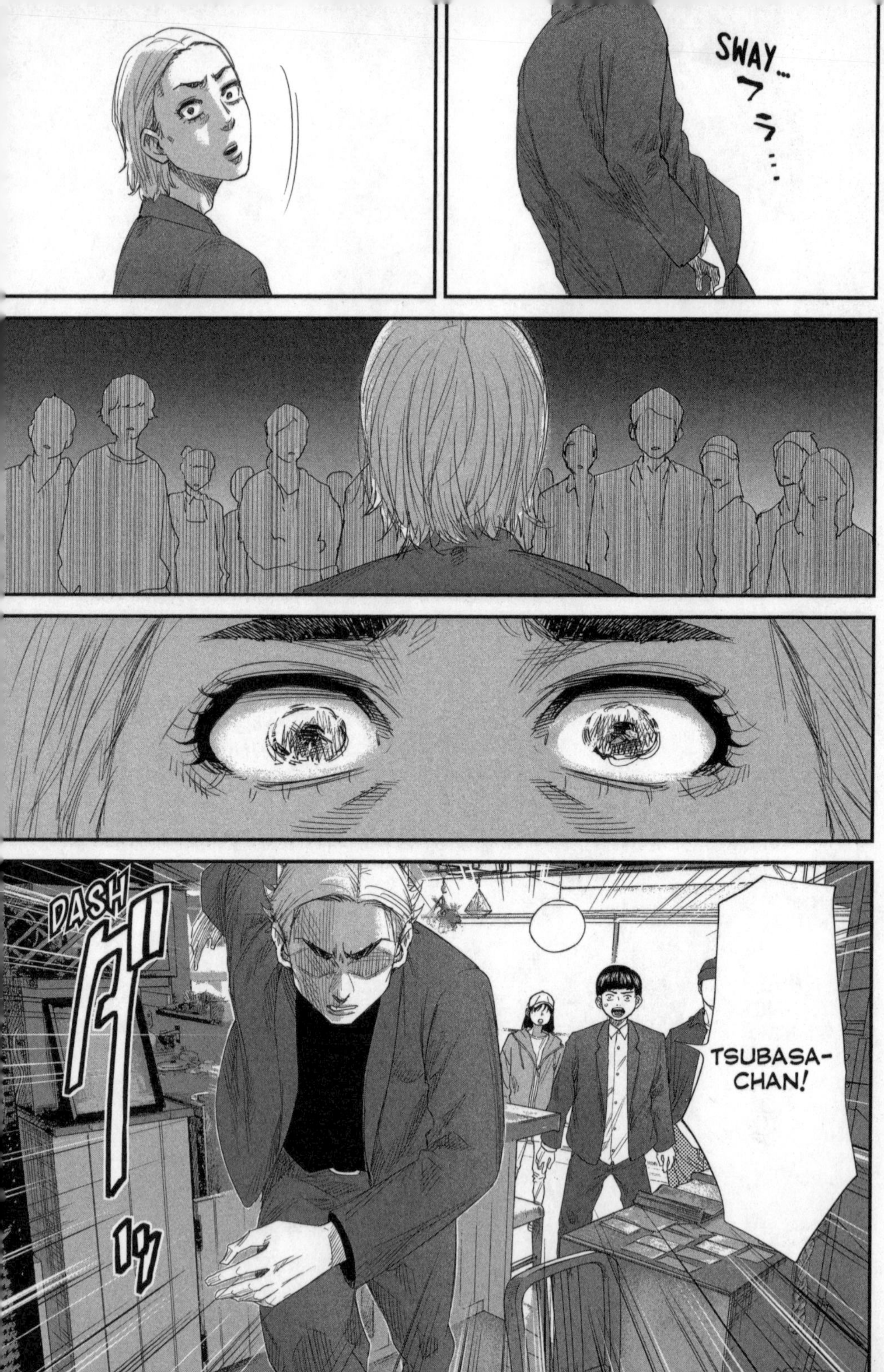
SWAY...
フラ…
TSUBASA-CHAN!
DASH
ダッ

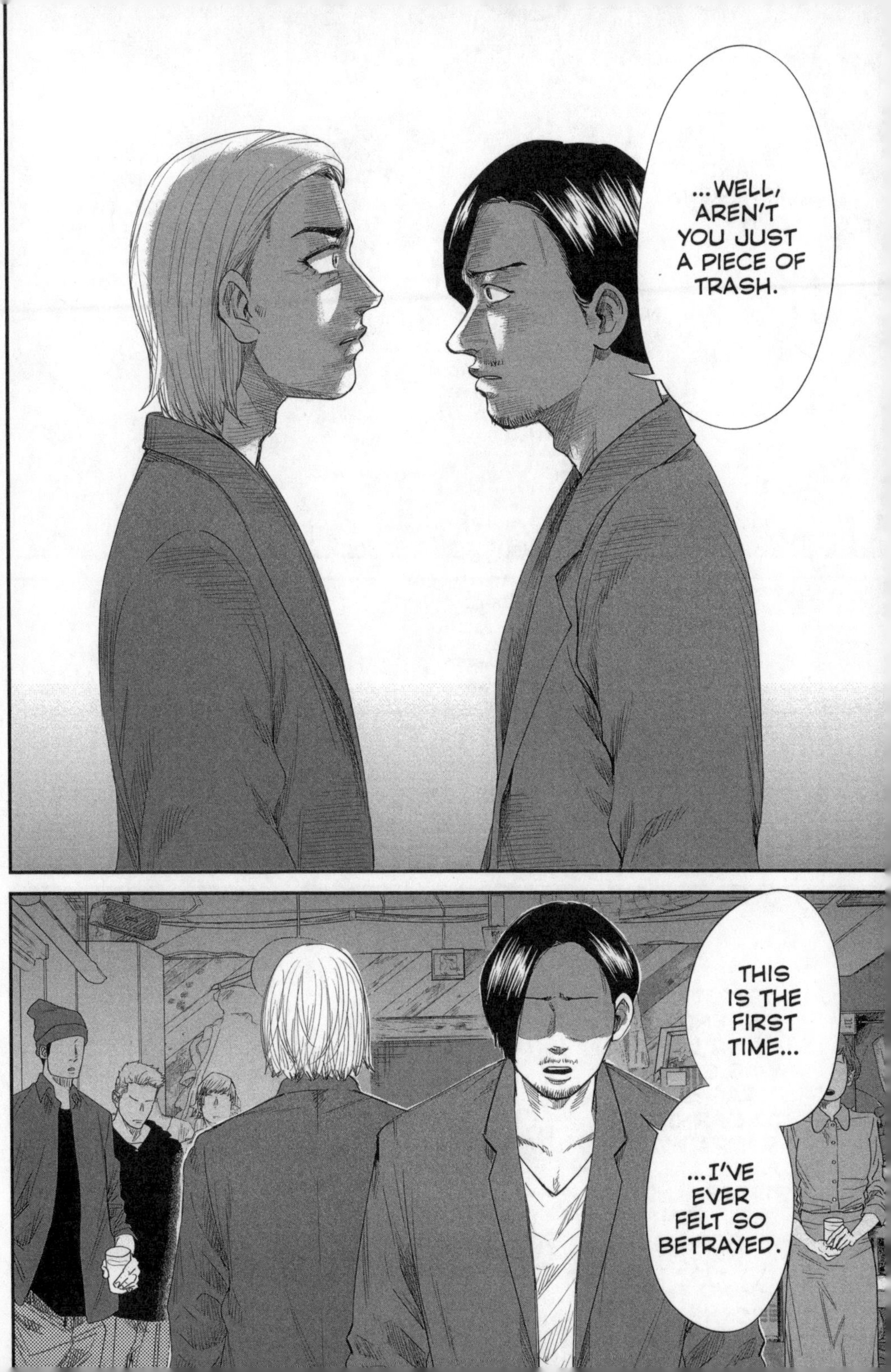
...WELL, AREN'T YOU JUST A PIECE OF TRASH.
THIS IS THE FIRST TIME...
...I'VE EVER FELT SO BETRAYED.

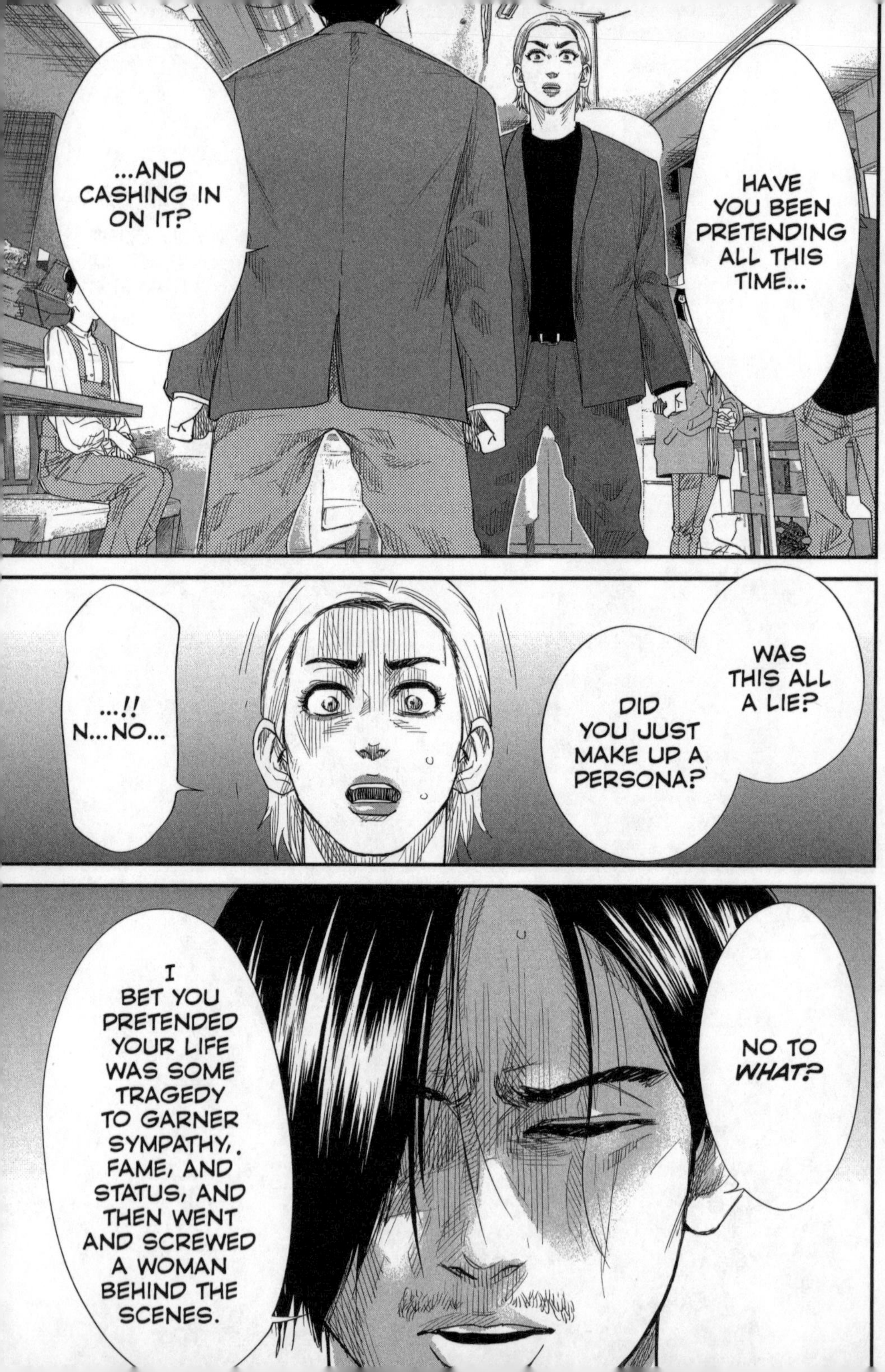
HAVE YOU BEEN PRETENDING ALL THIS TIME...
...AND CASHING IN ON IT?
WAS THIS ALL A LIE?
DID YOU JUST MAKE UP A PERSONA?
...!! N...NO...
NO TO *WHAT?*
I BET YOU PRETENDED YOUR LIFE WAS SOME TRAGEDY TO GARNER SYMPATHY, FAME, AND STATUS, AND THEN WENT AND SCREWED A WOMAN BEHIND THE SCENES.

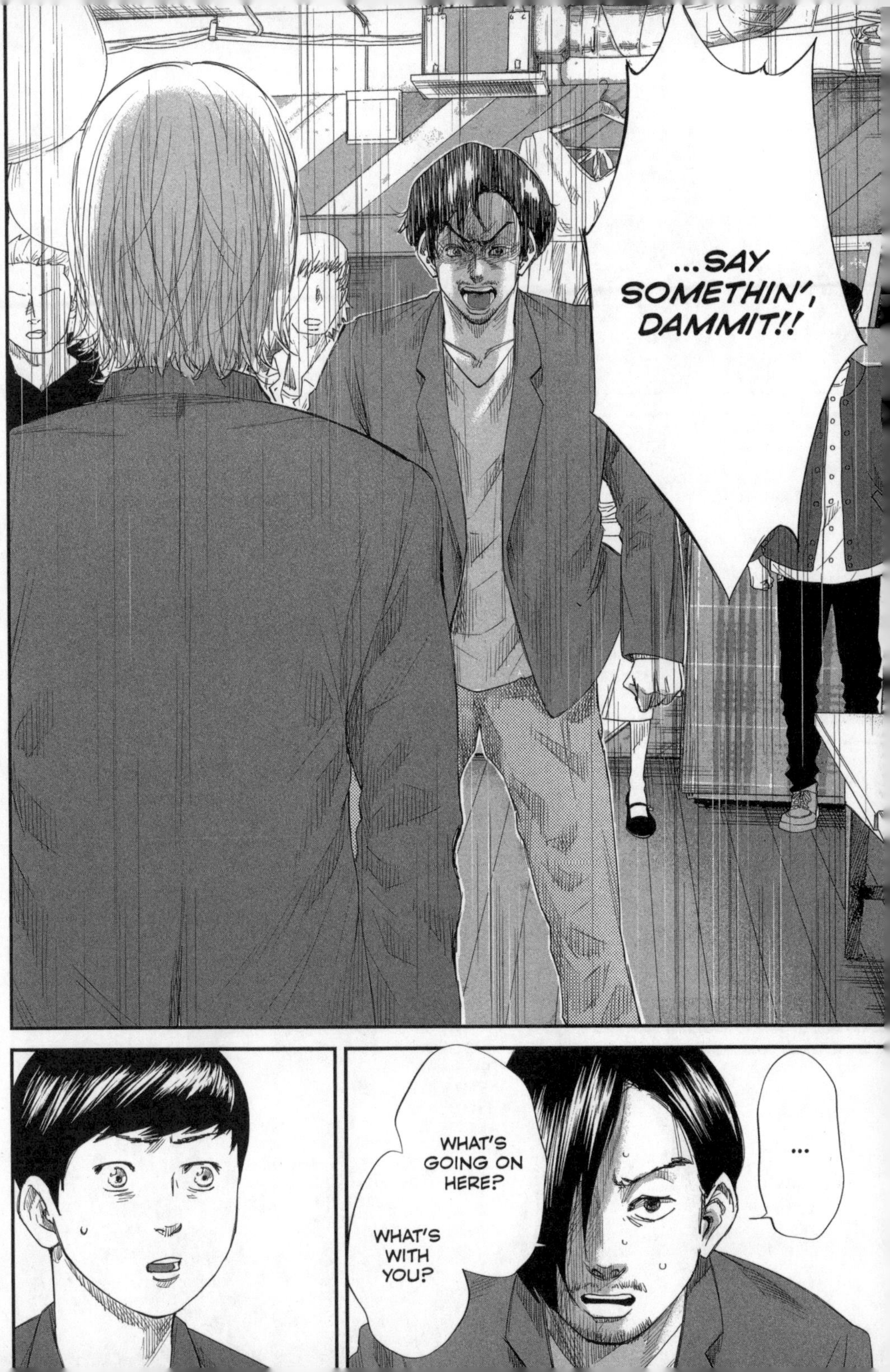
...SAY SOMETHIN', DAMMIT!!
...
WHAT'S GOING ON HERE?
WHAT'S WITH YOU?

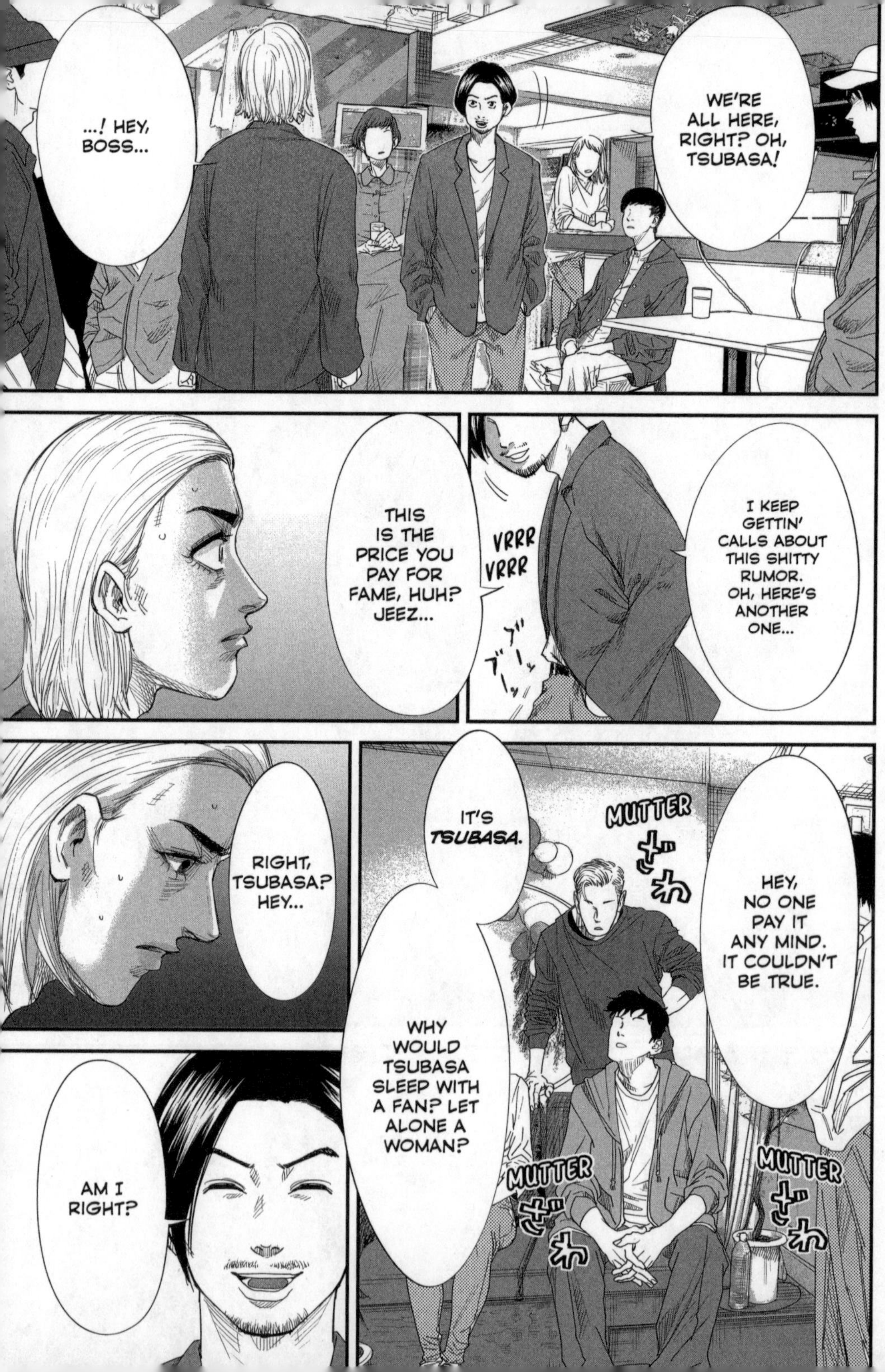
WE'RE ALL HERE, RIGHT? OH, TSUBASA!
...! HEY, BOSS...
I KEEP GETTIN' CALLS ABOUT THIS SHITTY RUMOR. OH, HERE'S ANOTHER ONE...
VRRR VRRR
ブーッ ブーッ
THIS IS THE PRICE YOU PAY FOR FAME, HUH? JEEZ...
HEY, NO ONE PAY IT ANY MIND. IT COULDN'T BE TRUE.
MUTTER ざわ
IT'S *TSUBASA.*
WHY WOULD TSUBASA SLEEP WITH A FAN? LET ALONE A WOMAN?
MUTTER ざわ
MUTTER ざわ
RIGHT, TSUBASA? HEY...
AM I RIGHT?

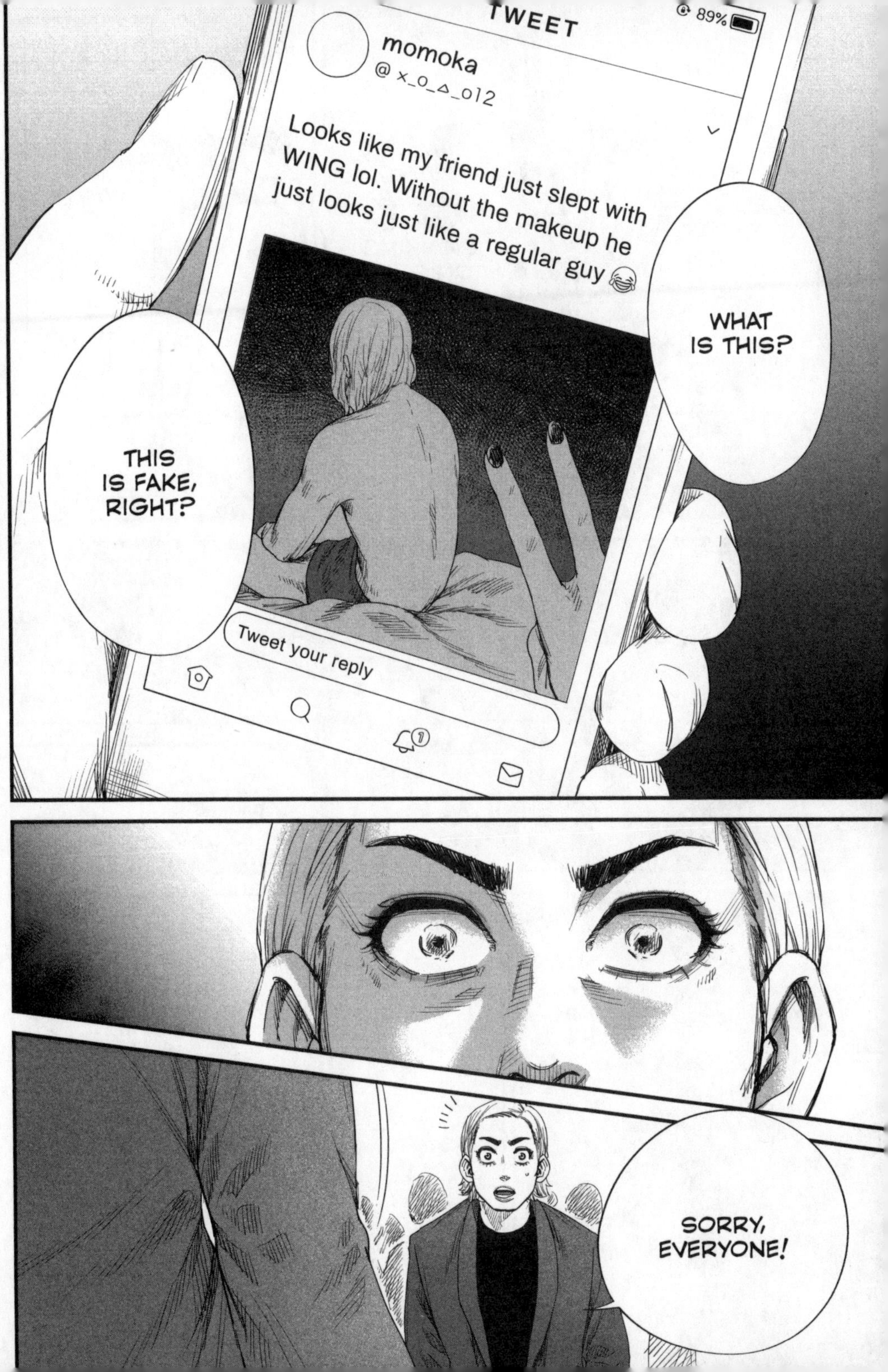
TWEET
89%
momoka
@ x_o_△_o12
Looks like my friend just slept with WING lol. Without the makeup he just looks just like a regular guy 😂
WHAT IS THIS?
THIS IS FAKE, RIGHT?
Tweet your reply
SORRY, EVERYONE!

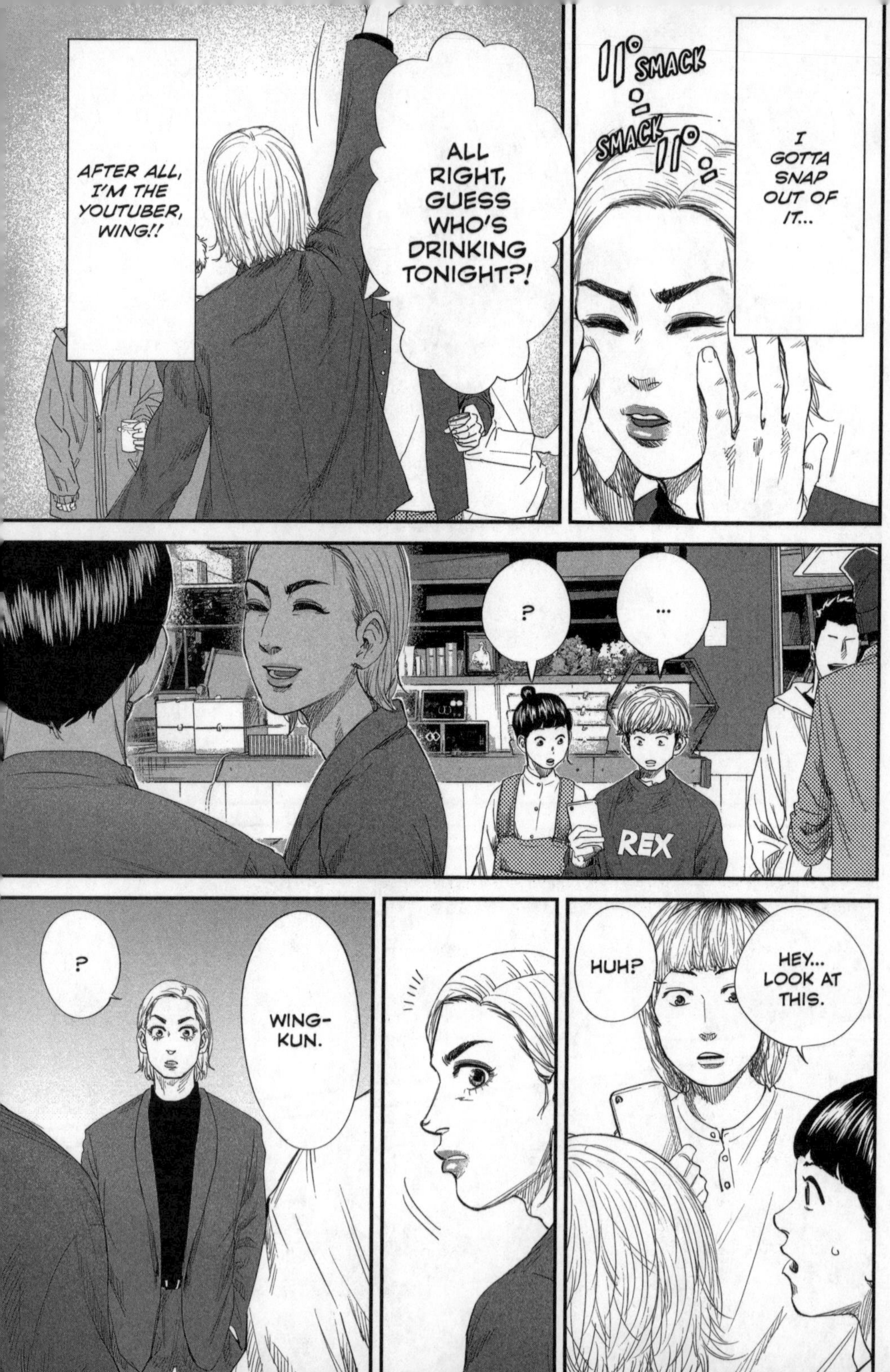

I GOTTA SNAP OUT OF IT...
SMACK
SMACK
ALL RIGHT, GUESS WHO'S DRINKING TONIGHT?!
AFTER ALL, I'M THE YOUTUBER, WING!!
...
?
REX
HEY... LOOK AT THIS.
HUH?
WING-KUN.
?

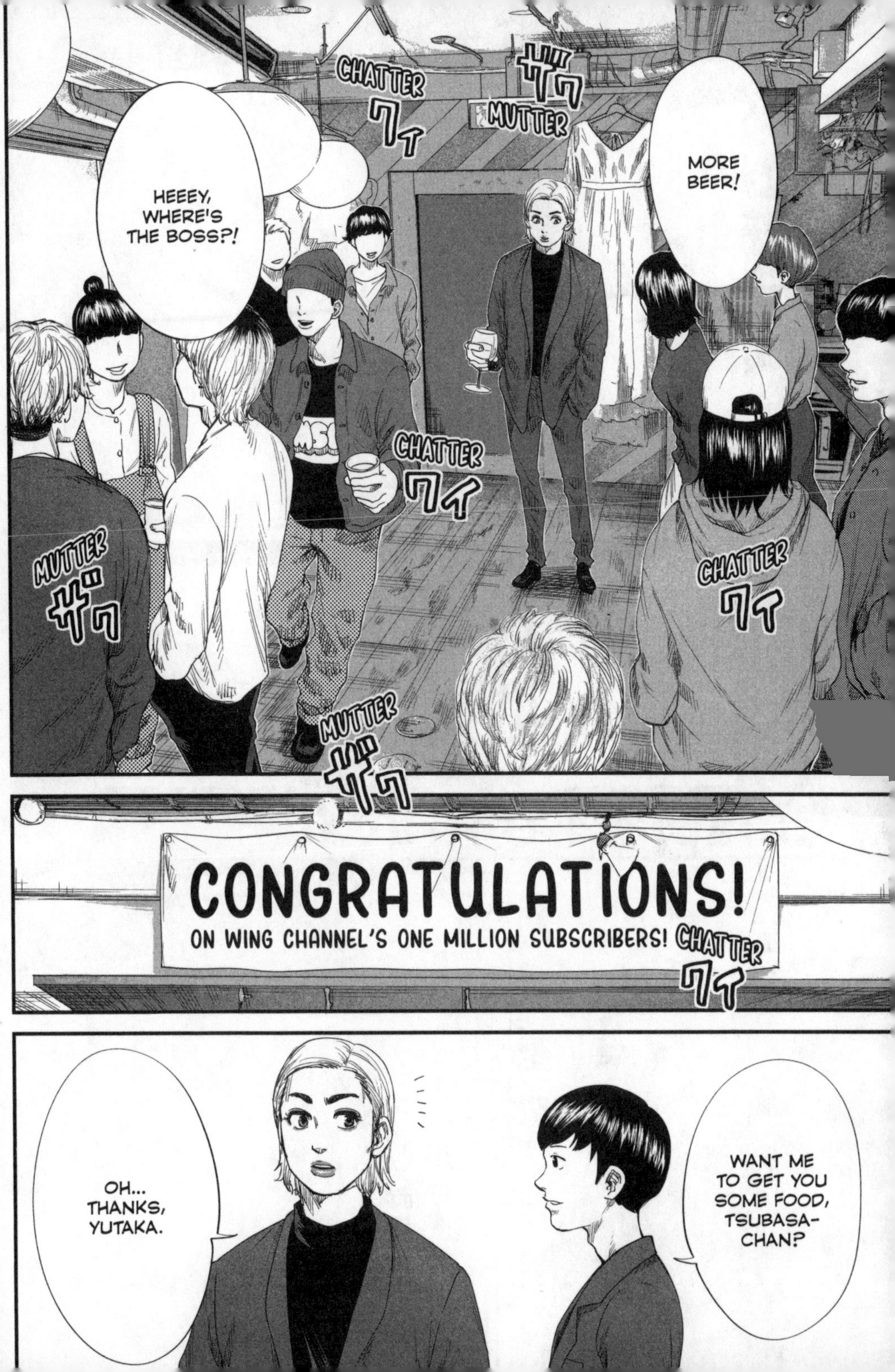

ザワ MUTTER
MORE BEER!
CHATTER ワイ
HEEEY, WHERE'S THE BOSS?!
CHATTER ワイ
CHATTER ワイ
MUTTER ザワ
MUTTER ザワ
CONGRATULATIONS!
ON WING CHANNEL'S ONE MILLION SUBSCRIBERS!
CHATTER ワイ
WANT ME TO GET YOU SOME FOOD, TSUBASA-CHAN?
OH... THANKS, YUTAKA.

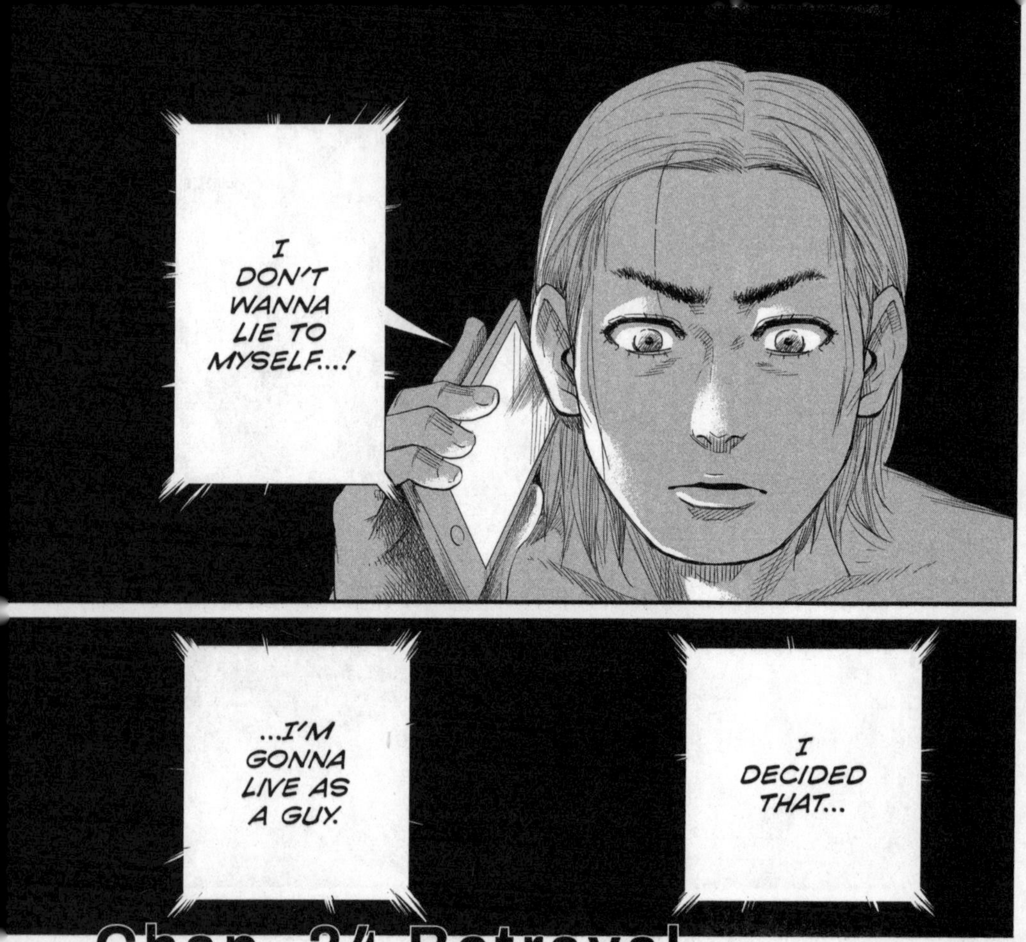
I DON'T WANNA LIE TO MYSELF...!
I DECIDED THAT...
...I'M GONNA LIVE AS A GUY.

Chap. 24 Betrayal

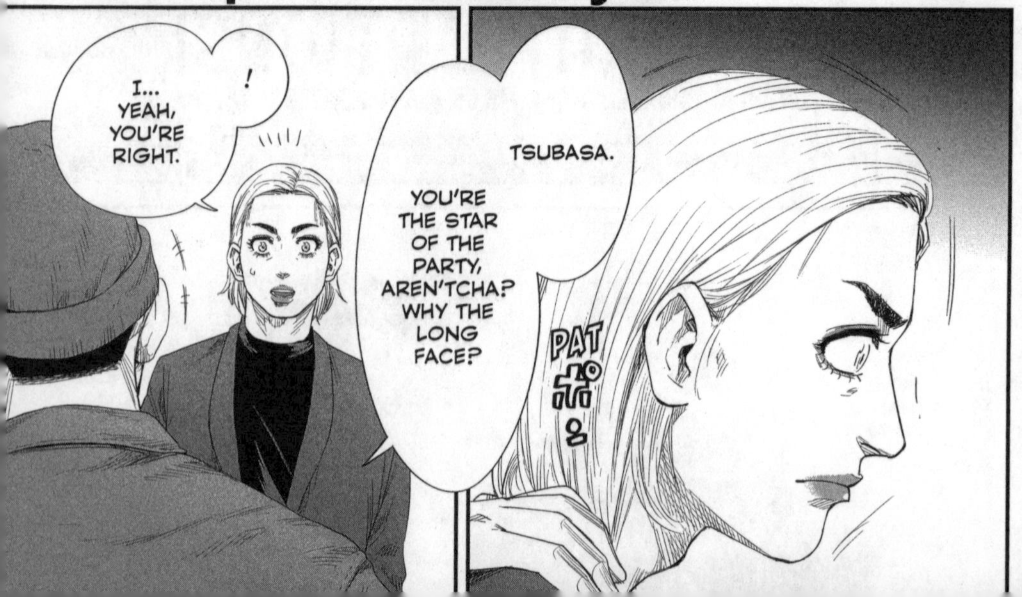
TSUBASA.
YOU'RE THE STAR OF THE PARTY, AREN'TCHA? WHY THE LONG FACE?
PAT
!
I... YEAH, YOU'RE RIGHT.

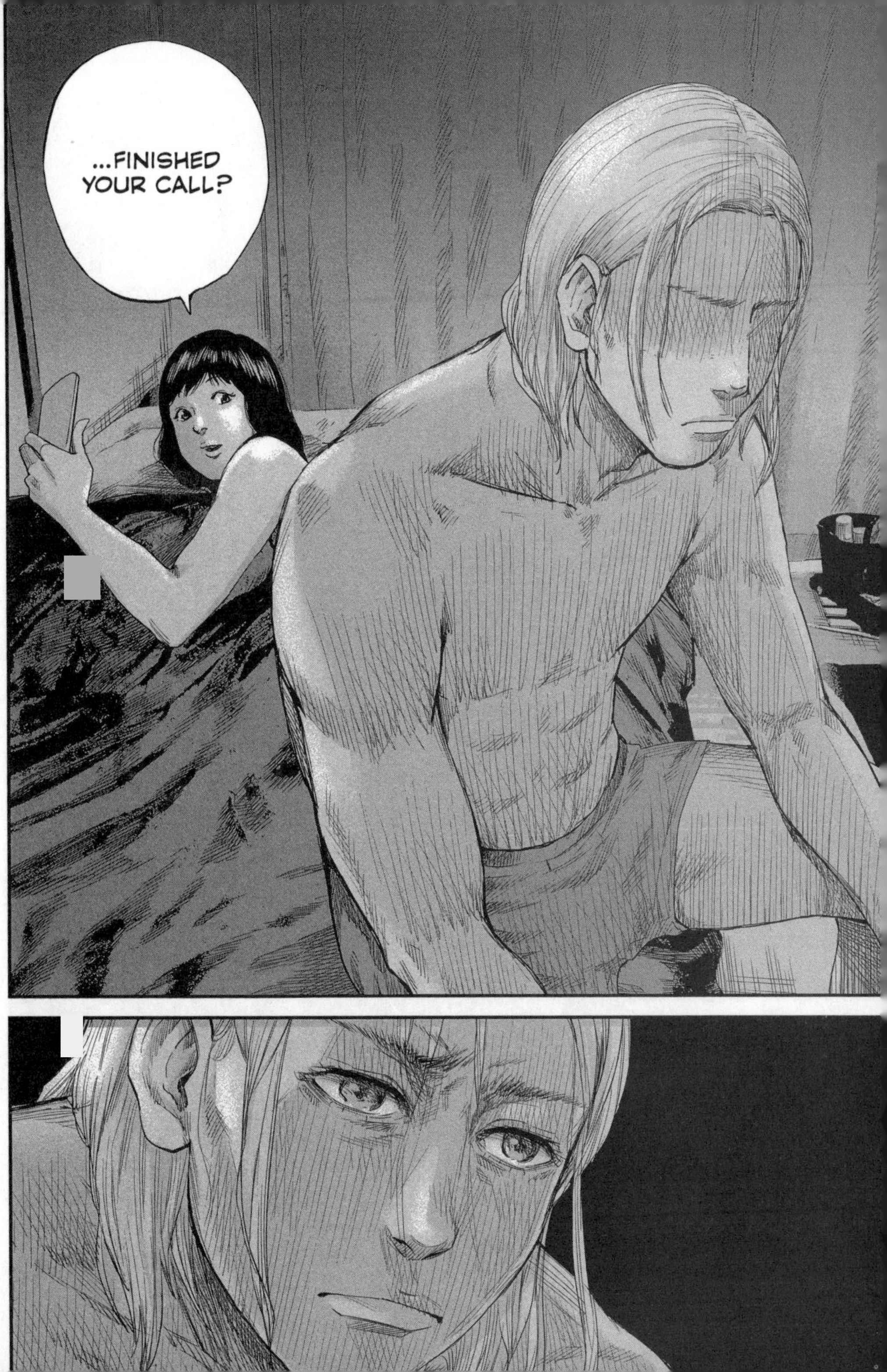
...FINISHED YOUR CALL?

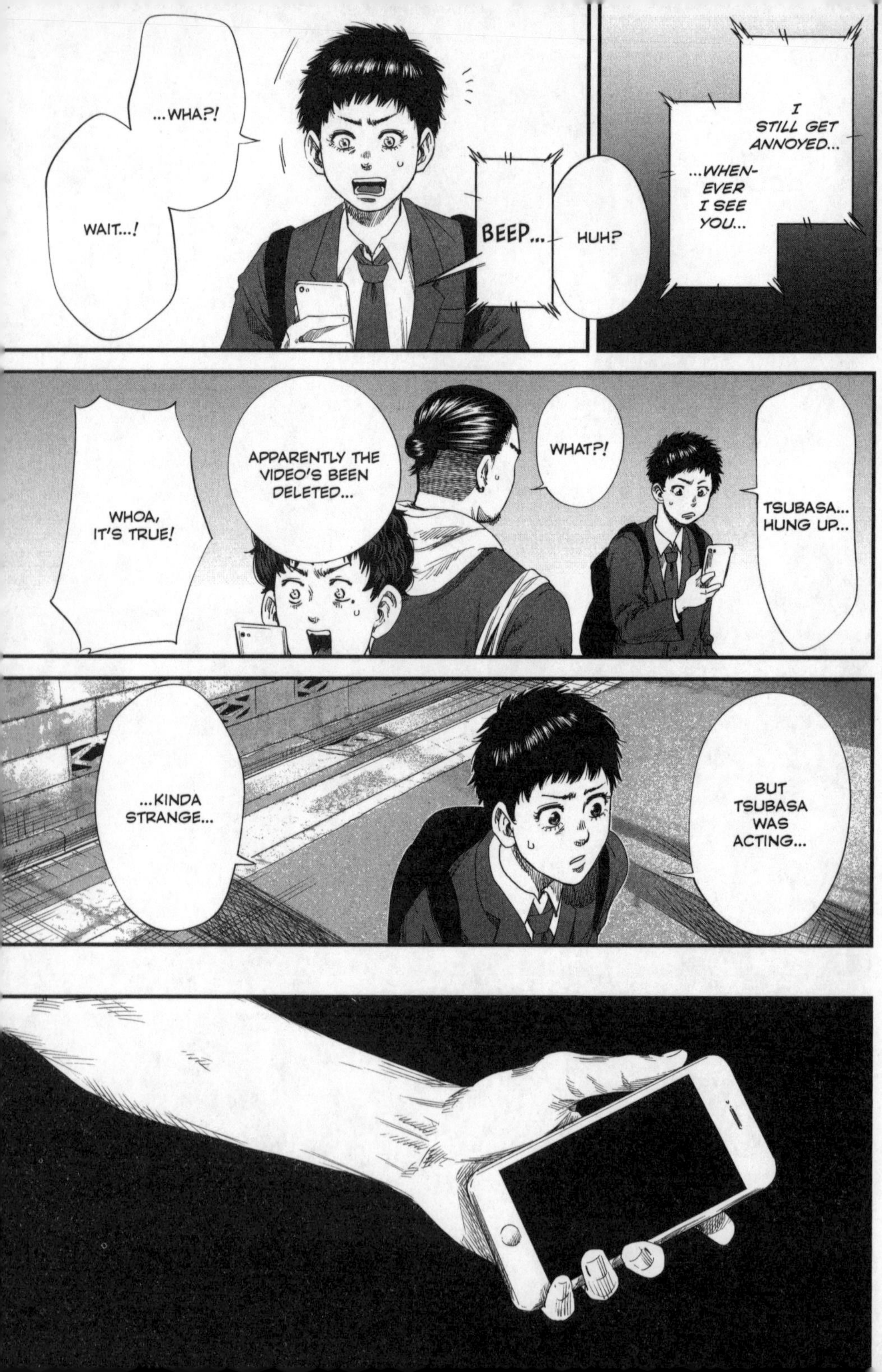
I STILL GET ANNOYED...
...WHEN-EVER I SEE YOU...
HUH?
BEEP...
...WHA?!
WAIT...!
TSUBASA... HUNG UP...
WHAT?!
APPARENTLY THE VIDEO'S BEEN DELETED...
WHOA, IT'S TRUE!
BUT TSUBASA WAS ACTING...
...KINDA STRANGE...

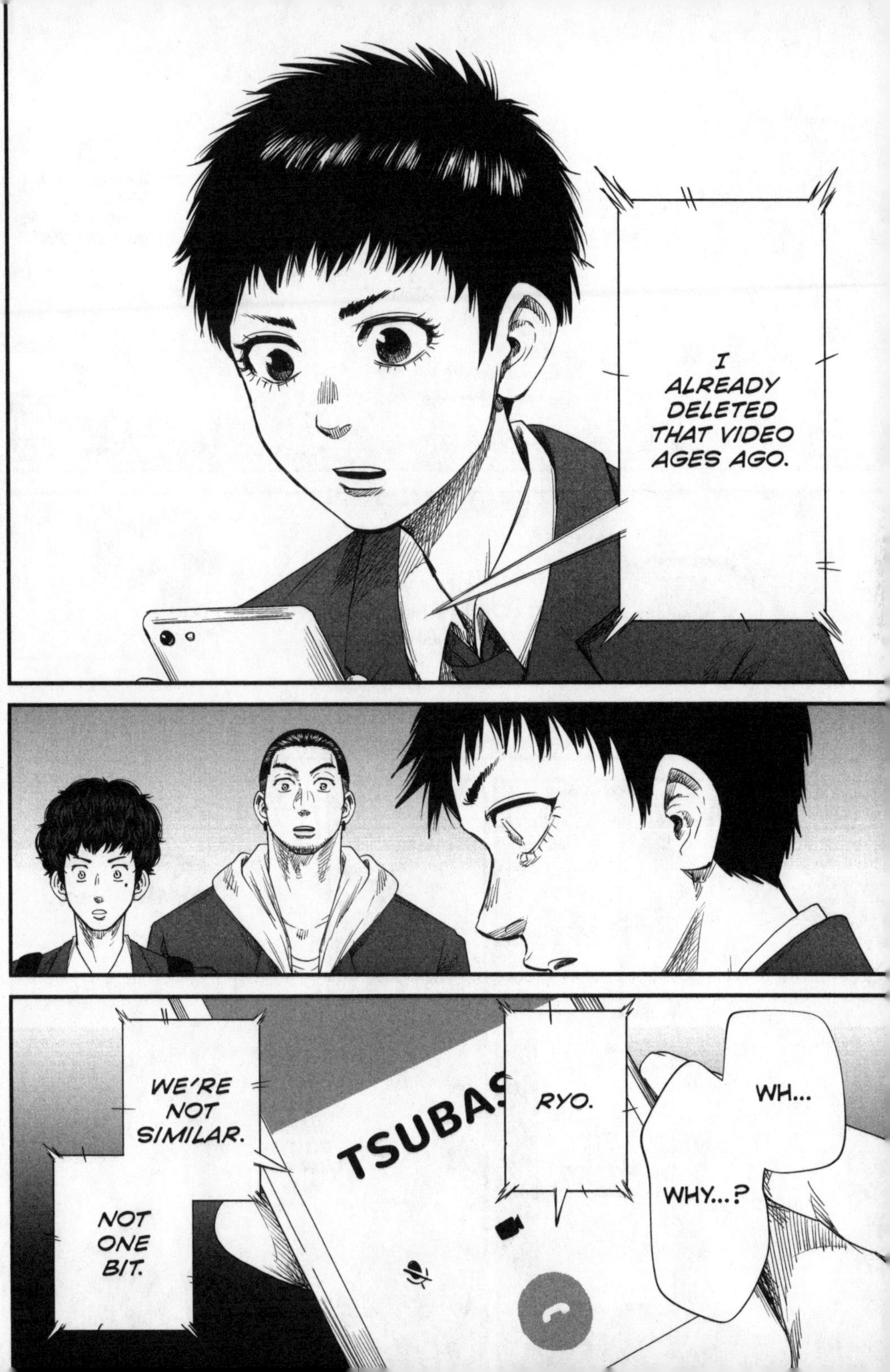
I ALREADY DELETED THAT VIDEO AGES AGO.
WH...
WHY...?
TSUBAS
RYO.
WE'RE NOT SIMILAR.
NOT ONE BIT.

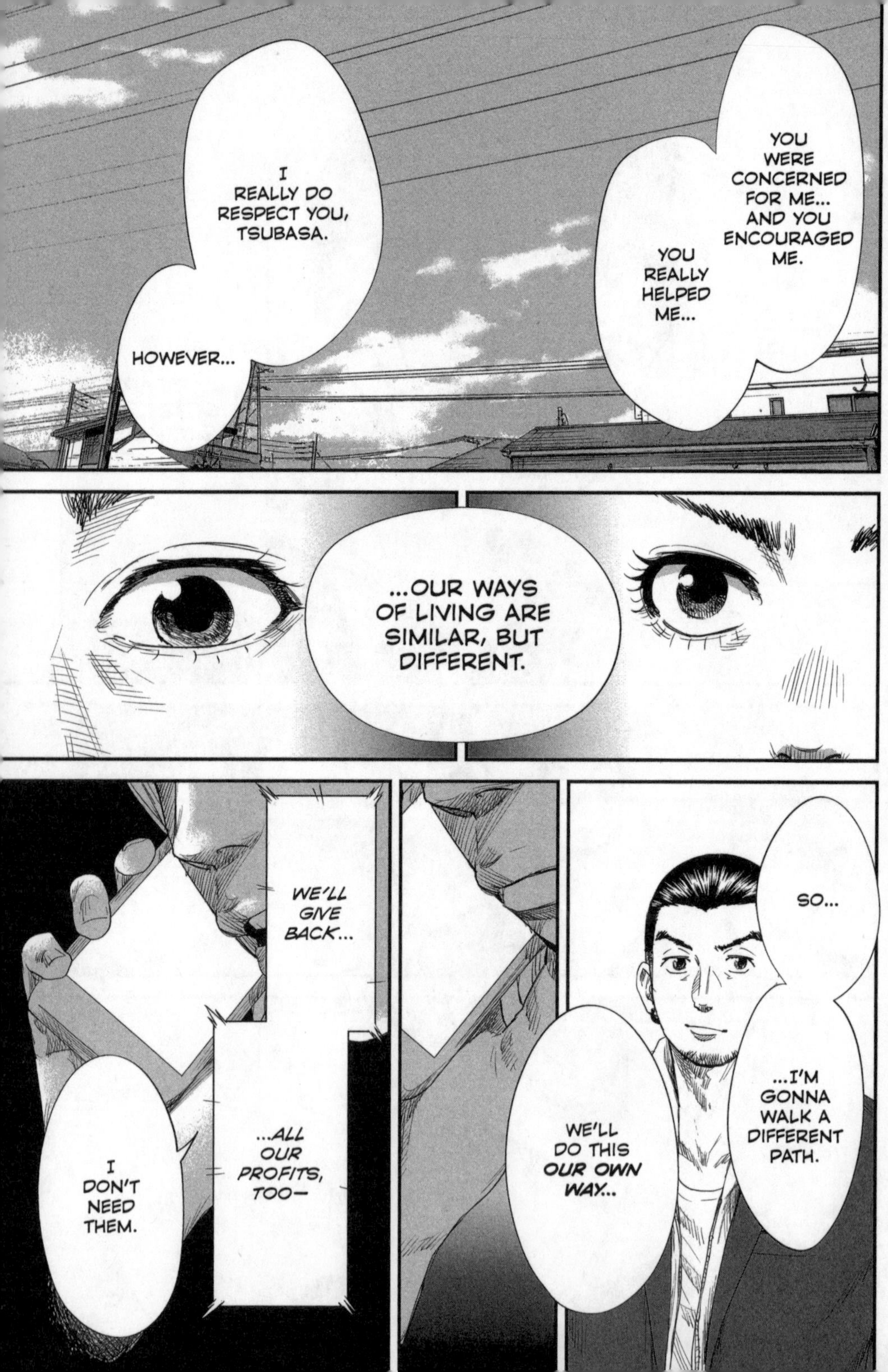
YOU WERE CONCERNED FOR ME... AND YOU ENCOURAGED ME.
YOU REALLY HELPED ME...
I REALLY DO RESPECT YOU, TSUBASA.
HOWEVER...
...OUR WAYS OF LIVING ARE SIMILAR, BUT DIFFERENT.
SO...
...I'M GONNA WALK A DIFFERENT PATH.
WE'LL DO THIS *OUR OWN WAY*...
WE'LL GIVE BACK...
...ALL OUR PROFITS, TOO—
I DON'T NEED THEM.

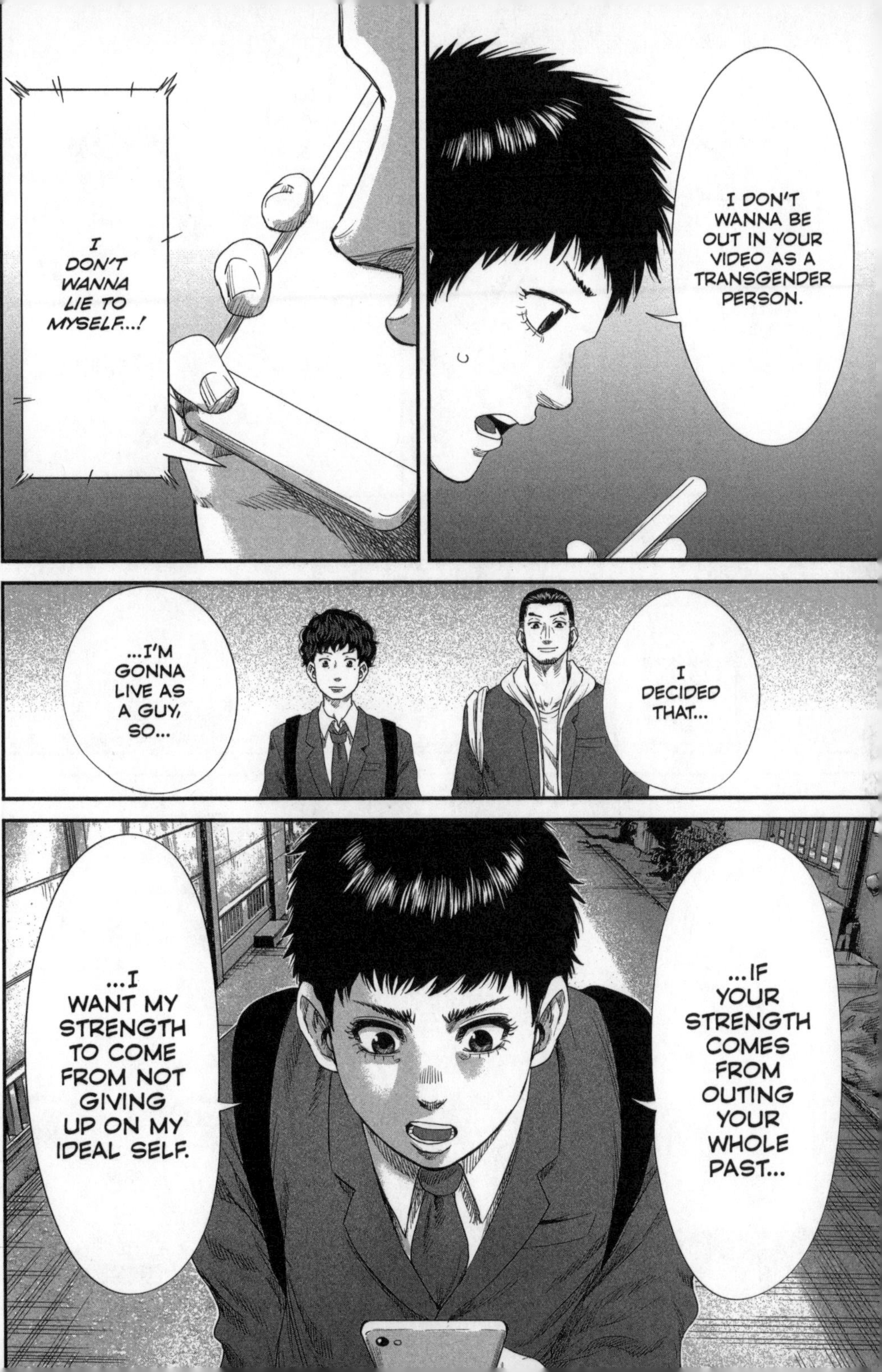
I DON'T WANNA BE OUT IN YOUR VIDEO AS A TRANSGENDER PERSON.
I DON'T WANNA LIE TO MYSELF...!
I DECIDED THAT...
...I'M GONNA LIVE AS A GUY, SO...
...IF YOUR STRENGTH COMES FROM OUTING YOUR WHOLE PAST...
...I WANT MY STRENGTH TO COME FROM NOT GIVING UP ON MY IDEAL SELF.

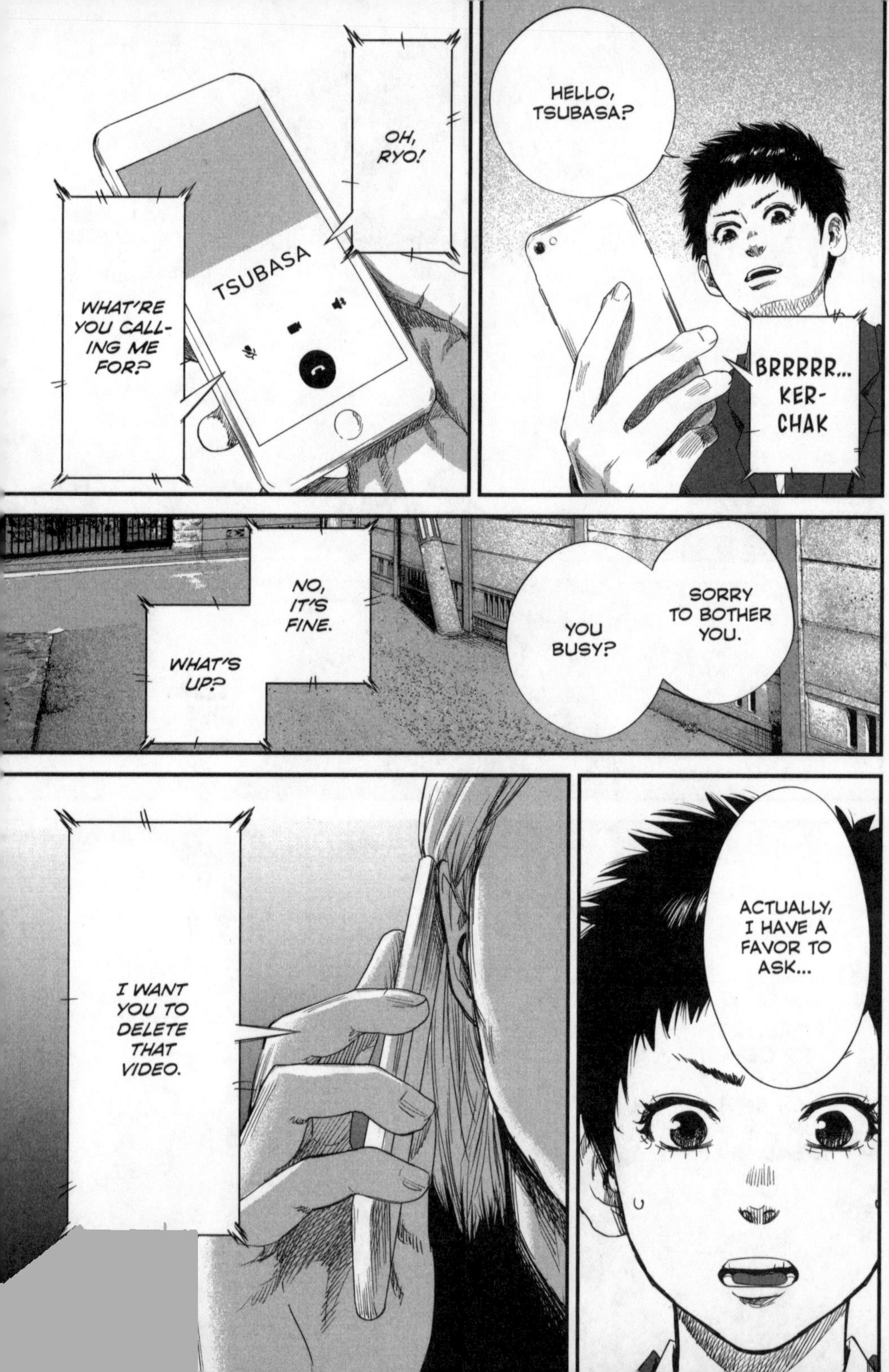
HELLO, TSUBASA?
BRRRRR... KER-CHAK
OH, RYO!
TSUBASA
WHAT'RE YOU CALL-ING ME FOR?
SORRY TO BOTHER YOU.
YOU BUSY?
NO, IT'S FINE.
WHAT'S UP?
ACTUALLY, I HAVE A FAVOR TO ASK...
I WANT YOU TO DELETE THAT VIDEO.

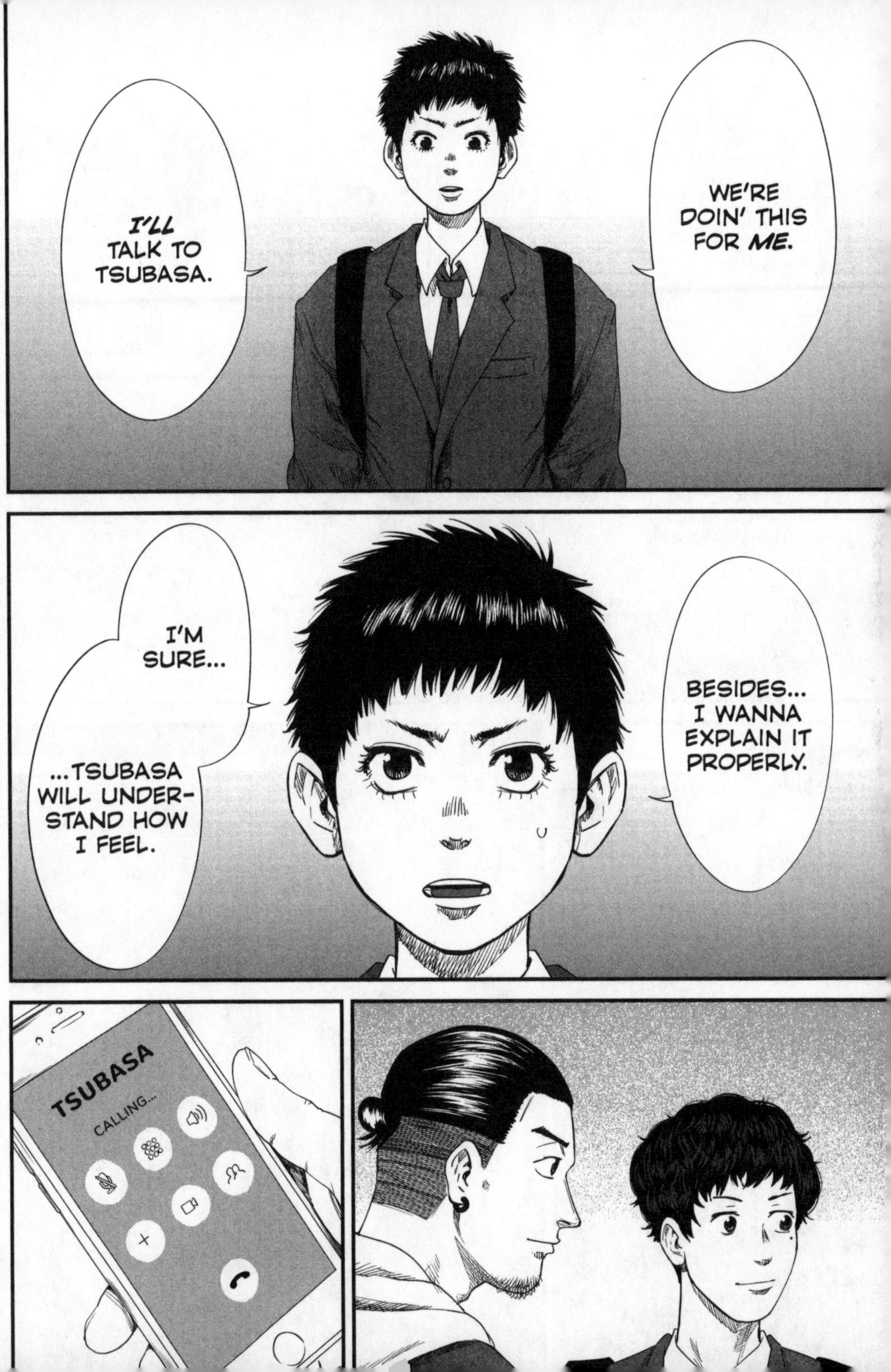
WE'RE DOIN' THIS FOR *ME*.
I'LL TALK TO TSUBASA.
BESIDES... I WANNA EXPLAIN IT PROPERLY.
I'M SURE...
...TSUBASA WILL UNDER-STAND HOW I FEEL.
TSUBASA
CALLING...

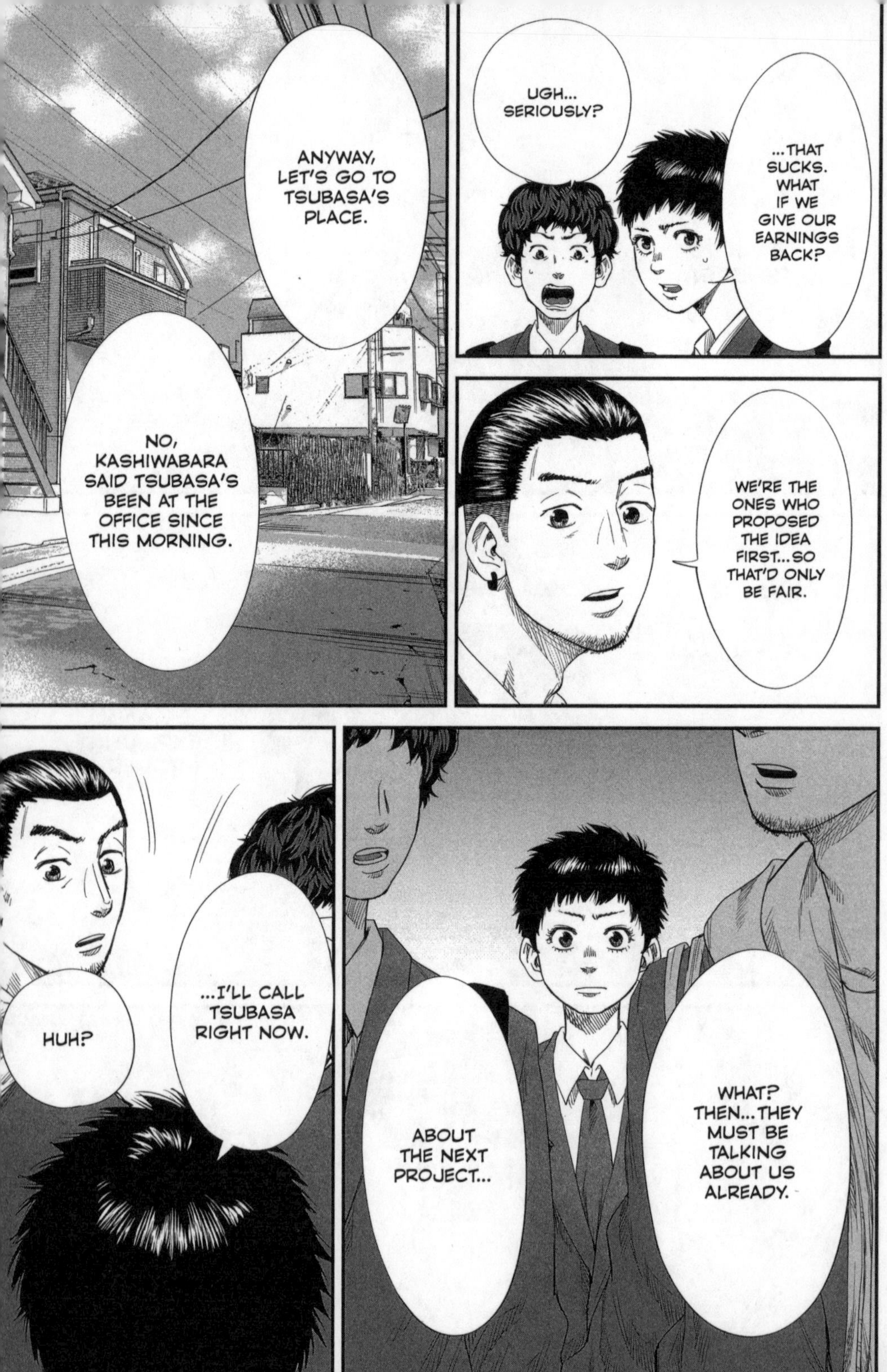
UGH... SERIOUSLY?
...THAT SUCKS. WHAT IF WE GIVE OUR EARNINGS BACK?
WE'RE THE ONES WHO PROPOSED THE IDEA FIRST...SO THAT'D ONLY BE FAIR.
ANYWAY, LET'S GO TO TSUBASA'S PLACE.
NO, KASHIWABARA SAID TSUBASA'S BEEN AT THE OFFICE SINCE THIS MORNING.
WHAT? THEN...THEY MUST BE TALKING ABOUT US ALREADY.
ABOUT THE NEXT PROJECT...
...I'LL CALL TSUBASA RIGHT NOW.
HUH?

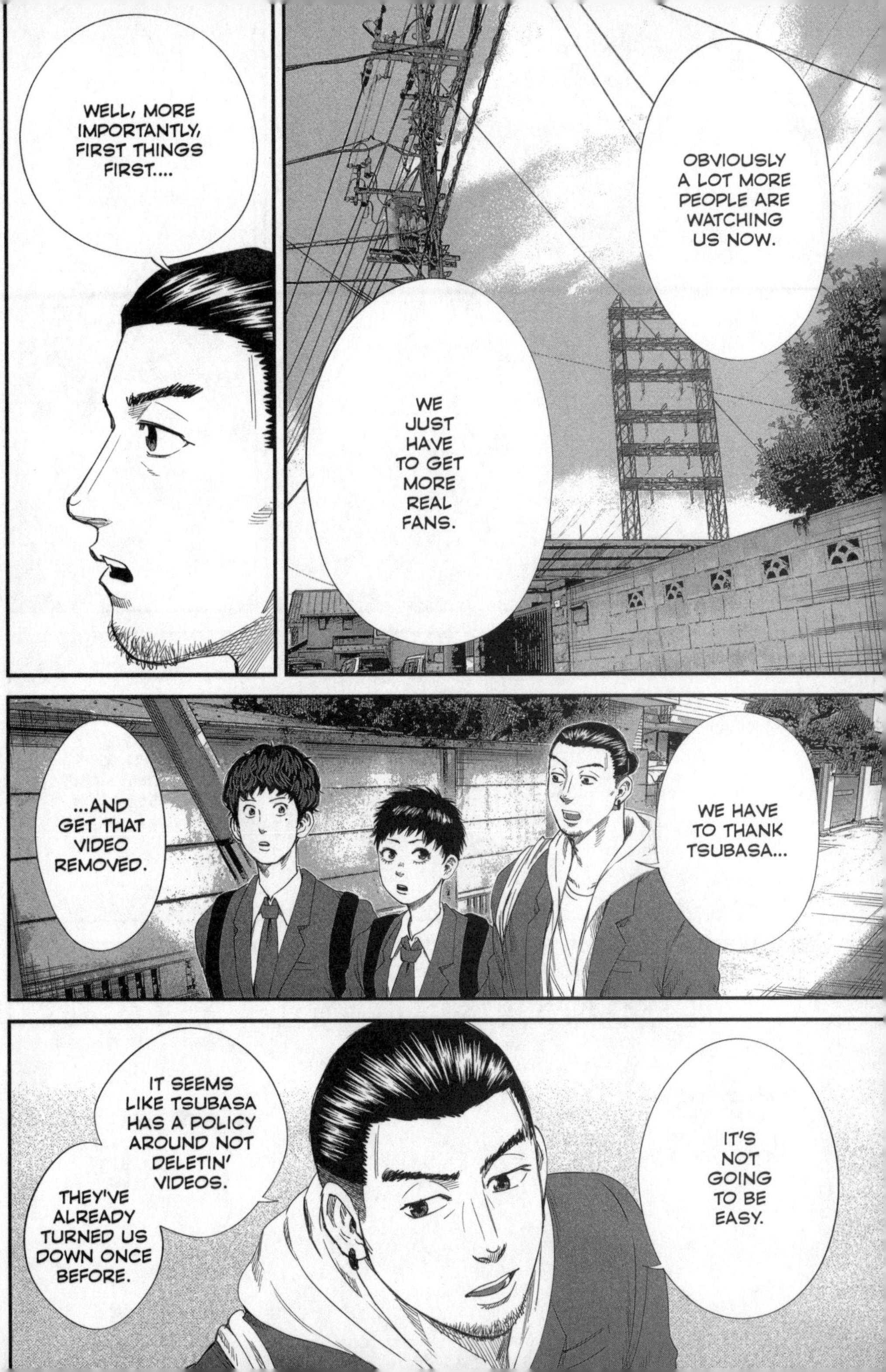
OBVIOUSLY A LOT MORE PEOPLE ARE WATCHING US NOW.
WE JUST HAVE TO GET MORE REAL FANS.
WELL, MORE IMPORTANTLY, FIRST THINGS FIRST....
WE HAVE TO THANK TSUBASA...
...AND GET THAT VIDEO REMOVED.
IT'S NOT GOING TO BE EASY.
IT SEEMS LIKE TSUBASA HAS A POLICY AROUND NOT DELETIN' VIDEOS.
THEY'VE ALREADY TURNED US DOWN ONCE BEFORE.

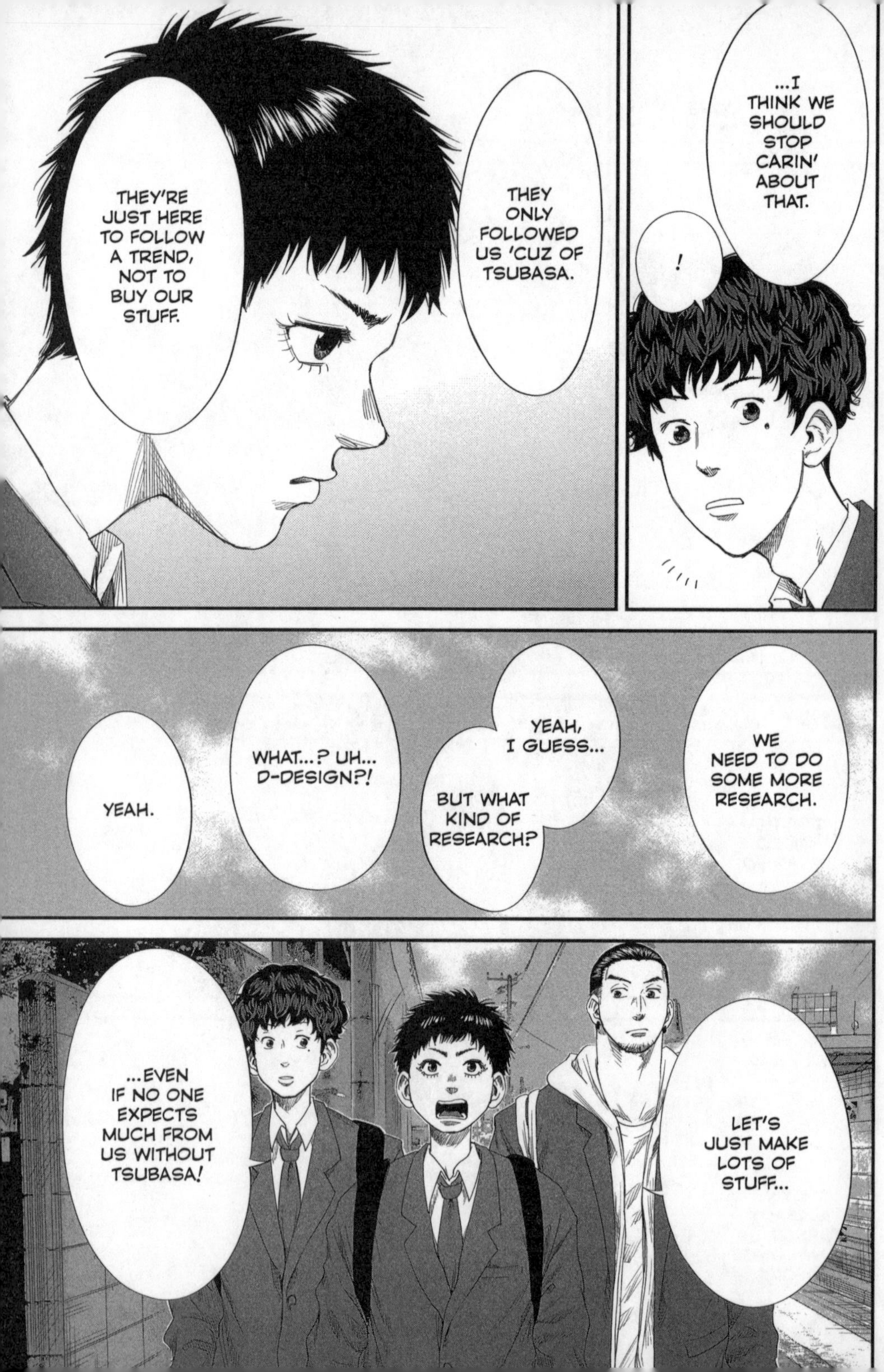
...I THINK WE SHOULD STOP CARIN' ABOUT THAT.
!
THEY ONLY FOLLOWED US 'CUZ OF TSUBASA.
THEY'RE JUST HERE TO FOLLOW A TREND, NOT TO BUY OUR STUFF.
WE NEED TO DO SOME MORE RESEARCH.
YEAH, I GUESS...
BUT WHAT KIND OF RESEARCH?
WHAT...? UH... D-DESIGN?!
YEAH.
LET'S JUST MAKE LOTS OF STUFF...
...EVEN IF NO ONE EXPECTS MUCH FROM US WITHOUT TSUBASA!

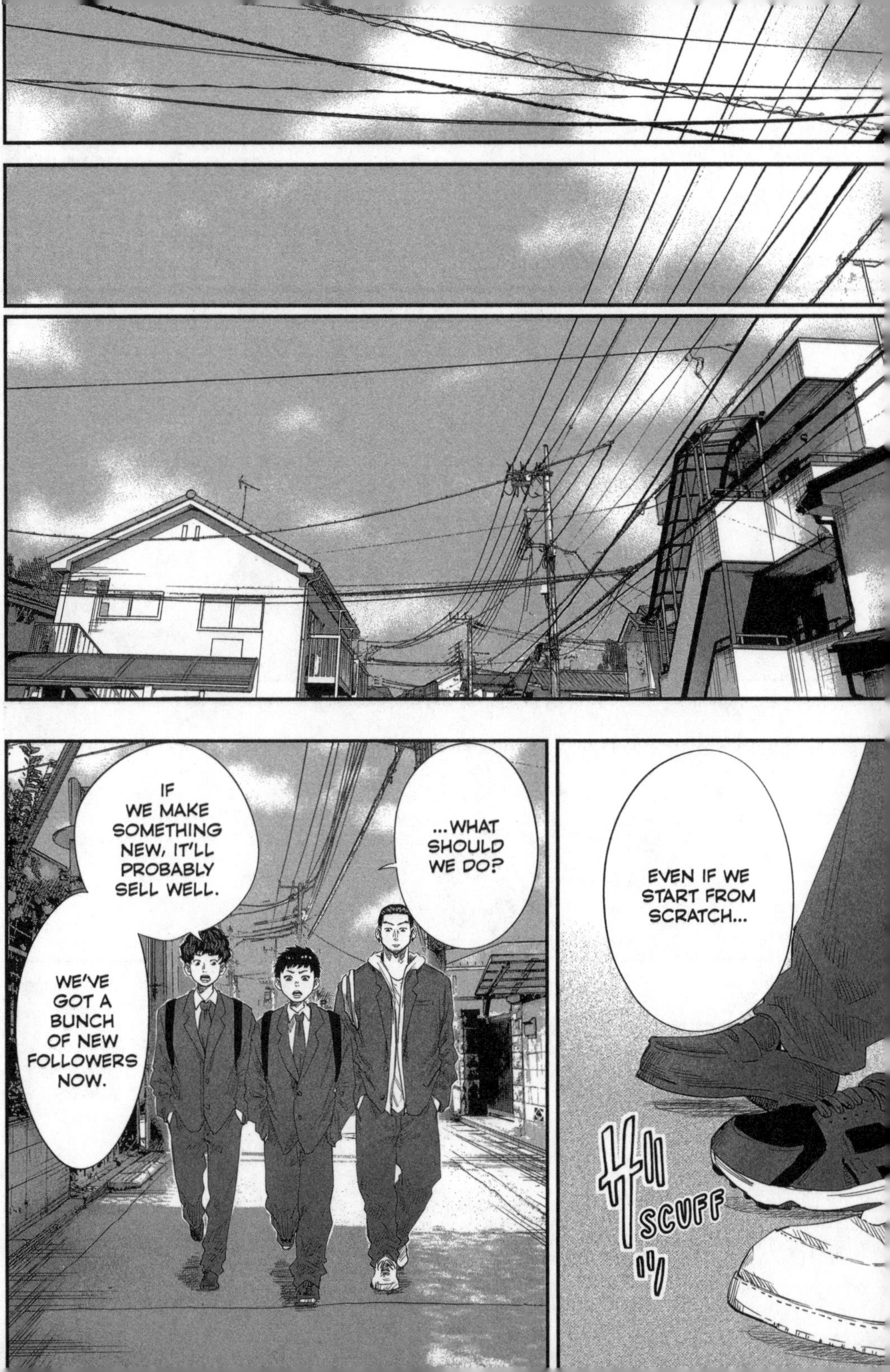
EVEN IF WE START FROM SCRATCH...
SCUFF
...WHAT SHOULD WE DO?
IF WE MAKE SOMETHING NEW, IT'LL PROBABLY SELL WELL.
WE'VE GOT A BUNCH OF NEW FOLLOWERS NOW.

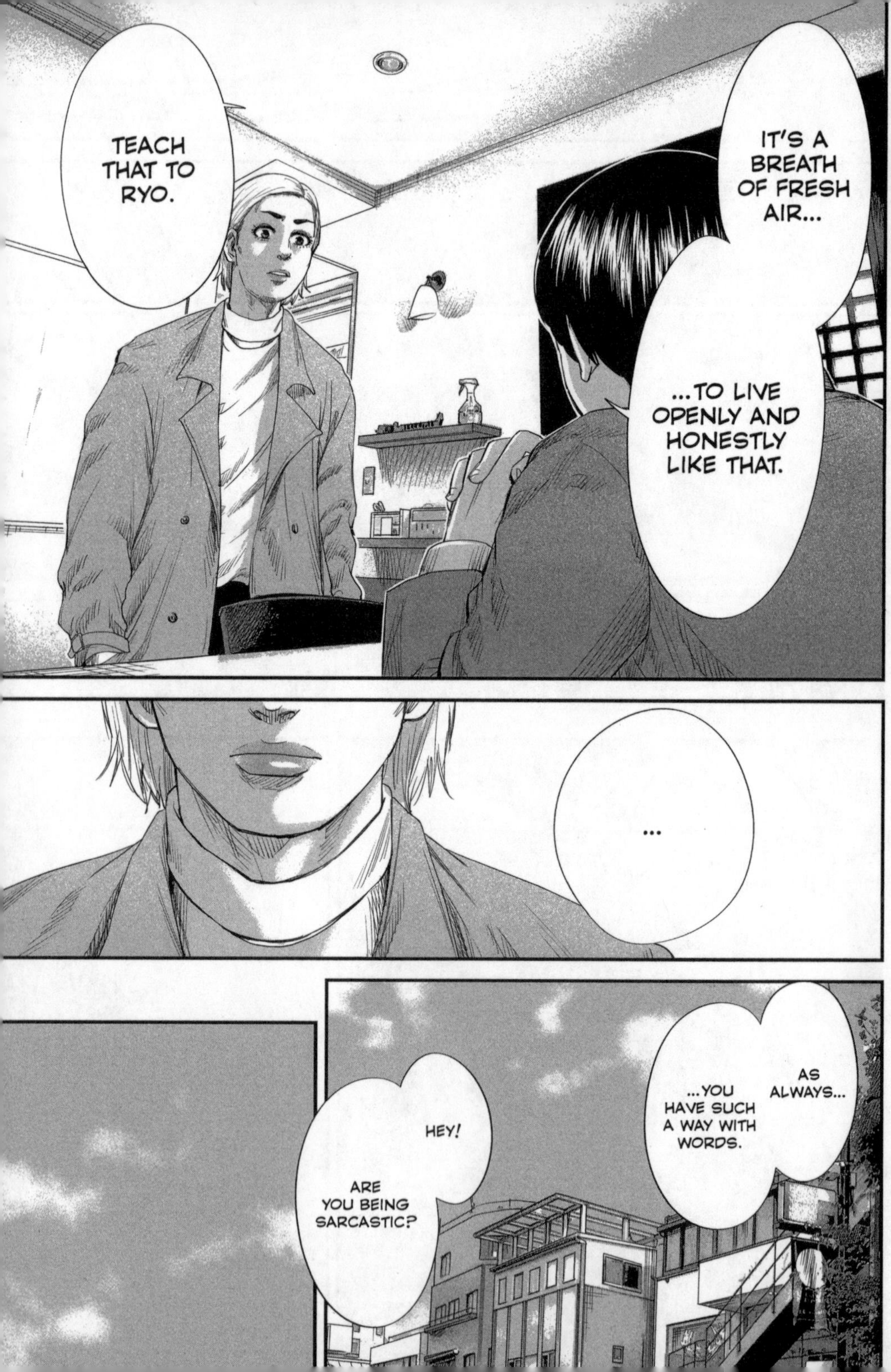
IT'S A BREATH OF FRESH AIR...
...TO LIVE OPENLY AND HONESTLY LIKE THAT.
TEACH THAT TO RYO.
...
AS ALWAYS...
...YOU HAVE SUCH A WAY WITH WORDS.
HEY!
ARE YOU BEING SARCASTIC?

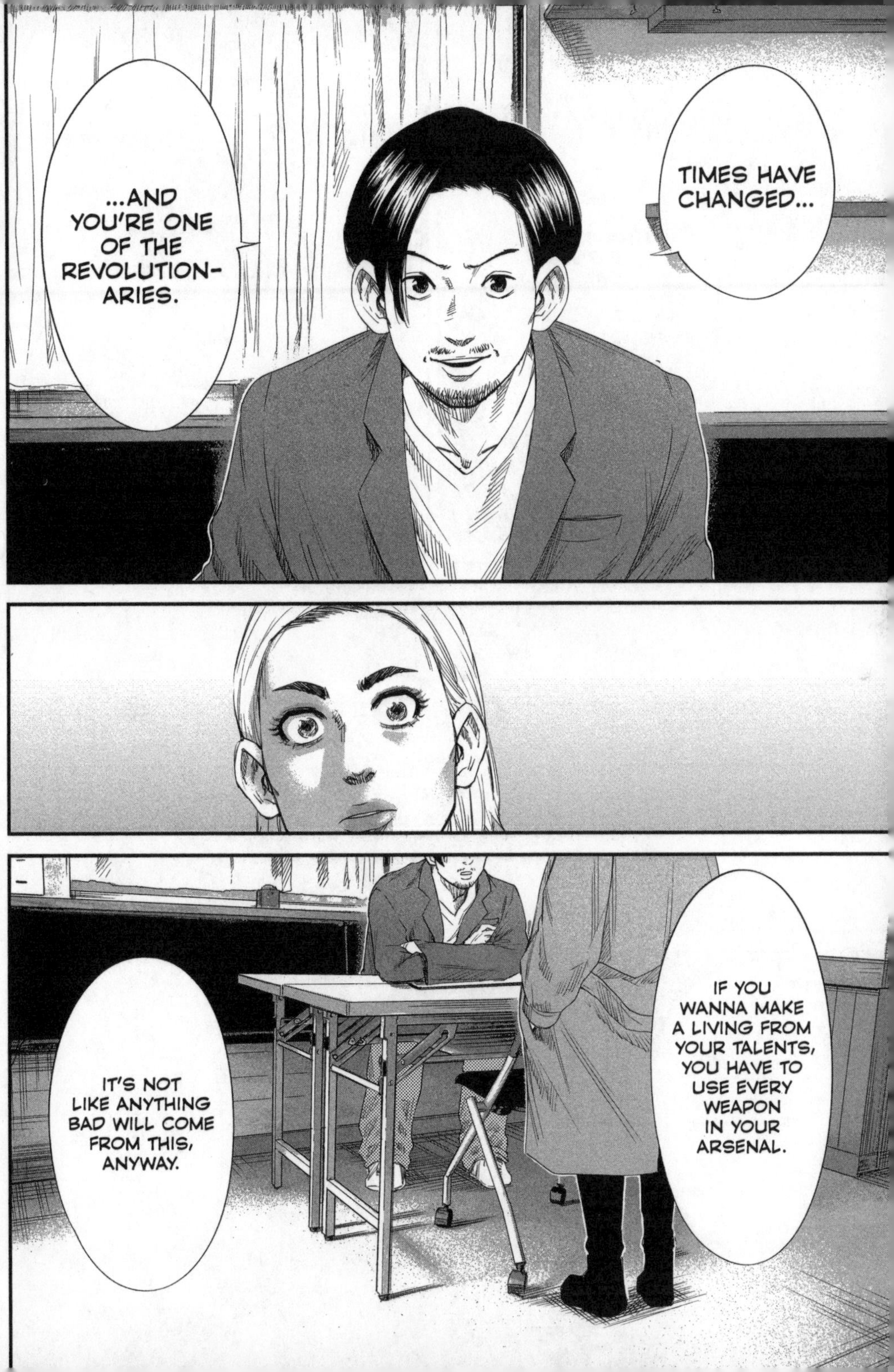
TIMES HAVE CHANGED...
...AND YOU'RE ONE OF THE REVOLUTION-ARIES.
IF YOU WANNA MAKE A LIVING FROM YOUR TALENTS, YOU HAVE TO USE EVERY WEAPON IN YOUR ARSENAL.
IT'S NOT LIKE ANYTHING BAD WILL COME FROM THIS, ANYWAY.

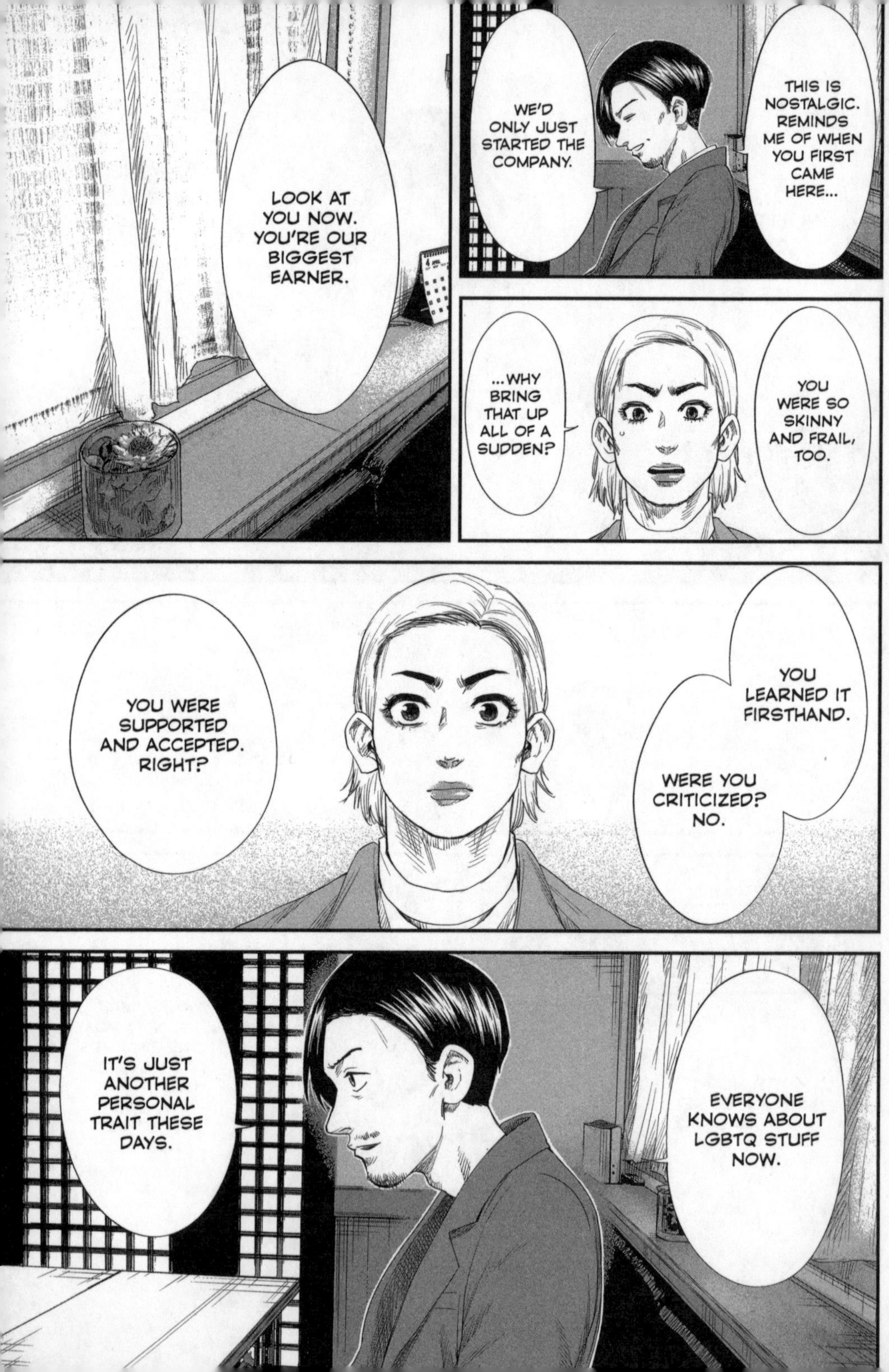
THIS IS NOSTALGIC. REMINDS ME OF WHEN YOU FIRST CAME HERE...
WE'D ONLY JUST STARTED THE COMPANY.
YOU WERE SO SKINNY AND FRAIL, TOO.
...WHY BRING THAT UP ALL OF A SUDDEN?
LOOK AT YOU NOW. YOU'RE OUR BIGGEST EARNER.
YOU LEARNED IT FIRSTHAND.
WERE YOU CRITICIZED? NO.
YOU WERE SUPPORTED AND ACCEPTED. RIGHT?
EVERYONE KNOWS ABOUT LGBTQ STUFF NOW.
IT'S JUST ANOTHER PERSONAL TRAIT THESE DAYS.

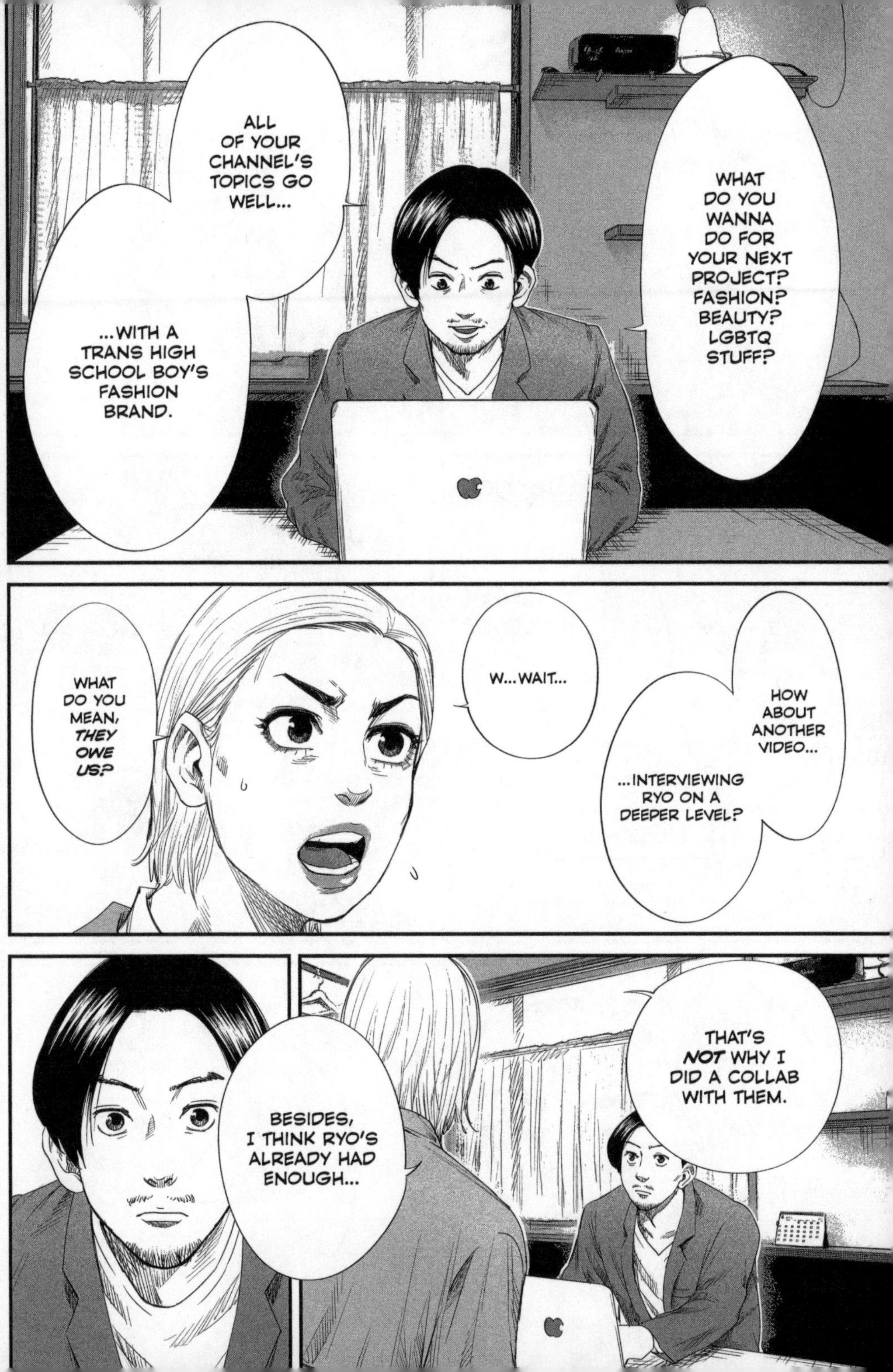
WHAT DO YOU WANNA DO FOR YOUR NEXT PROJECT? FASHION? BEAUTY? LGBTQ STUFF?
ALL OF YOUR CHANNEL'S TOPICS GO WELL...
...WITH A TRANS HIGH SCHOOL BOY'S FASHION BRAND.
HOW ABOUT ANOTHER VIDEO...
...INTERVIEWING RYO ON A DEEPER LEVEL?
W...WAIT...
WHAT DO YOU MEAN, *THEY OWE US?*
THAT'S *NOT* WHY I DID A COLLAB WITH THEM.
BESIDES, I THINK RYO'S ALREADY HAD ENOUGH...

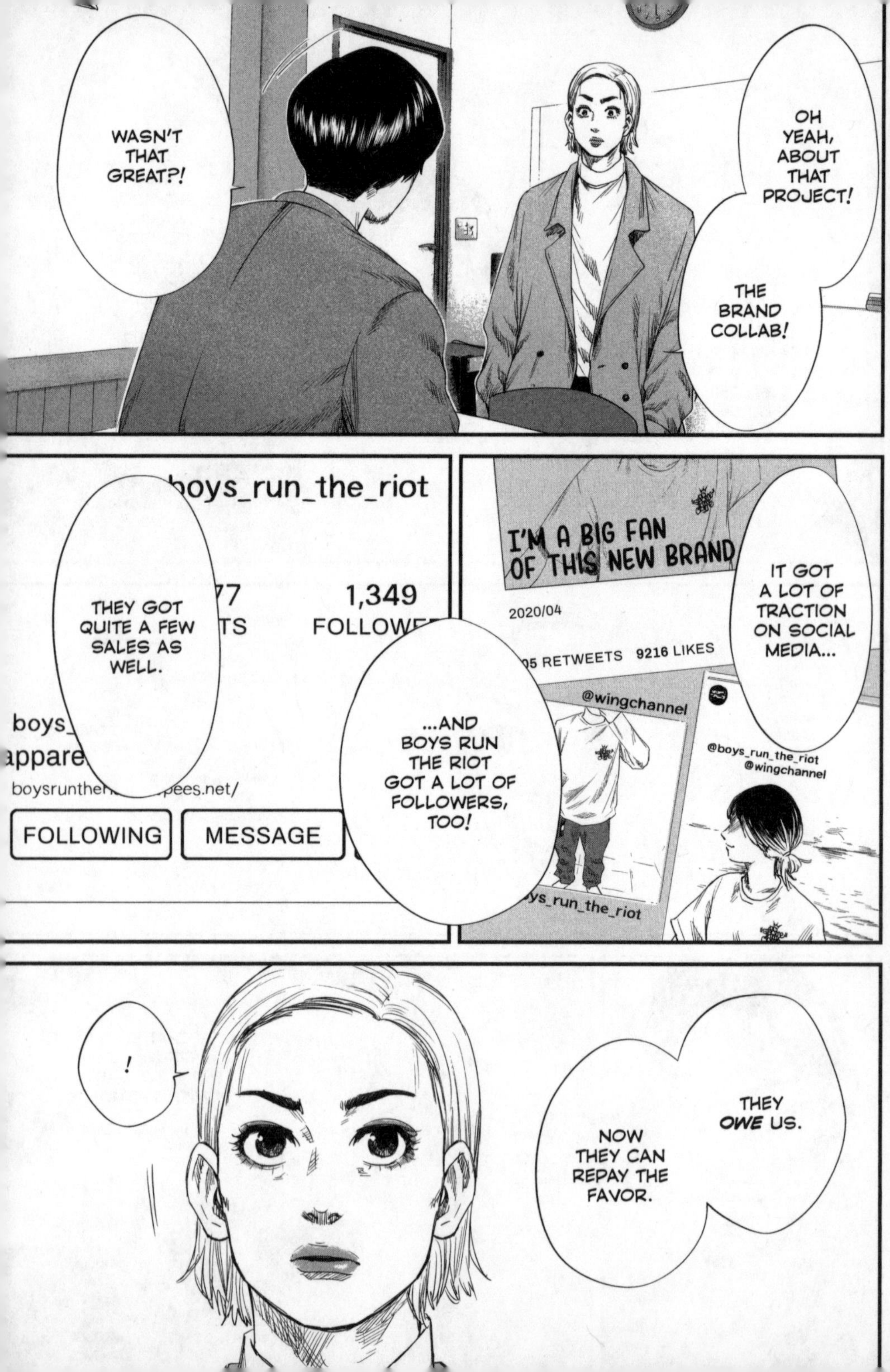
OH YEAH, ABOUT THAT PROJECT!
THE BRAND COLLAB!
WASN'T THAT GREAT?!
I'M A BIG FAN OF THIS NEW BRAND
2020/04
9216 LIKES
@wingchannel
@boys_run_the_riot @wingchannel
IT GOT A LOT OF TRACTION ON SOCIAL MEDIA...
...AND BOYS RUN THE RIOT GOT A LOT OF FOLLOWERS, TOO!
boys_run_the_riot
1,349
FOLLOWING
MESSAGE
THEY GOT QUITE A FEW SALES AS WELL.
THEY *OWE* US.
NOW THEY CAN REPAY THE FAVOR.
!

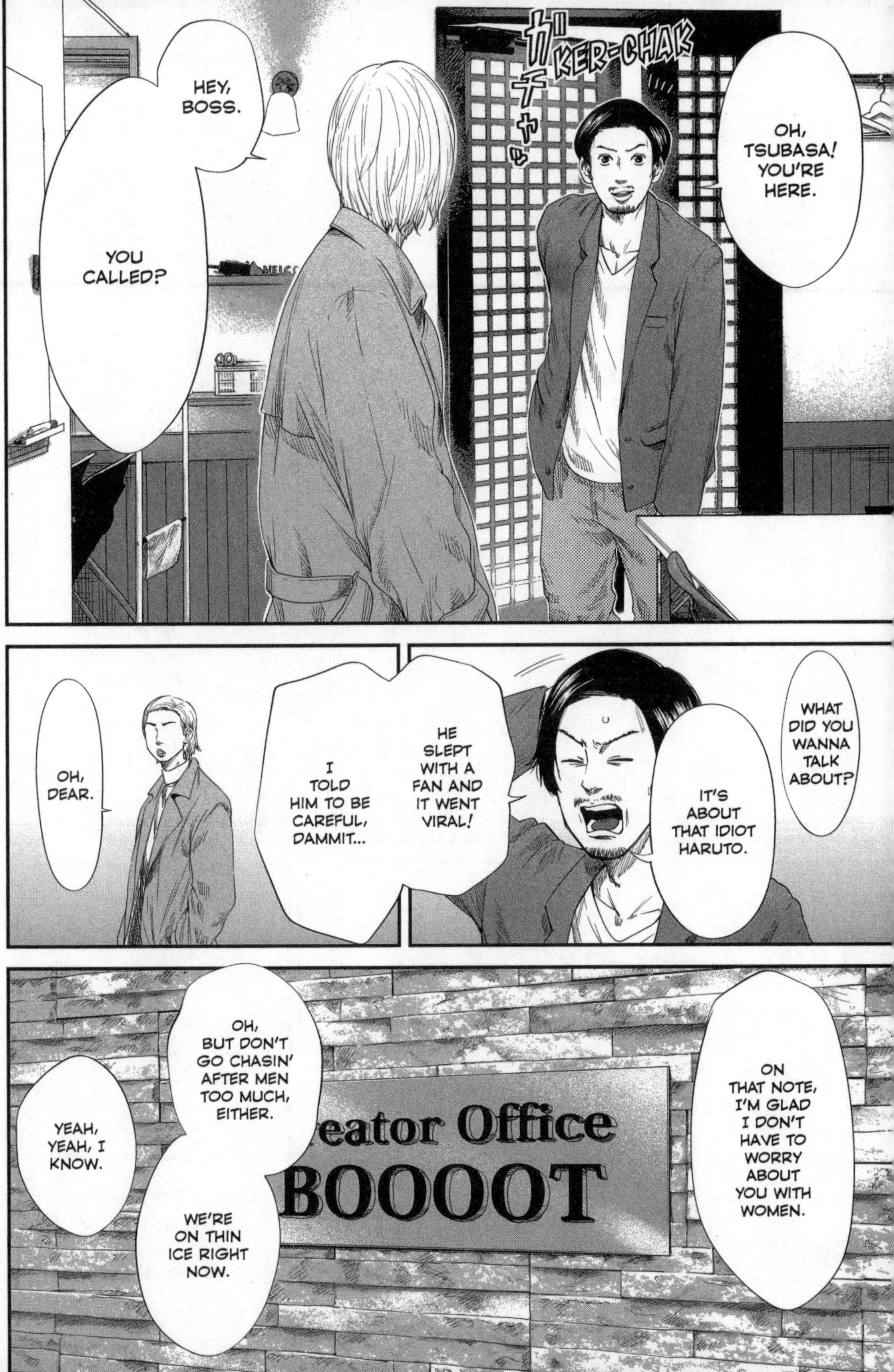
ガチャ
KER-CHAK
OH, TSUBASA! YOU'RE HERE.
HEY, BOSS.
YOU CALLED?
WHAT DID YOU WANNA TALK ABOUT?
IT'S ABOUT THAT IDIOT HARUTO.
HE SLEPT WITH A FAN AND IT WENT VIRAL!
I TOLD HIM TO BE CAREFUL, DAMMIT...
OH, DEAR.
reator Office BOOOOT
ON THAT NOTE, I'M GLAD I DON'T HAVE TO WORRY ABOUT YOU WITH WOMEN.
OH, BUT DON'T GO CHASIN' AFTER MEN TOO MUCH, EITHER.
WE'RE ON THIN ICE RIGHT NOW.
YEAH, YEAH, I KNOW.

Chap. 23 Scandal

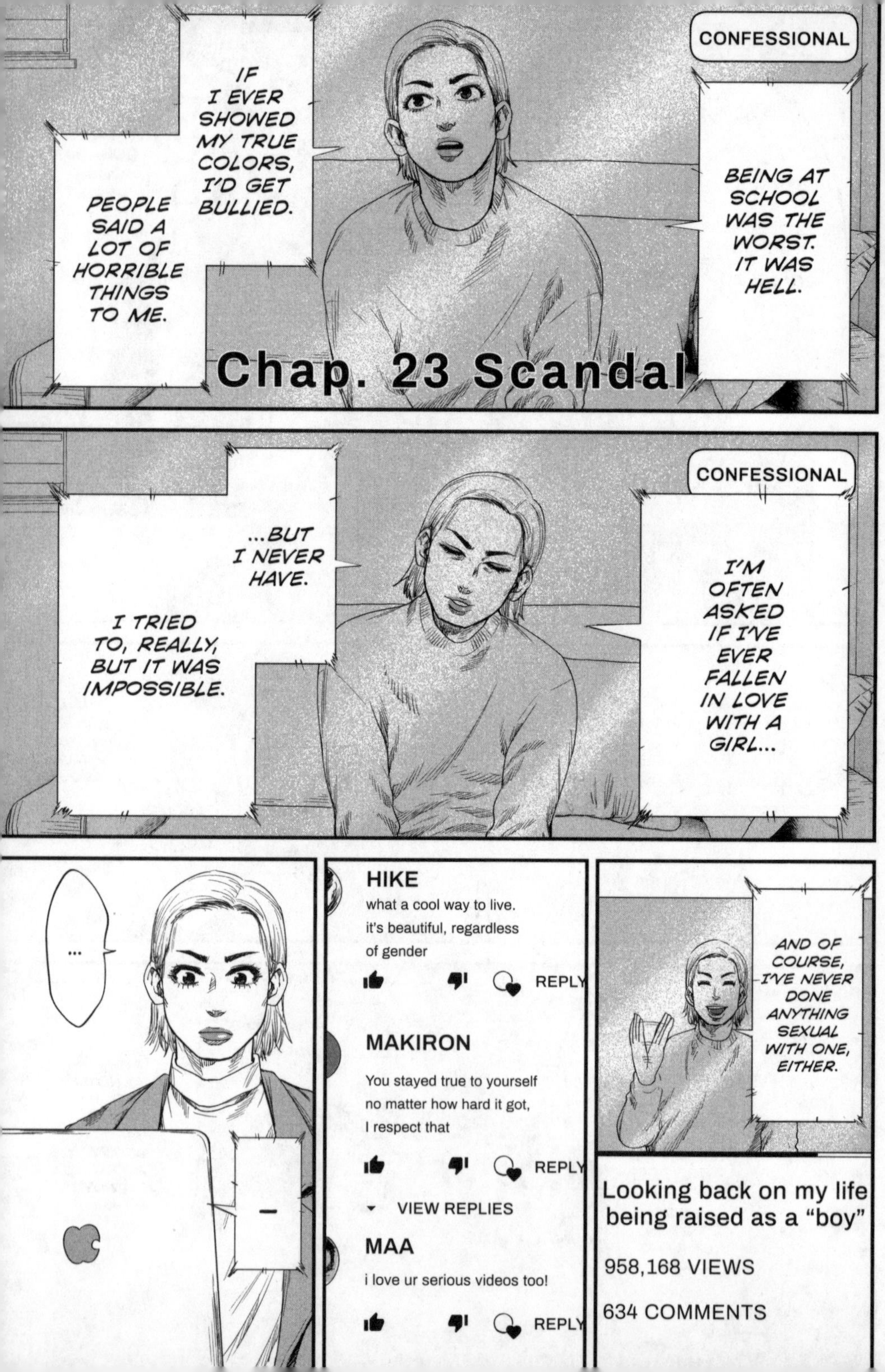
CONFESSIONAL
BEING AT SCHOOL WAS THE WORST. IT WAS HELL.
IF I EVER SHOWED MY TRUE COLORS, I'D GET BULLIED.
PEOPLE SAID A LOT OF HORRIBLE THINGS TO ME.
CONFESSIONAL
I'M OFTEN ASKED IF I'VE EVER FALLEN IN LOVE WITH A GIRL...
...BUT I NEVER HAVE.
I TRIED TO, REALLY, BUT IT WAS IMPOSSIBLE.
AND OF COURSE, I'VE NEVER DONE ANYTHING SEXUAL WITH ONE, EITHER.
Looking back on my life being raised as a "boy"
958,168 VIEWS
634 COMMENTS
HIKE
what a cool way to live. it's beautiful, regardless of gender
REPLY
MAKIRON
You stayed true to yourself no matter how hard it got, I respect that
REPLY
VIEW REPLIES
MAA
i love ur serious videos too!
REPLY
...
—

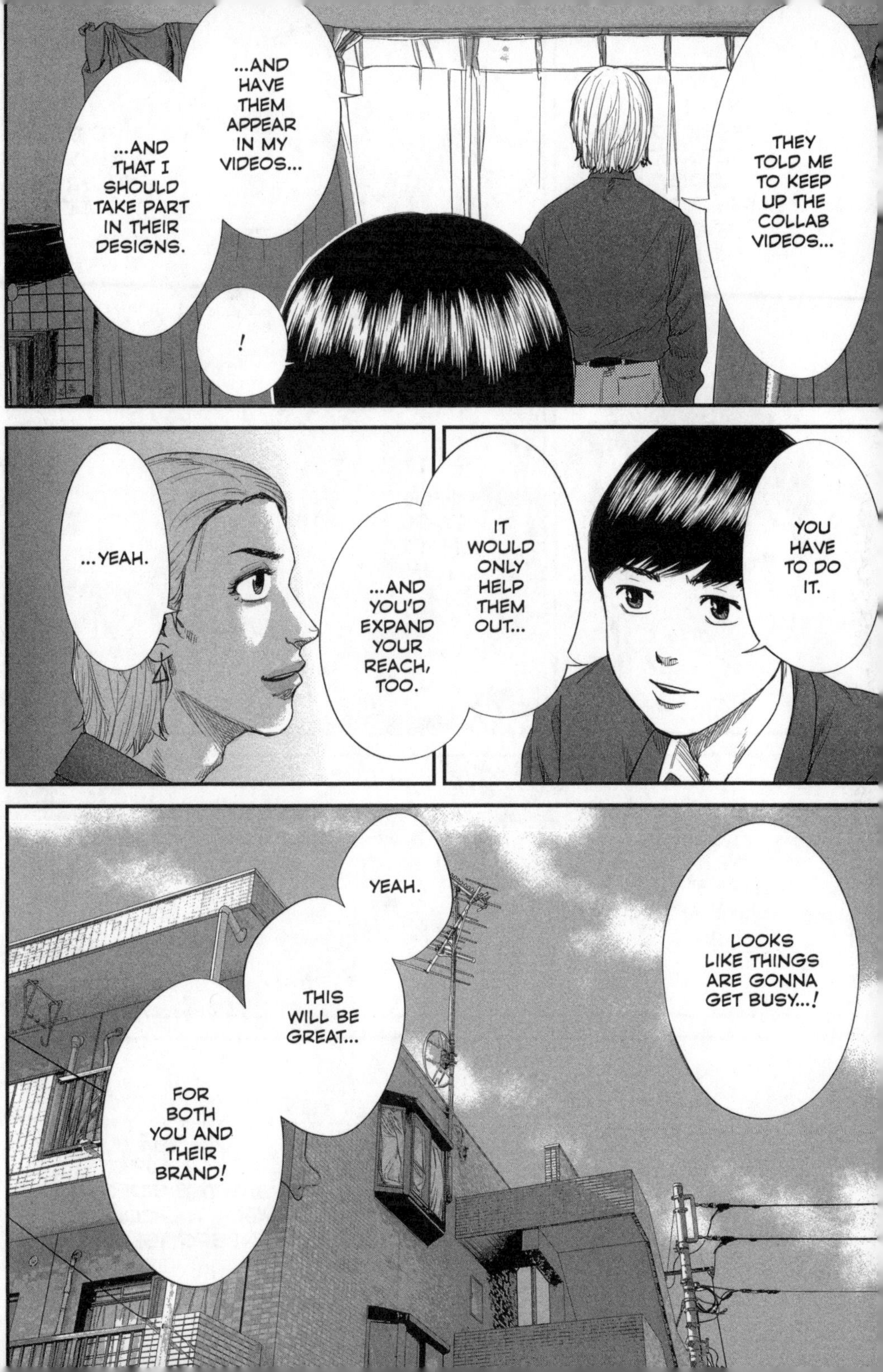
THEY TOLD ME TO KEEP UP THE COLLAB VIDEOS...
...AND HAVE THEM APPEAR IN MY VIDEOS...
...AND THAT I SHOULD TAKE PART IN THEIR DESIGNS.
!
YOU HAVE TO DO IT.
IT WOULD ONLY HELP THEM OUT...
...AND YOU'D EXPAND YOUR REACH, TOO.
...YEAH.
LOOKS LIKE THINGS ARE GONNA GET BUSY...!
YEAH.
THIS WILL BE GREAT...
FOR BOTH YOU AND THEIR BRAND!

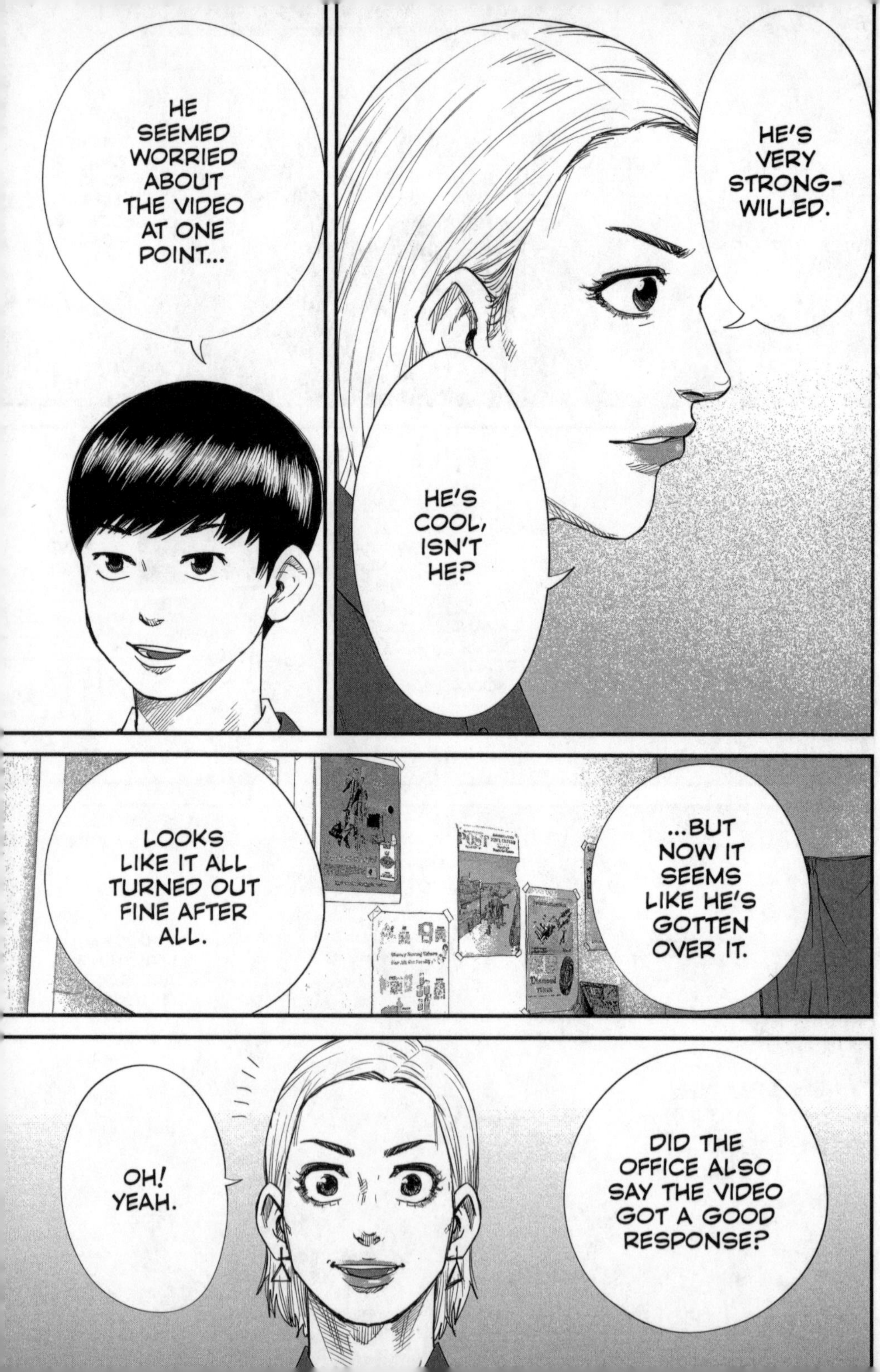
HE'S VERY STRONG-WILLED.
HE'S COOL, ISN'T HE?
HE SEEMED WORRIED ABOUT THE VIDEO AT ONE POINT...
...BUT NOW IT SEEMS LIKE HE'S GOTTEN OVER IT.
LOOKS LIKE IT ALL TURNED OUT FINE AFTER ALL.
DID THE OFFICE ALSO SAY THE VIDEO GOT A GOOD RESPONSE?
OH! YEAH.

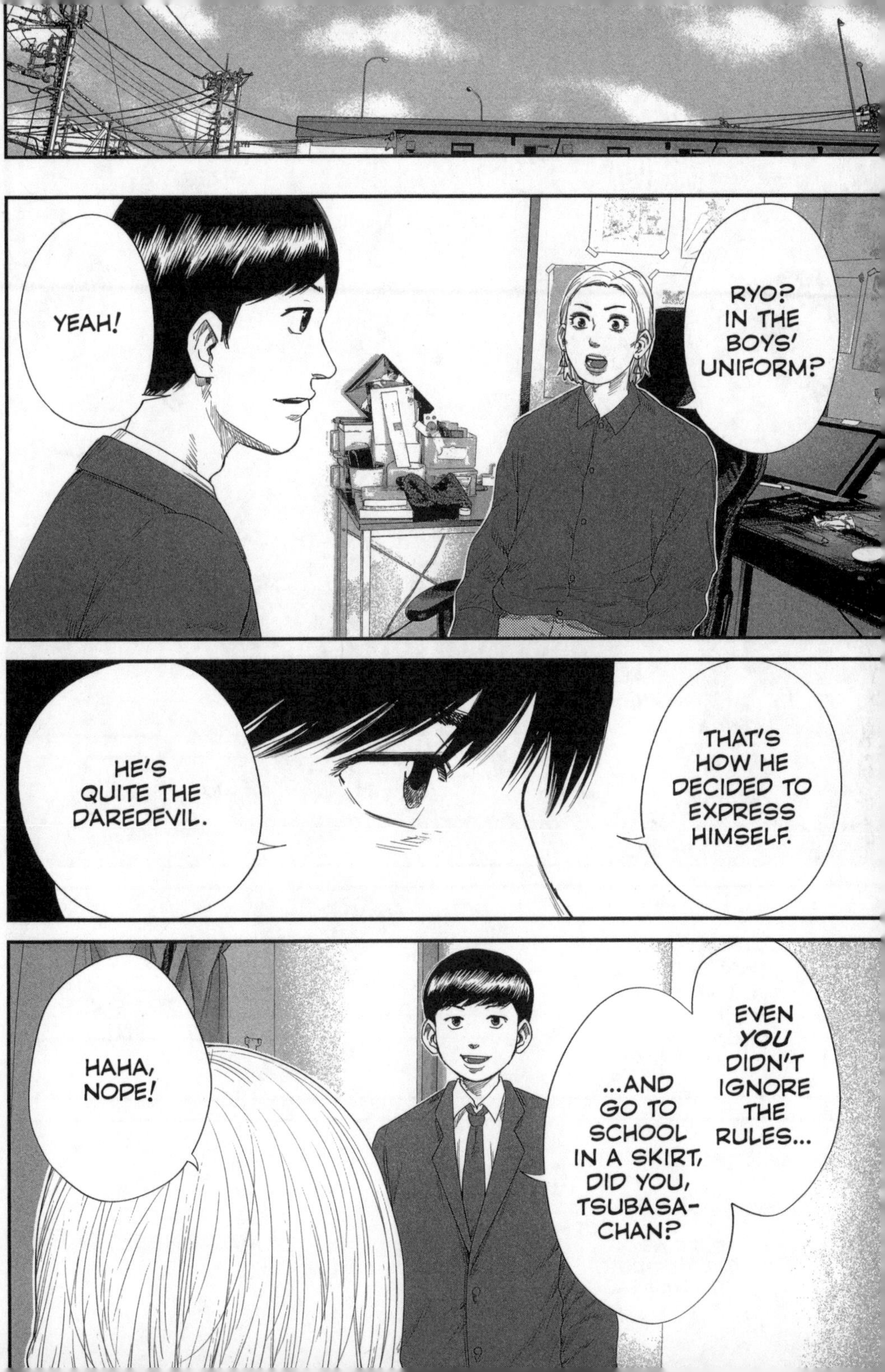
RYO? IN THE BOYS' UNIFORM?
YEAH!
THAT'S HOW HE DECIDED TO EXPRESS HIMSELF.
HE'S QUITE THE DAREDEVIL.
EVEN *YOU* DIDN'T IGNORE THE RULES...
...AND GO TO SCHOOL IN A SKIRT, DID YOU, TSUBASA-CHAN?
HAHA, NOPE!

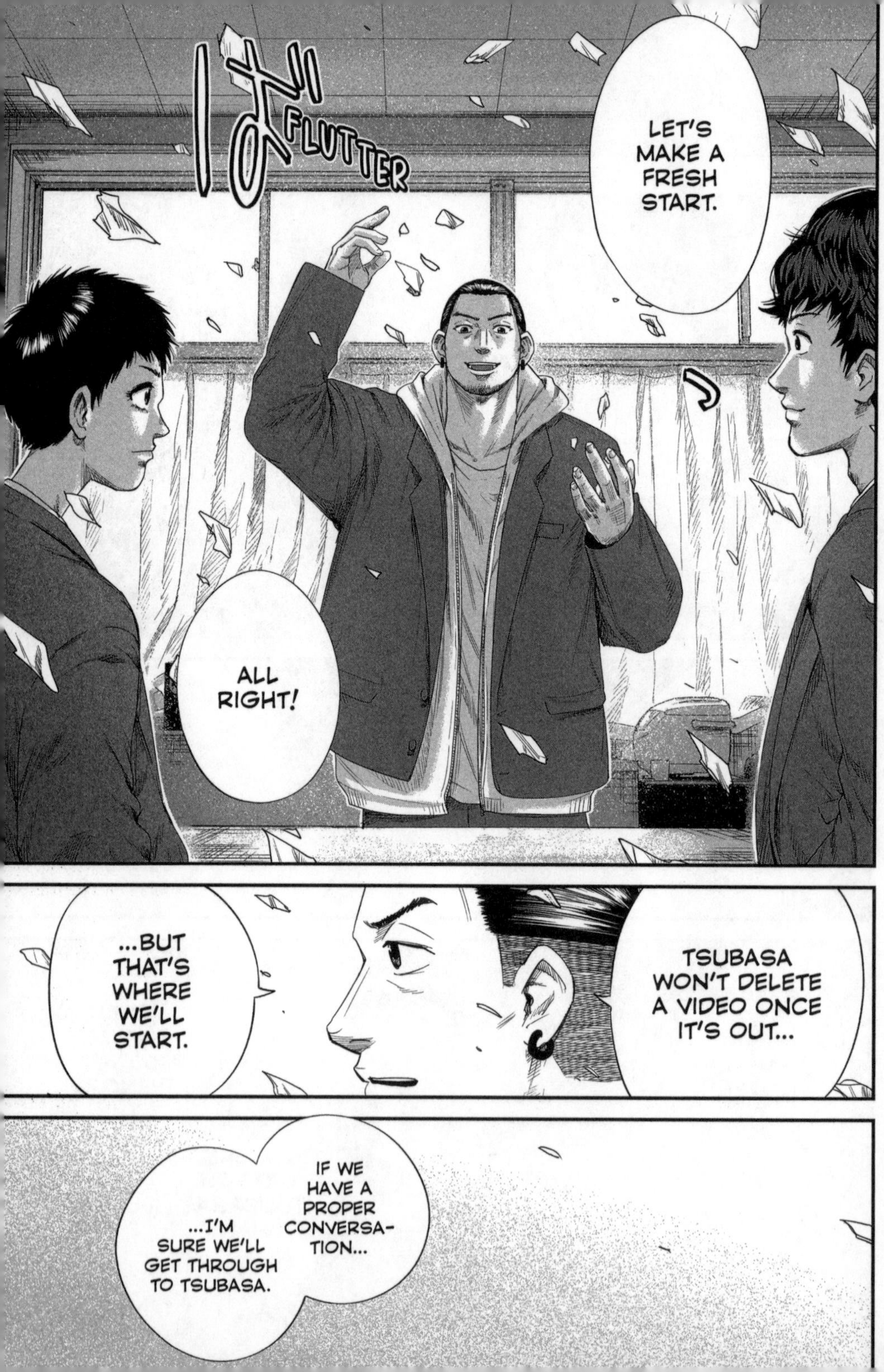
LET'S MAKE A FRESH START.
FLUTTER
ALL RIGHT!
TSUBASA WON'T DELETE A VIDEO ONCE IT'S OUT...
...BUT THAT'S WHERE WE'LL START.
IF WE HAVE A PROPER CONVERSA-TION...
...I'M SURE WE'LL GET THROUGH TO TSUBASA.

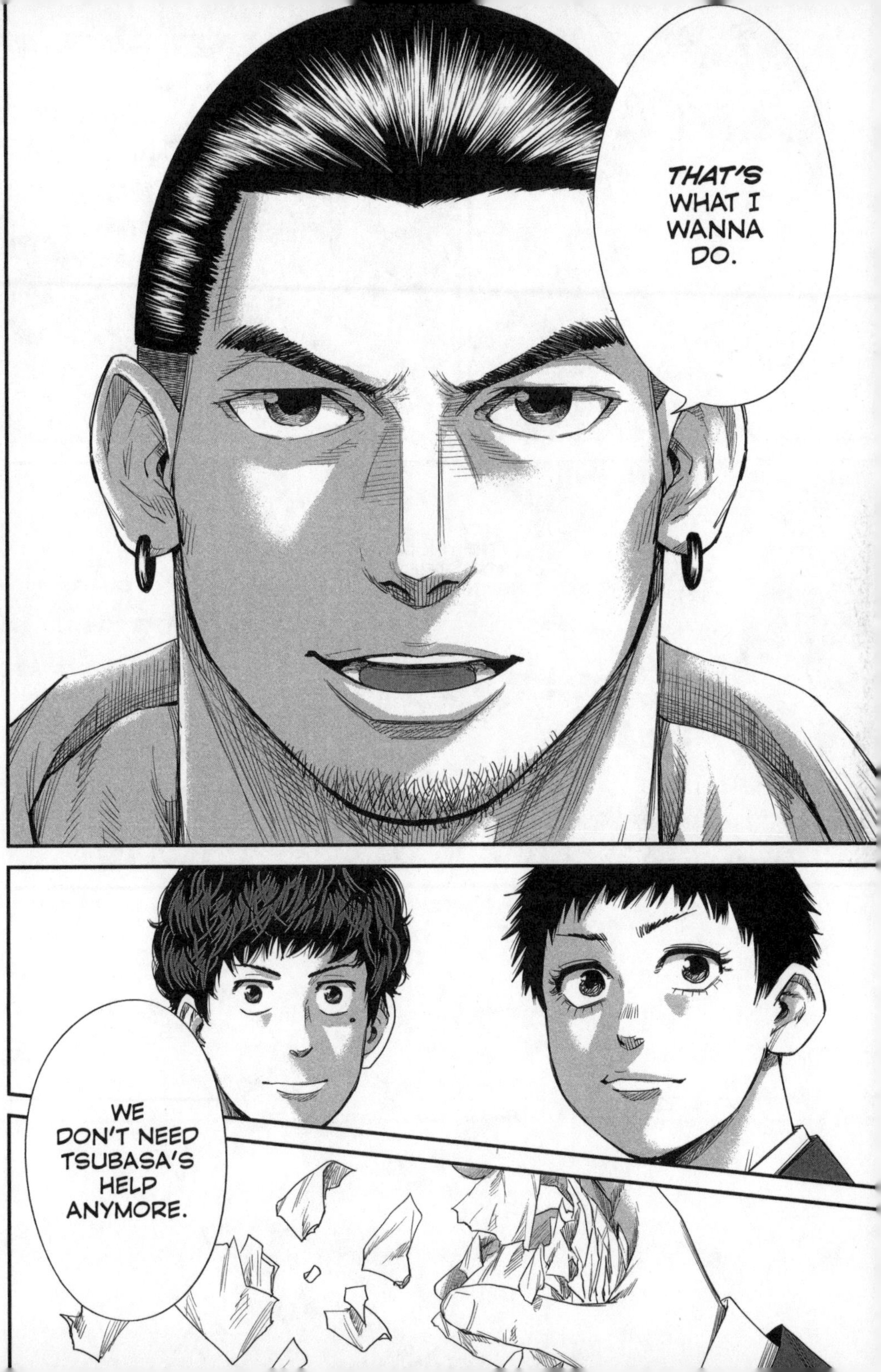
THAT'S WHAT I WANNA DO.
WE DON'T NEED TSUBASA'S HELP ANYMORE.

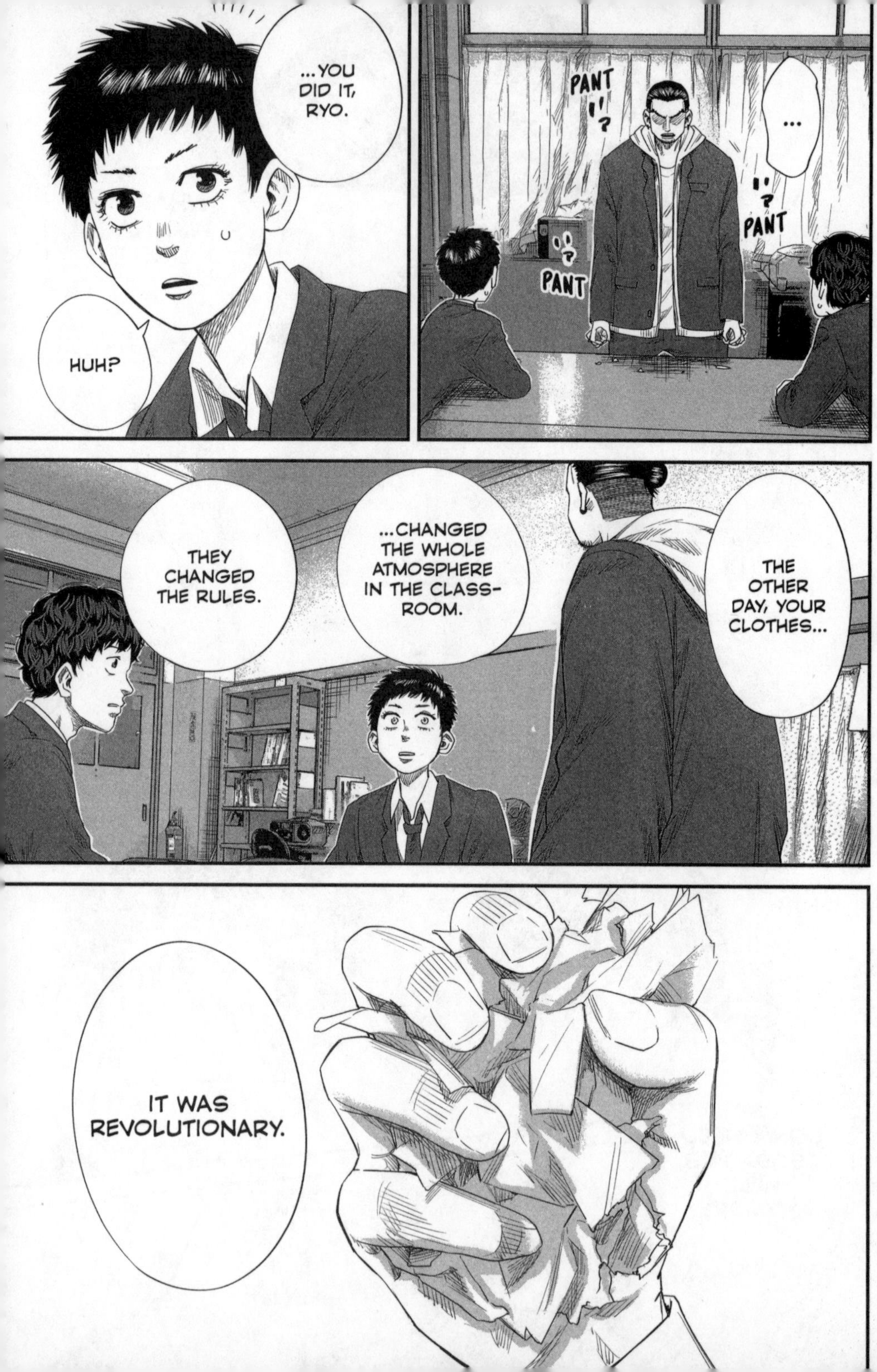
...
PANT
PANT
PANT
...YOU DID IT, RYO.
HUH?
THE OTHER DAY, YOUR CLOTHES...
...CHANGED THE WHOLE ATMOSPHERE IN THE CLASSROOM.
THEY CHANGED THE RULES.
IT WAS REVOLUTIONARY.

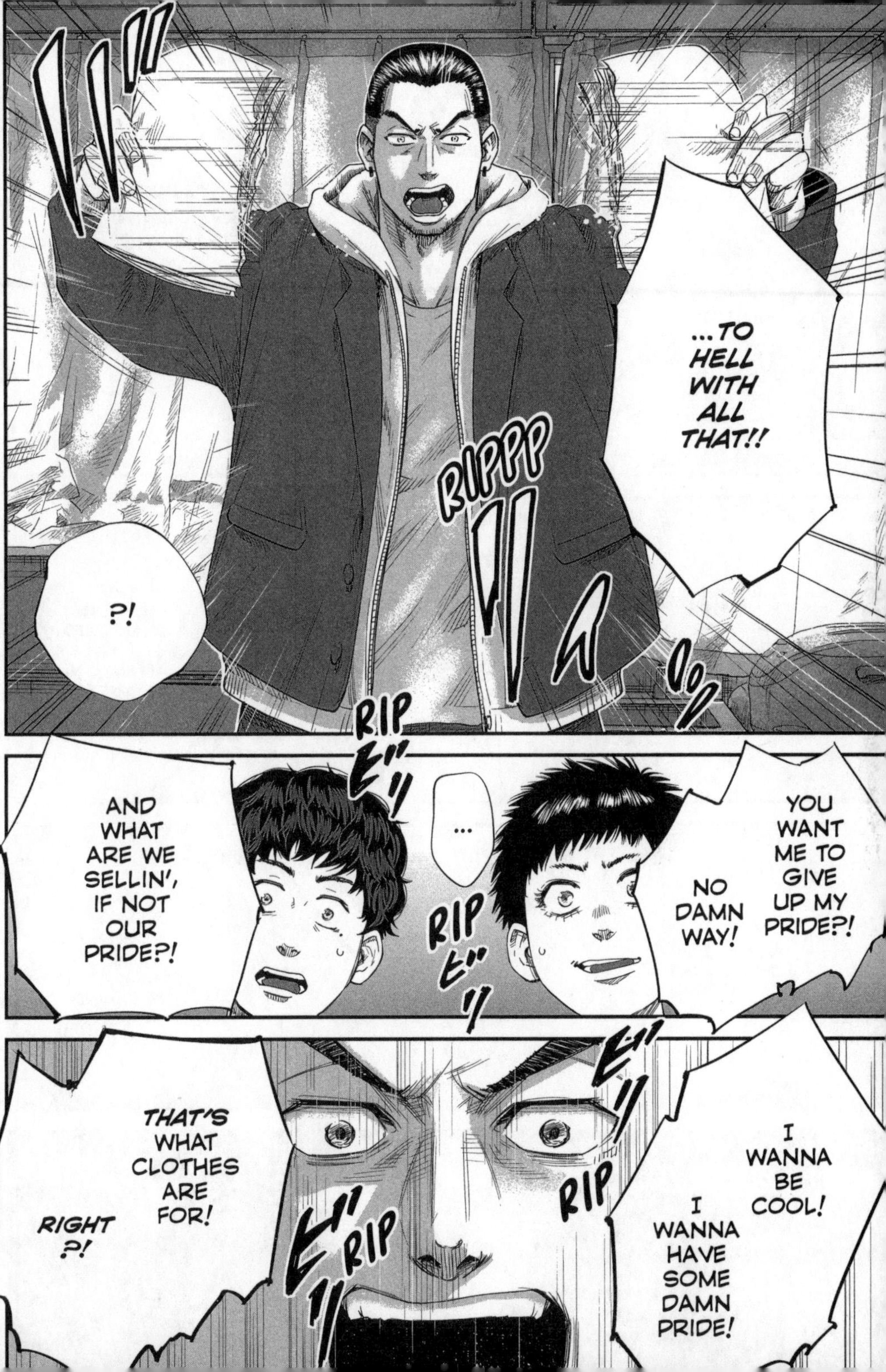
...TO HELL WITH ALL THAT!!
RIPPP
?!
RIP
YOU WANT ME TO GIVE UP MY PRIDE?!
NO DAMN WAY!
...
RIP
AND WHAT ARE WE SELLIN', IF NOT OUR PRIDE?!
I WANNA BE COOL!
I WANNA HAVE SOME DAMN PRIDE!
RIP
RIP
THAT'S WHAT CLOTHES ARE FOR!
RIGHT?!

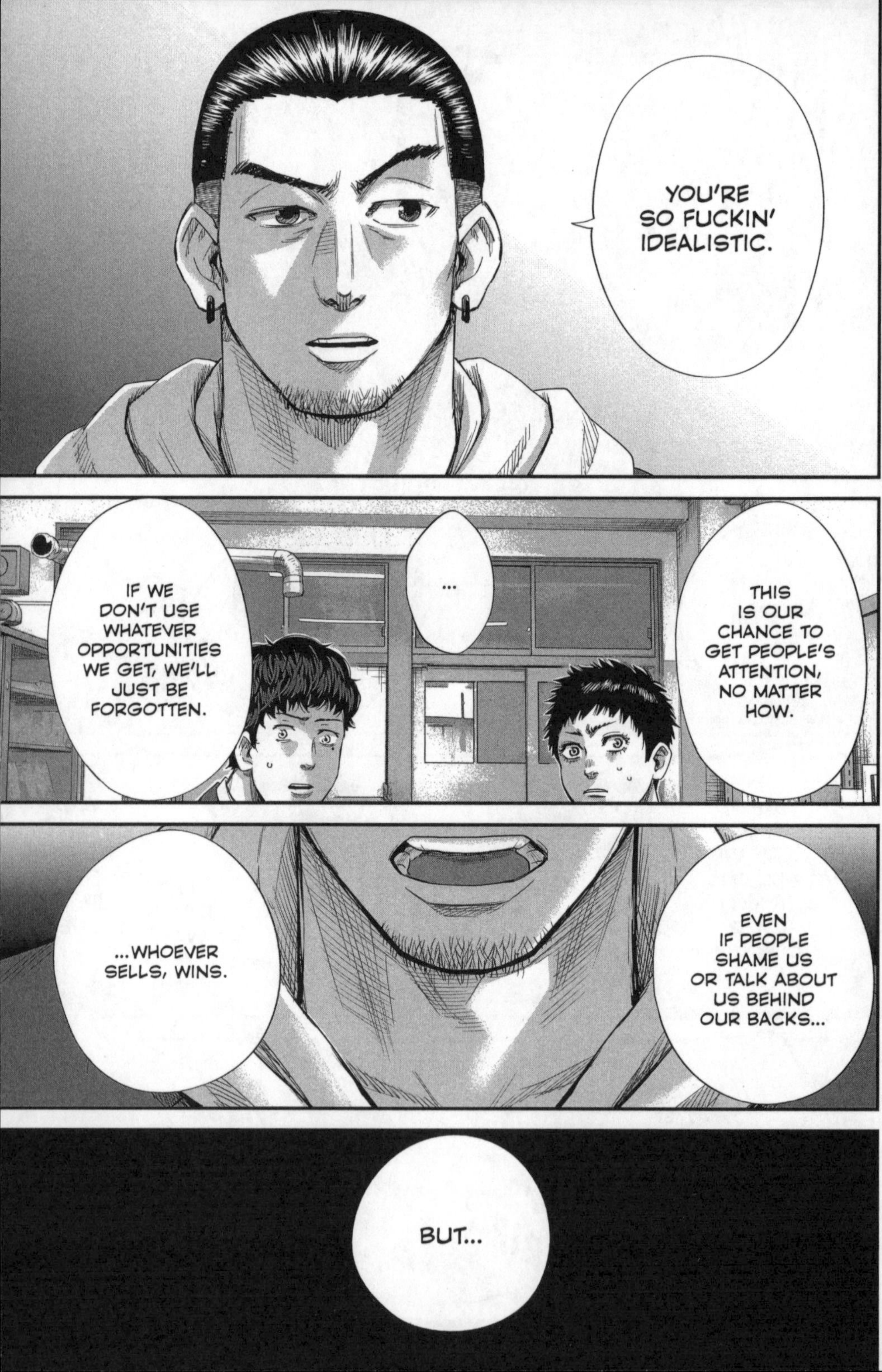
YOU'RE SO FUCKIN' IDEALISTIC.
THIS IS OUR CHANCE TO GET PEOPLE'S ATTENTION, NO MATTER HOW.
...
IF WE DON'T USE WHATEVER OPPORTUNITIES WE GET, WE'LL JUST BE FORGOTTEN.
EVEN IF PEOPLE SHAME US OR TALK ABOUT US BEHIND OUR BACKS...
...WHOEVER SELLS, WINS.
BUT...

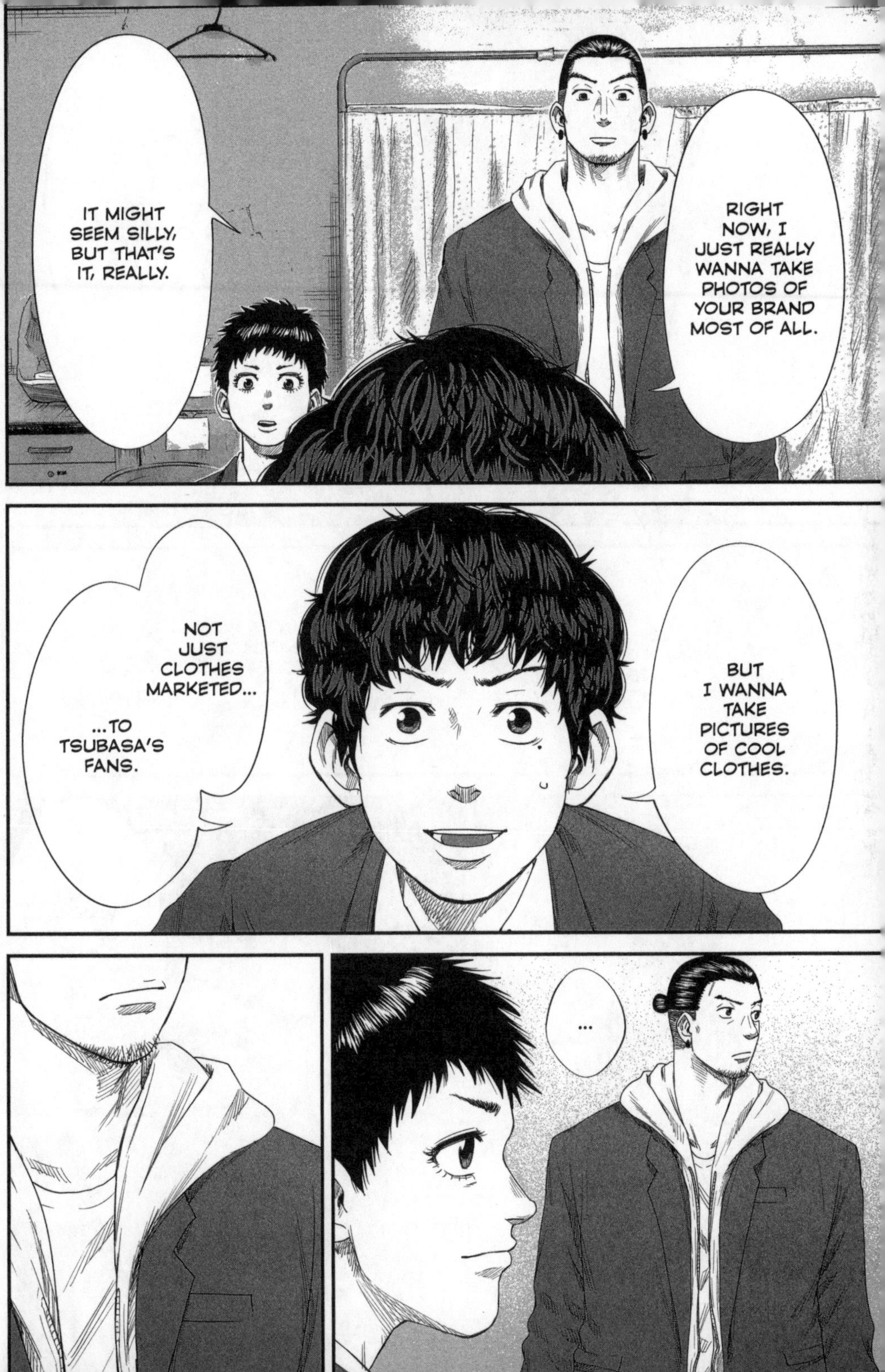
RIGHT NOW, I JUST REALLY WANNA TAKE PHOTOS OF YOUR BRAND MOST OF ALL.
IT MIGHT SEEM SILLY, BUT THAT'S IT, REALLY.
BUT I WANNA TAKE PICTURES OF COOL CLOTHES.
NOT JUST CLOTHES MARKETED...
...TO TSUBASA'S FANS.
...

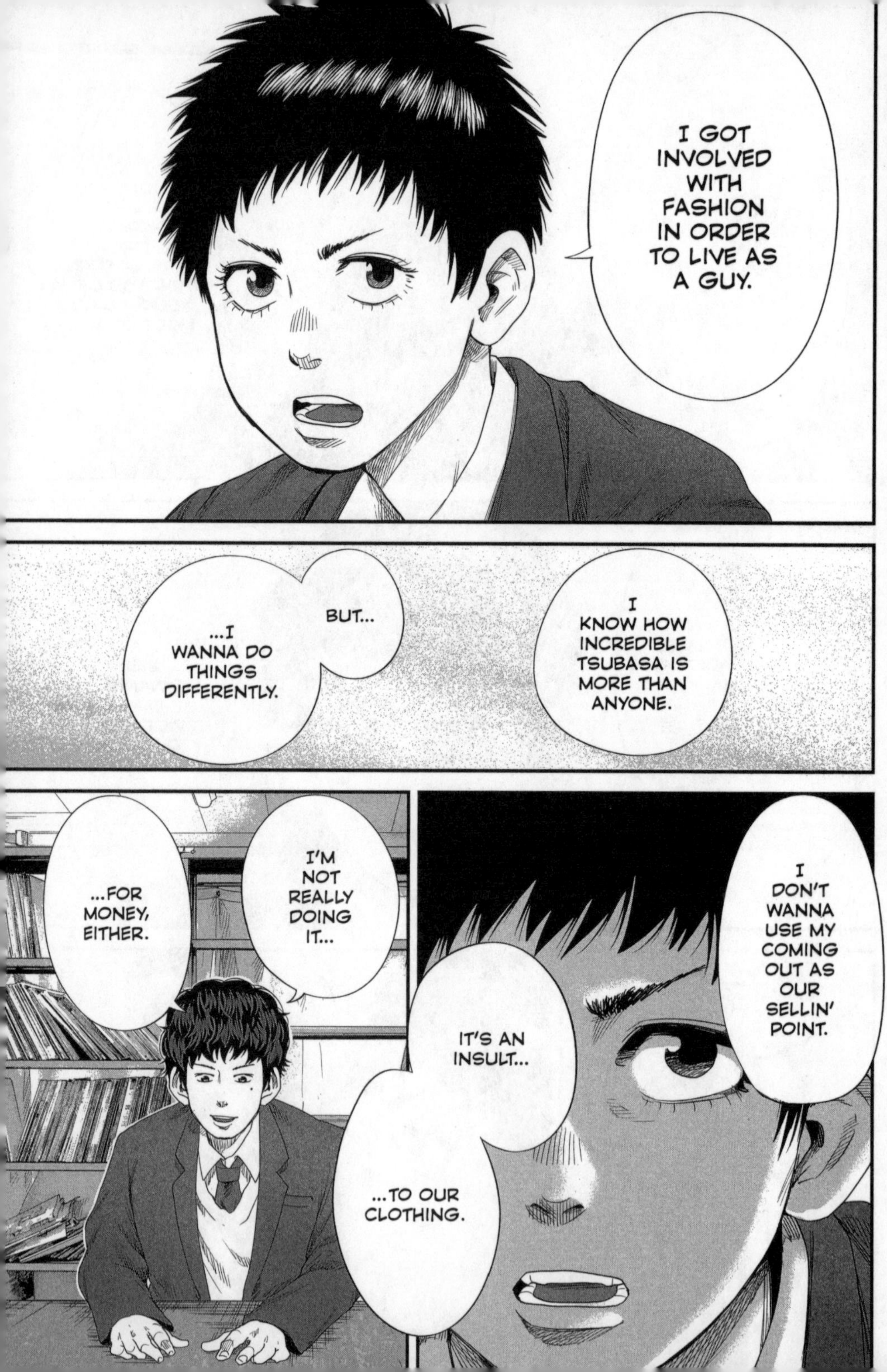
I GOT INVOLVED WITH FASHION IN ORDER TO LIVE AS A GUY.
I KNOW HOW INCREDIBLE TSUBASA IS MORE THAN ANYONE.
BUT...
...I WANNA DO THINGS DIFFERENTLY.
I DON'T WANNA USE MY COMING OUT AS OUR SELLIN' POINT.
IT'S AN INSULT...
...TO OUR CLOTHING.
I'M NOT REALLY DOING IT...
...FOR MONEY, EITHER.

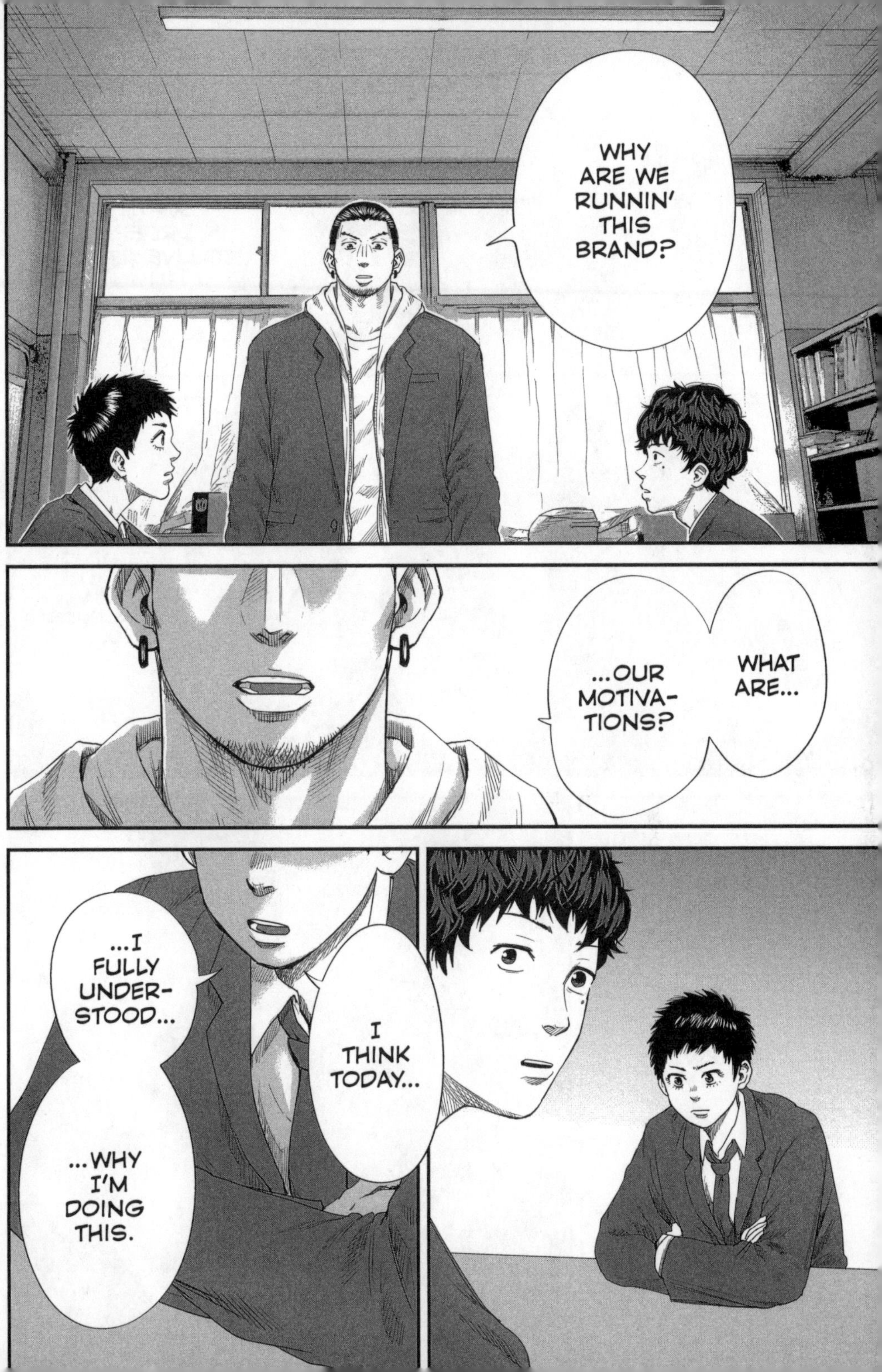
WHY ARE WE RUNNIN' THIS BRAND?
WHAT ARE...
...OUR MOTIVA-TIONS?
I THINK TODAY...
...I FULLY UNDER-STOOD...
...WHY I'M DOING THIS.

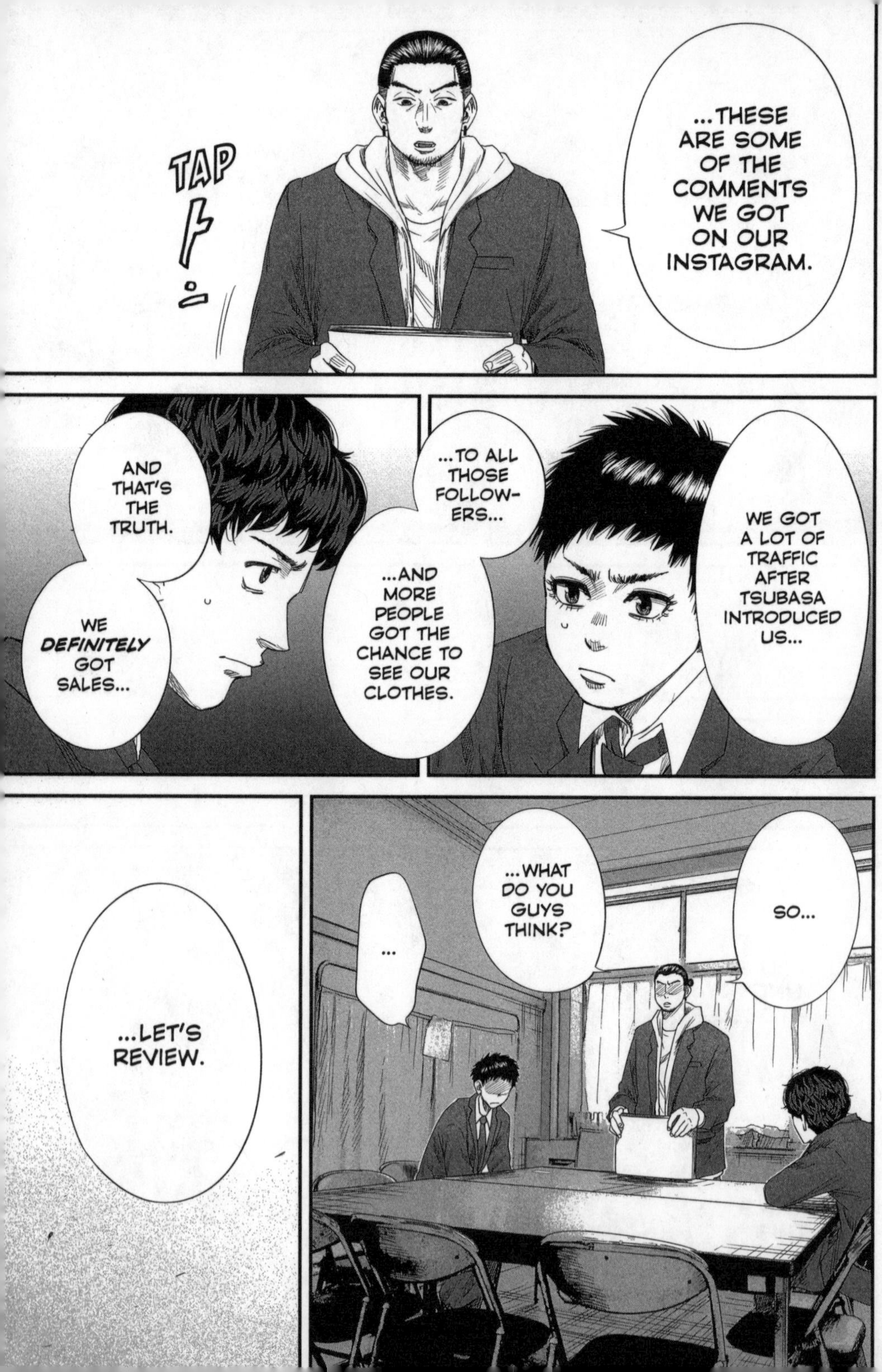
TAP
ト
...THESE ARE SOME OF THE COMMENTS WE GOT ON OUR INSTAGRAM.
WE GOT A LOT OF TRAFFIC AFTER TSUBASA INTRODUCED US...
...TO ALL THOSE FOLLOWERS...
...AND MORE PEOPLE GOT THE CHANCE TO SEE OUR CLOTHES.
AND THAT'S THE TRUTH.
WE *DEFINITELY* GOT SALES...
SO...
...WHAT DO YOU GUYS THINK?
...
...LET'S REVIEW.

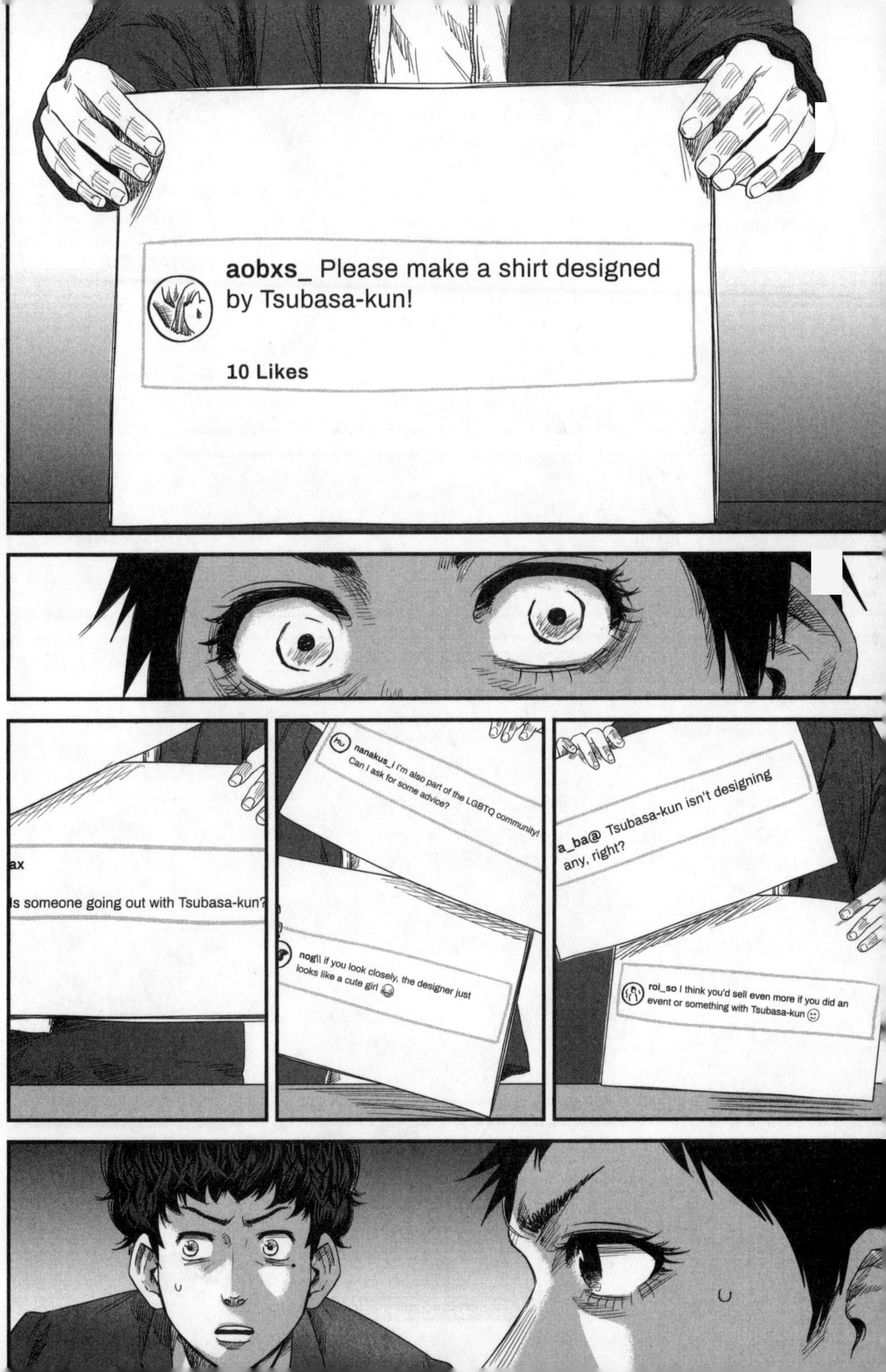
aobxs_ Please make a shirt designed by Tsubasa-kun!
10 Likes
a_ba@ Tsubasa-kun isn't designing any, right?
roi_so I think you'd sell even more if you did an event or something with Tsubasa-kun
nanakus_i I'm also part of the LGBTQ community! Can I ask for some advice?
nog\\ if you look closely, the designer just looks like a cute girl
ax
Is someone going out with Tsubasa-kun?

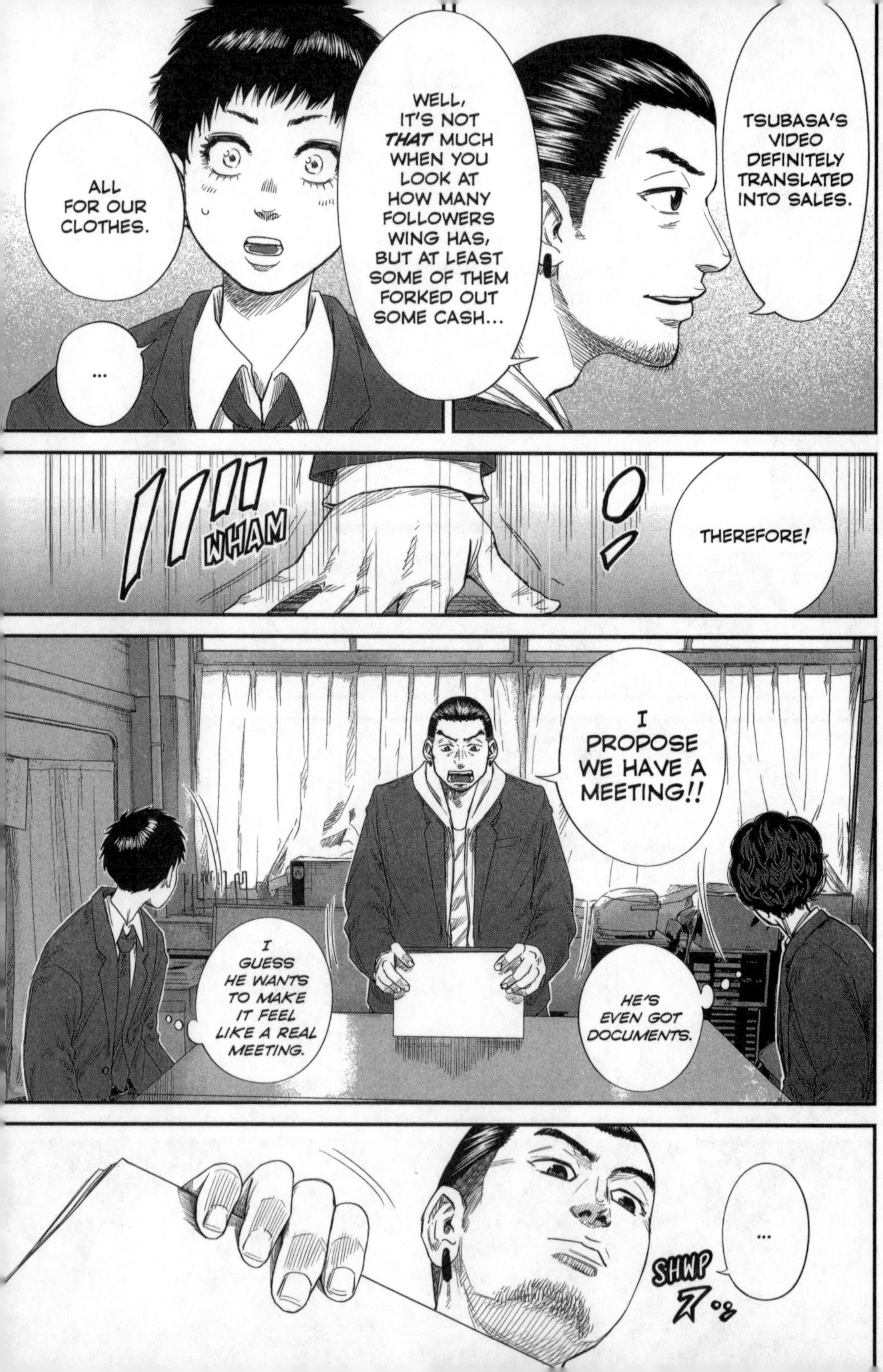
TSUBASA'S VIDEO DEFINITELY TRANSLATED INTO SALES.
WELL, IT'S NOT *THAT* MUCH WHEN YOU LOOK AT HOW MANY FOLLOWERS WING HAS, BUT AT LEAST SOME OF THEM FORKED OUT SOME CASH...
ALL FOR OUR CLOTHES.
...
THEREFORE!
WHAM
I PROPOSE WE HAVE A MEETING!!
HE'S EVEN GOT DOCUMENTS.
I GUESS HE WANTS TO MAKE IT FEEL LIKE A REAL MEETING.
...
SHWP

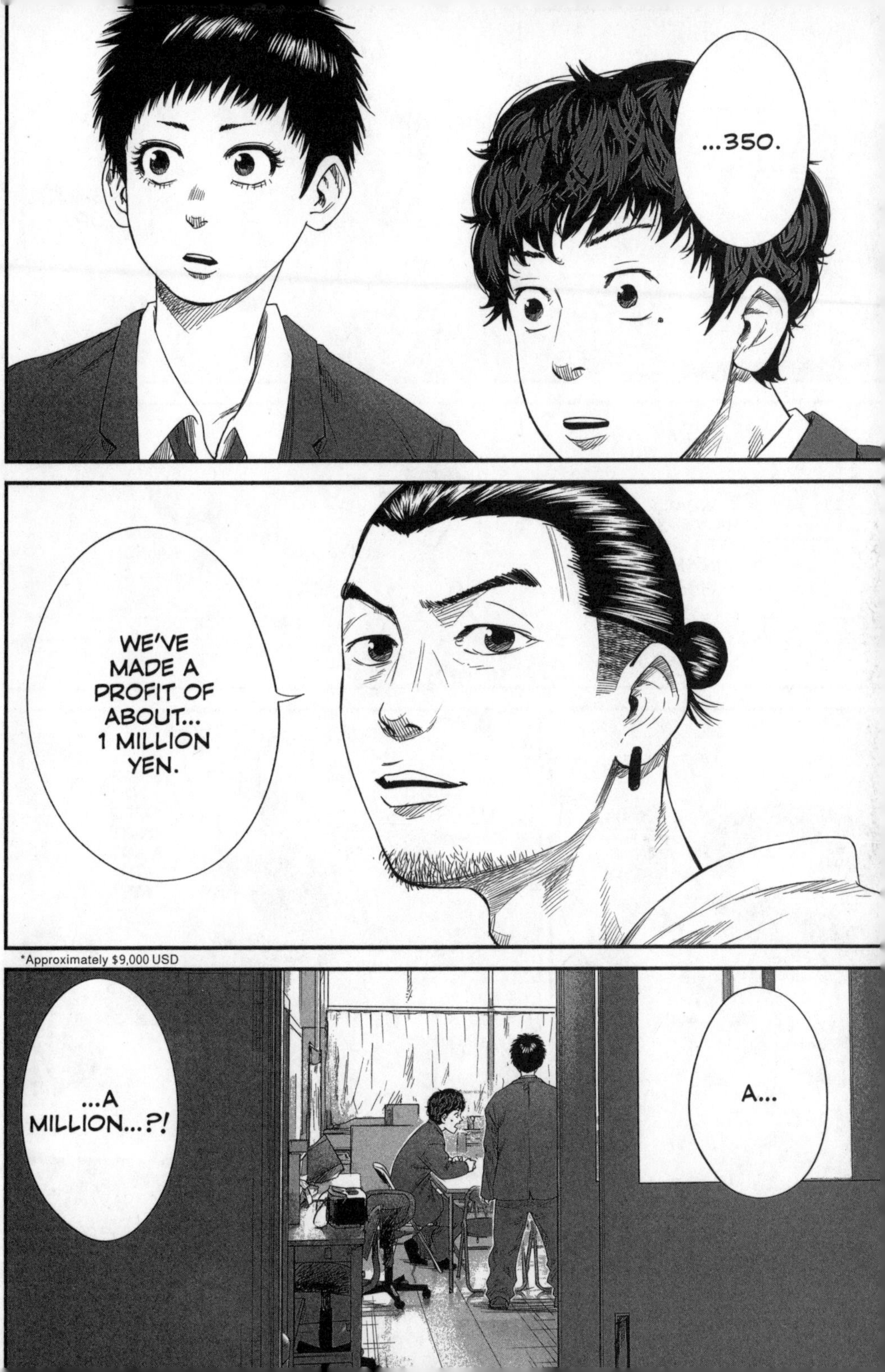
...350.
WE'VE MADE A PROFIT OF ABOUT... 1 MILLION YEN.
A...
...A MILLION...?!
*Approximately $9,000 USD

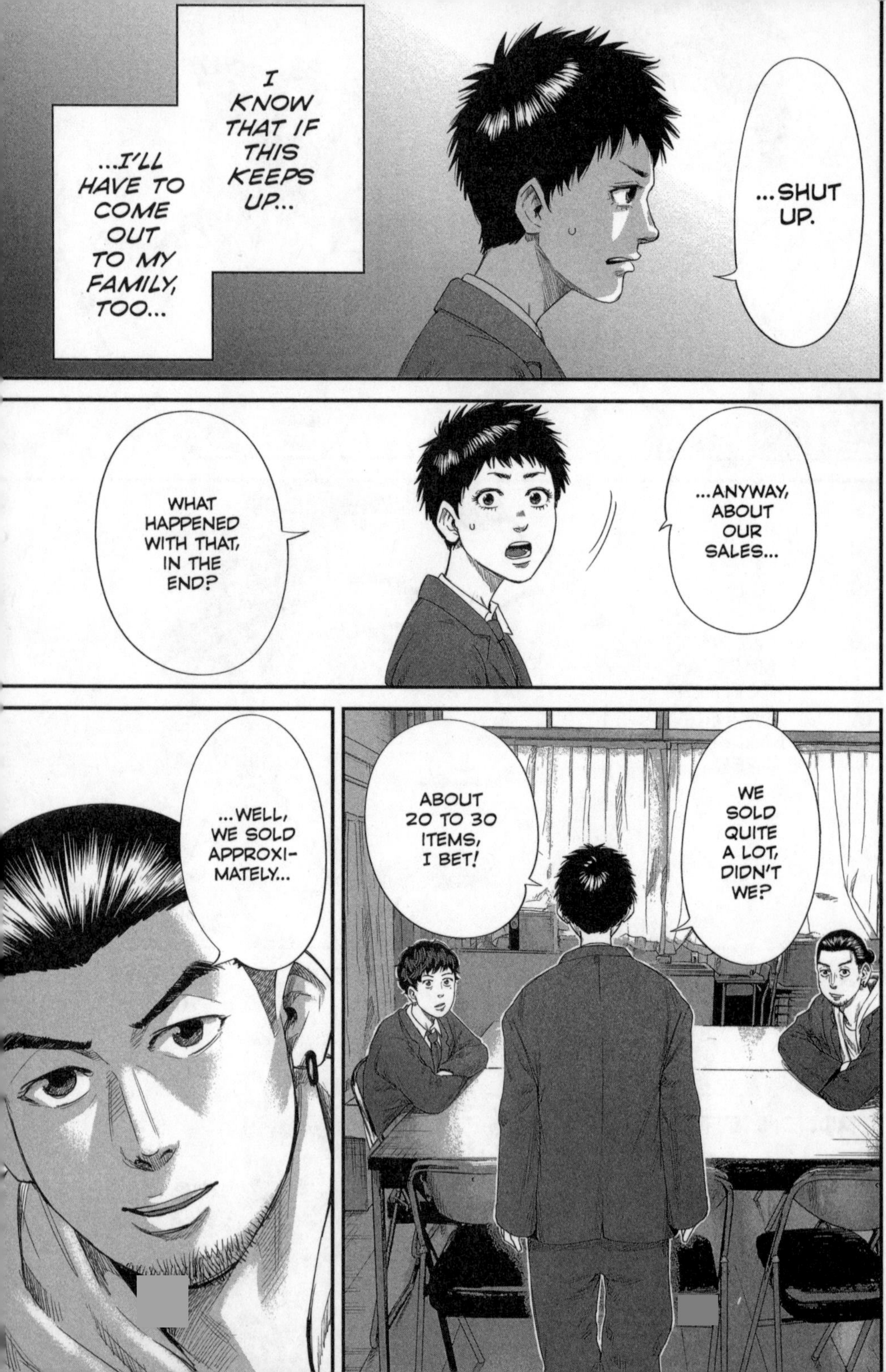
...SHUT UP.
I KNOW THAT IF THIS KEEPS UP...
...I'LL HAVE TO COME OUT TO MY FAMILY, TOO...
...ANYWAY, ABOUT OUR SALES...
WHAT HAPPENED WITH THAT, IN THE END?
WE SOLD QUITE A LOT, DIDN'T WE?
ABOUT 20 TO 30 ITEMS, I BET!
...WELL, WE SOLD APPROXI-MATELY...

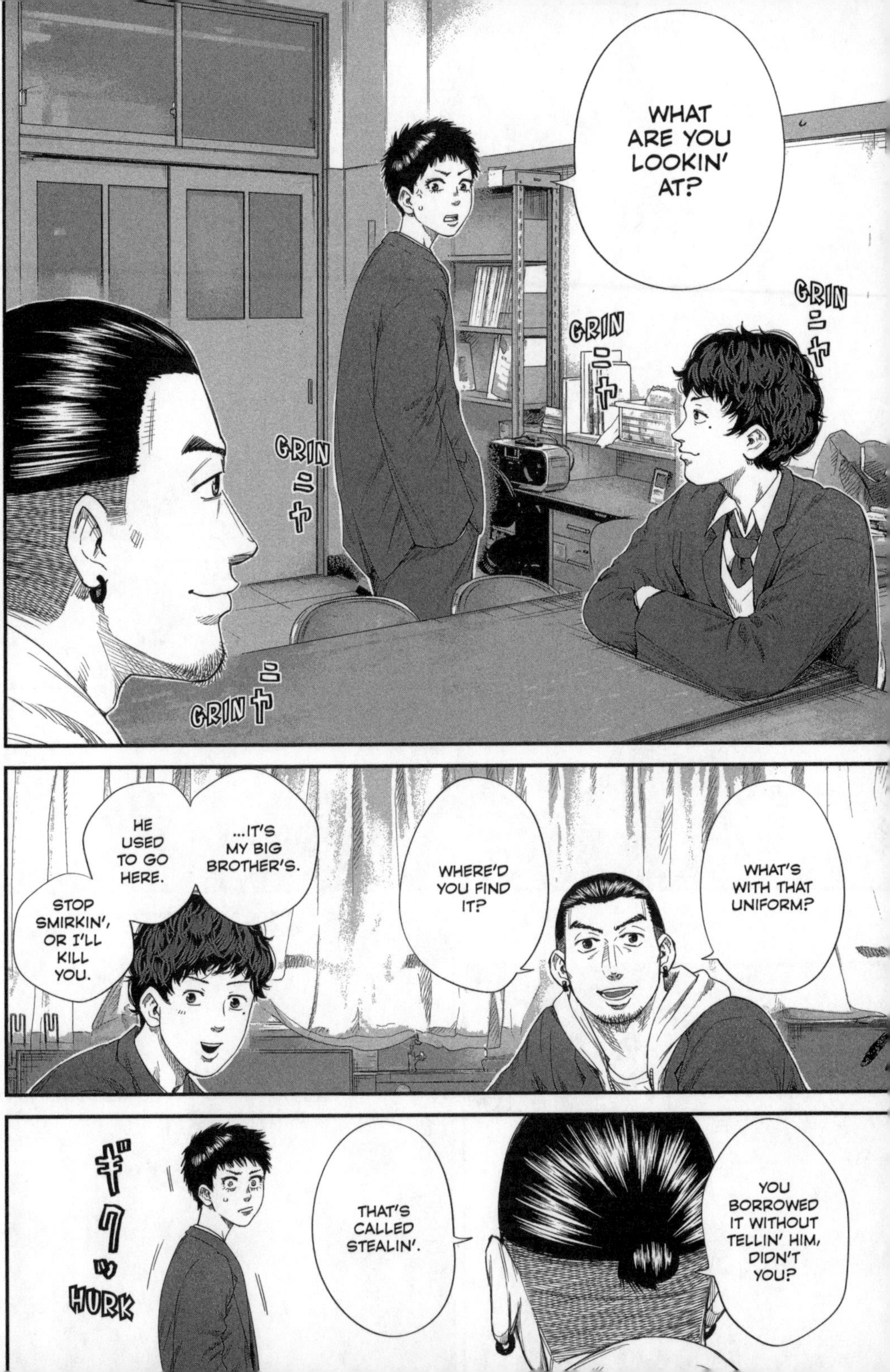
WHAT ARE YOU LOOKIN' AT?
GRIN ニヤ
GRIN ニヤ
GRIN ニヤ
GRIN ニヤ
WHAT'S WITH THAT UNIFORM?
WHERE'D YOU FIND IT?
...IT'S MY BIG BROTHER'S.
HE USED TO GO HERE.
STOP SMIRKIN', OR I'LL KILL YOU.
YOU BORROWED IT WITHOUT TELLIN' HIM, DIDN'T YOU?
THAT'S CALLED STEALIN'.
ギクッ HURK

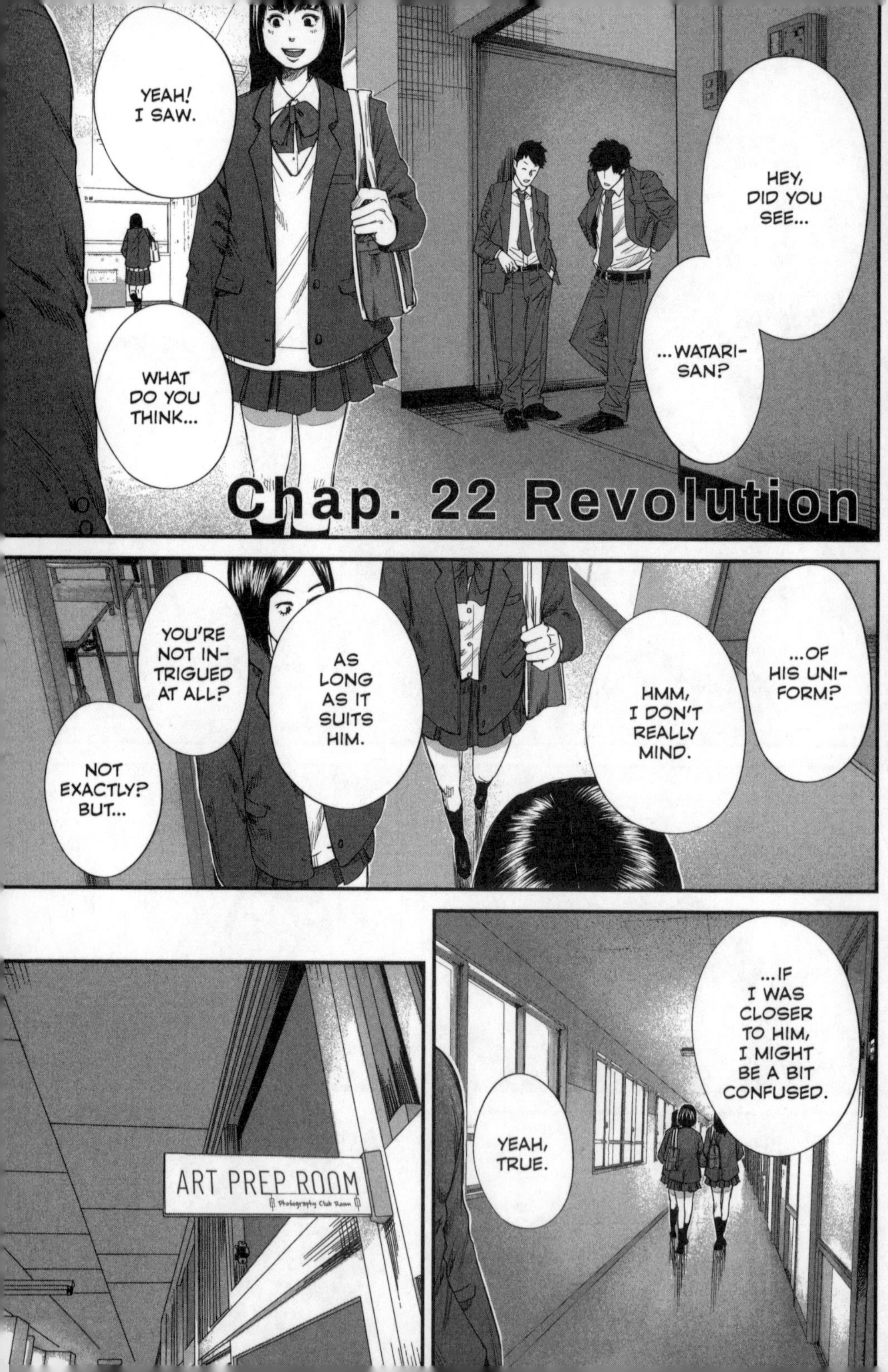
HEY, DID YOU SEE...
...WATARI-SAN?
YEAH! I SAW.
WHAT DO YOU THINK...
Chap. 22 Revolution
...OF HIS UNI-FORM?
HMM, I DON'T REALLY MIND.
AS LONG AS IT SUITS HIM.
YOU'RE NOT IN-TRIGUED AT ALL?
NOT EXACTLY? BUT...
...IF I WAS CLOSER TO HIM, I MIGHT BE A BIT CONFUSED.
YEAH, TRUE.
ART PREP ROOM
Photography Club Room

BOYS RUN
ボーイズ・ラン・ザ・ライオット
THE RIOT

BOYS RUN

ボーイズ・ラン・ザ・ライオット

THE RIOT

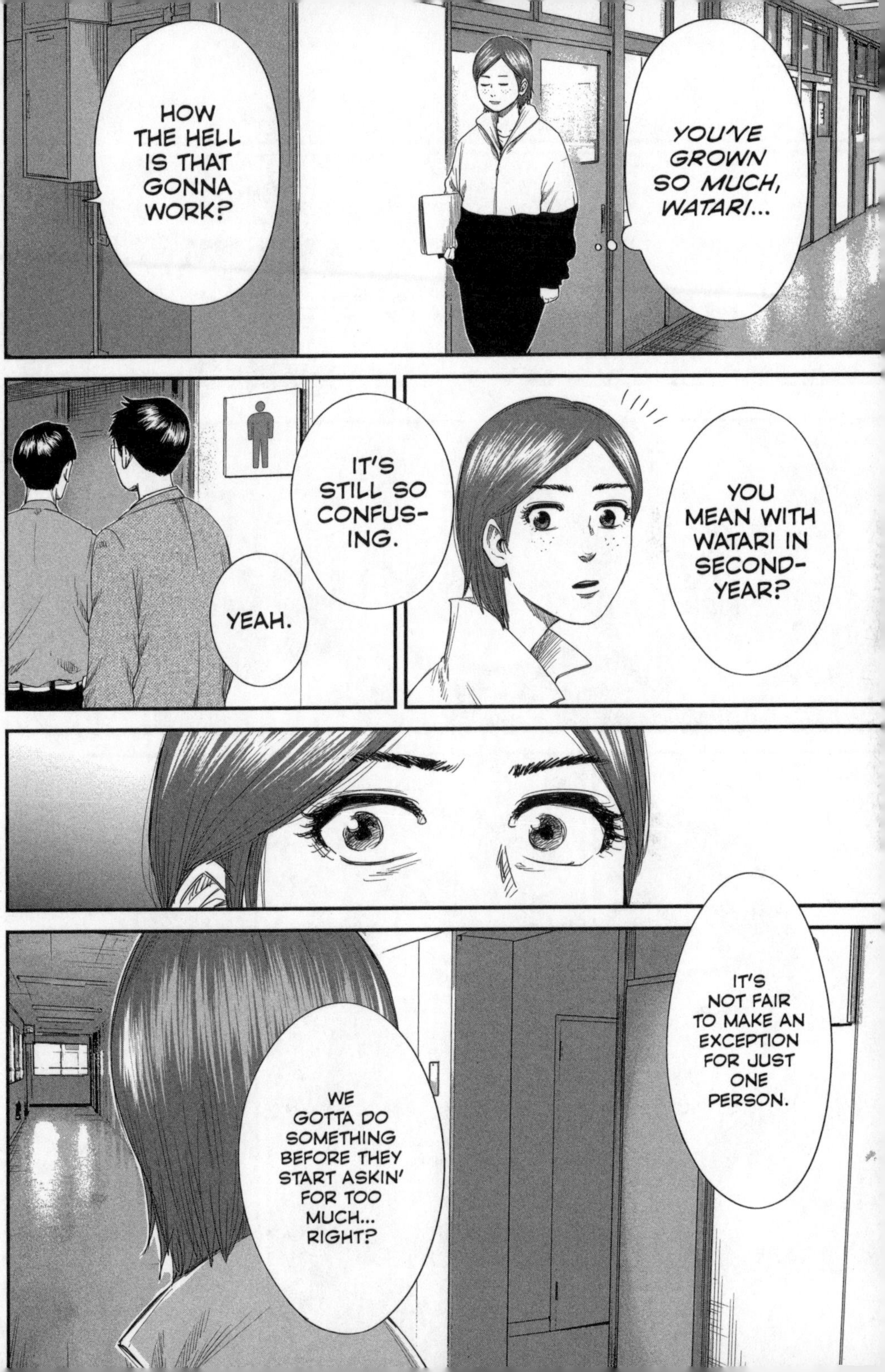
YOU'VE GROWN SO MUCH, WATARI...
HOW THE HELL IS THAT GONNA WORK?
YOU MEAN WITH WATARI IN SECOND-YEAR?
IT'S STILL SO CONFUS-ING.
YEAH.
IT'S NOT FAIR TO MAKE AN EXCEPTION FOR JUST ONE PERSON.
WE GOTTA DO SOMETHING BEFORE THEY START ASKIN' FOR TOO MUCH... RIGHT?

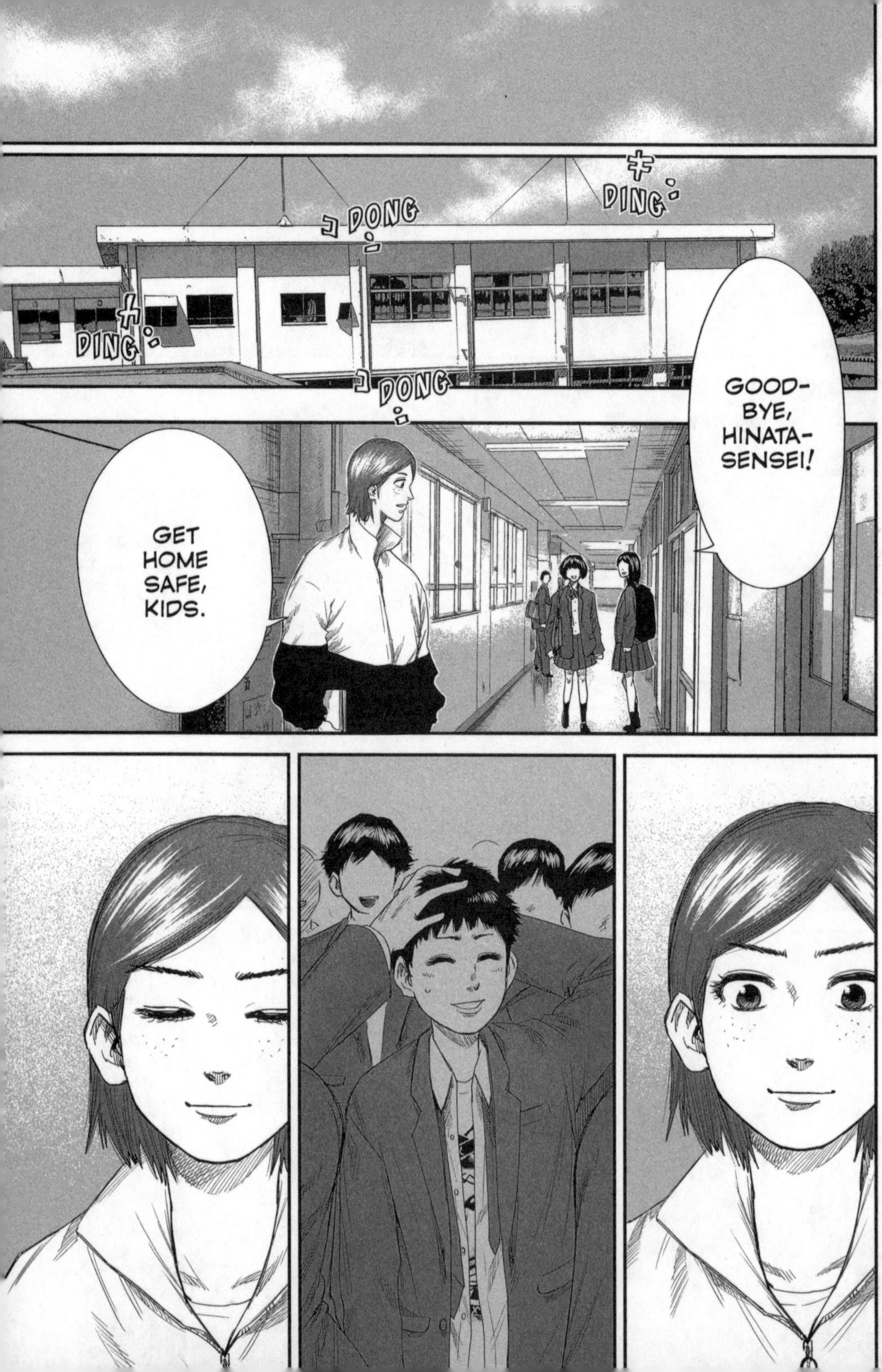
DING
DONG
DING
DONG
GOOD-BYE, HINATA-SENSEI!
GET HOME SAFE, KIDS.

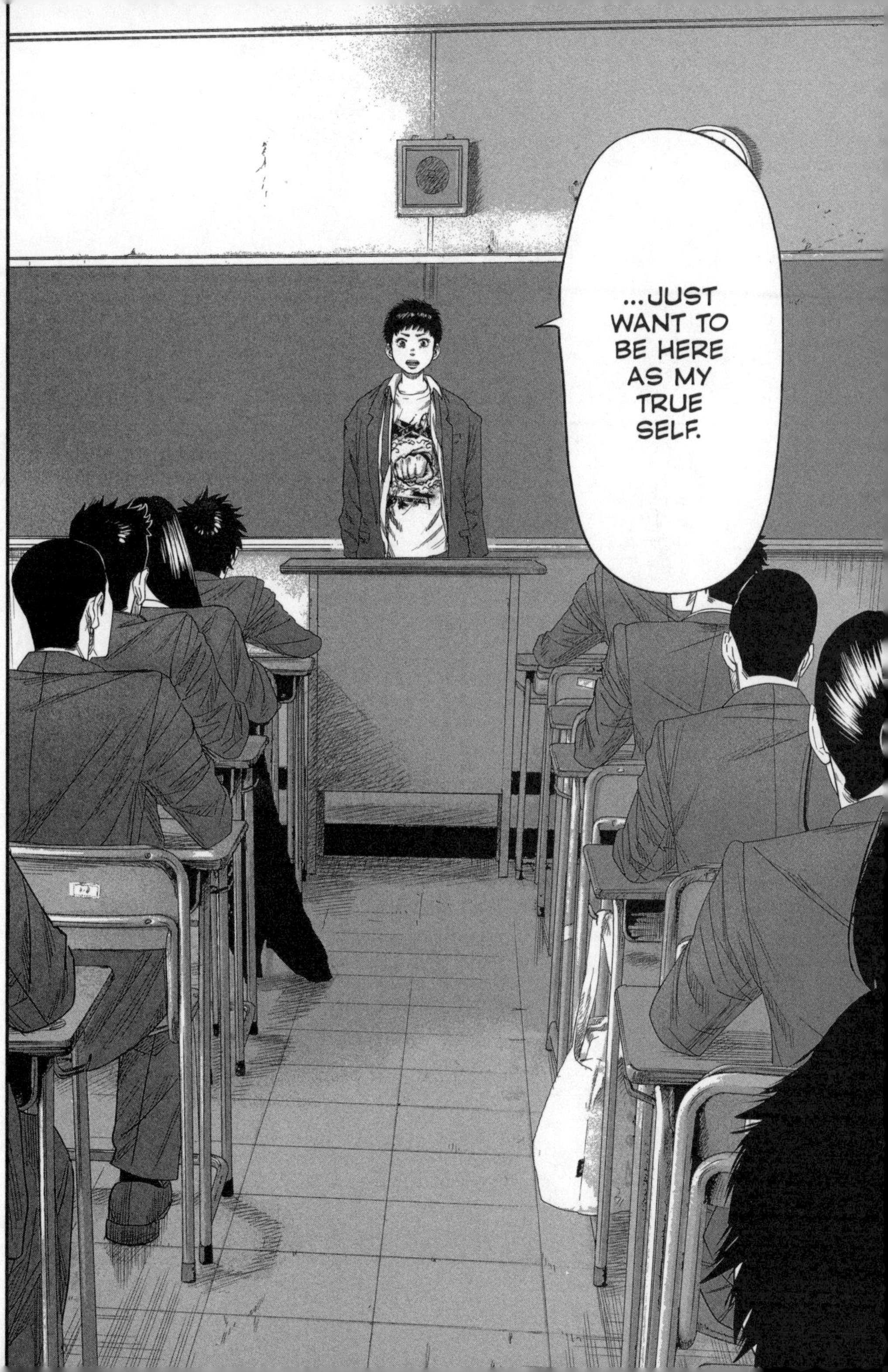
...JUST WANT TO BE HERE AS MY TRUE SELF.

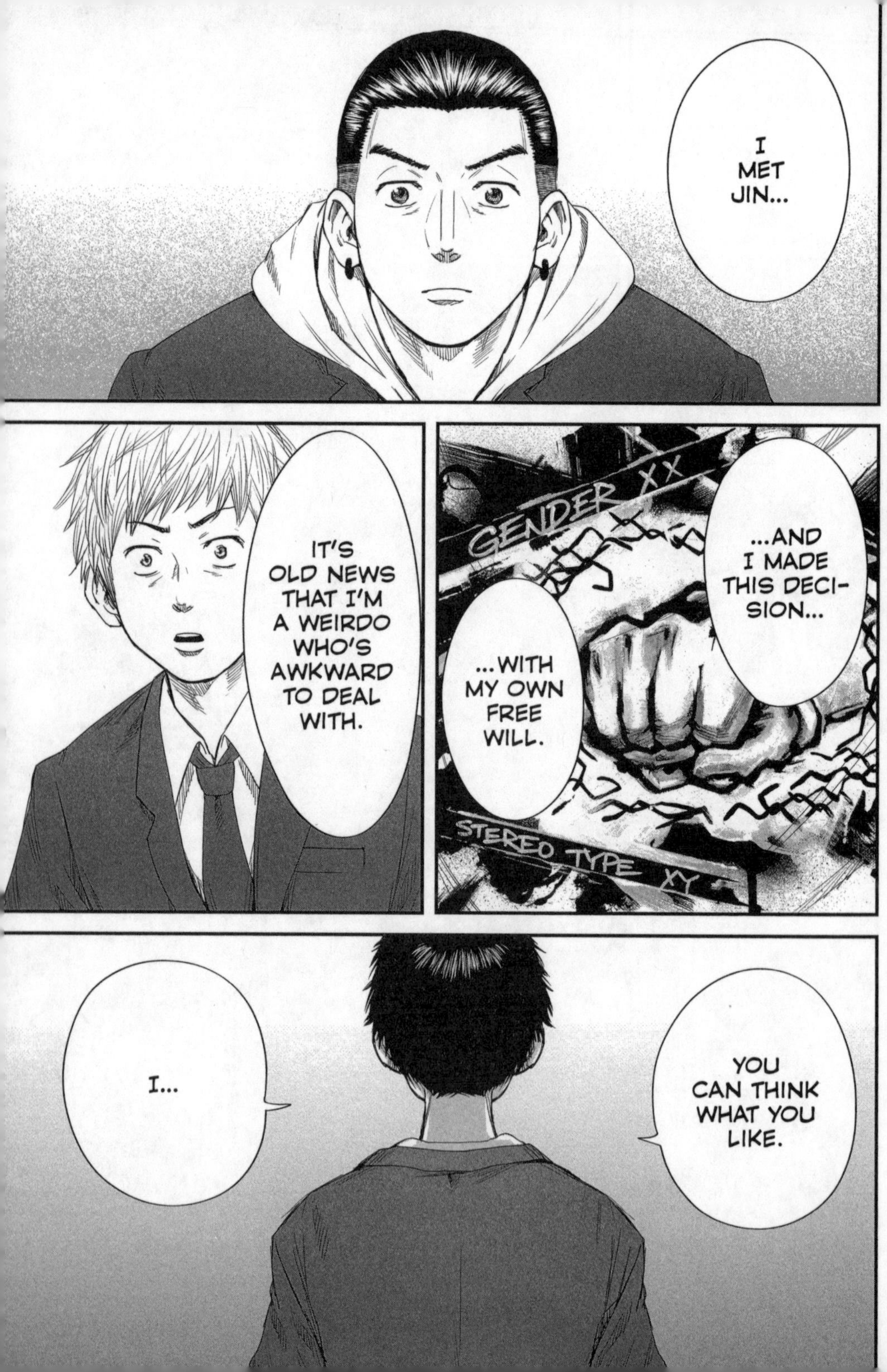
I MET JIN...
...AND I MADE THIS DECISION...
GENDER XX
...WITH MY OWN FREE WILL.
STEREO TYPE XY
IT'S OLD NEWS THAT I'M A WEIRDO WHO'S AWKWARD TO DEAL WITH.
YOU CAN THINK WHAT YOU LIKE.
I...

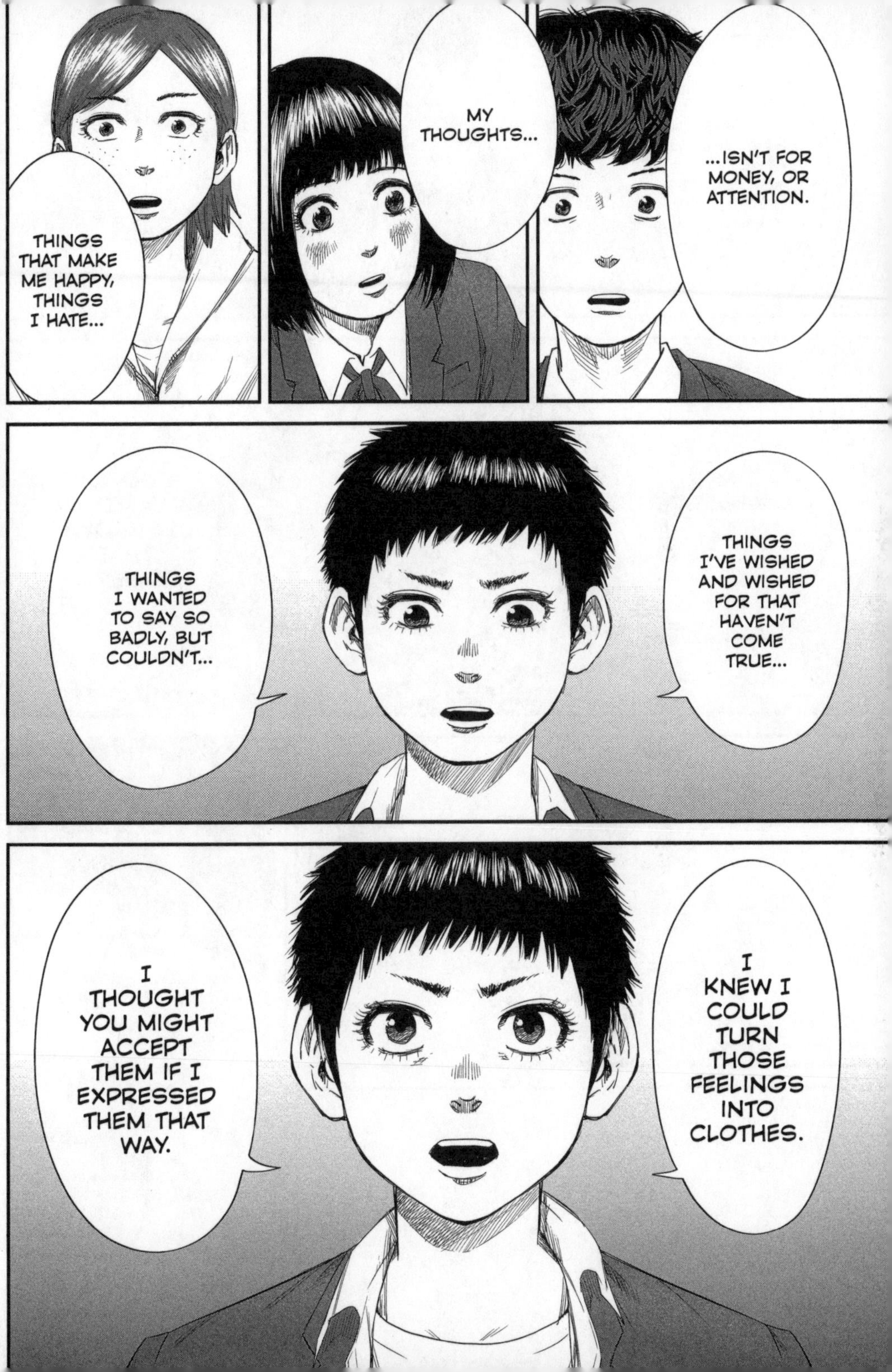

...ISN'T FOR MONEY, OR ATTENTION.
MY THOUGHTS...
THINGS THAT MAKE ME HAPPY, THINGS I HATE...
THINGS I'VE WISHED AND WISHED FOR THAT HAVEN'T COME TRUE...
THINGS I WANTED TO SAY SO BADLY, BUT COULDN'T...
I KNEW I COULD TURN THOSE FEELINGS INTO CLOTHES.
I THOUGHT YOU MIGHT ACCEPT THEM IF I EXPRESSED THEM THAT WAY.

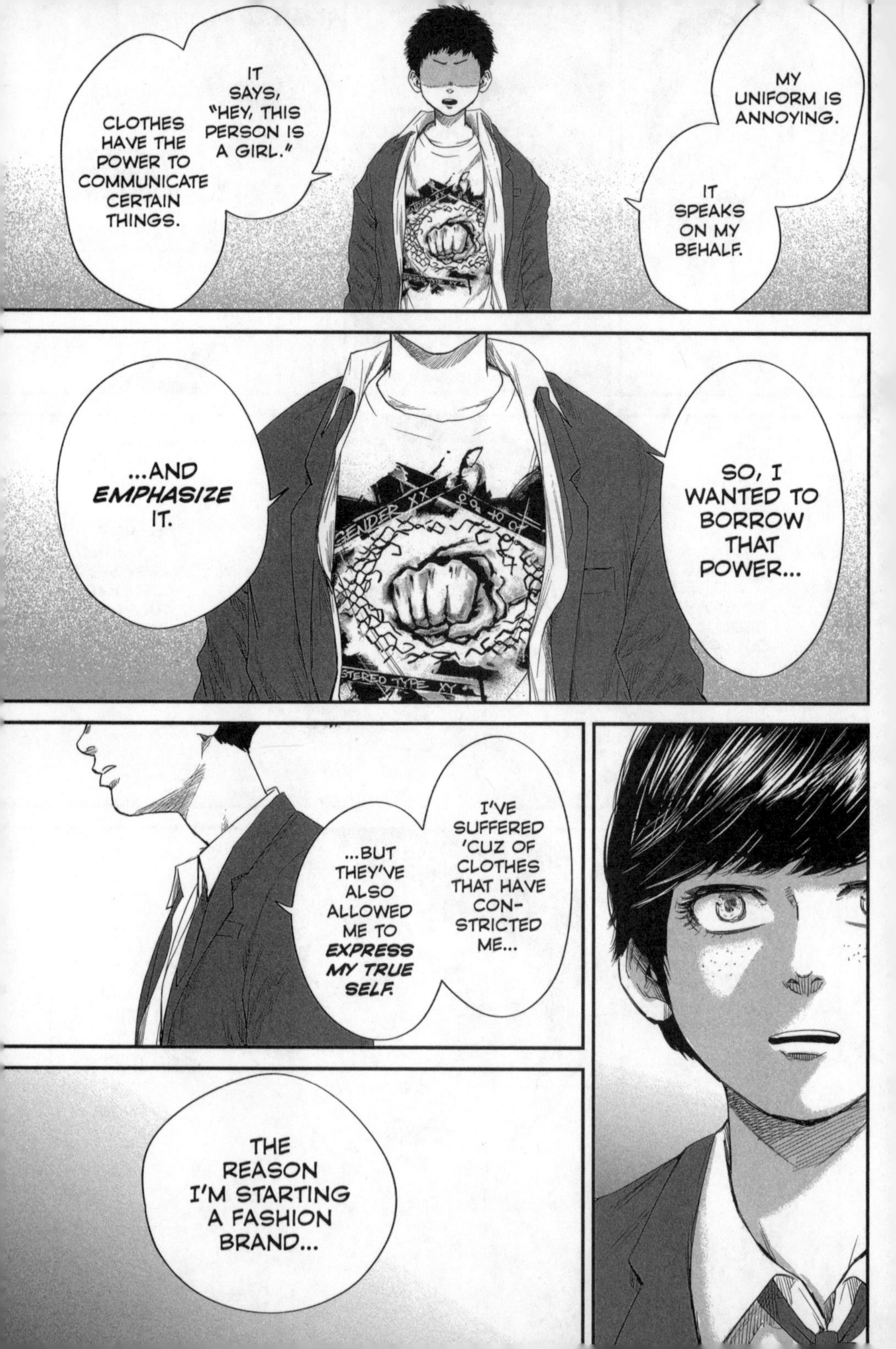
MY UNIFORM IS ANNOYING.
IT SPEAKS ON MY BEHALF.
IT SAYS, "HEY, THIS PERSON IS A GIRL."
CLOTHES HAVE THE POWER TO COMMUNICATE CERTAIN THINGS.
SO, I WANTED TO BORROW THAT POWER...
...AND *EMPHASIZE* IT.
GENDER XX
STEREO TYPE XY
I'VE SUFFERED 'CUZ OF CLOTHES THAT HAVE CON-STRICTED ME...
...BUT THEY'VE ALSO ALLOWED ME TO *EXPRESS MY TRUE SELF.*
THE REASON I'M STARTING A FASHION BRAND...

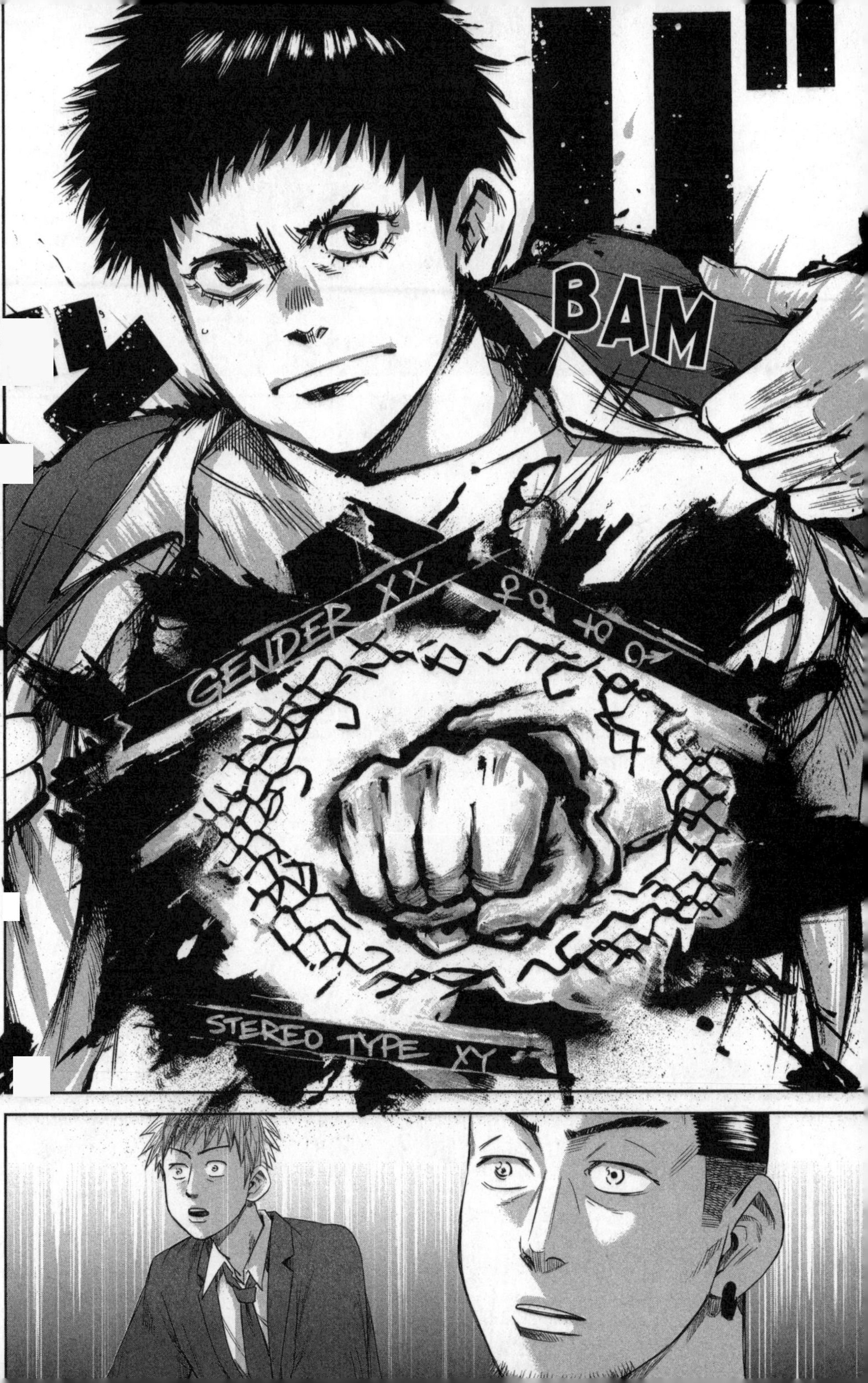
BAM
GENDER XX
STEREO TYPE XY

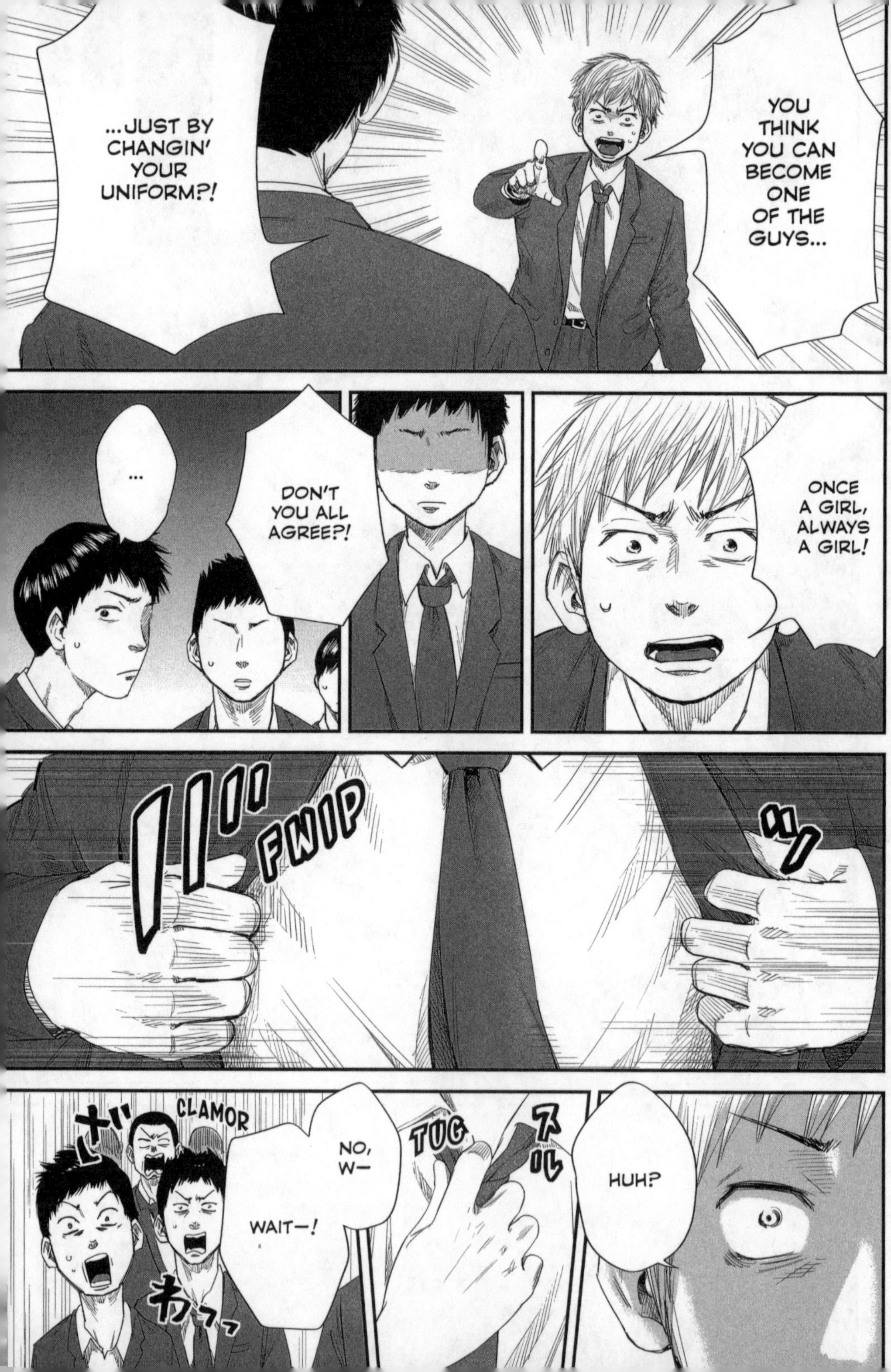
YOU THINK YOU CAN BECOME ONE OF THE GUYS...
...JUST BY CHANGIN' YOUR UNIFORM?!
ONCE A GIRL, ALWAYS A GIRL!
DON'T YOU ALL AGREE?!
...
FWIP
HUH?
TUG
スル
NO, W—
WAIT—!
CLAMOR

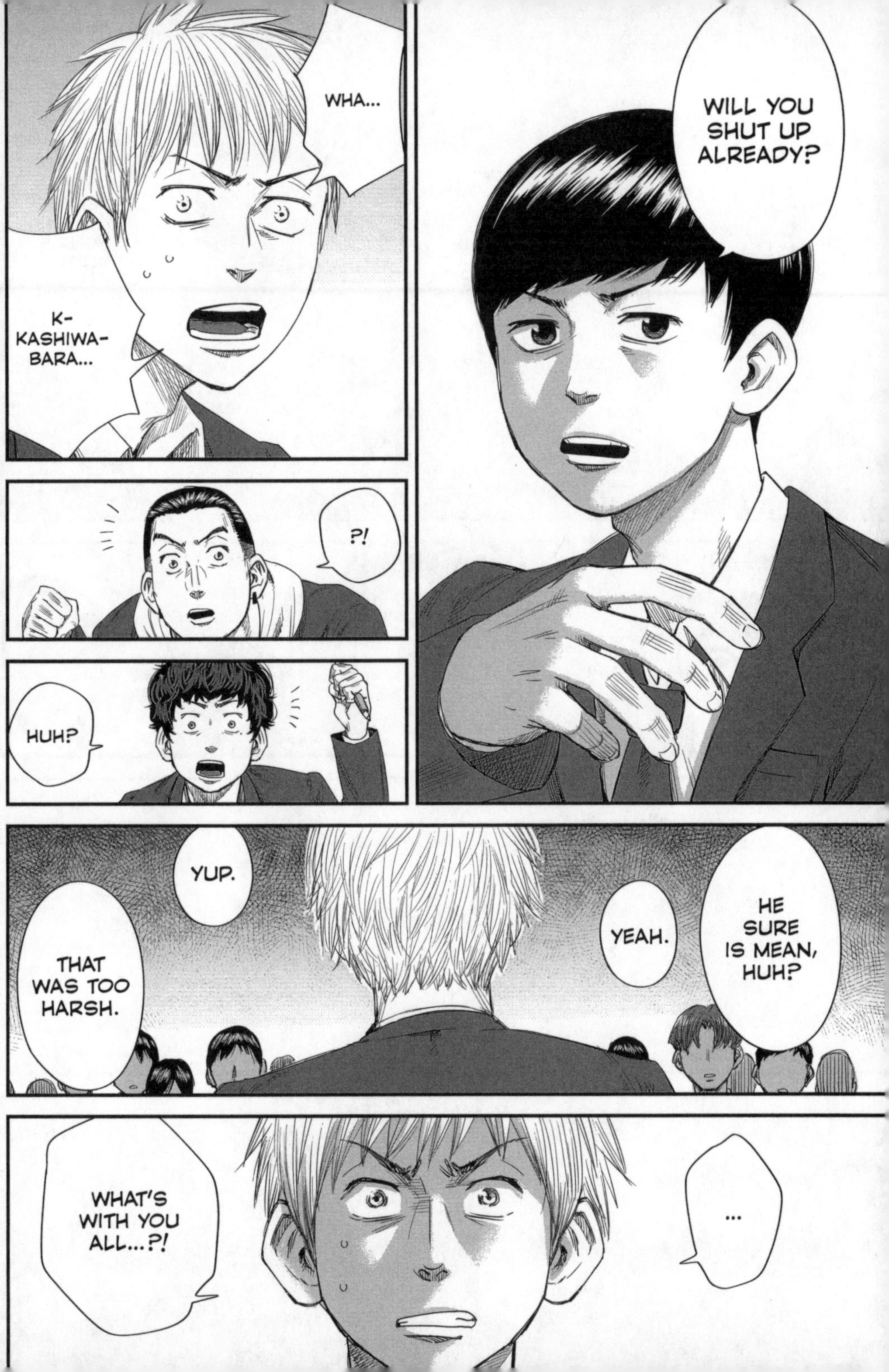
WILL YOU SHUT UP ALREADY?
WHA...
K-KASHIWA-BARA...
?!
HUH?
HE SURE IS MEAN, HUH?
YEAH.
YUP.
THAT WAS TOO HARSH.
...
WHAT'S WITH YOU ALL...?!

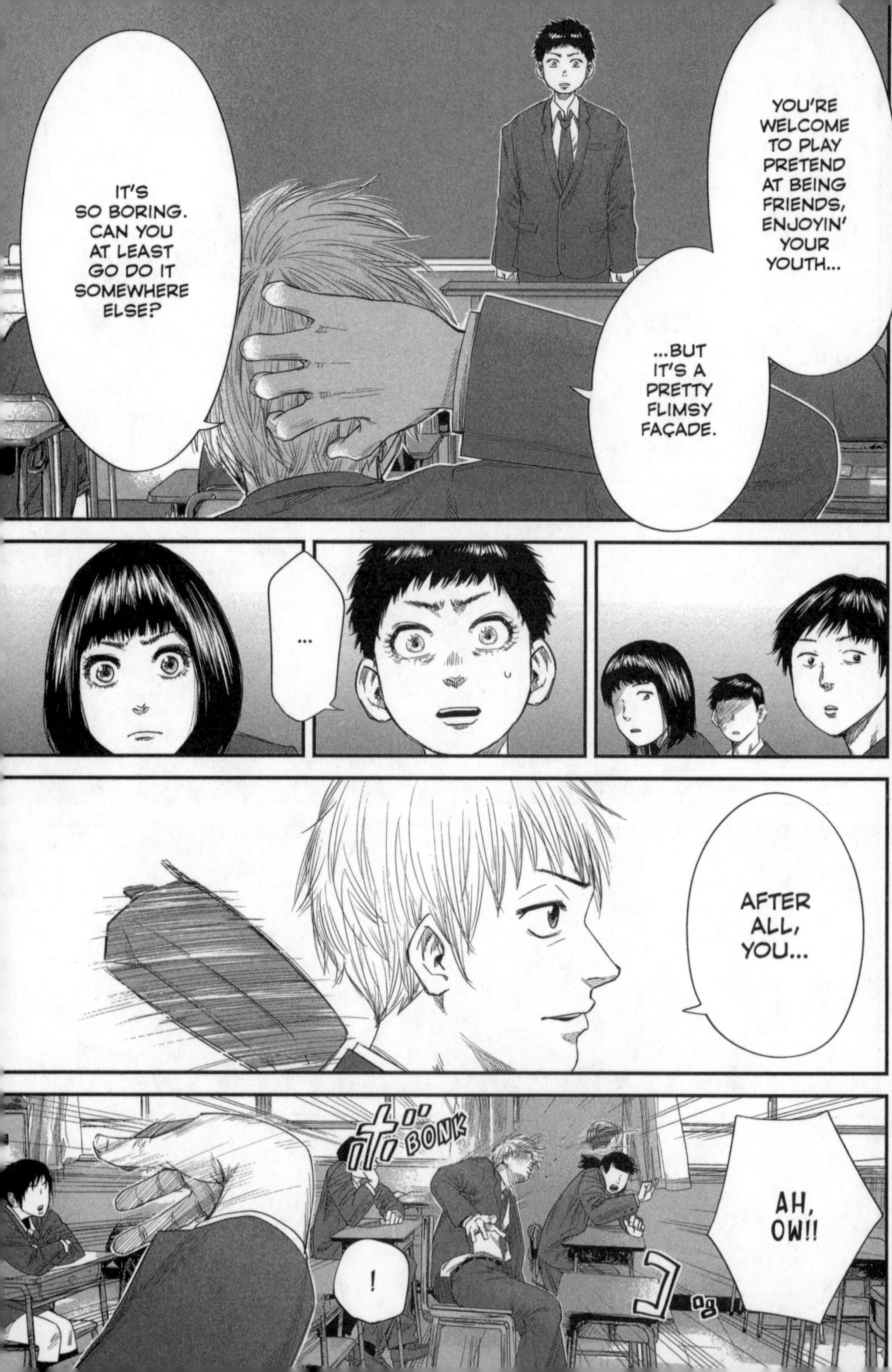
YOU'RE WELCOME TO PLAY PRETEND AT BEING FRIENDS, ENJOYIN' YOUR YOUTH...
...BUT IT'S A PRETTY FLIMSY FAÇADE.
IT'S SO BORING. CAN YOU AT LEAST GO DO IT SOMEWHERE ELSE?
...
AFTER ALL, YOU...
AH, OW!!
BONK
!

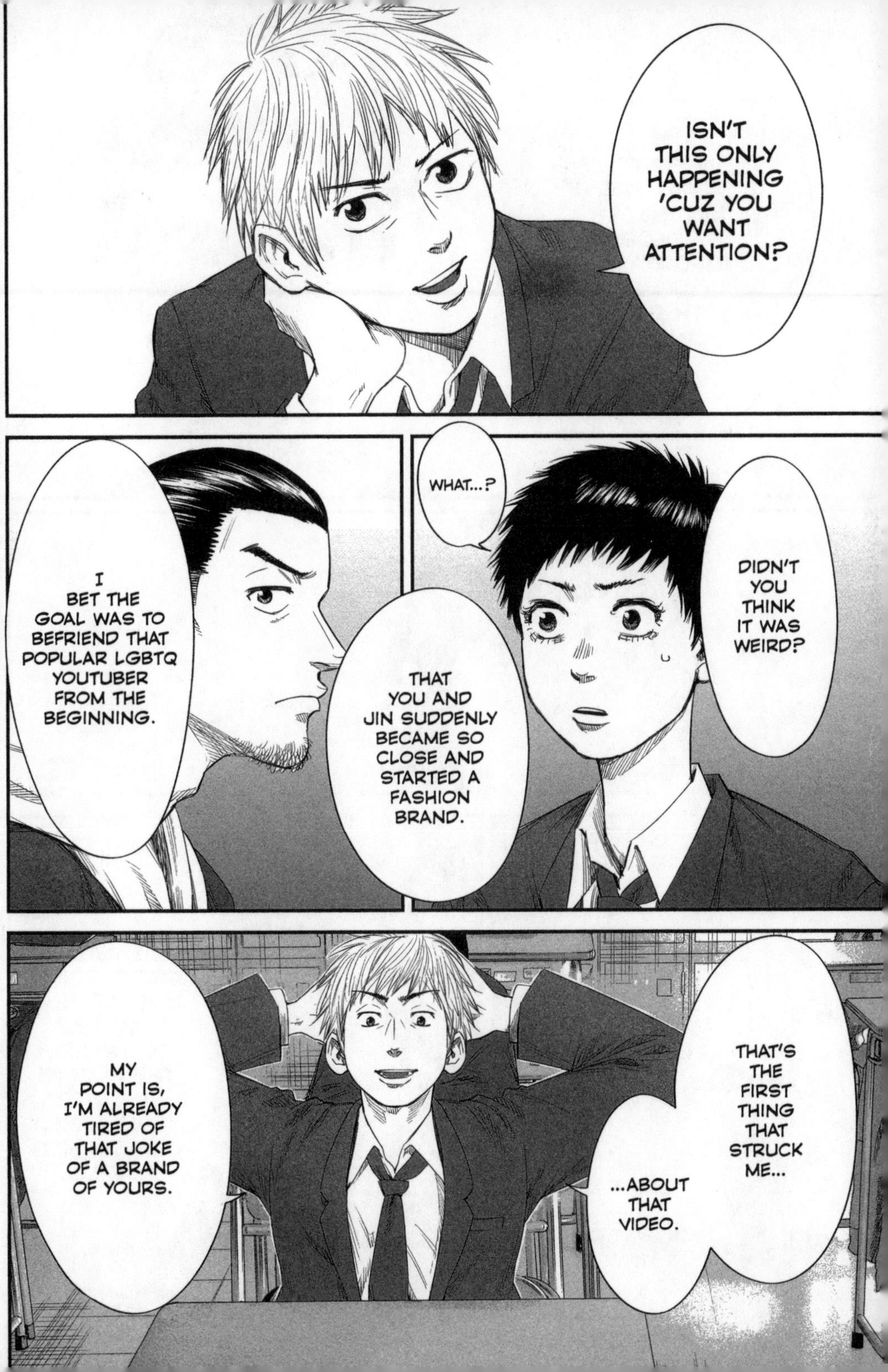
ISN'T THIS ONLY HAPPENING 'CUZ YOU WANT ATTENTION?
WHAT...?
DIDN'T YOU THINK IT WAS WEIRD?
THAT YOU AND JIN SUDDENLY BECAME SO CLOSE AND STARTED A FASHION BRAND.
I BET THE GOAL WAS TO BEFRIEND THAT POPULAR LGBTQ YOUTUBER FROM THE BEGINNING.
THAT'S THE FIRST THING THAT STRUCK ME...
...ABOUT THAT VIDEO.
MY POINT IS, I'M ALREADY TIRED OF THAT JOKE OF A BRAND OF YOURS.

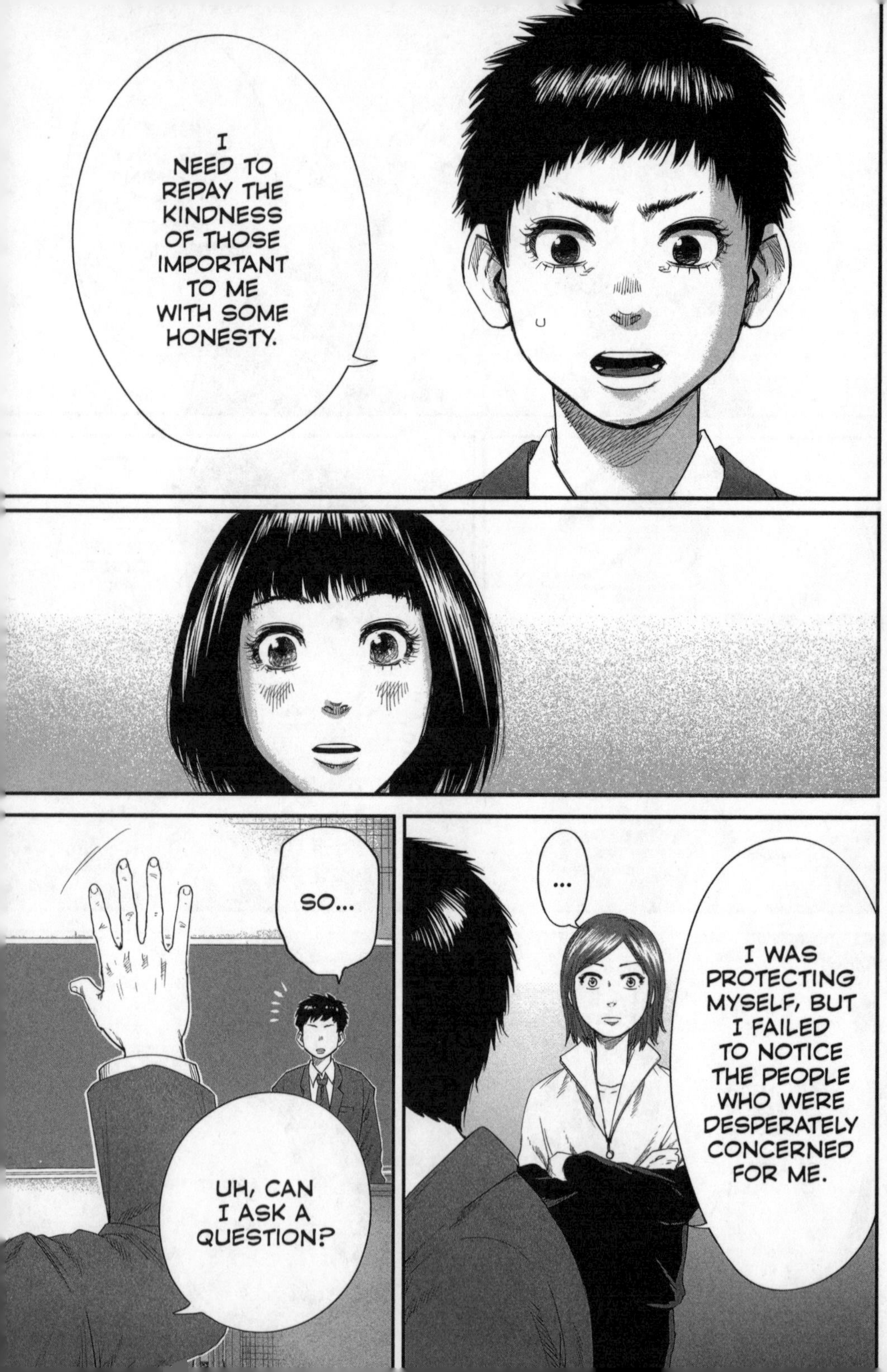
I NEED TO REPAY THE KINDNESS OF THOSE IMPORTANT TO ME WITH SOME HONESTY.
I WAS PROTECTING MYSELF, BUT I FAILED TO NOTICE THE PEOPLE WHO WERE DESPERATELY CONCERNED FOR ME.
...
SO...
UH, CAN I ASK A QUESTION?

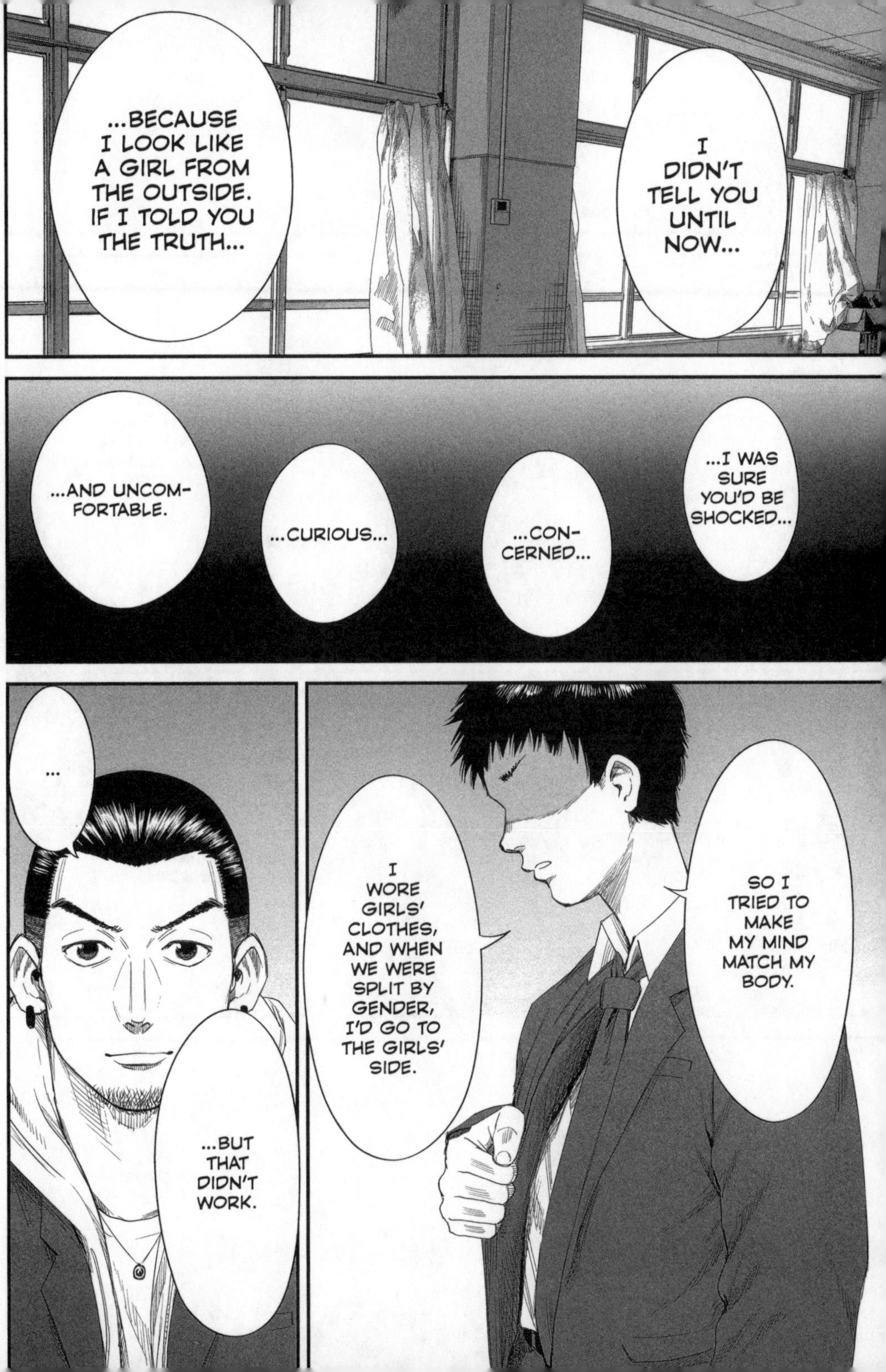
I DIDN'T TELL YOU UNTIL NOW...
...BECAUSE I LOOK LIKE A GIRL FROM THE OUTSIDE. IF I TOLD YOU THE TRUTH...
...I WAS SURE YOU'D BE SHOCKED...
...CON-CERNED...
...CURIOUS...
...AND UNCOM-FORTABLE.
SO I TRIED TO MAKE MY MIND MATCH MY BODY.
I WORE GIRLS' CLOTHES, AND WHEN WE WERE SPLIT BY GENDER, I'D GO TO THE GIRLS' SIDE.
...BUT THAT DIDN'T WORK.
...

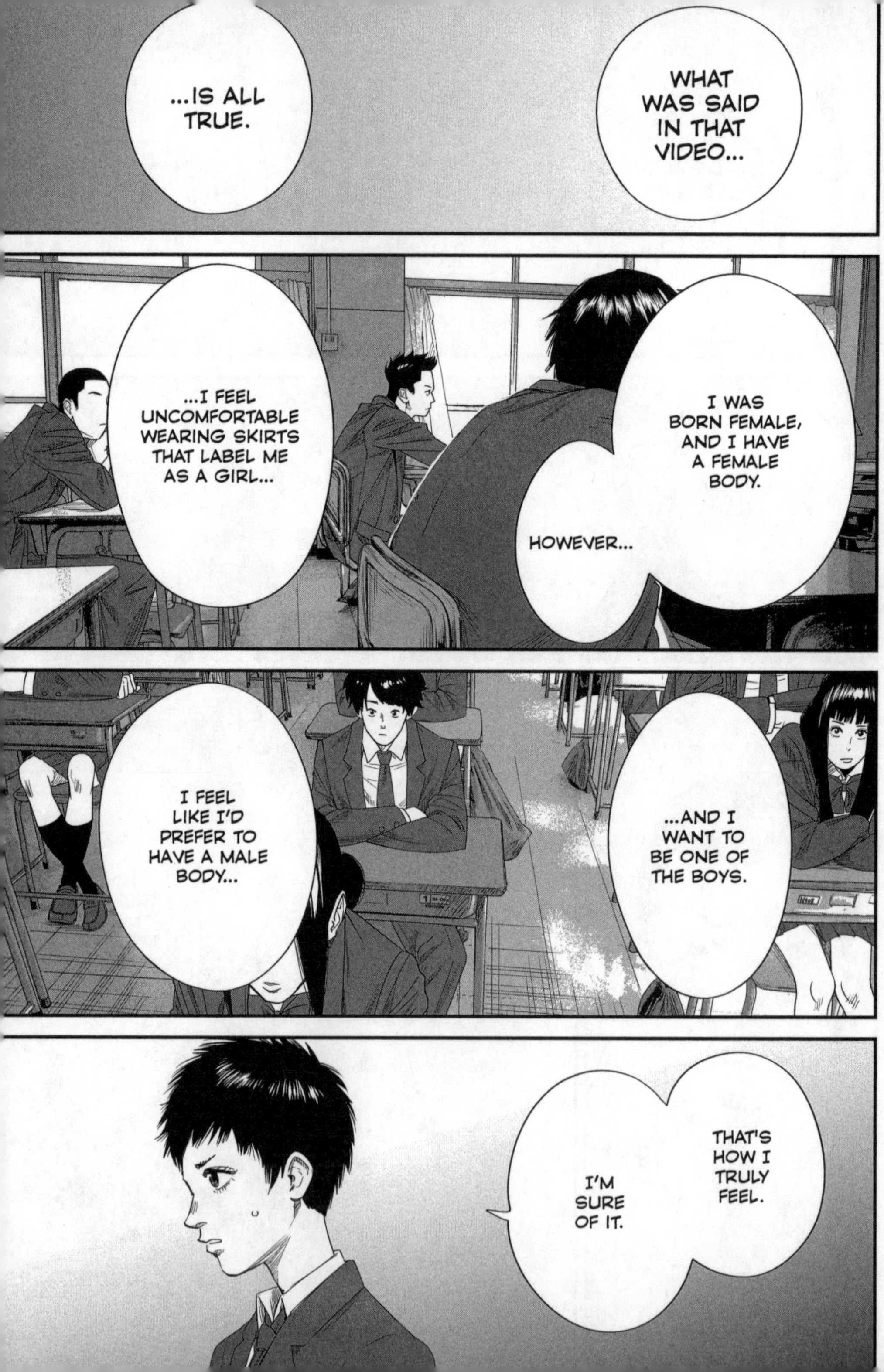
WHAT WAS SAID IN THAT VIDEO...
...IS ALL TRUE.
I WAS BORN FEMALE, AND I HAVE A FEMALE BODY.
HOWEVER...
...I FEEL UNCOMFORTABLE WEARING SKIRTS THAT LABEL ME AS A GIRL...
...AND I WANT TO BE ONE OF THE BOYS.
I FEEL LIKE I'D PREFER TO HAVE A MALE BODY...
THAT'S HOW I TRULY FEEL.
I'M SURE OF IT.

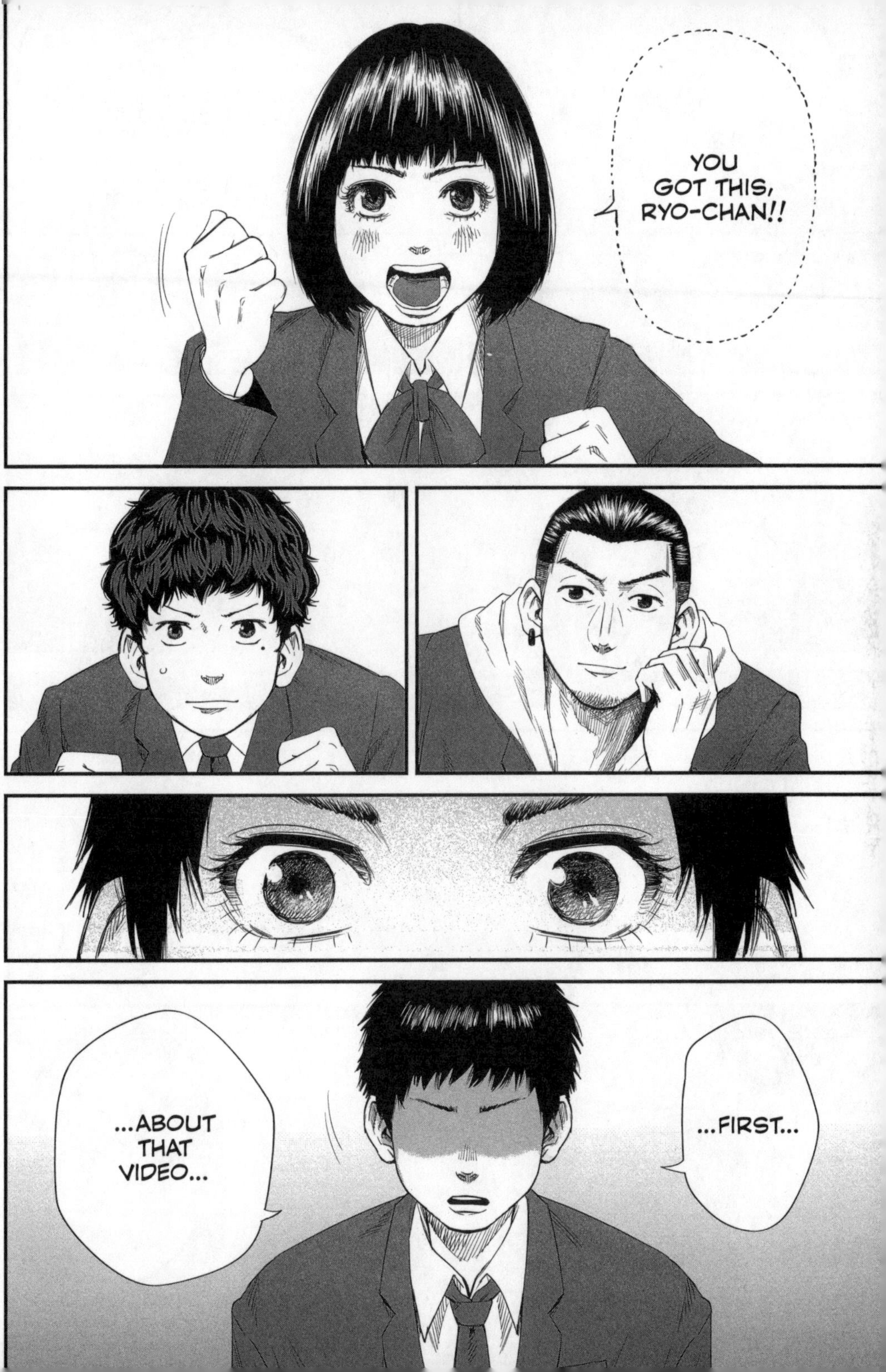
YOU GOT THIS, RYO-CHAN!!
...FIRST...
...ABOUT THAT VIDEO...

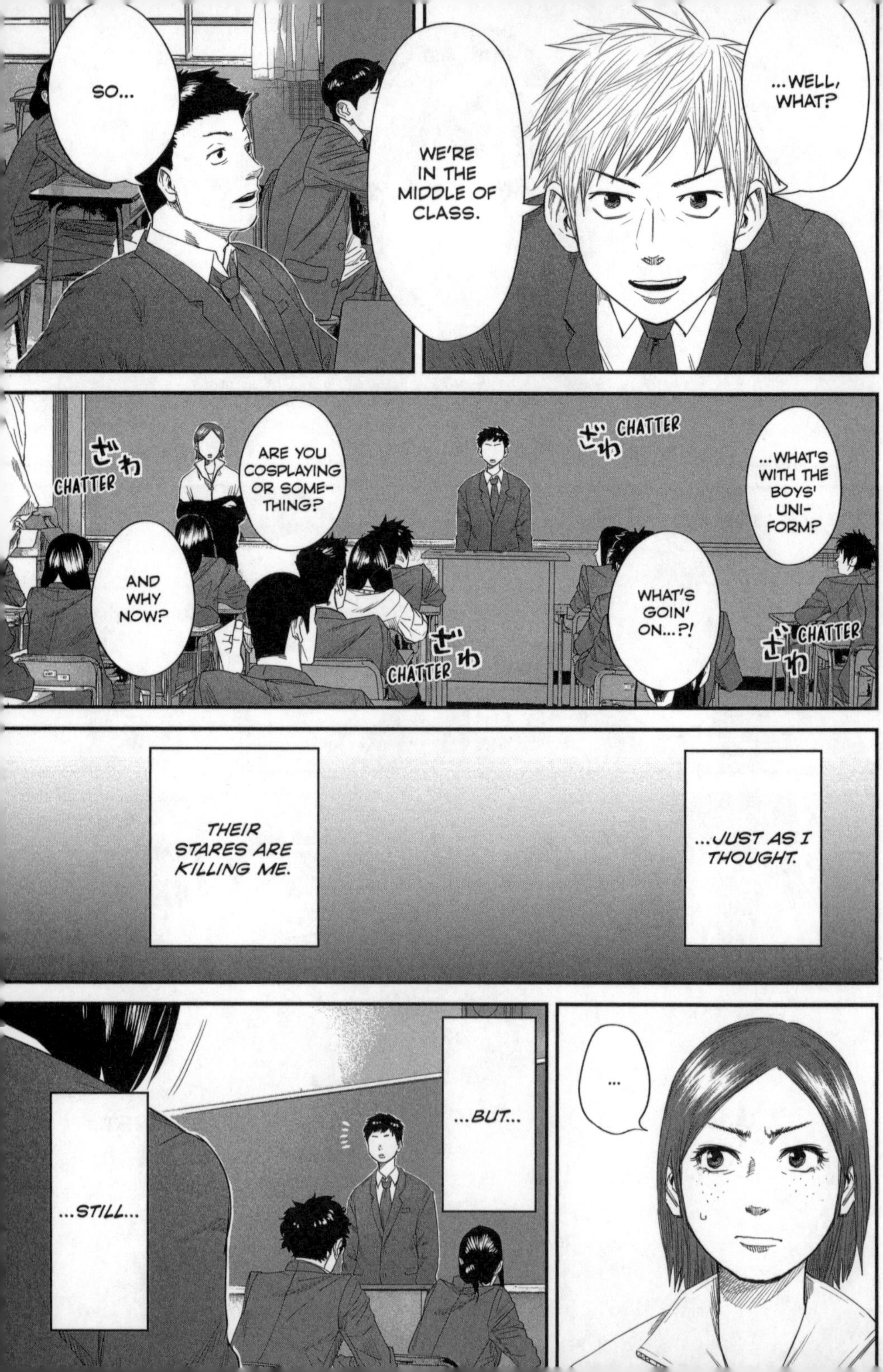
...WELL, WHAT?
WE'RE IN THE MIDDLE OF CLASS.
SO...
...WHAT'S WITH THE BOYS' UNI-FORM?
ざわ CHATTER
ざわ CHATTER
WHAT'S GOIN' ON...?!
ARE YOU COSPLAYING OR SOME-THING?
ざわ CHATTER
AND WHY NOW?
ざわ CHATTER
...JUST AS I THOUGHT.
THEIR STARES ARE KILLING ME.
...
...BUT...
...STILL...

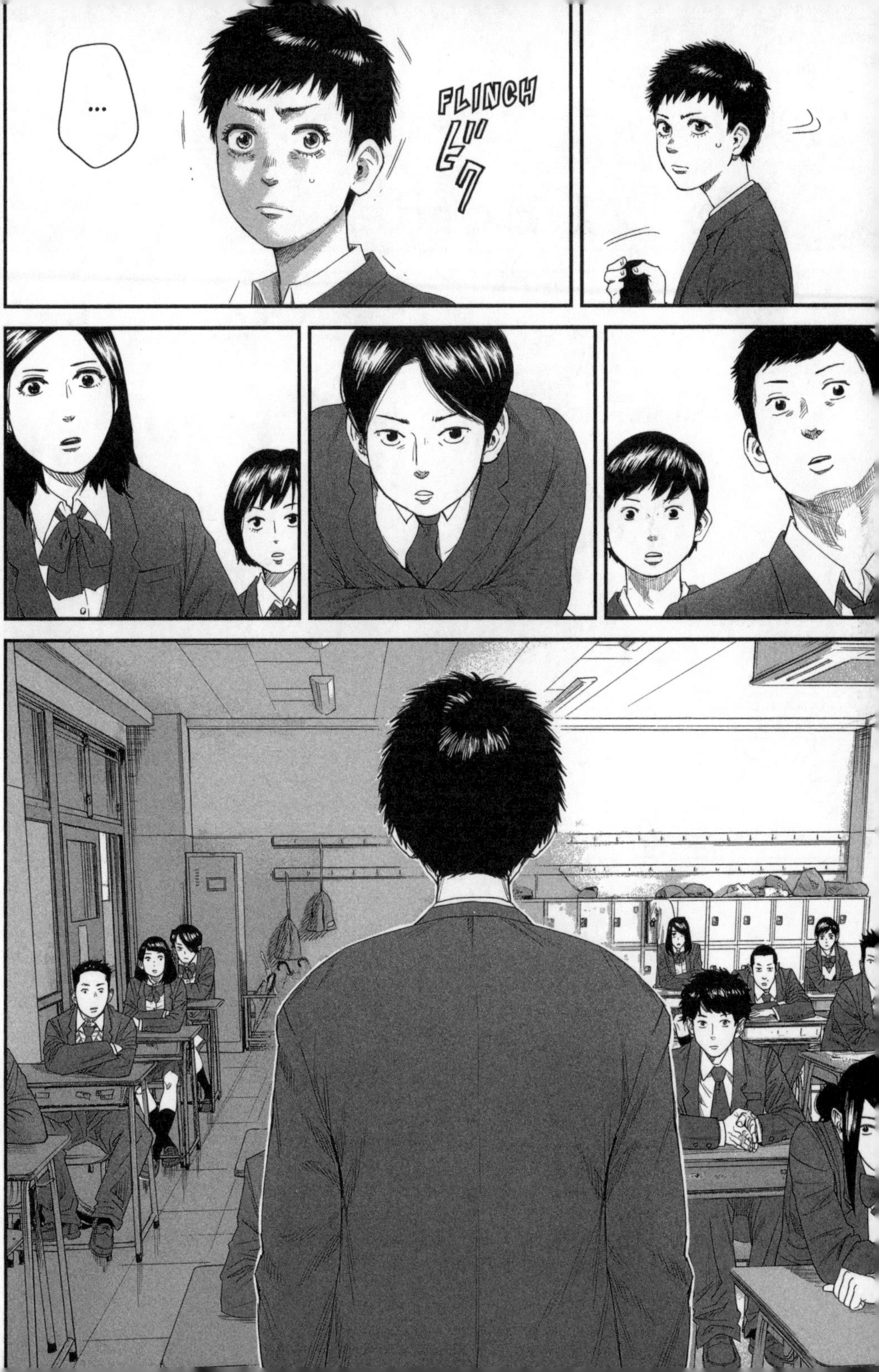
...
FLINCH
ビクッ

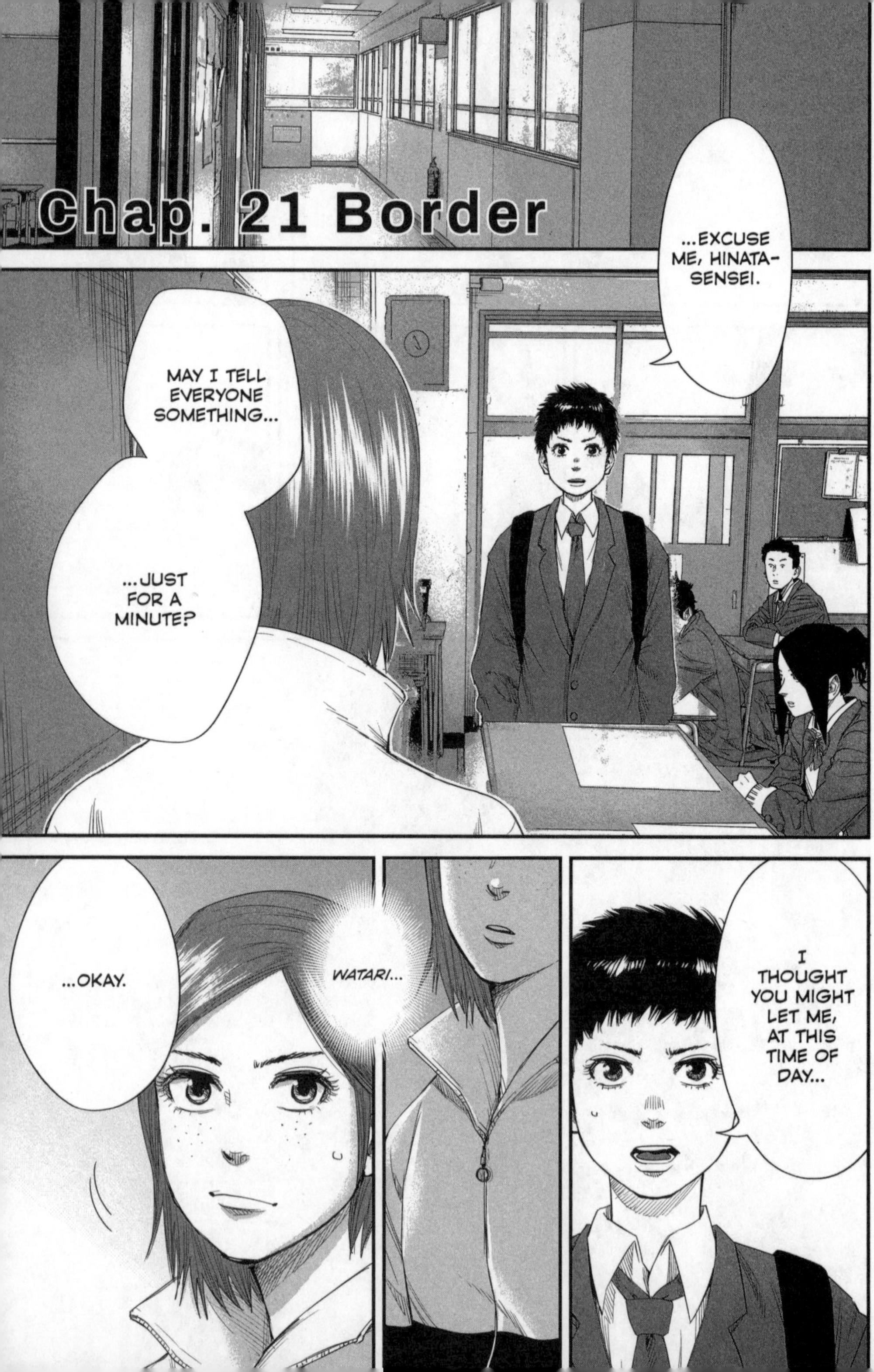
Chap. 21 Border
...EXCUSE ME, HINATA-SENSEI.
MAY I TELL EVERYONE SOMETHING...
...JUST FOR A MINUTE?
I THOUGHT YOU MIGHT LET ME, AT THIS TIME OF DAY...
WATARI...
...OKAY.

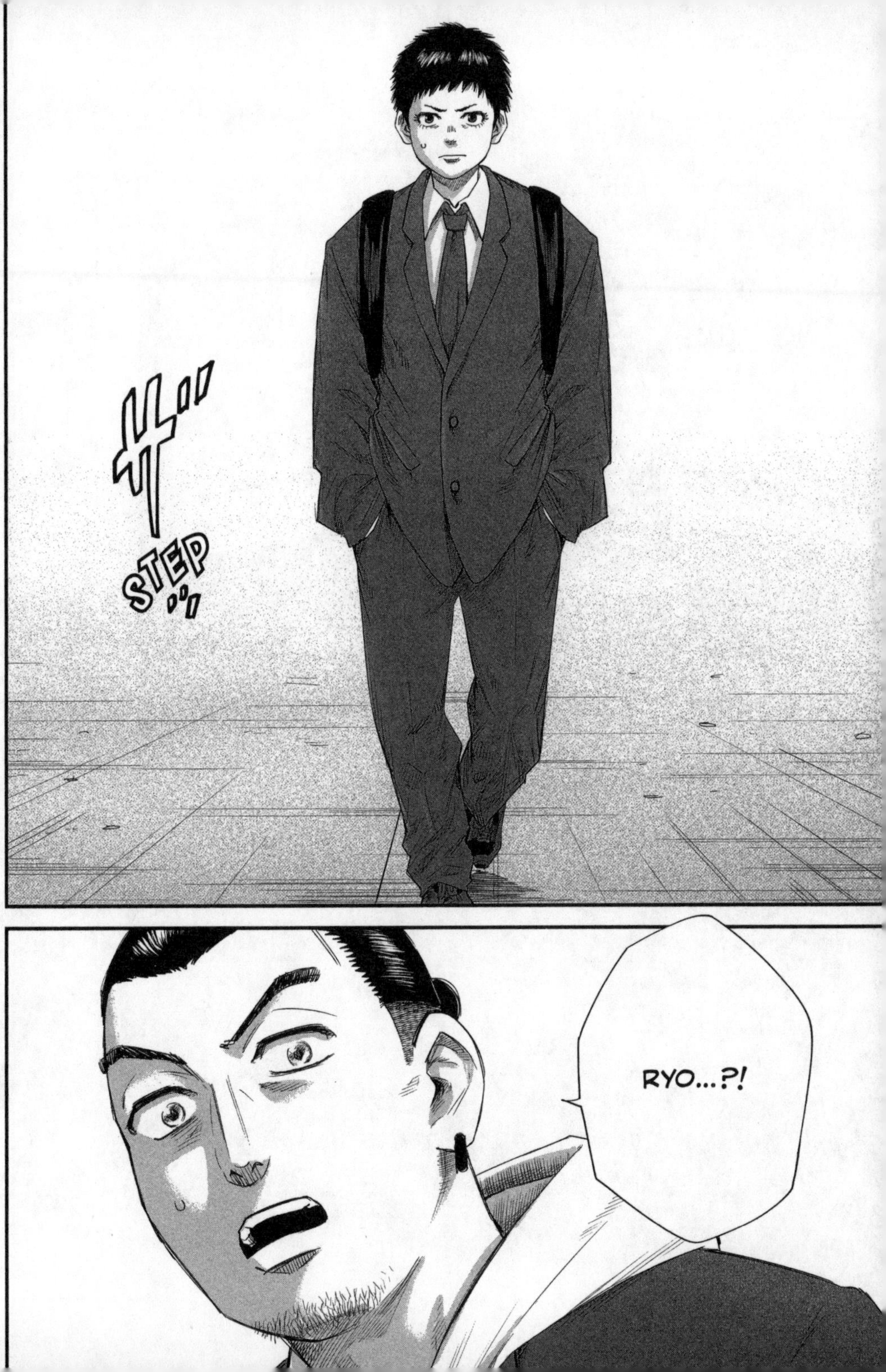
STEP
STEP
RYO...?!

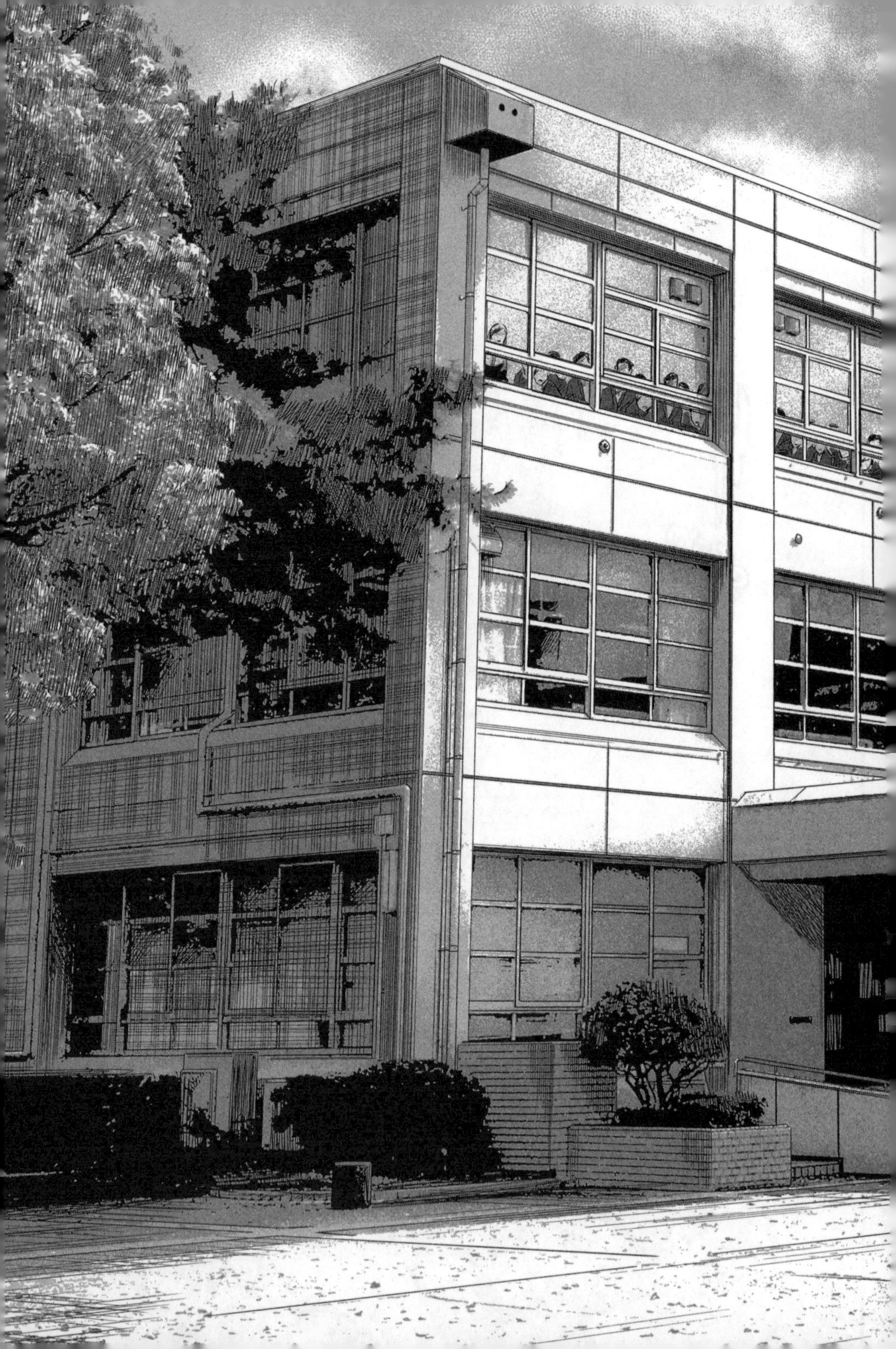

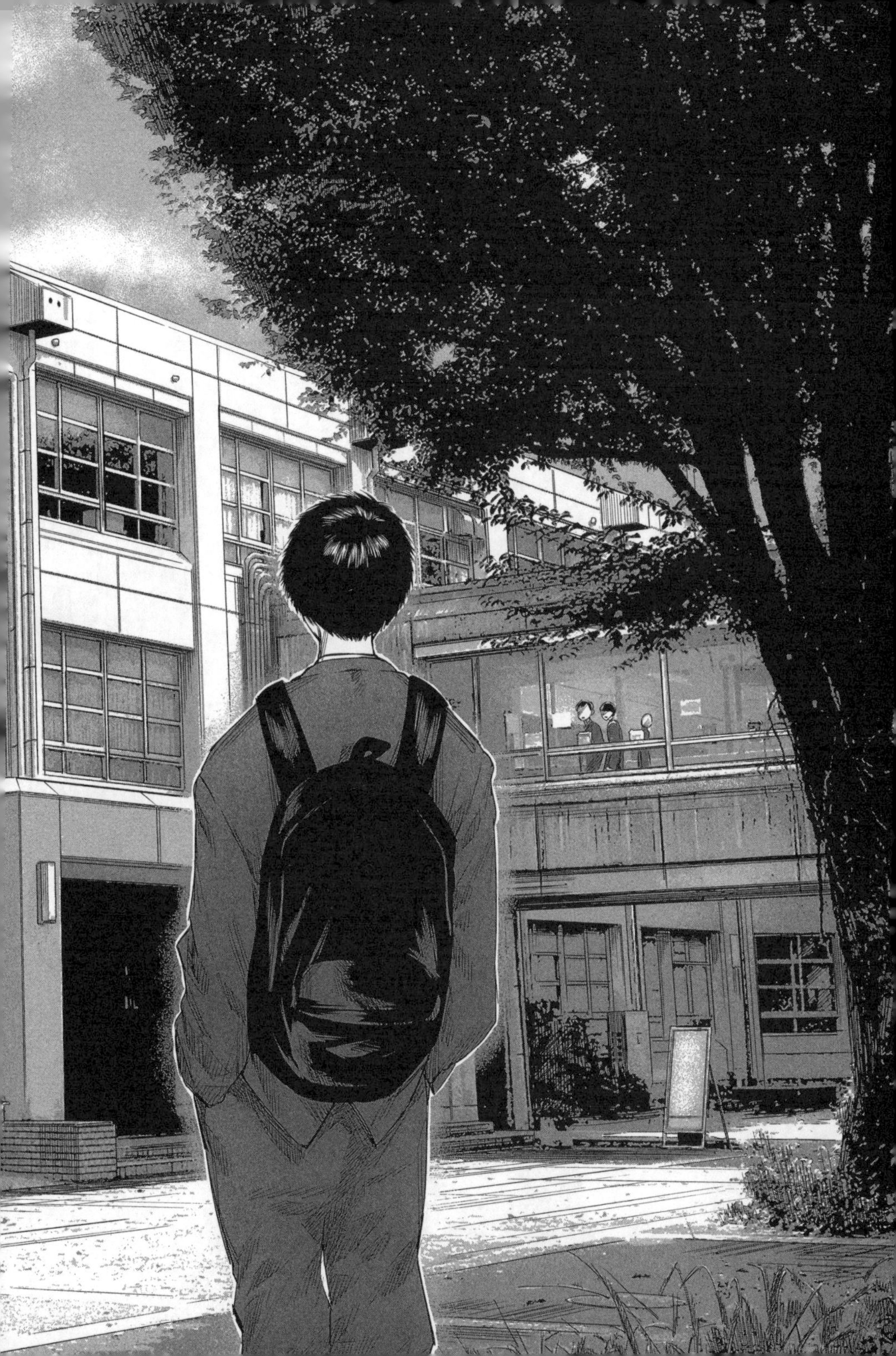

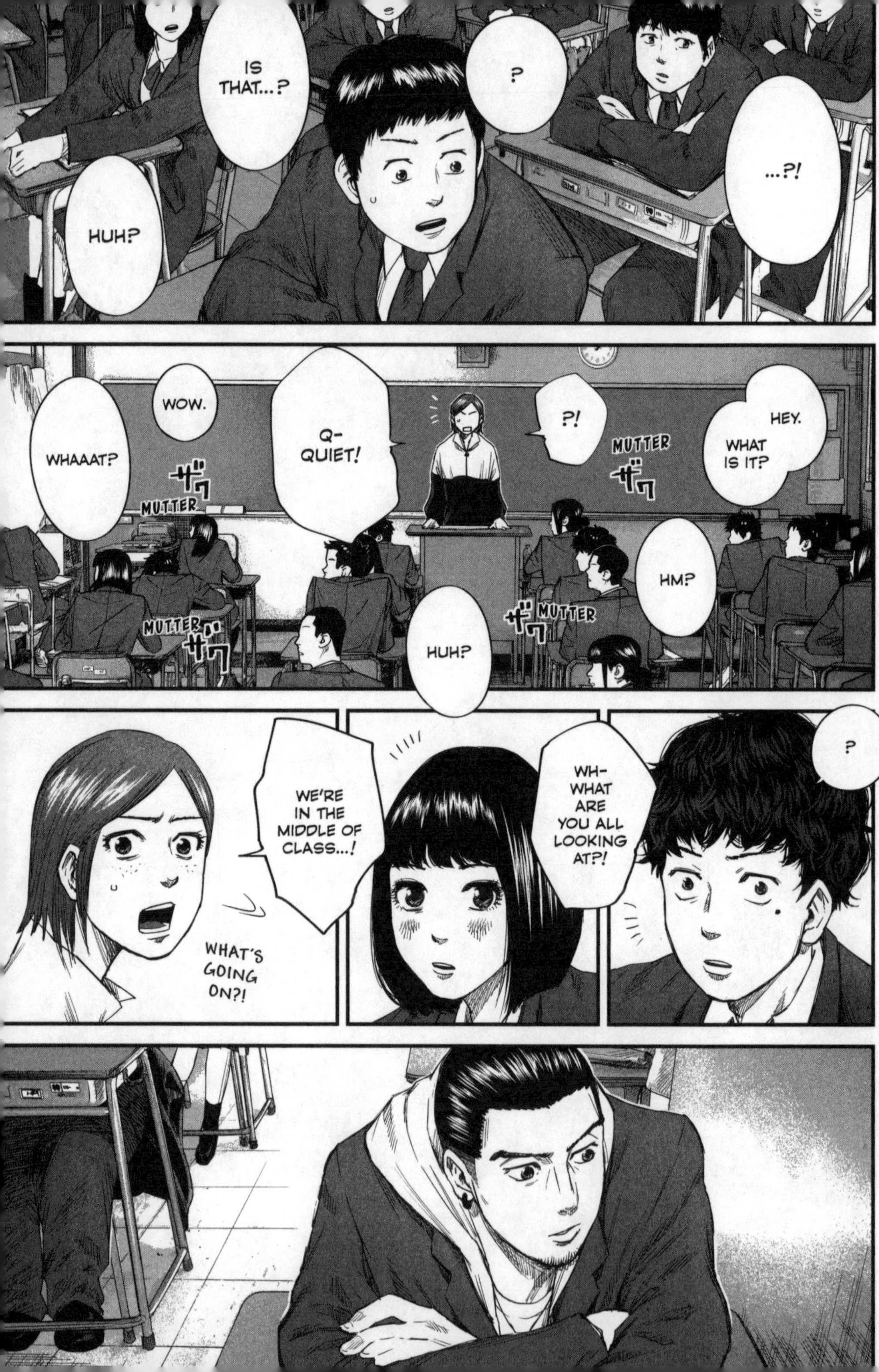

...?!
?
IS THAT...?
HUH?
HEY.
WHAT IS IT?
MUTTER
ザワ
HM?
?!
Q-
QUIET!
MUTTER
ザワ
HUH?
WOW.
WHAAAT?
MUTTER
ザワ
MUTTER
ザワ
?
WH-
WHAT
ARE
YOU ALL
LOOKING
AT?!
WE'RE
IN THE
MIDDLE OF
CLASS...!
WHAT'S
GOING
ON?!

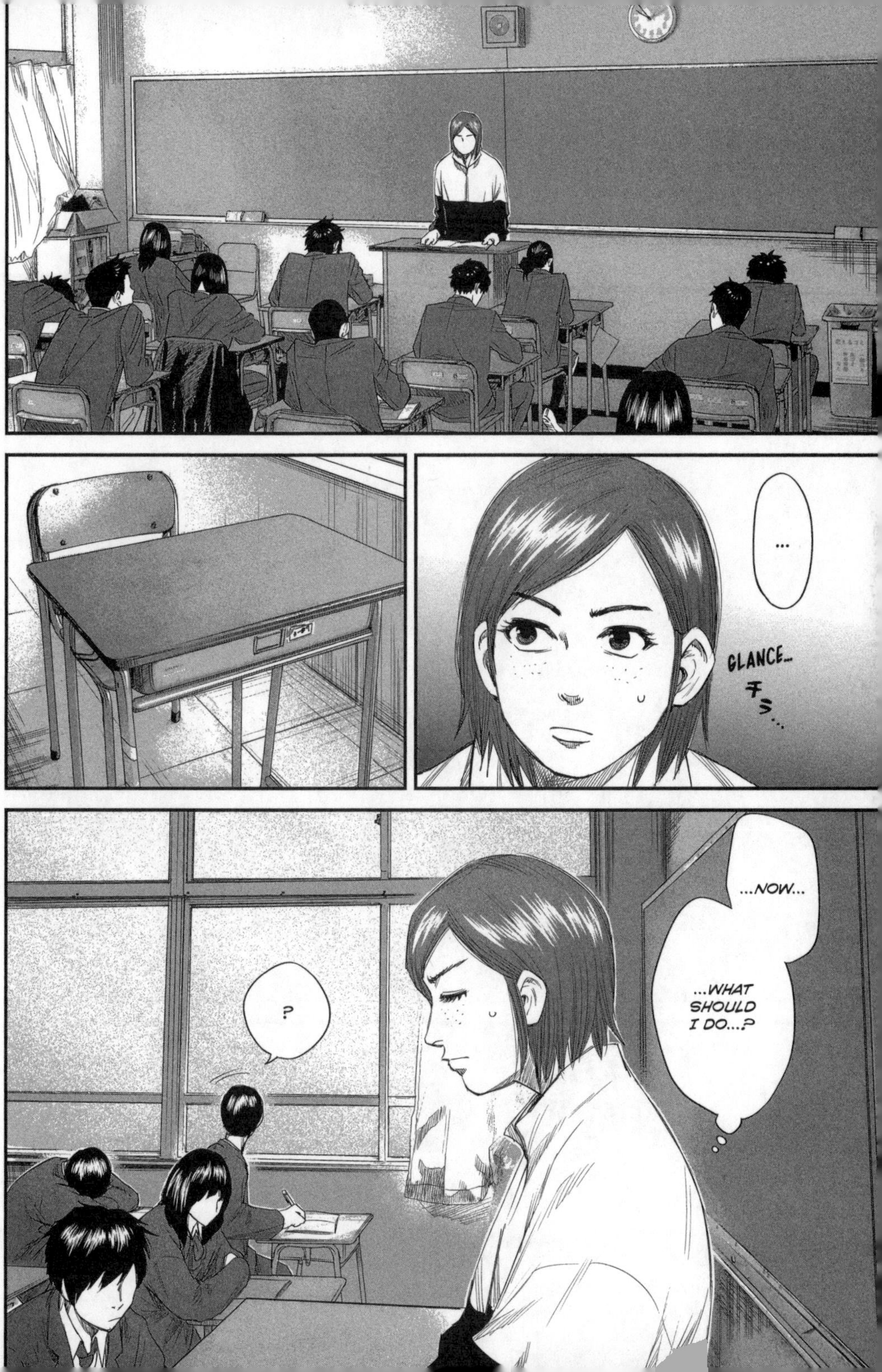
...
GLANCE...
チラ...
...NOW...
...WHAT SHOULD I DO...?
?

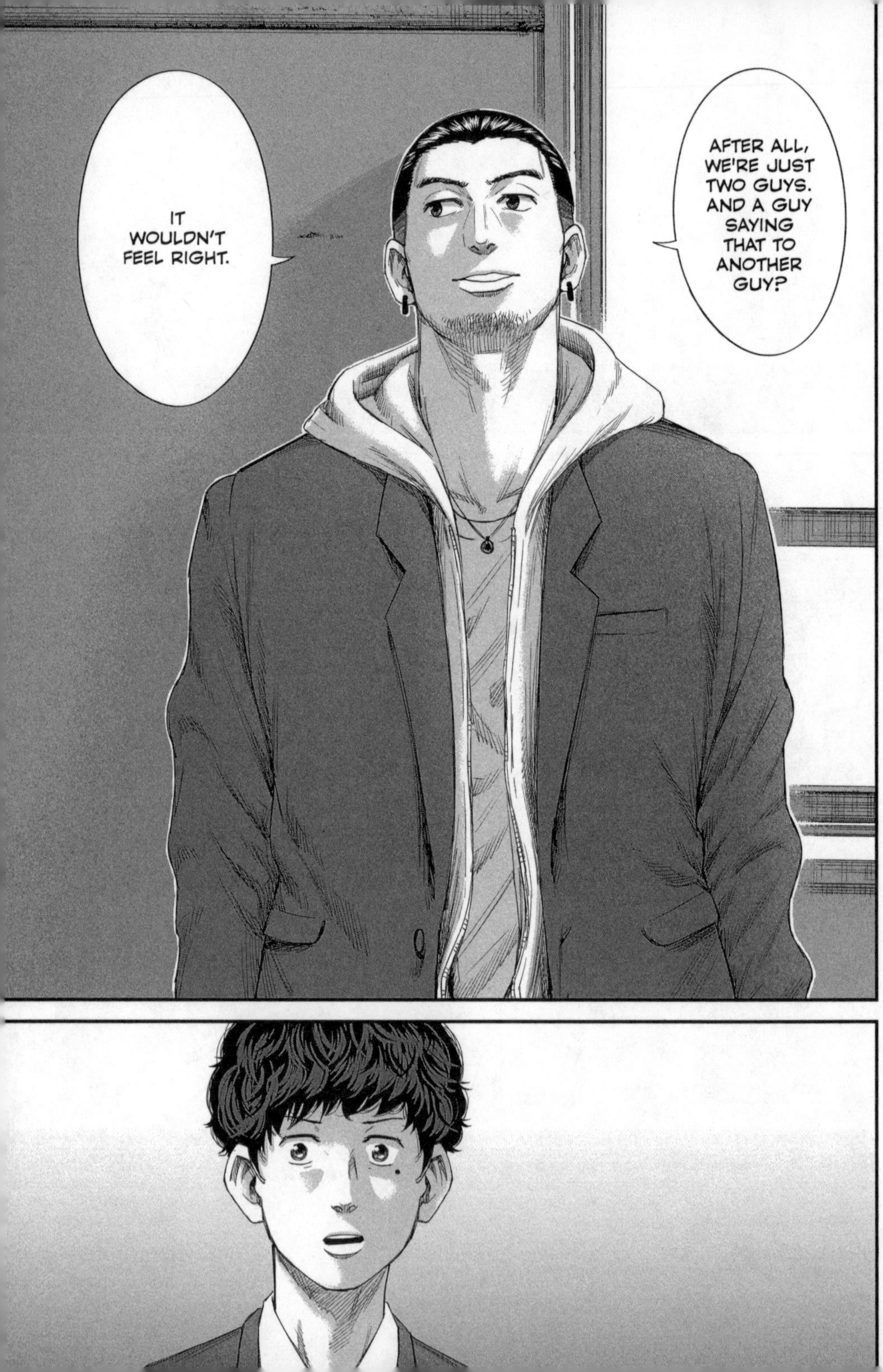
AFTER ALL, WE'RE JUST TWO GUYS. AND A GUY SAYING THAT TO ANOTHER GUY?
IT WOULDN'T FEEL RIGHT.

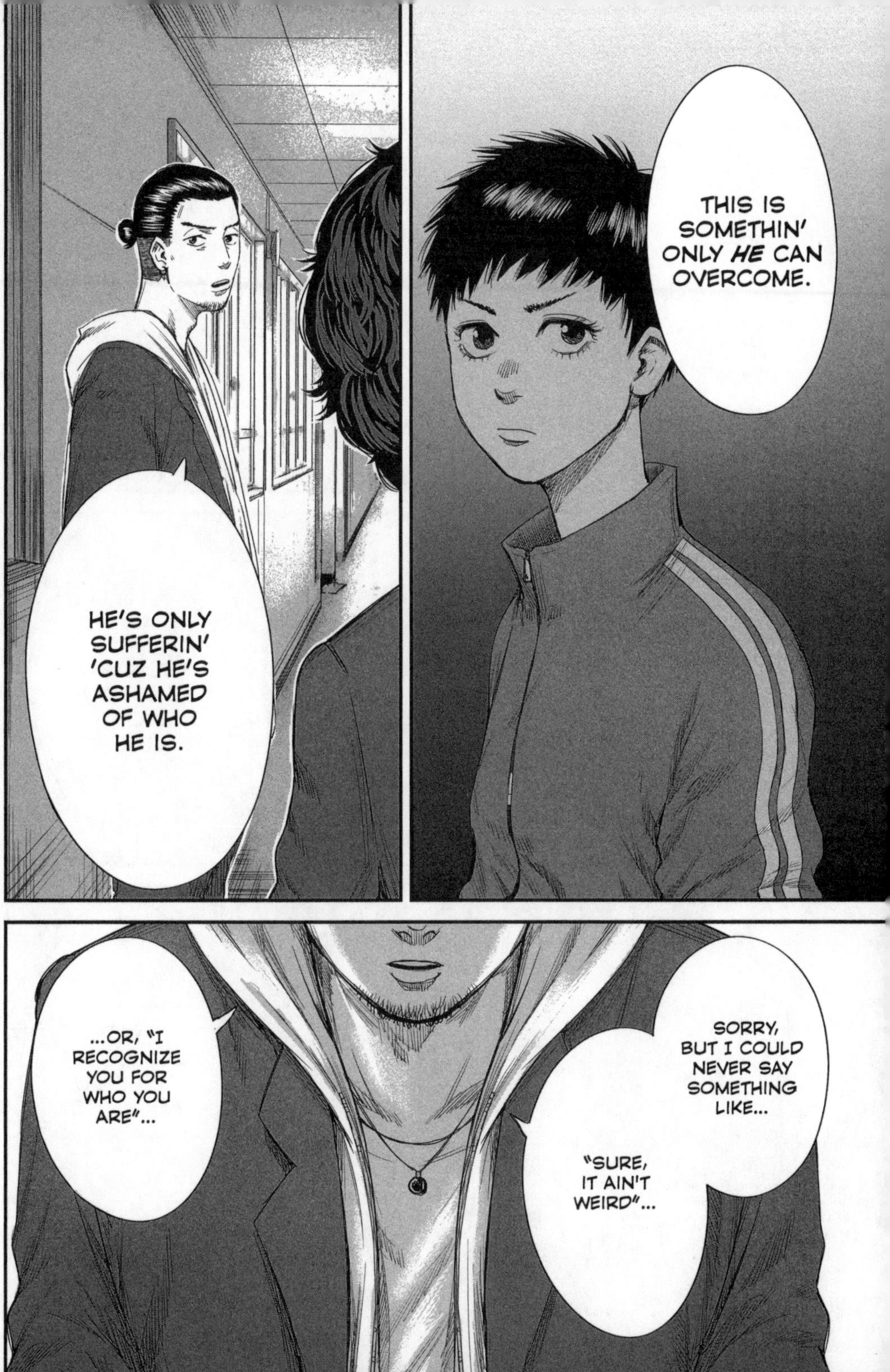
THIS IS SOMETHIN' ONLY *HE* CAN OVERCOME.
HE'S ONLY SUFFERIN' 'CUZ HE'S ASHAMED OF WHO HE IS.
SORRY, BUT I COULD NEVER SAY SOMETHING LIKE...
"SURE, IT AIN'T WEIRD"...
...OR, "I RECOGNIZE YOU FOR WHO YOU ARE"...

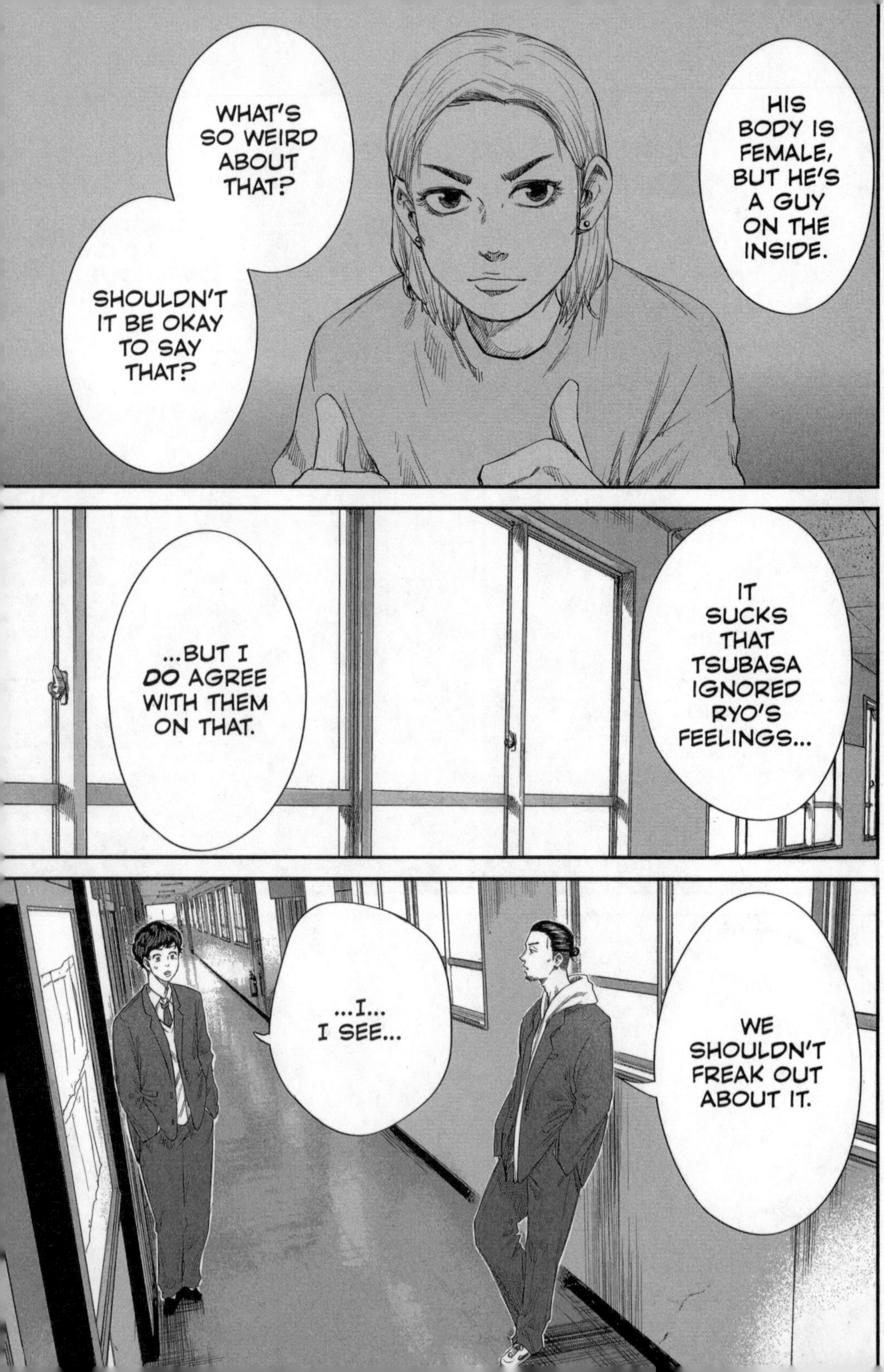
HIS BODY IS FEMALE, BUT HE'S A GUY ON THE INSIDE.
WHAT'S SO WEIRD ABOUT THAT?
SHOULDN'T IT BE OKAY TO SAY THAT?
IT SUCKS THAT TSUBASA IGNORED RYO'S FEELINGS...
...BUT I *DO* AGREE WITH THEM ON THAT.
WE SHOULDN'T FREAK OUT ABOUT IT.
...I... I SEE...

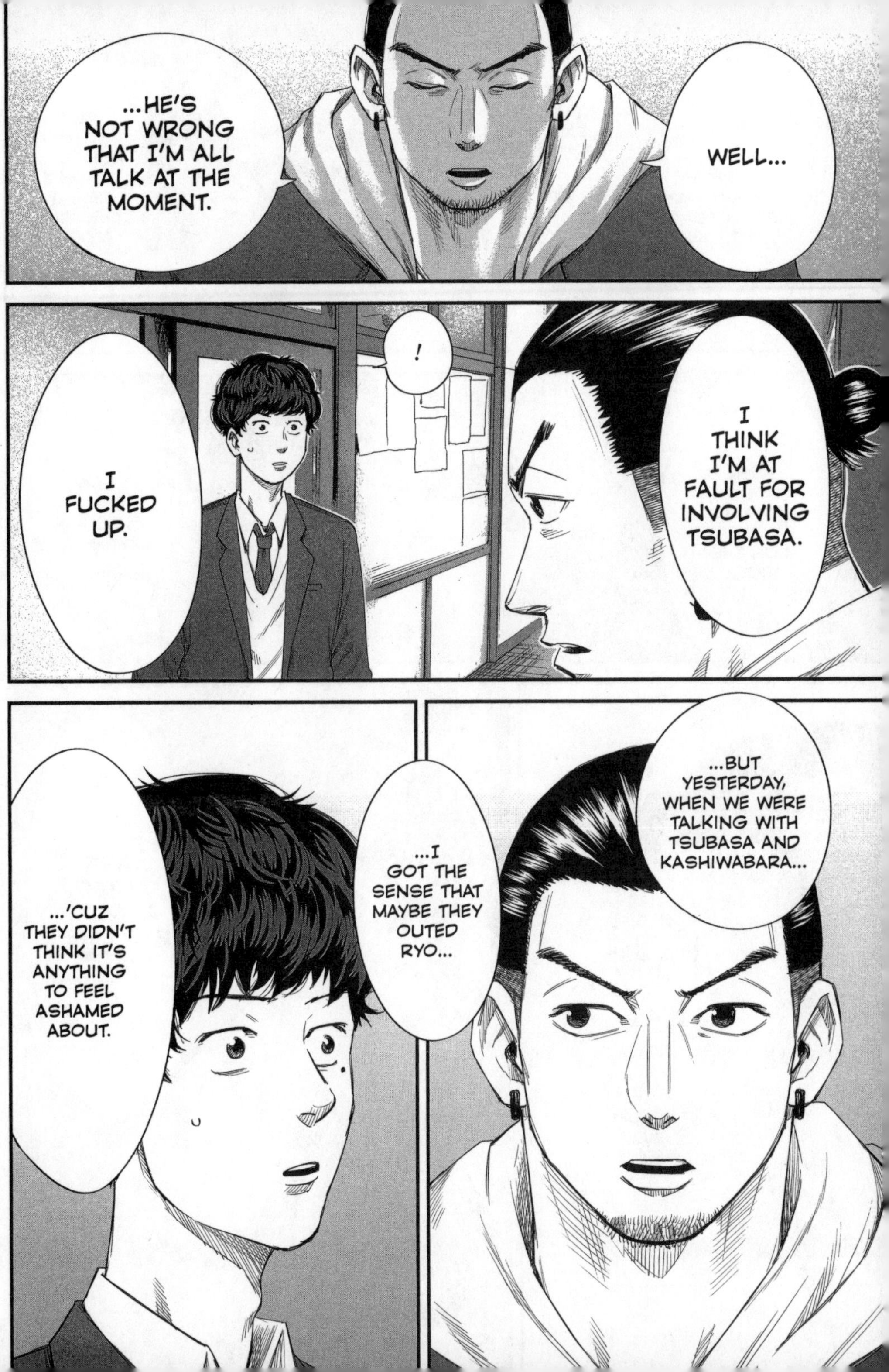
WELL...
...HE'S NOT WRONG THAT I'M ALL TALK AT THE MOMENT.
I THINK I'M AT FAULT FOR INVOLVING TSUBASA.
!
I FUCKED UP.
...BUT YESTERDAY, WHEN WE WERE TALKING WITH TSUBASA AND KASHIWABARA...
...I GOT THE SENSE THAT MAYBE THEY OUTED RYO...
...'CUZ THEY DIDN'T THINK IT'S ANYTHING TO FEEL ASHAMED ABOUT.

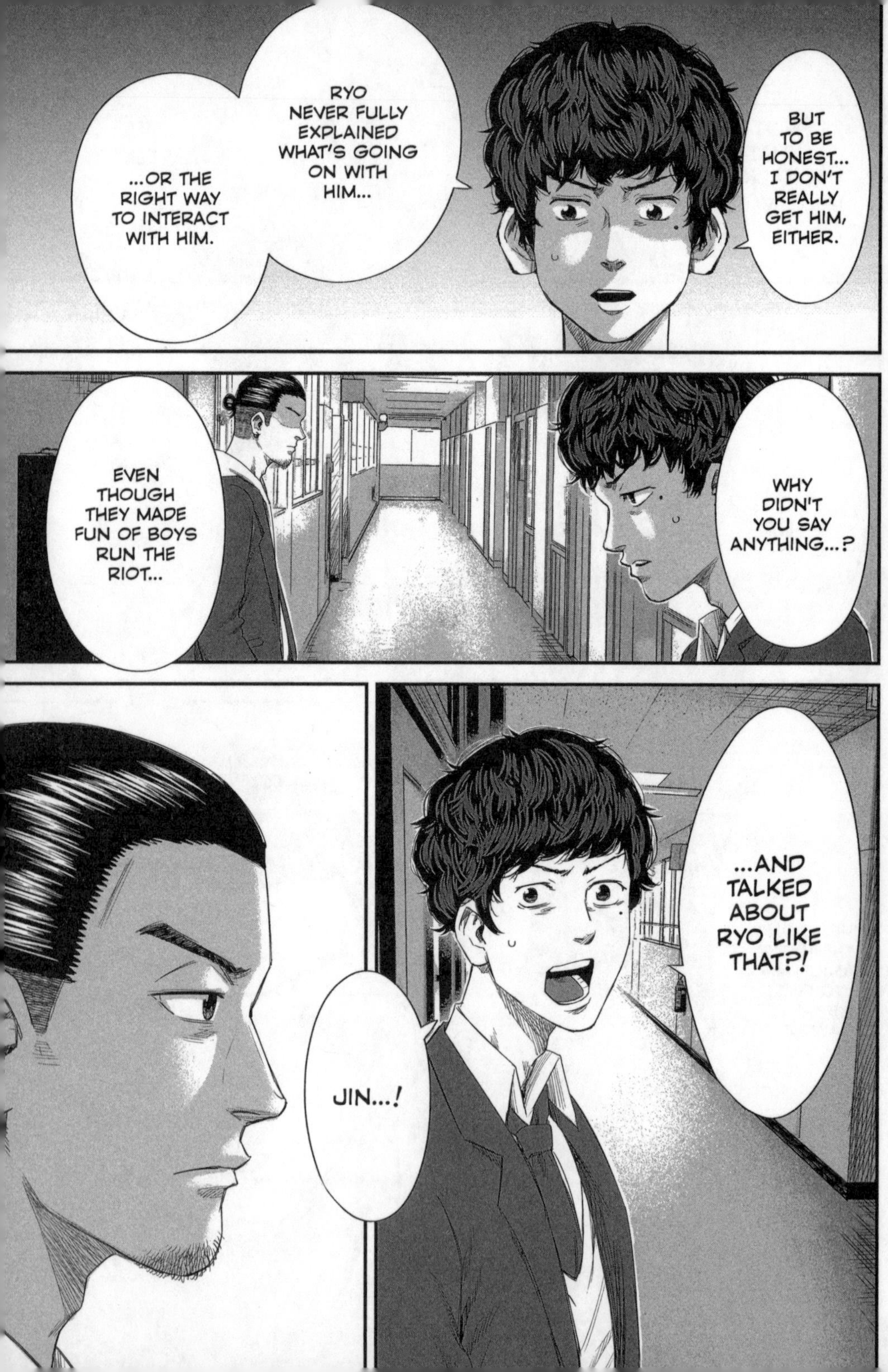
BUT TO BE HONEST... I DON'T REALLY GET HIM, EITHER.
RYO NEVER FULLY EXPLAINED WHAT'S GOING ON WITH HIM...
...OR THE RIGHT WAY TO INTERACT WITH HIM.
WHY DIDN'T YOU SAY ANYTHING...?
EVEN THOUGH THEY MADE FUN OF BOYS RUN THE RIOT...
...AND TALKED ABOUT RYO LIKE THAT?!
JIN...!

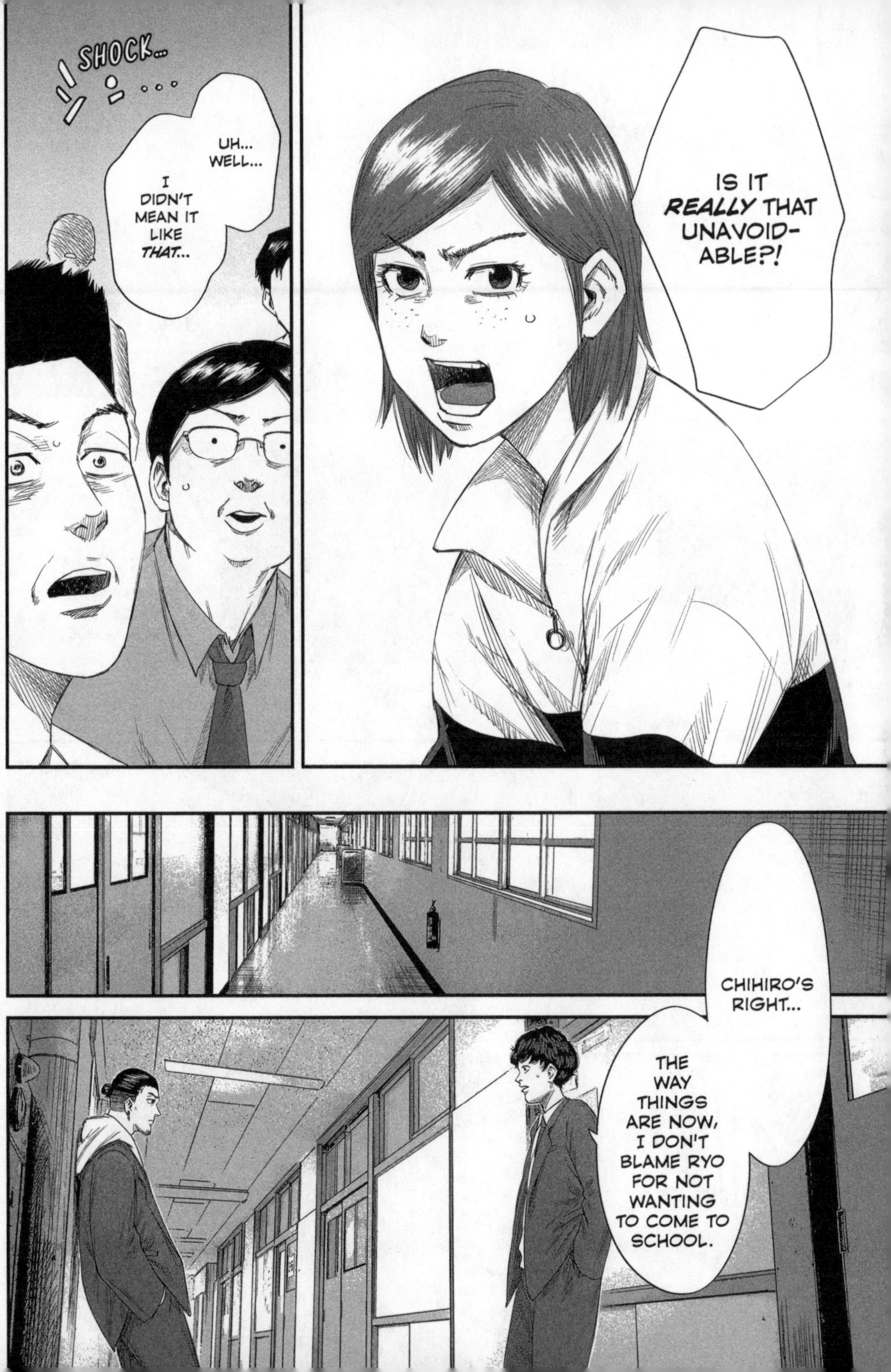
IS IT REALLY THAT UNAVOIDABLE?!
SHOCK...
UH... WELL...
I DIDN'T MEAN IT LIKE THAT...
CHIHIRO'S RIGHT...
THE WAY THINGS ARE NOW, I DON'T BLAME RYO FOR NOT WANTING TO COME TO SCHOOL.

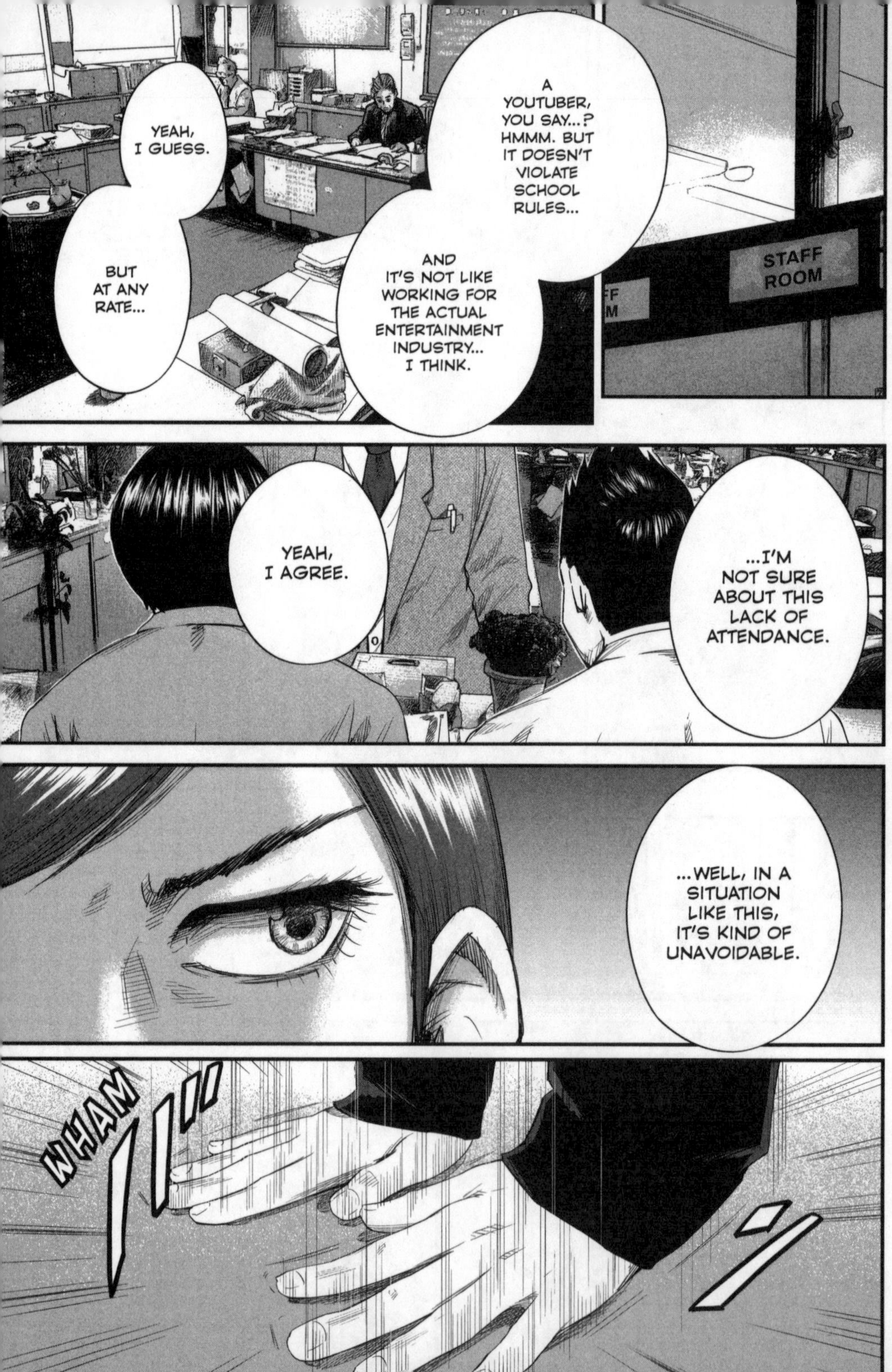
STAFF ROOM
A YOUTUBER, YOU SAY...? HMMM. BUT IT DOESN'T VIOLATE SCHOOL RULES...
AND IT'S NOT LIKE WORKING FOR THE ACTUAL ENTERTAINMENT INDUSTRY... I THINK.
YEAH, I GUESS.
BUT AT ANY RATE...
...I'M NOT SURE ABOUT THIS LACK OF ATTENDANCE.
YEAH, I AGREE.
...WELL, IN A SITUATION LIKE THIS, IT'S KIND OF UNAVOIDABLE.
WHAM

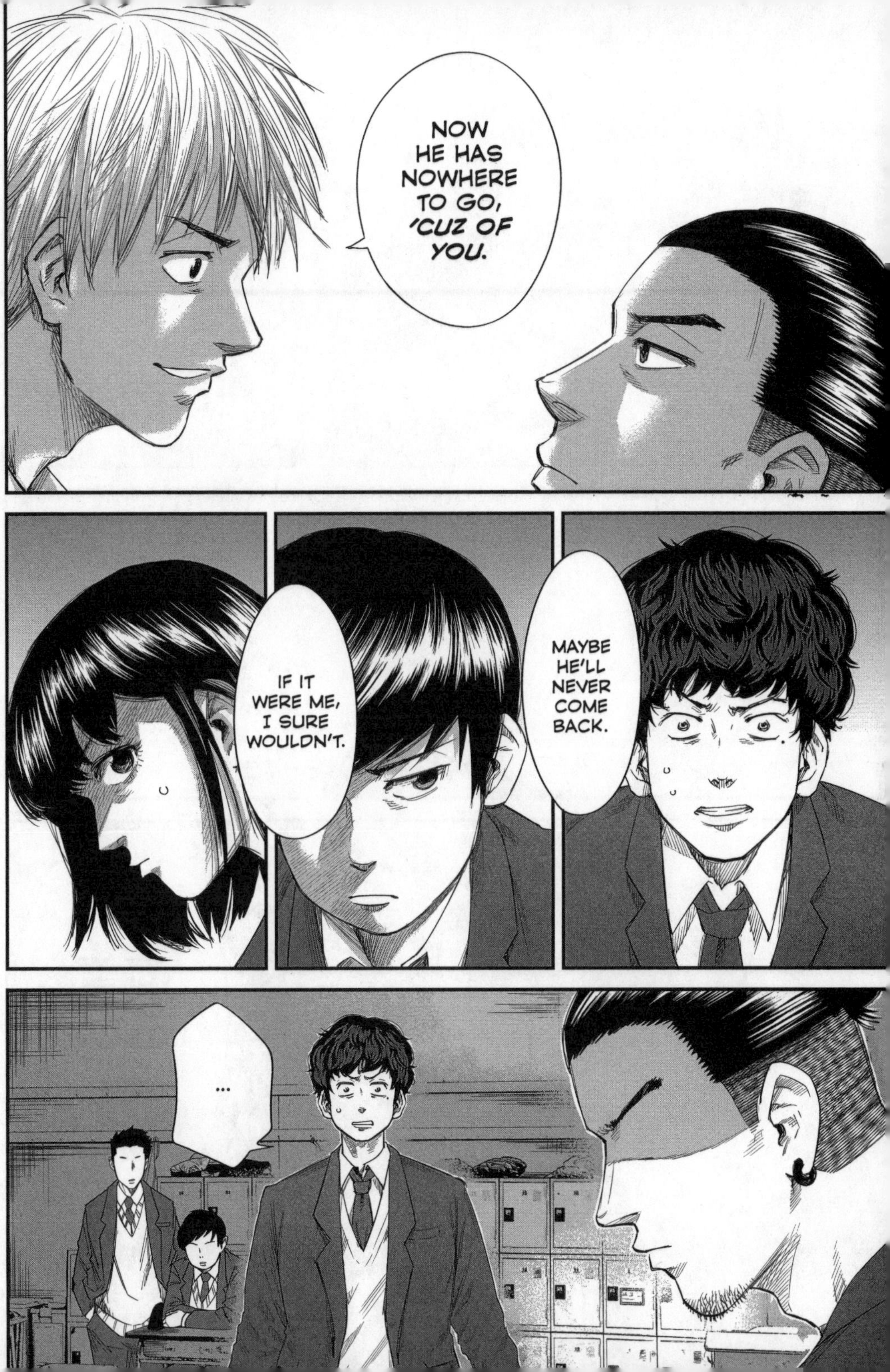
NOW HE HAS NOWHERE TO GO, 'CUZ OF YOU.
MAYBE HE'LL NEVER COME BACK.
IF IT WERE ME, I SURE WOULDN'T.
...

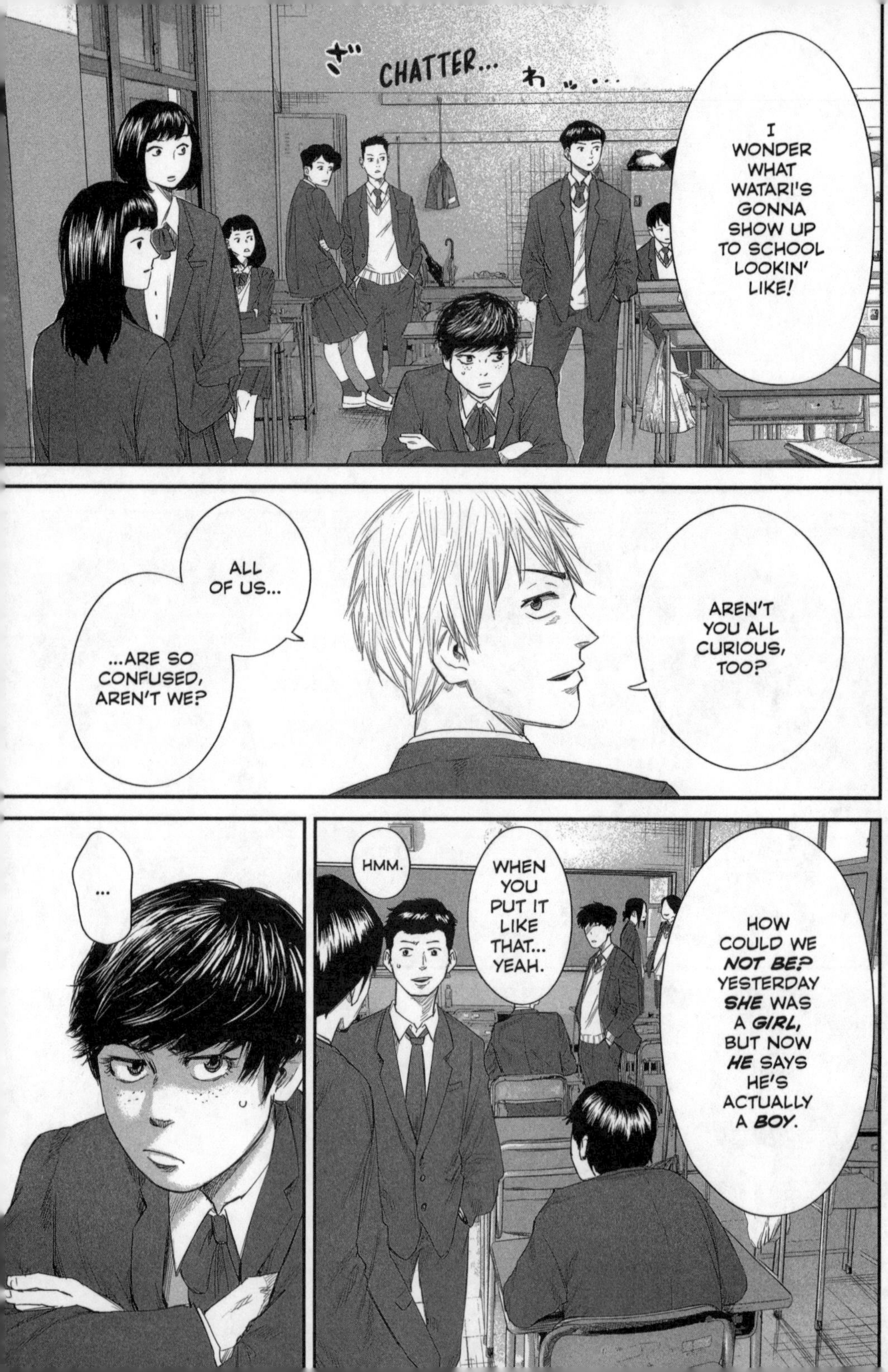
CHATTER...
I WONDER WHAT WATARI'S GONNA SHOW UP TO SCHOOL LOOKIN' LIKE!
AREN'T YOU ALL CURIOUS, TOO?
ALL OF US...
...ARE SO CONFUSED, AREN'T WE?
HOW COULD WE *NOT BE?* YESTERDAY *SHE* WAS A *GIRL,* BUT NOW *HE* SAYS HE'S ACTUALLY A *BOY.*
WHEN YOU PUT IT LIKE THAT... YEAH.
HMM.
...

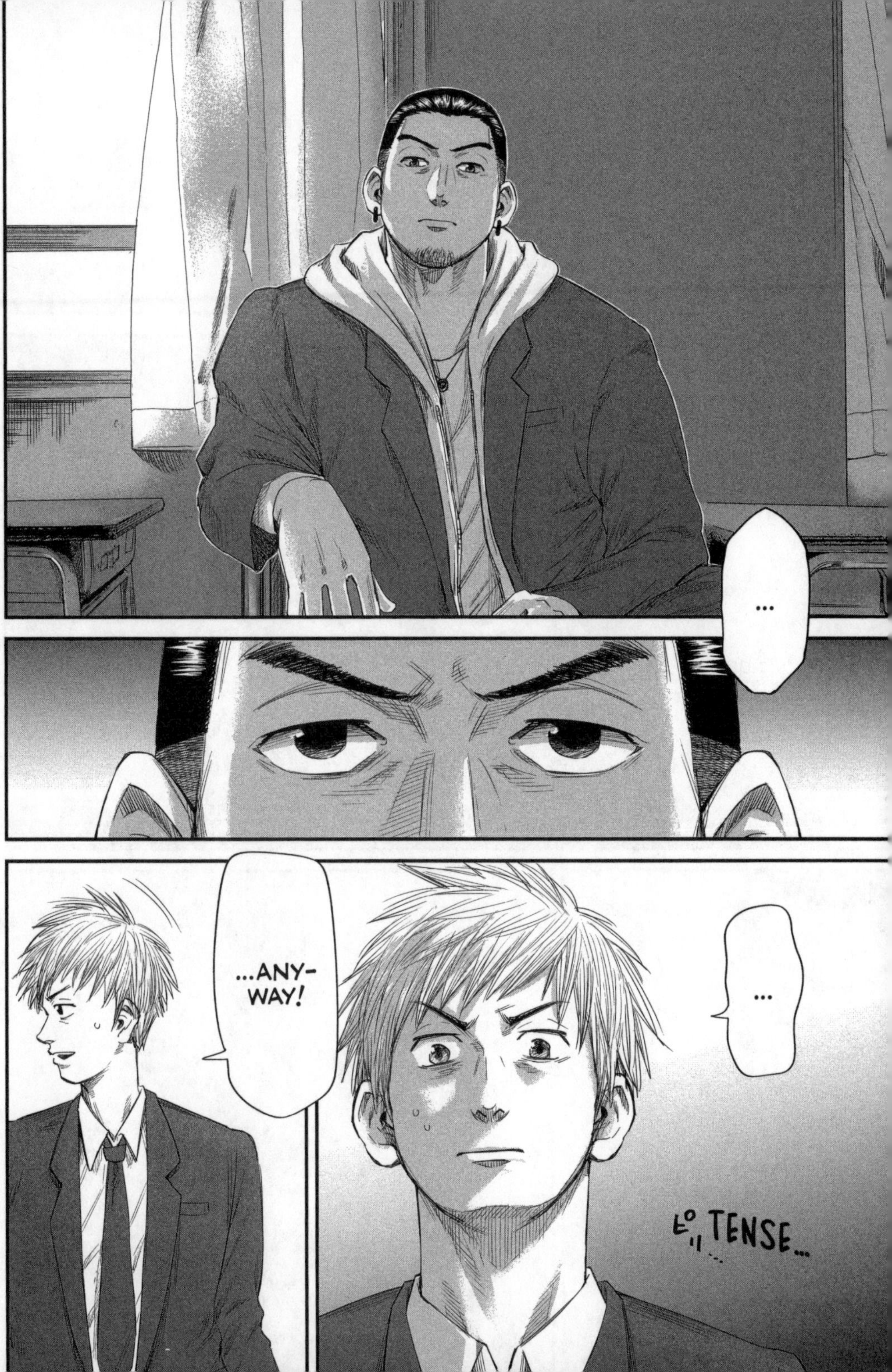
...
...
...ANY-WAY!
TENSE...

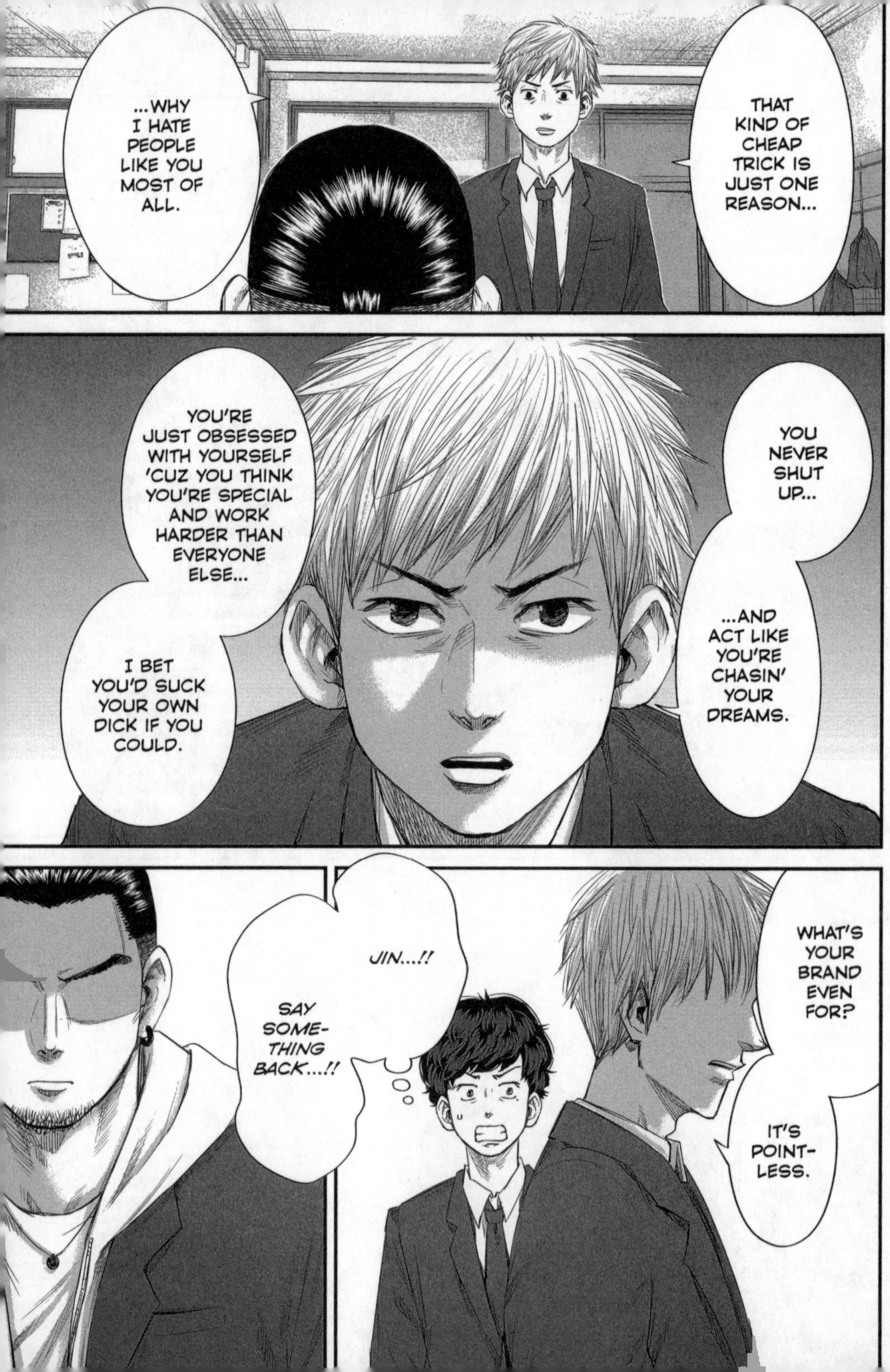
THAT KIND OF CHEAP TRICK IS JUST ONE REASON...
...WHY I HATE PEOPLE LIKE YOU MOST OF ALL.
YOU NEVER SHUT UP...
...AND ACT LIKE YOU'RE CHASIN' YOUR DREAMS.
YOU'RE JUST OBSESSED WITH YOURSELF 'CUZ YOU THINK YOU'RE SPECIAL AND WORK HARDER THAN EVERYONE ELSE...
I BET YOU'D SUCK YOUR OWN DICK IF YOU COULD.
WHAT'S YOUR BRAND EVEN FOR?
IT'S POINT-LESS.
JIN...!!
SAY SOME-THING BACK...!!

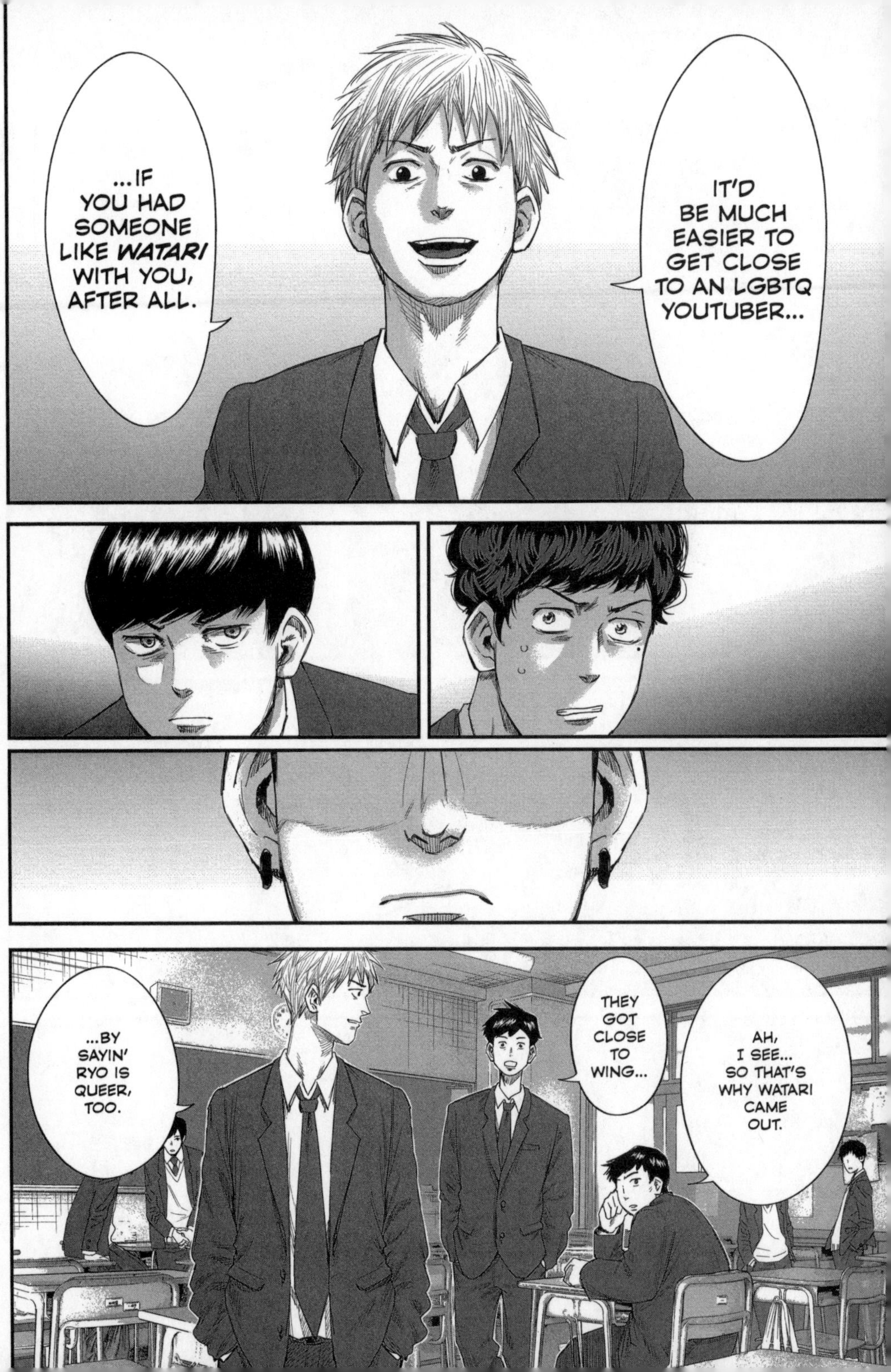
IT'D BE MUCH EASIER TO GET CLOSE TO AN LGBTQ YOUTUBER...
...IF YOU HAD SOMEONE LIKE *WATARI* WITH YOU, AFTER ALL.
AH, I SEE... SO THAT'S WHY WATARI CAME OUT.
THEY GOT CLOSE TO WING...
...BY SAYIN' RYO IS QUEER, TOO.

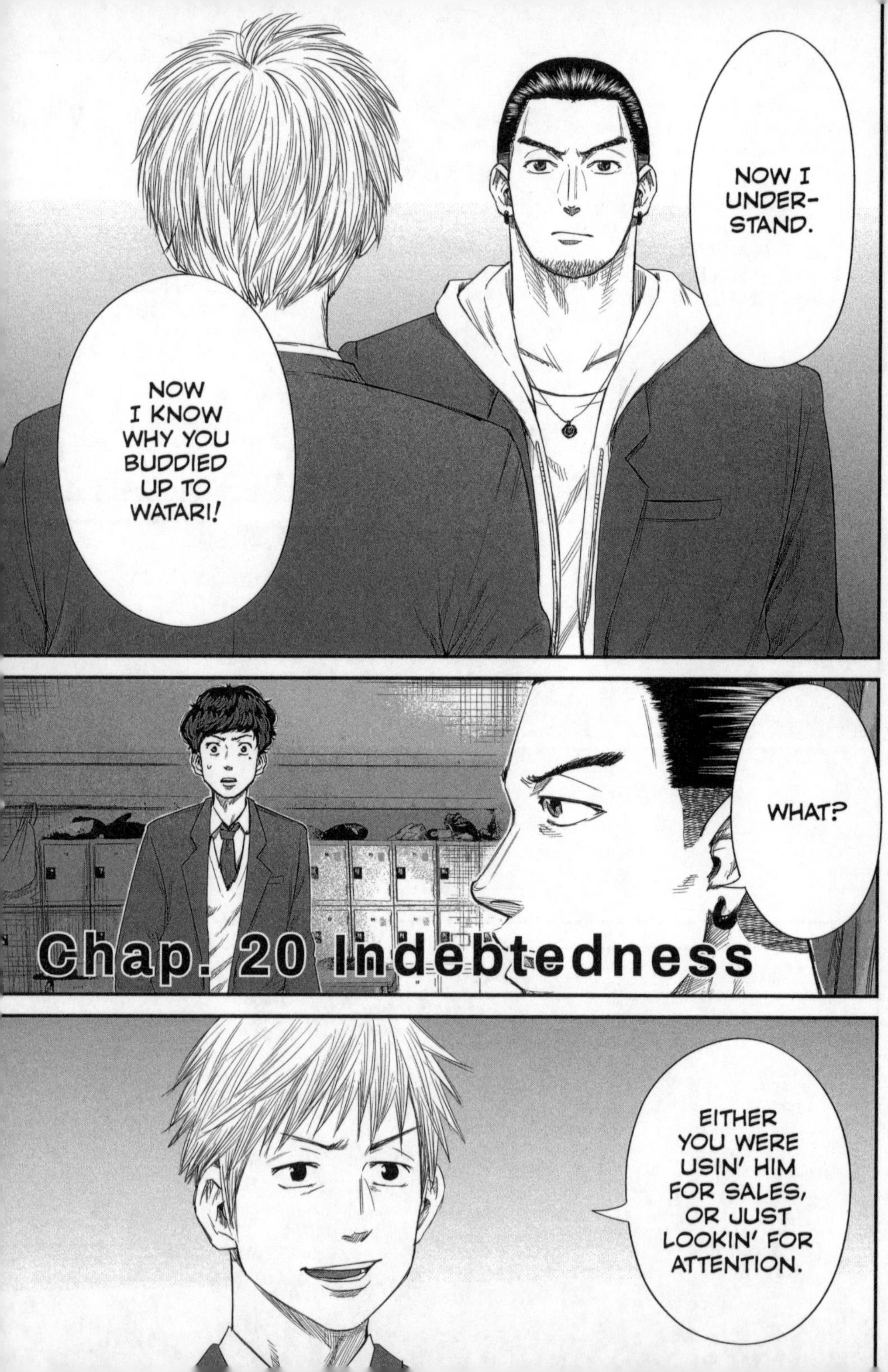
NOW I UNDER-STAND.
NOW I KNOW WHY YOU BUDDIED UP TO WATARI!
WHAT?
Chap. 20 Indebtedness
EITHER YOU WERE USIN' HIM FOR SALES, OR JUST LOOKIN' FOR ATTENTION.

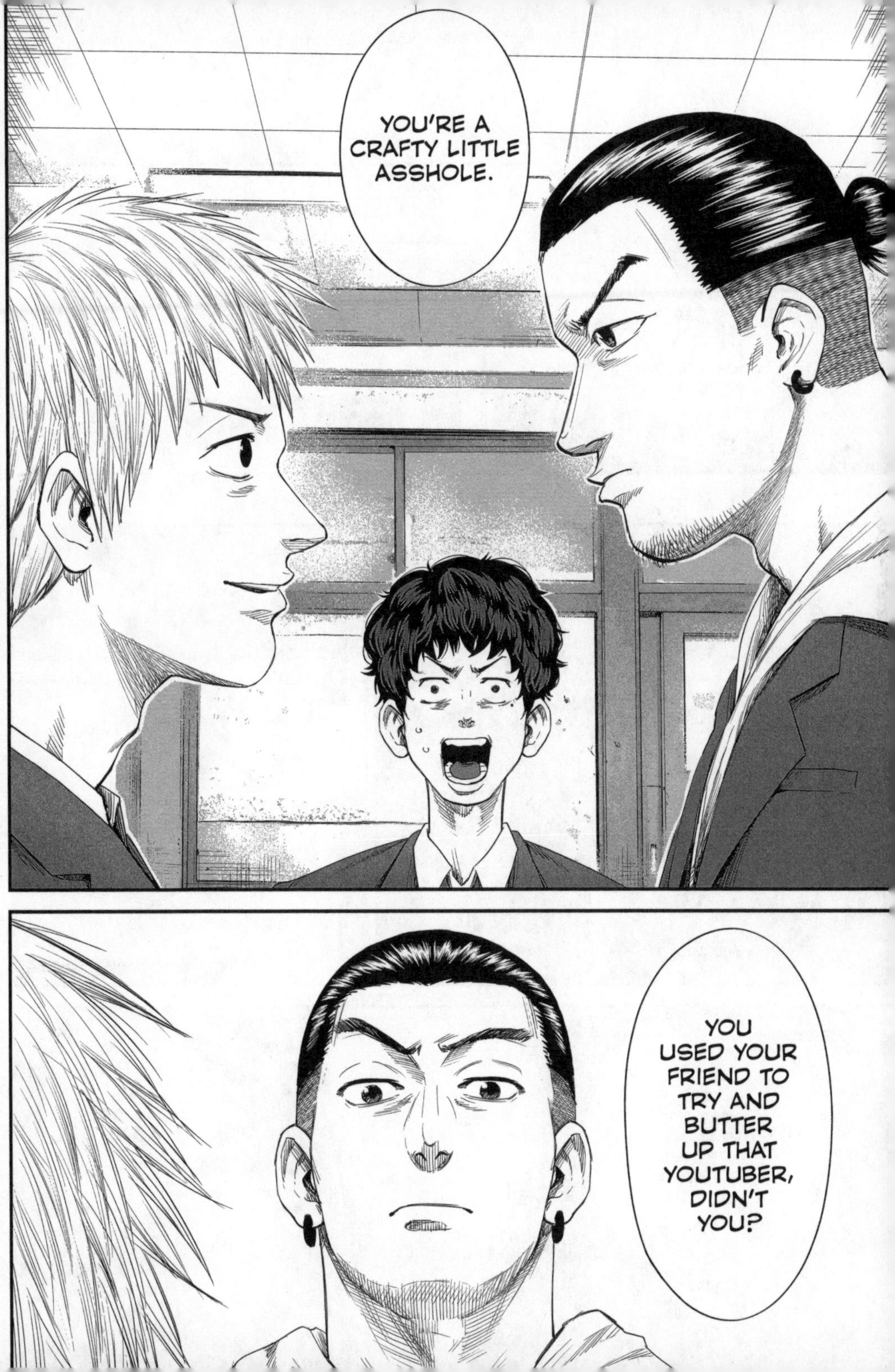
YOU'RE A CRAFTY LITTLE ASSHOLE.
YOU USED YOUR FRIEND TO TRY AND BUTTER UP THAT YOUTUBER, DIDN'T YOU?

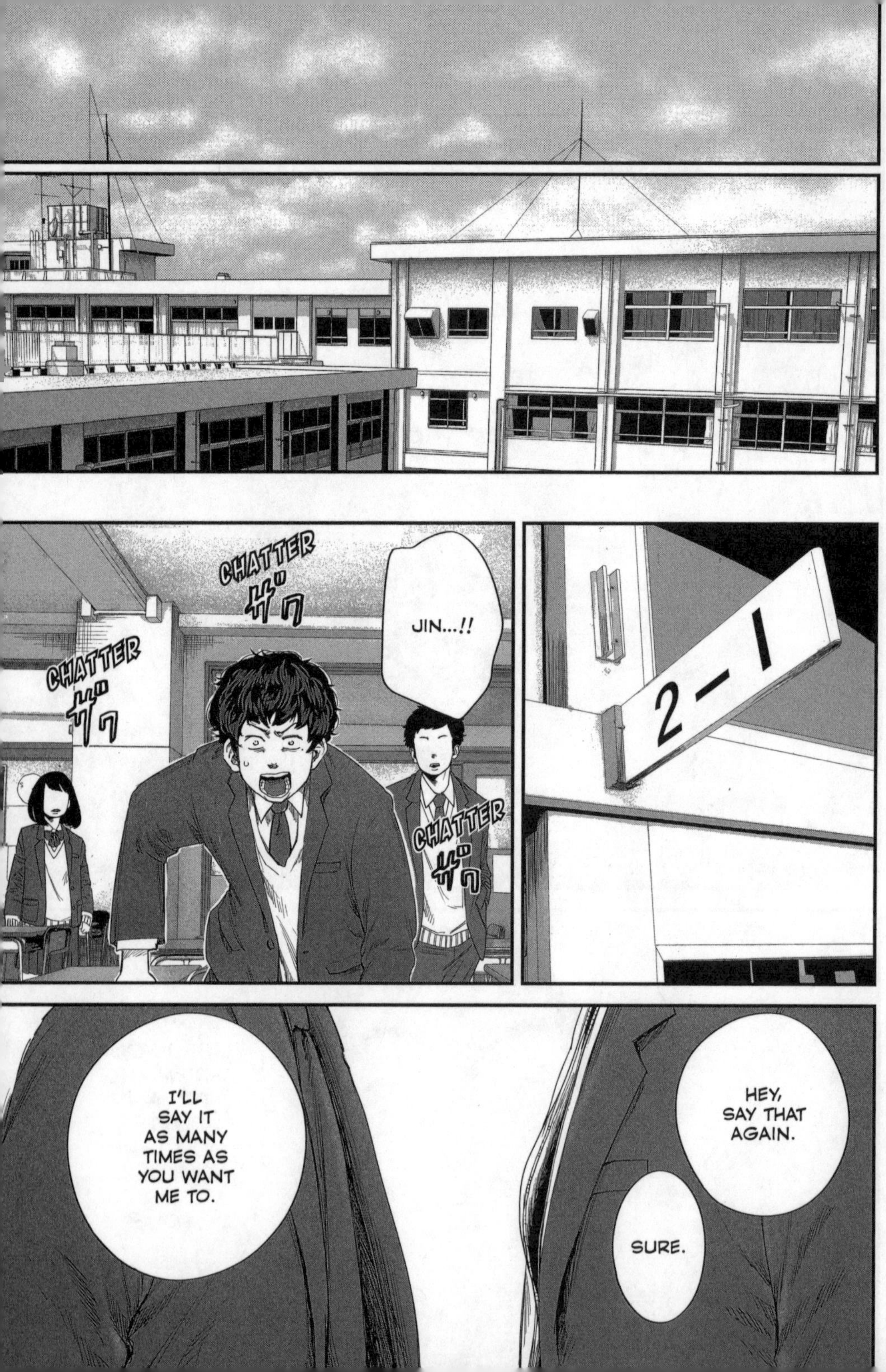
2-1
JIN...!!
CHATTER
ザワ
CHATTER
ザワ
CHATTER
ザワ
HEY, SAY THAT AGAIN.
SURE.
I'LL SAY IT AS MANY TIMES AS YOU WANT ME TO.

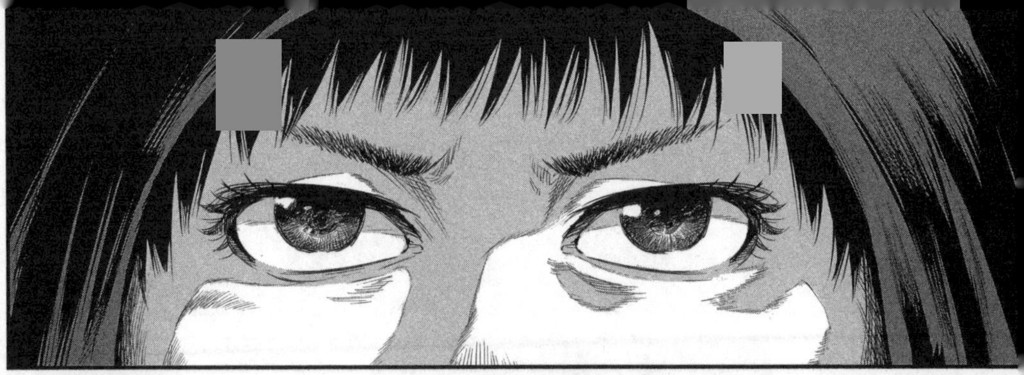

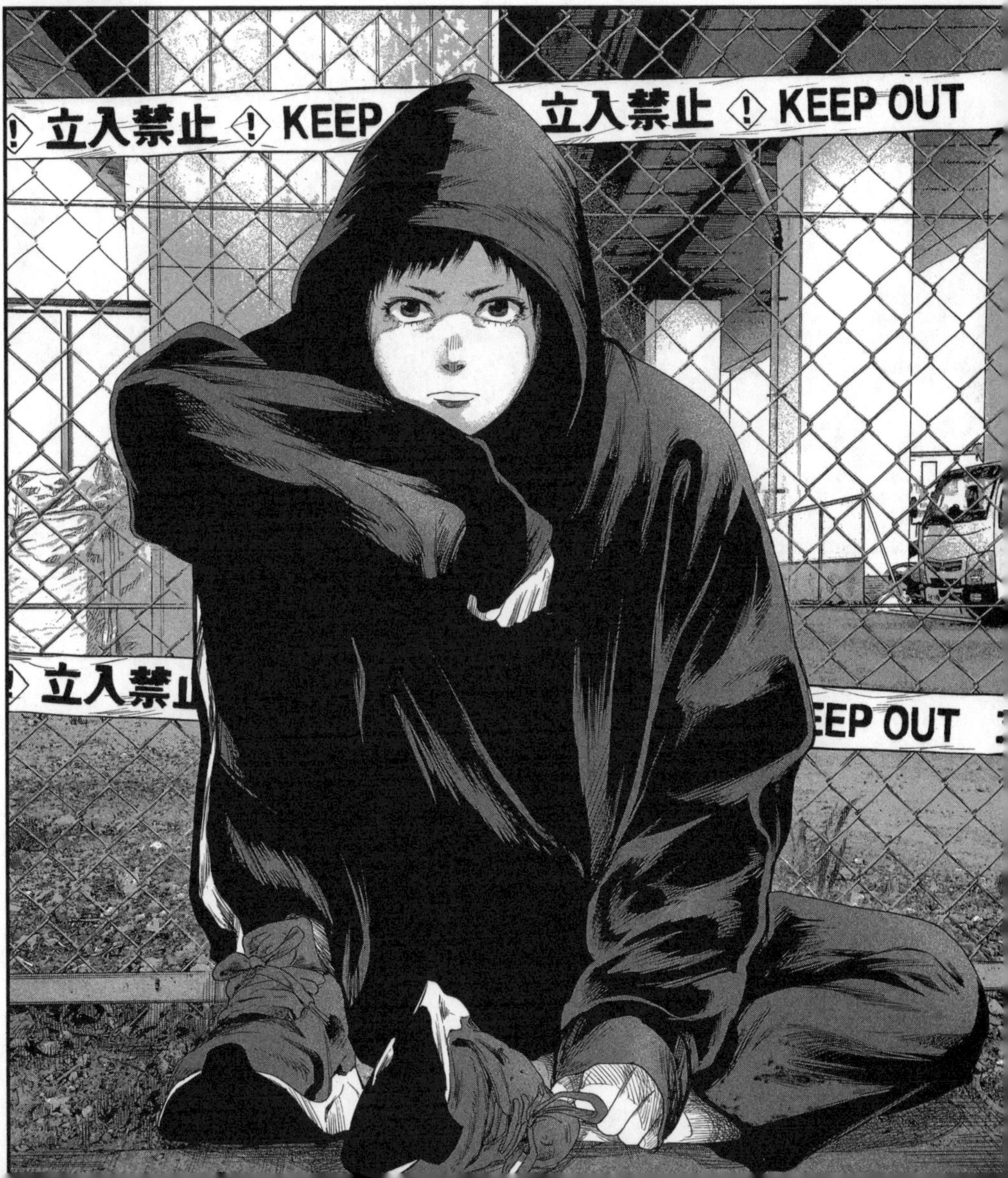
立入禁止
KEEP
立入禁止
KEEP OUT
立入禁止
EEP OUT

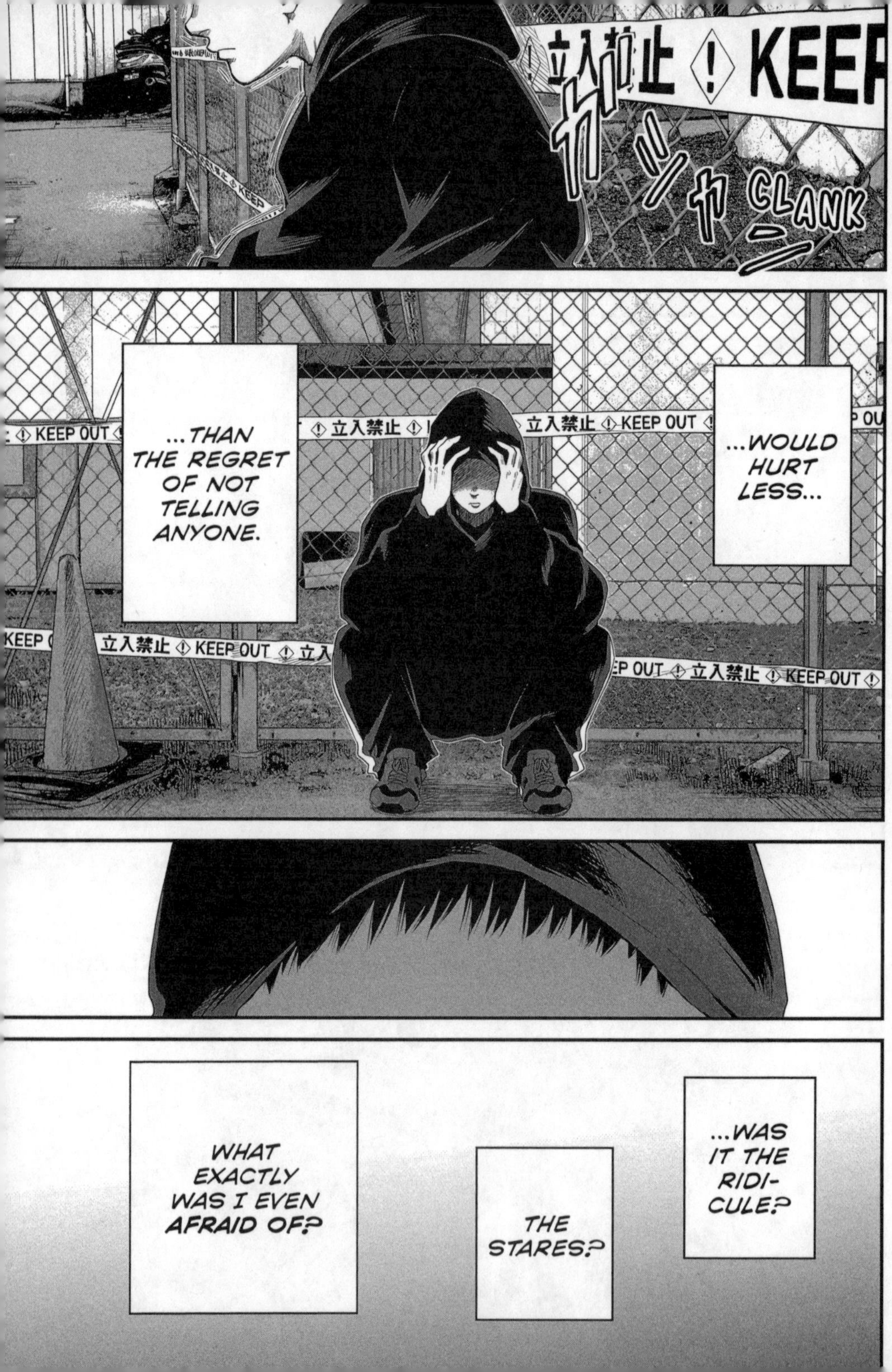
立入禁止 KEEP
CLANK
...WOULD HURT LESS...
...THAN THE REGRET OF NOT TELLING ANYONE.
...WAS IT THE RIDICULE?
THE STARES?
WHAT EXACTLY WAS I EVEN AFRAID OF?

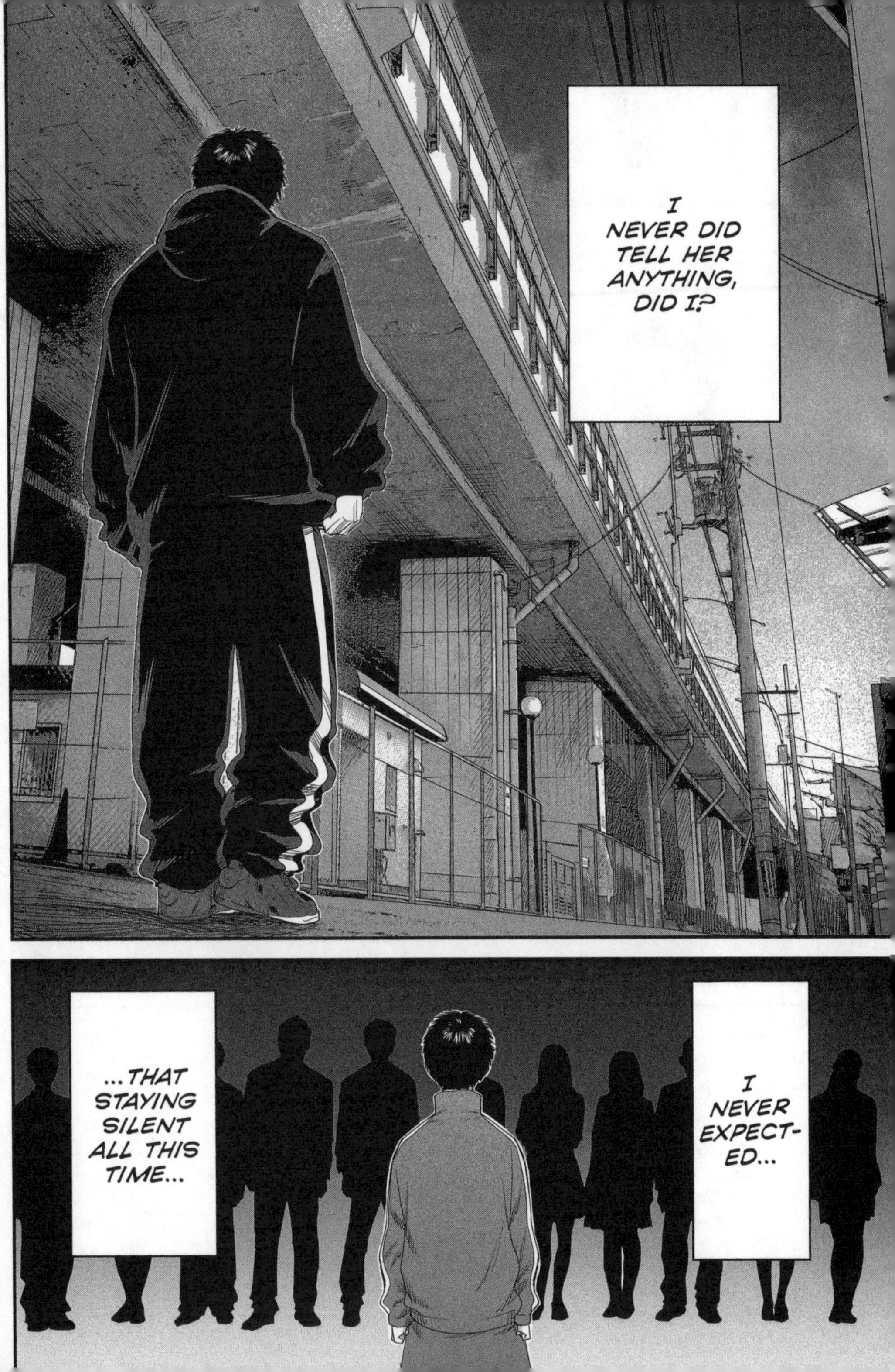
I NEVER DID TELL HER ANYTHING, DID I?
I NEVER EXPECT-ED...
...THAT STAYING SILENT ALL THIS TIME...

...EVEN THOUGH WE WERE ALWAYS SO CLOSE...

...I COULDN'T TELL HER A SINGLE THING.

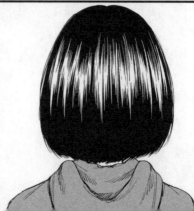

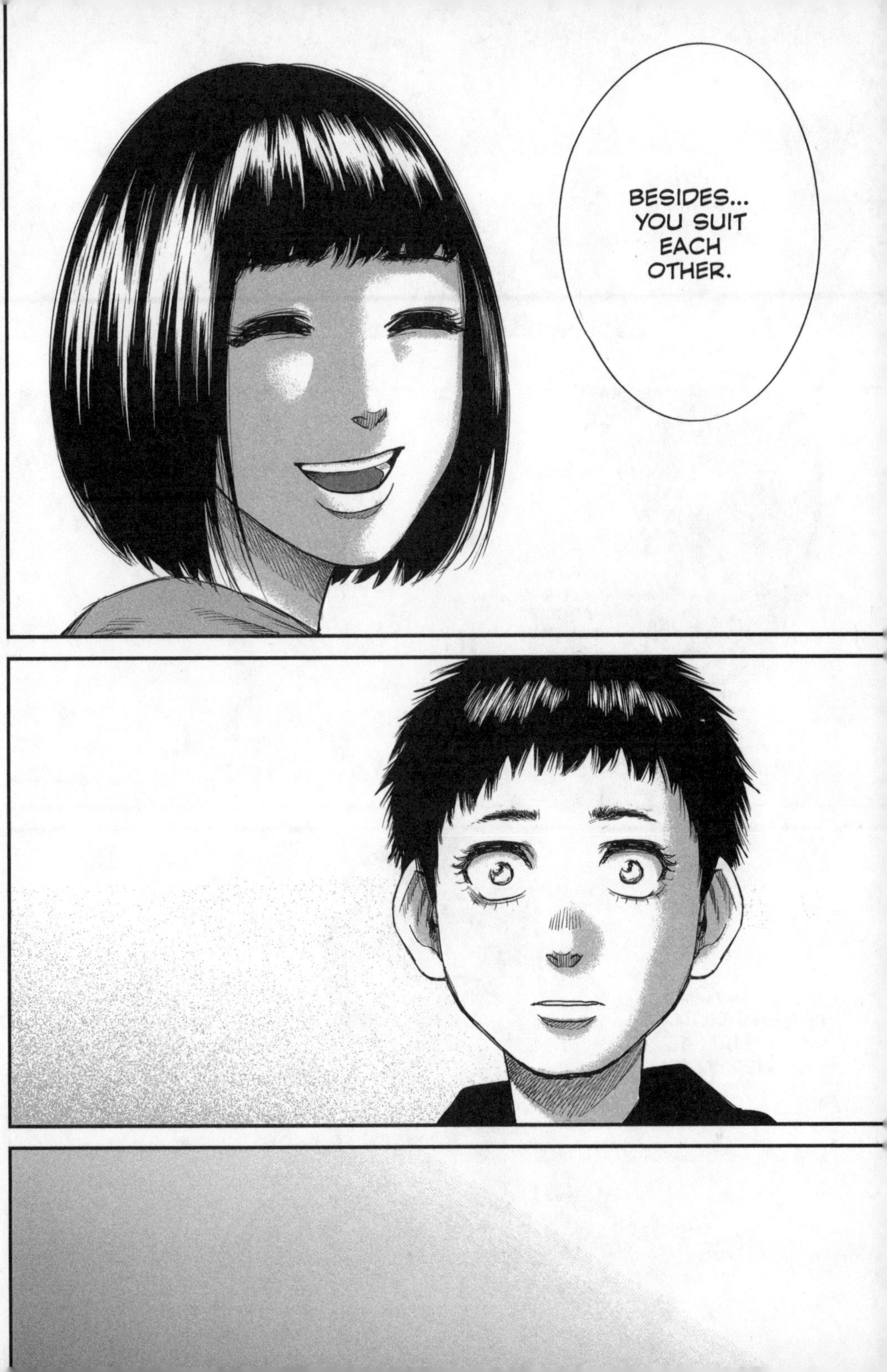
BESIDES... YOU SUIT EACH OTHER.

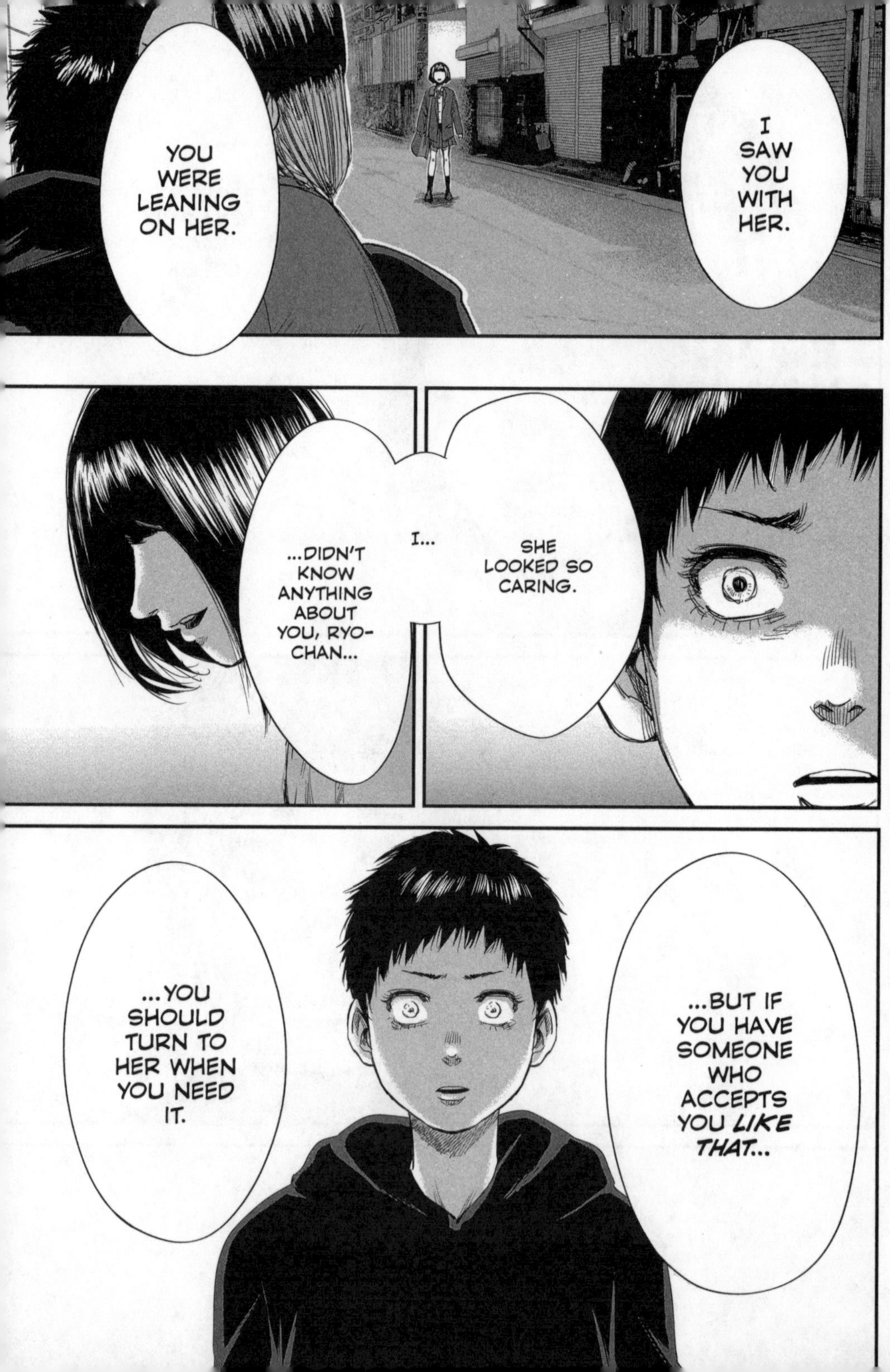
I SAW YOU WITH HER.
YOU WERE LEANING ON HER.
SHE LOOKED SO CARING.
I...
...DIDN'T KNOW ANYTHING ABOUT YOU, RYO-CHAN...
...BUT IF YOU HAVE SOMEONE WHO ACCEPTS YOU *LIKE THAT*...
...YOU SHOULD TURN TO HER WHEN YOU NEED IT.

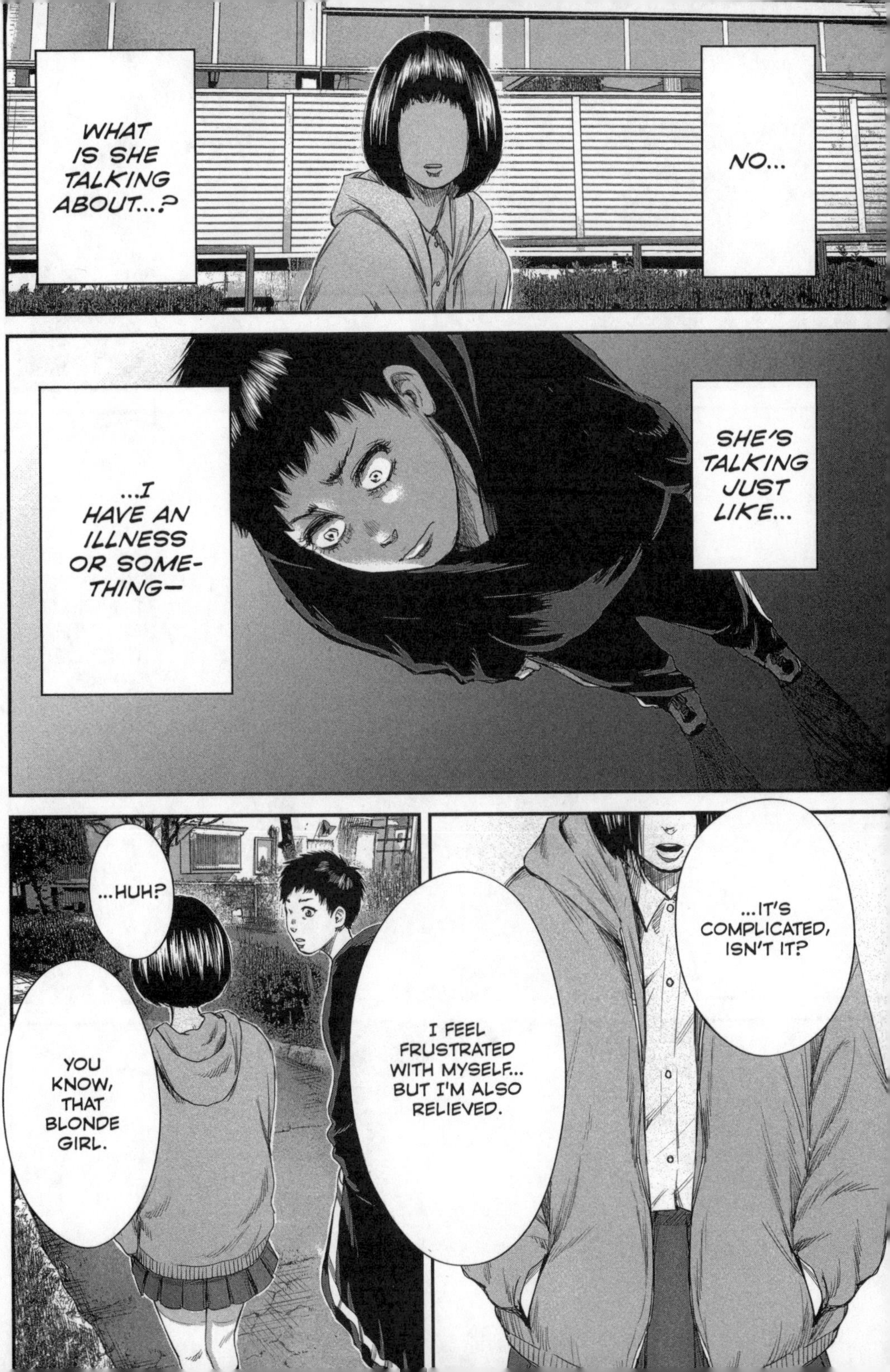
NO...
WHAT IS SHE TALKING ABOUT...?
SHE'S TALKING JUST LIKE...
...I HAVE AN ILLNESS OR SOME-THING—
...IT'S COMPLICATED, ISN'T IT?
I FEEL FRUSTRATED WITH MYSELF... BUT I'M ALSO RELIEVED.
...HUH?
YOU KNOW, THAT BLONDE GIRL.

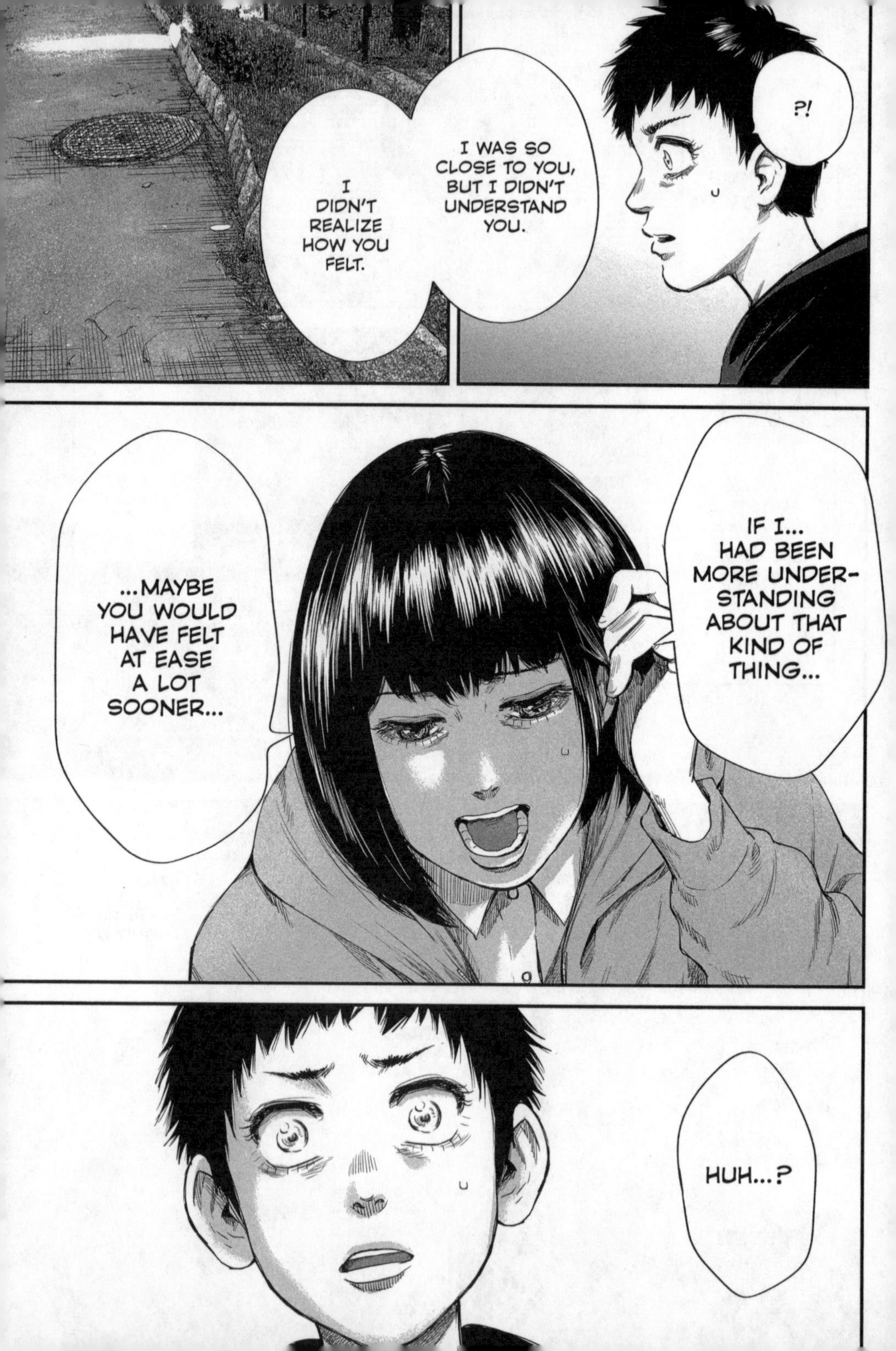
?!
I WAS SO CLOSE TO YOU, BUT I DIDN'T UNDERSTAND YOU.
I DIDN'T REALIZE HOW YOU FELT.
IF I... HAD BEEN MORE UNDER-STANDING ABOUT THAT KIND OF THING...
...MAYBE YOU WOULD HAVE FELT AT EASE A LOT SOONER...
HUH...?

NOT ONCE.

...YOU'VE NEVER TURNED TO ME FOR HELP, RYO-CHAN.

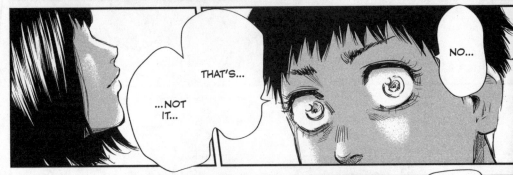

THAT'S...

...NOT IT...

NO...

WHOOSH

I'M SORRY!!!

CHIKA...

...I DIDN'T TELL YOU BECAUSE—

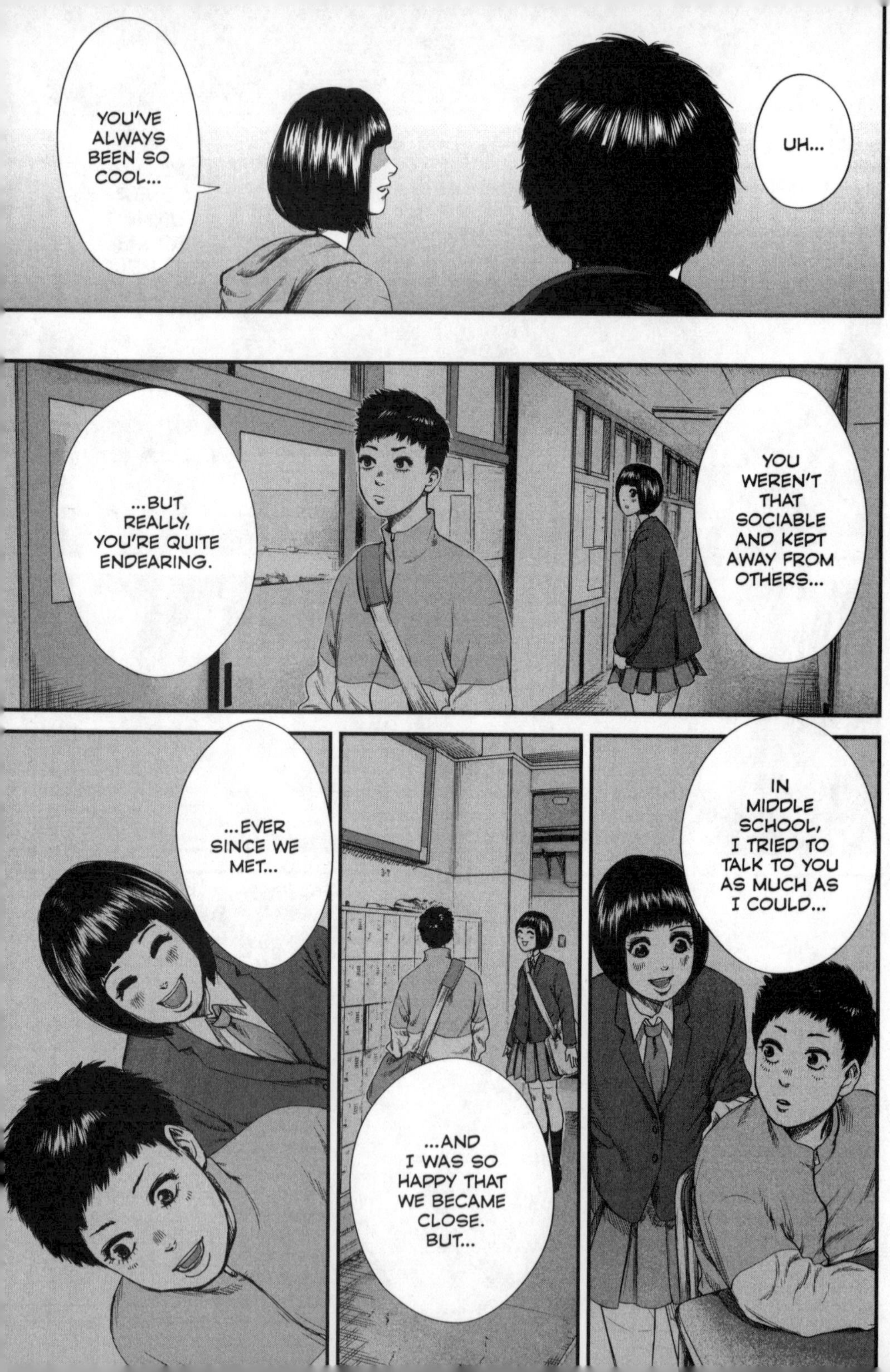
UH...
YOU'VE ALWAYS BEEN SO COOL...
YOU WEREN'T THAT SOCIABLE AND KEPT AWAY FROM OTHERS...
...BUT REALLY, YOU'RE QUITE ENDEARING.
IN MIDDLE SCHOOL, I TRIED TO TALK TO YOU AS MUCH AS I COULD...
...AND I WAS SO HAPPY THAT WE BECAME CLOSE. BUT...
...EVER SINCE WE MET...

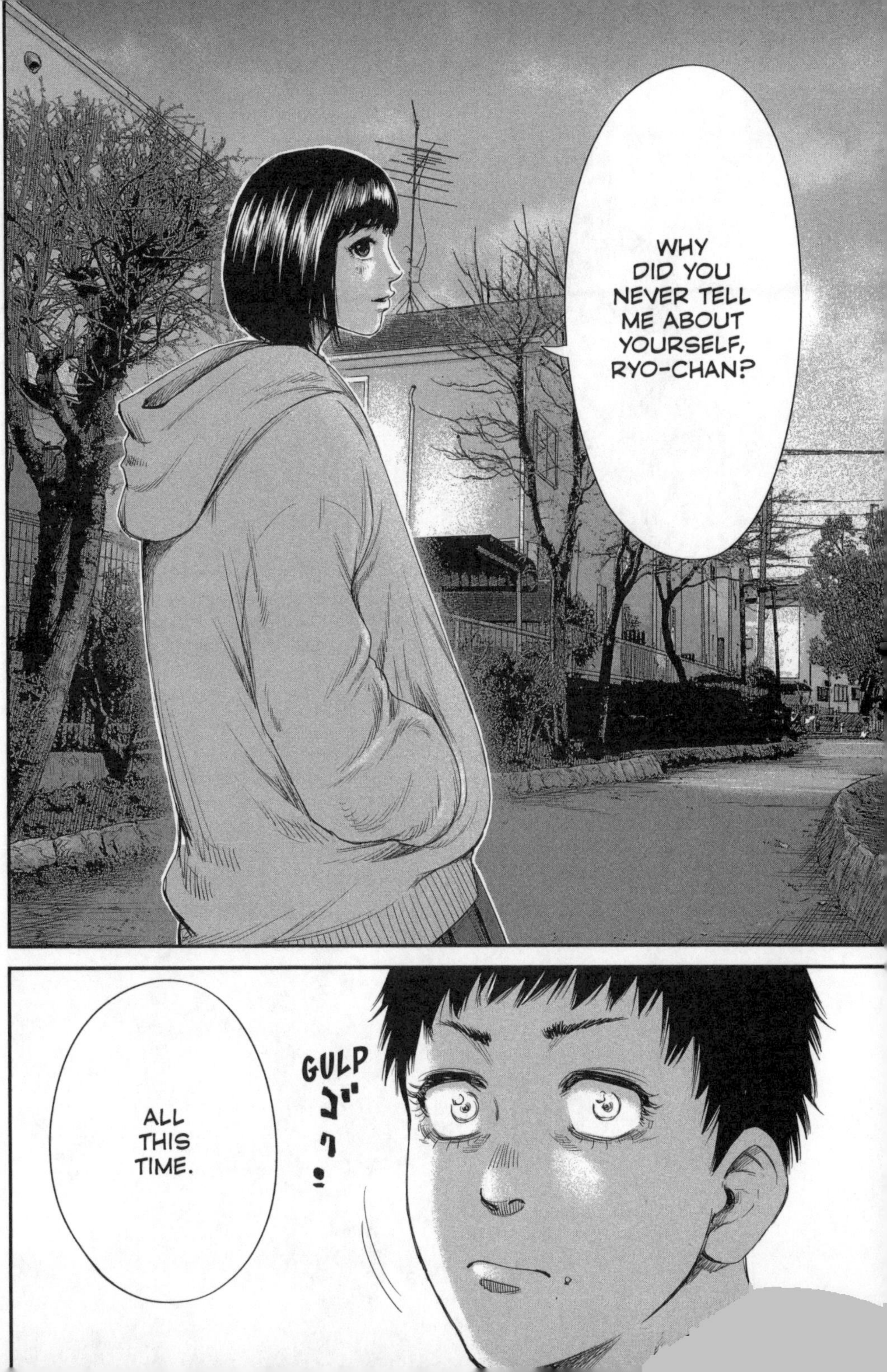
WHY DID YOU NEVER TELL ME ABOUT YOURSELF, RYO-CHAN?
GULP
ゴク
ALL THIS TIME.

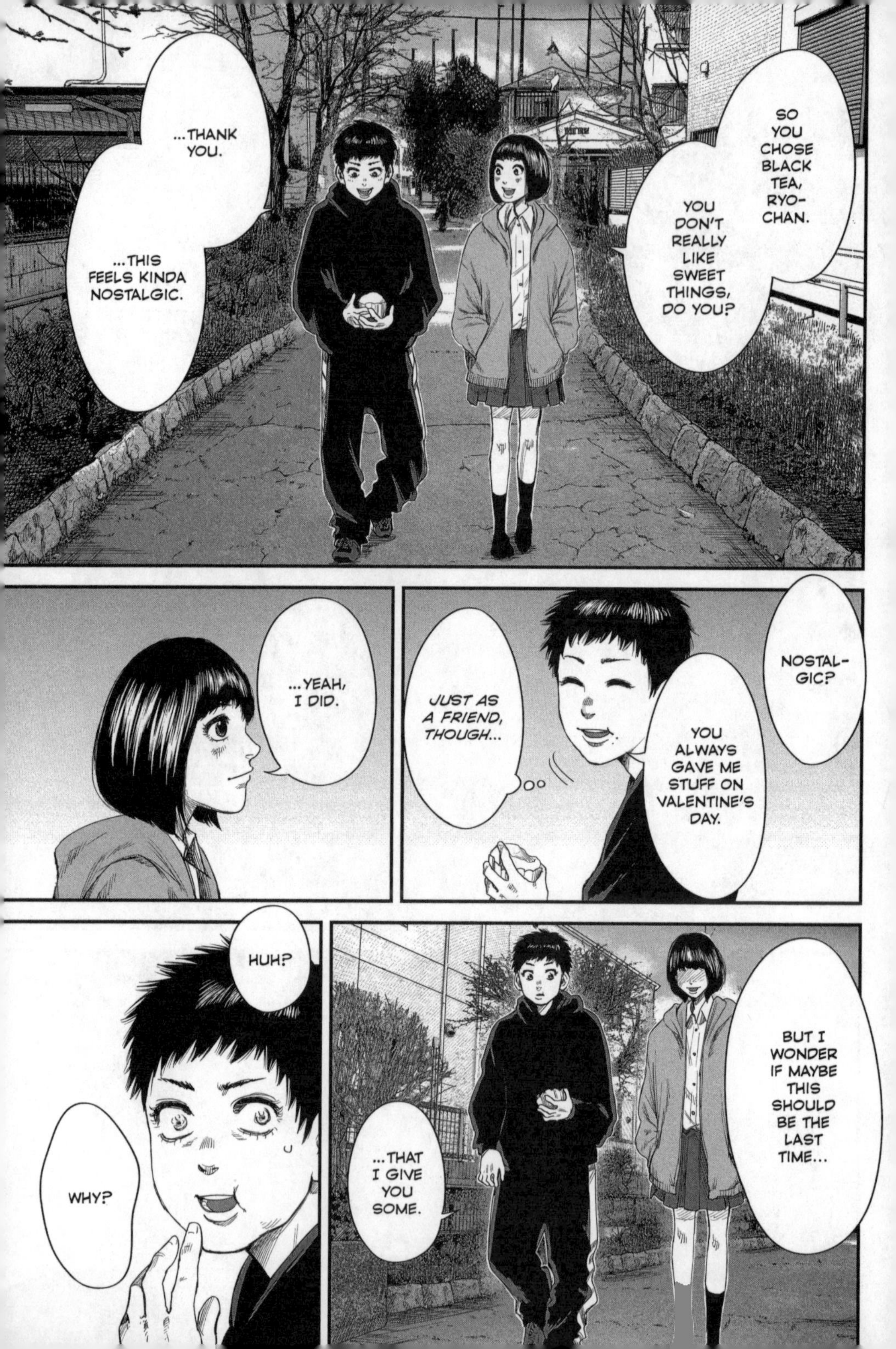
SO YOU CHOSE BLACK TEA, RYO-CHAN.
YOU DON'T REALLY LIKE SWEET THINGS, DO YOU?
...THANK YOU.
...THIS FEELS KINDA NOSTALGIC.
NOSTAL-GIC?
YOU ALWAYS GAVE ME STUFF ON VALENTINE'S DAY.
JUST AS A FRIEND, THOUGH...
...YEAH, I DID.
BUT I WONDER IF MAYBE THIS SHOULD BE THE LAST TIME...
...THAT I GIVE YOU SOME.
HUH?
WHY?

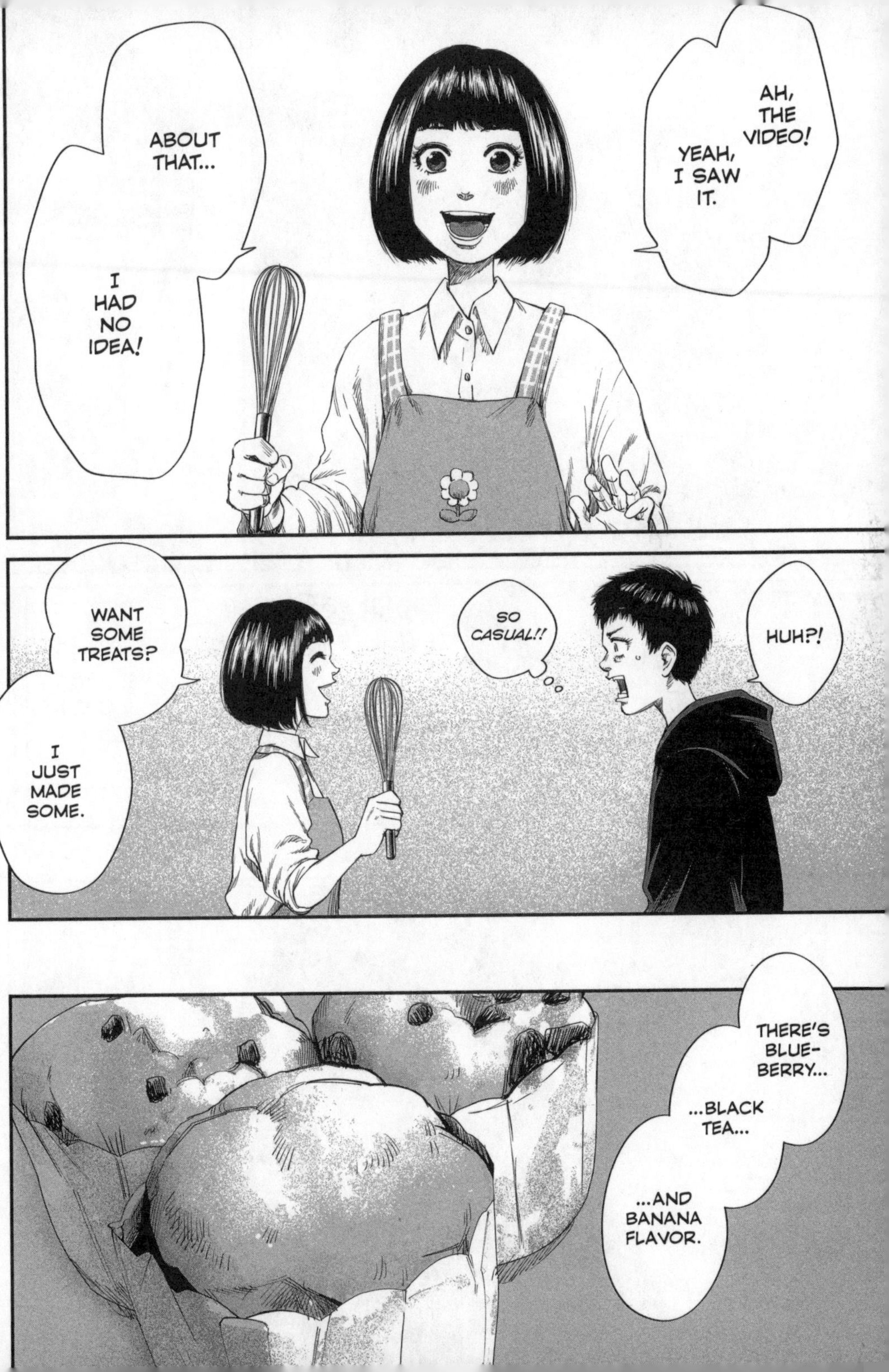
AH, THE VIDEO!
YEAH, I SAW IT.
ABOUT THAT...
I HAD NO IDEA!
HUH?!
SO CASUAL!!
WANT SOME TREATS?
I JUST MADE SOME.
THERE'S BLUE-BERRY...
...BLACK TEA...
...AND BANANA FLAVOR.

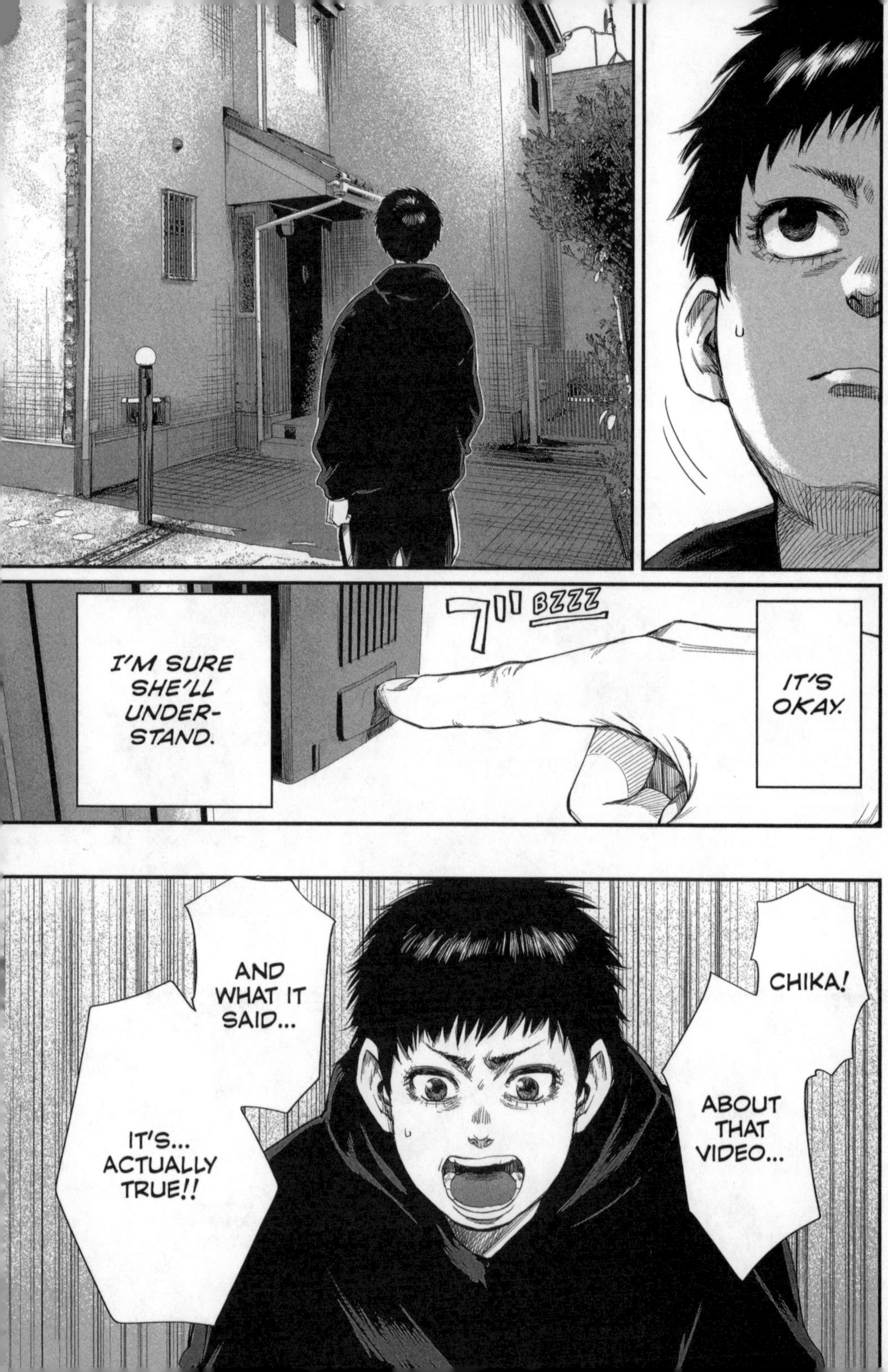
IT'S OKAY.
BZZZ
I'M SURE SHE'LL UNDER-STAND.
CHIKA!
ABOUT THAT VIDEO...
AND WHAT IT SAID...
IT'S... ACTUALLY TRUE!!

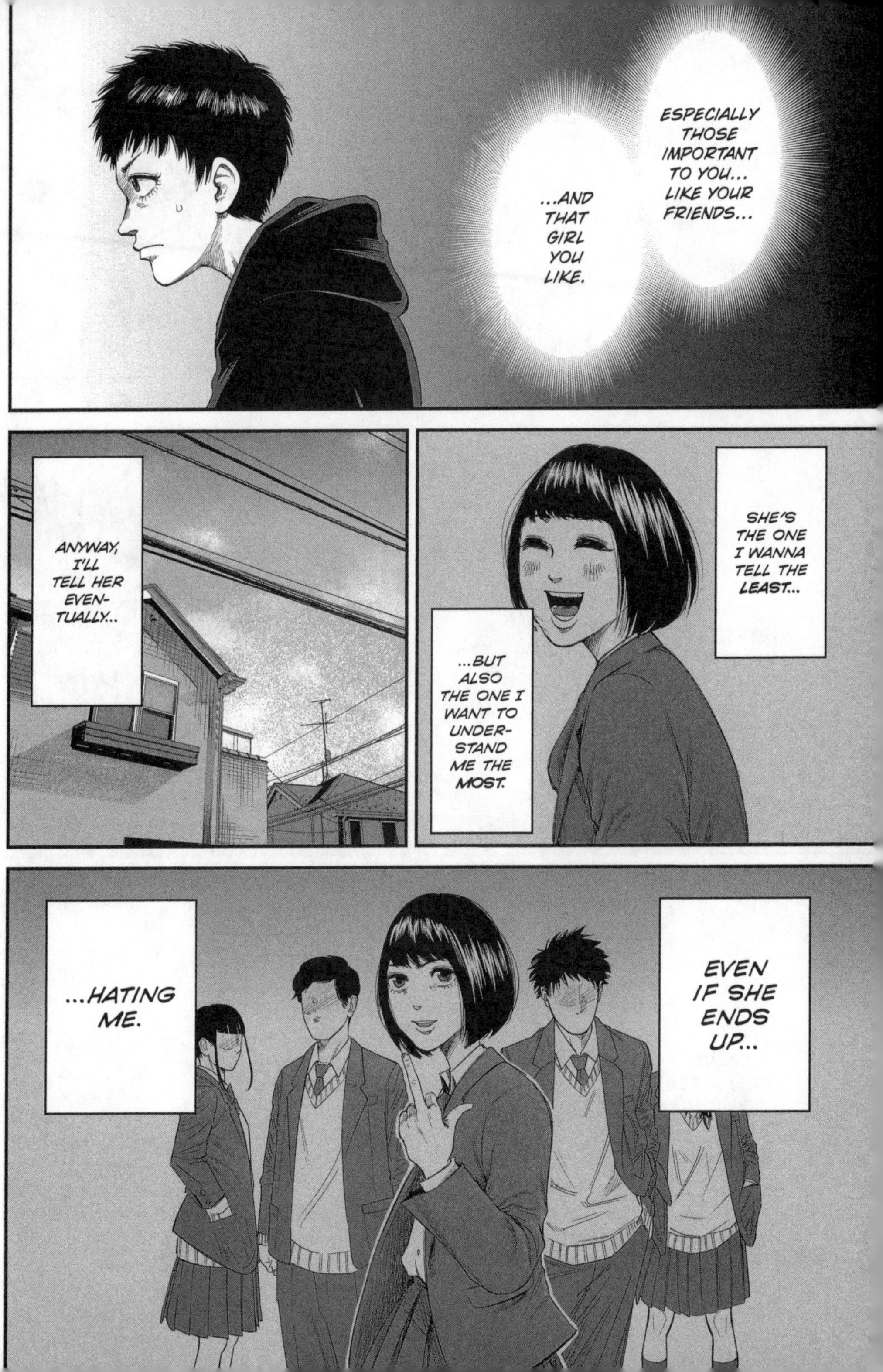
ESPECIALLY THOSE IMPORTANT TO YOU... LIKE YOUR FRIENDS...
...AND THAT GIRL YOU LIKE.
SHE'S THE ONE I WANNA TELL THE **LEAST**...
...BUT ALSO THE ONE I WANT TO UNDER-STAND ME THE **MOST**.
ANYWAY, I'LL TELL HER EVEN-TUALLY...
EVEN IF SHE ENDS UP...
...HATING ME.

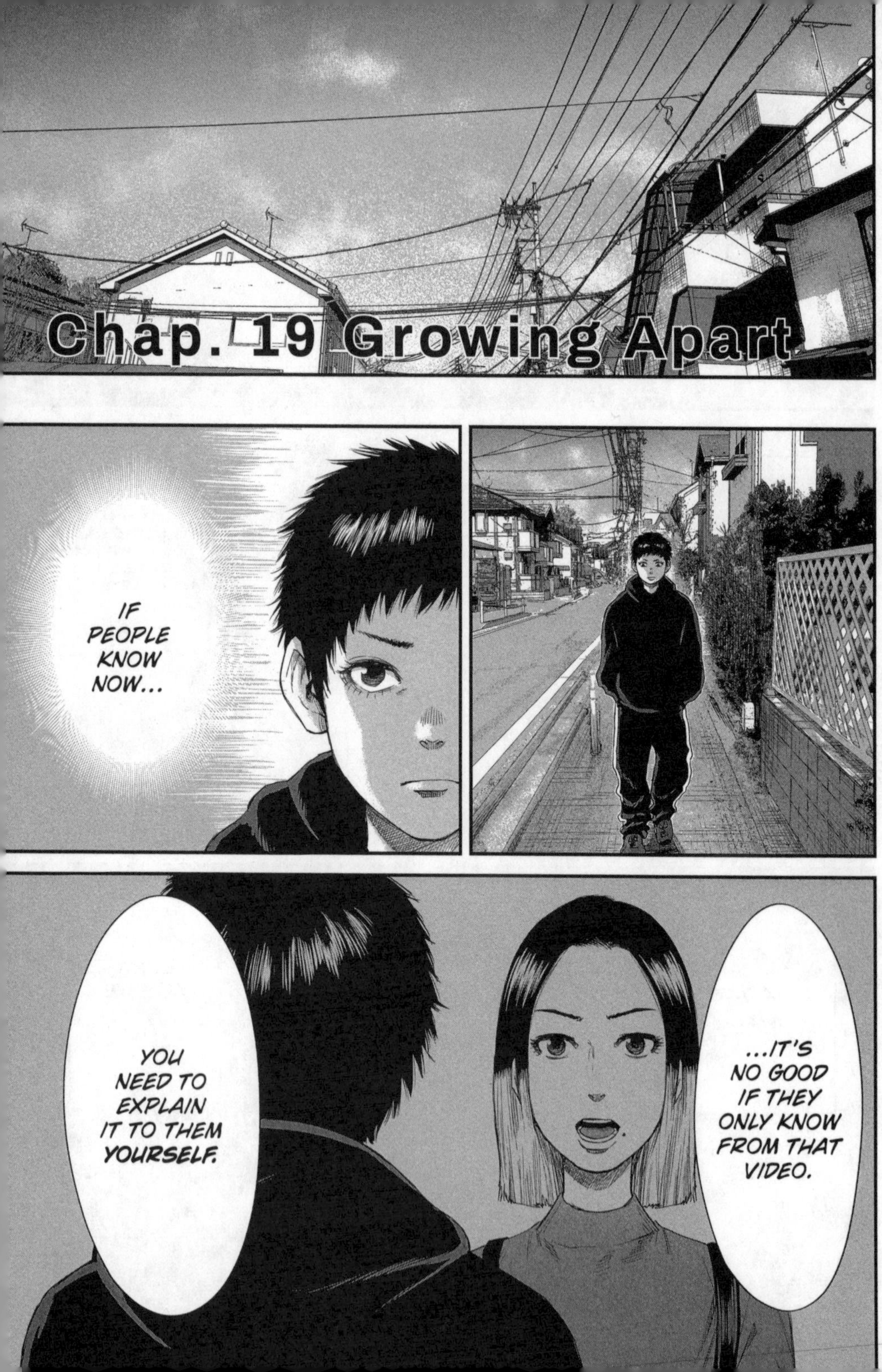
Chap. 19 Growing Apart
IF PEOPLE KNOW NOW...
...IT'S NO GOOD IF THEY ONLY KNOW FROM THAT VIDEO.
YOU NEED TO EXPLAIN IT TO THEM YOURSELF.

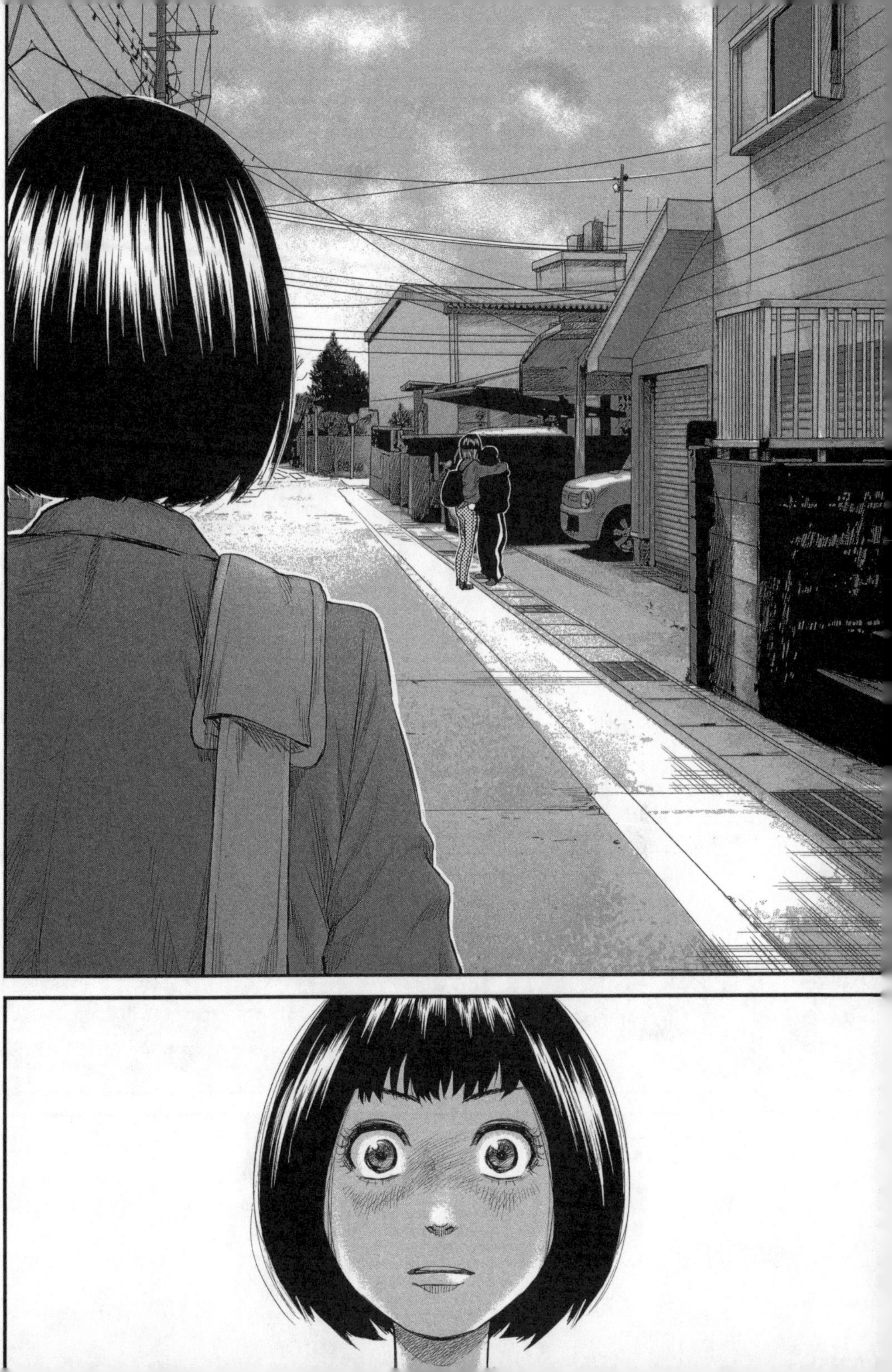

YOU'RE NOT WEIRD.

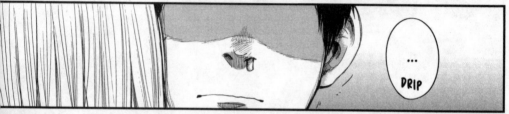

... DRIP

HEY, DON'T GET YOUR SNOT ON ME.

SNIFF

SNIFF

SOB

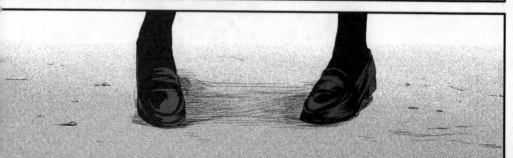

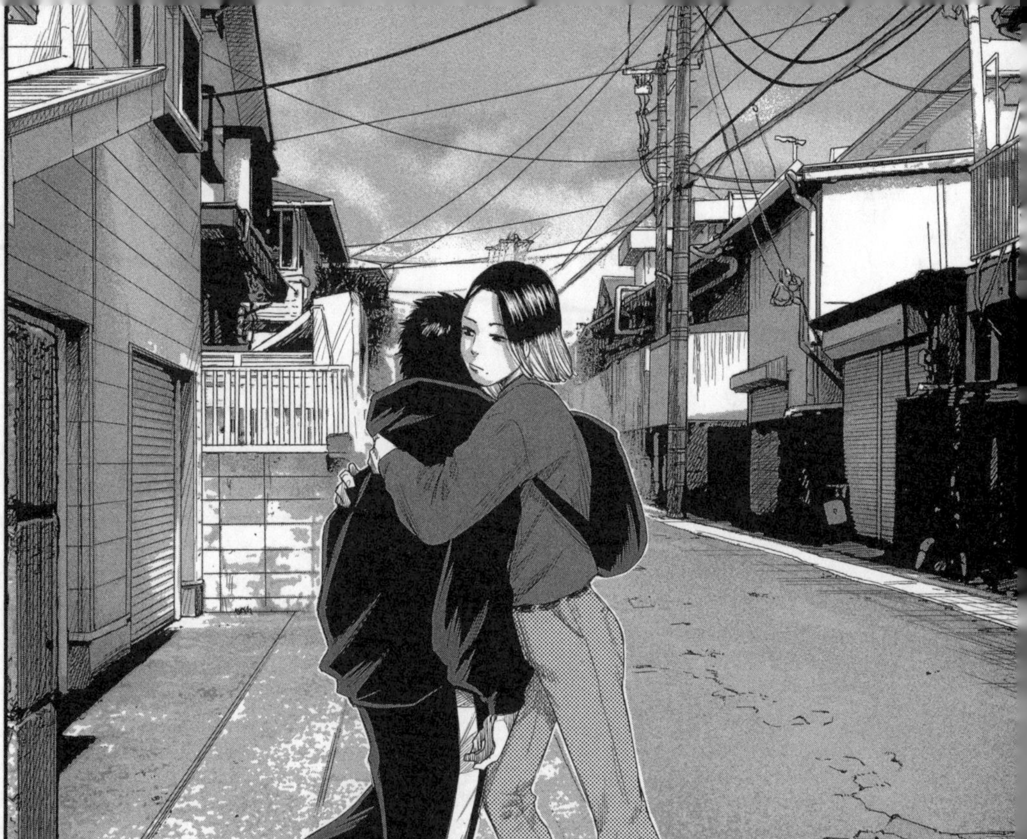

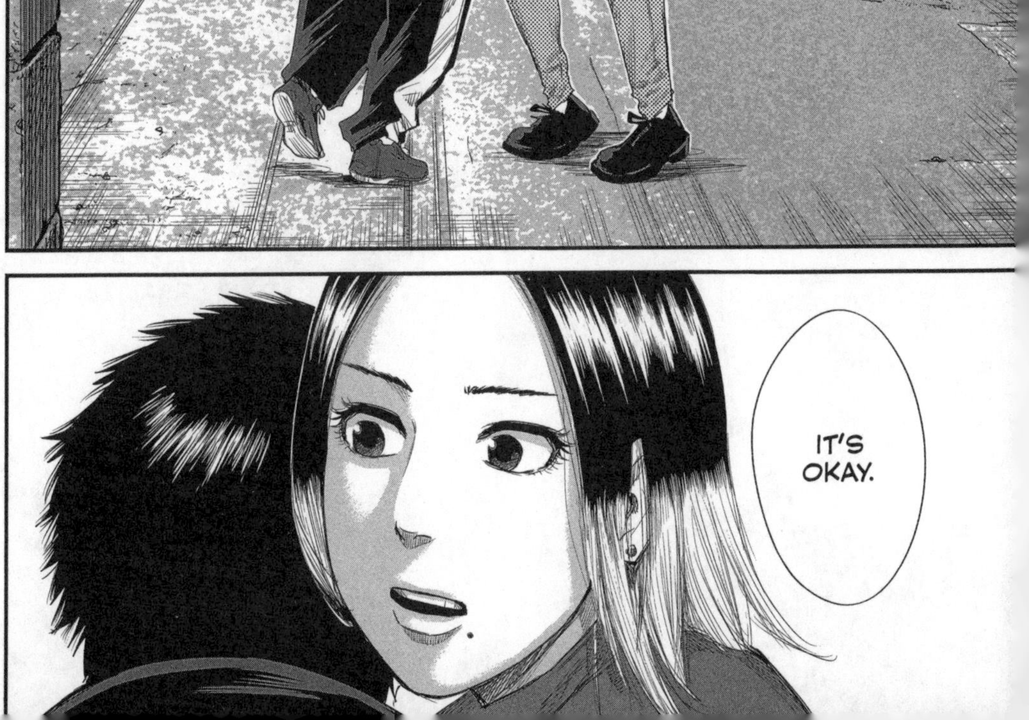
IT'S OKAY.

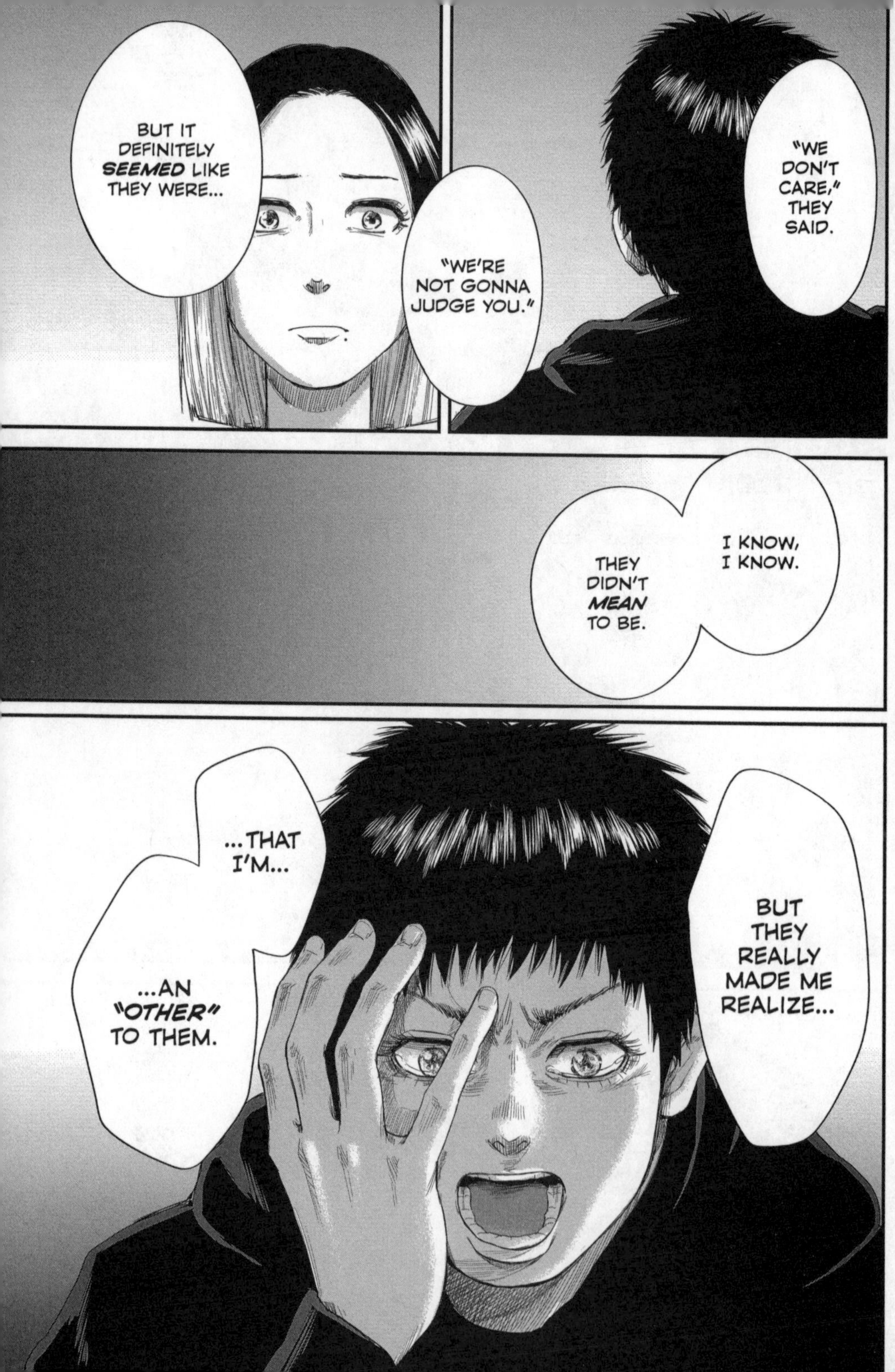
"WE DON'T CARE," THEY SAID.
"WE'RE NOT GONNA JUDGE YOU."
BUT IT DEFINITELY SEEMED LIKE THEY WERE...
I KNOW, I KNOW.
THEY DIDN'T MEAN TO BE.
BUT THEY REALLY MADE ME REALIZE...
...THAT I'M...
...AN "OTHER" TO THEM.

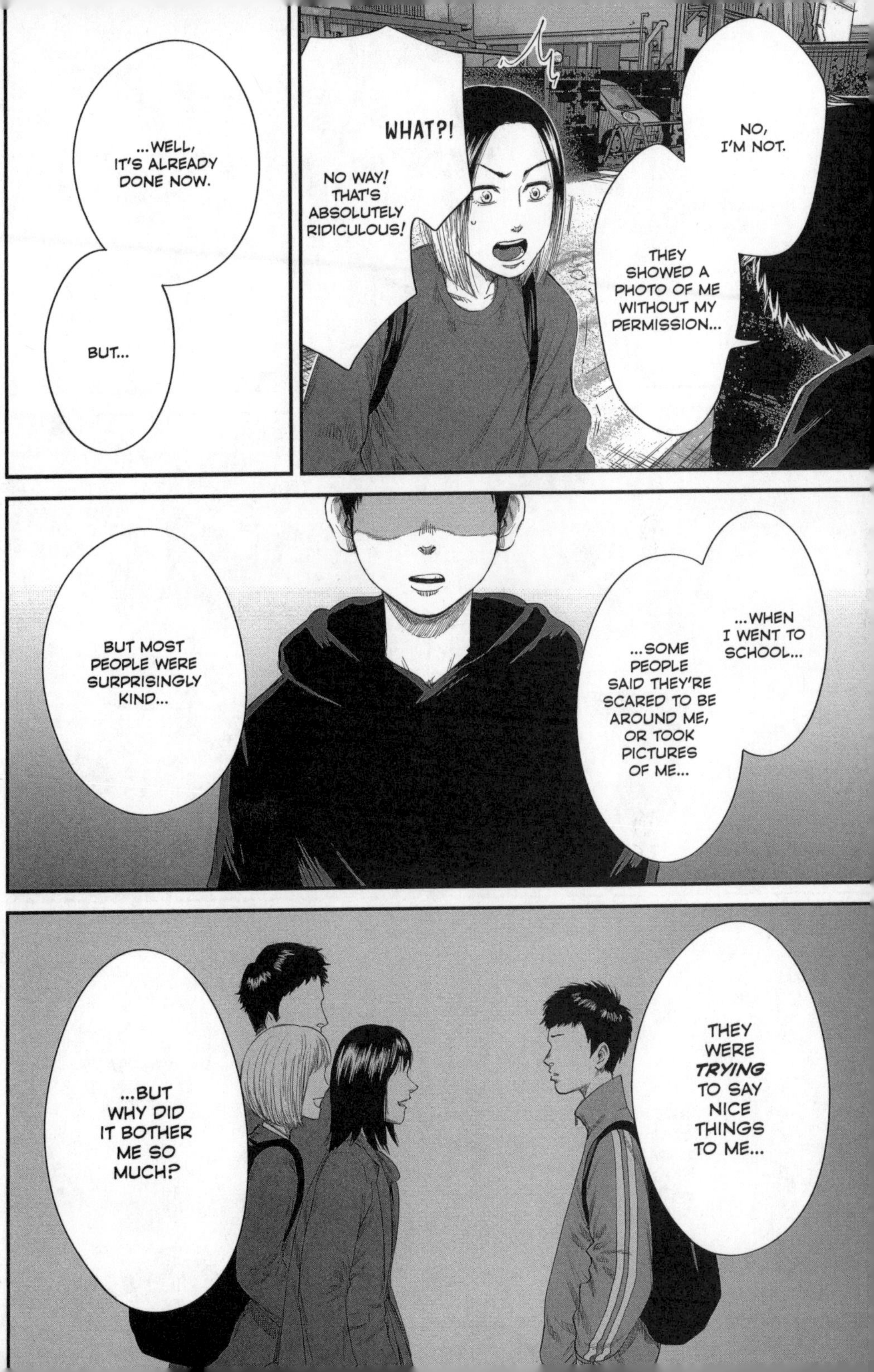
NO, I'M NOT.
THEY SHOWED A PHOTO OF ME WITHOUT MY PERMISSION...
WHAT?!
NO WAY! THAT'S ABSOLUTELY RIDICULOUS!
...WELL, IT'S ALREADY DONE NOW.
BUT...
...WHEN I WENT TO SCHOOL...
...SOME PEOPLE SAID THEY'RE SCARED TO BE AROUND ME, OR TOOK PICTURES OF ME...
BUT MOST PEOPLE WERE SURPRISINGLY KIND...
THEY WERE *TRYING* TO SAY NICE THINGS TO ME...
...BUT WHY DID IT BOTHER ME SO MUCH?

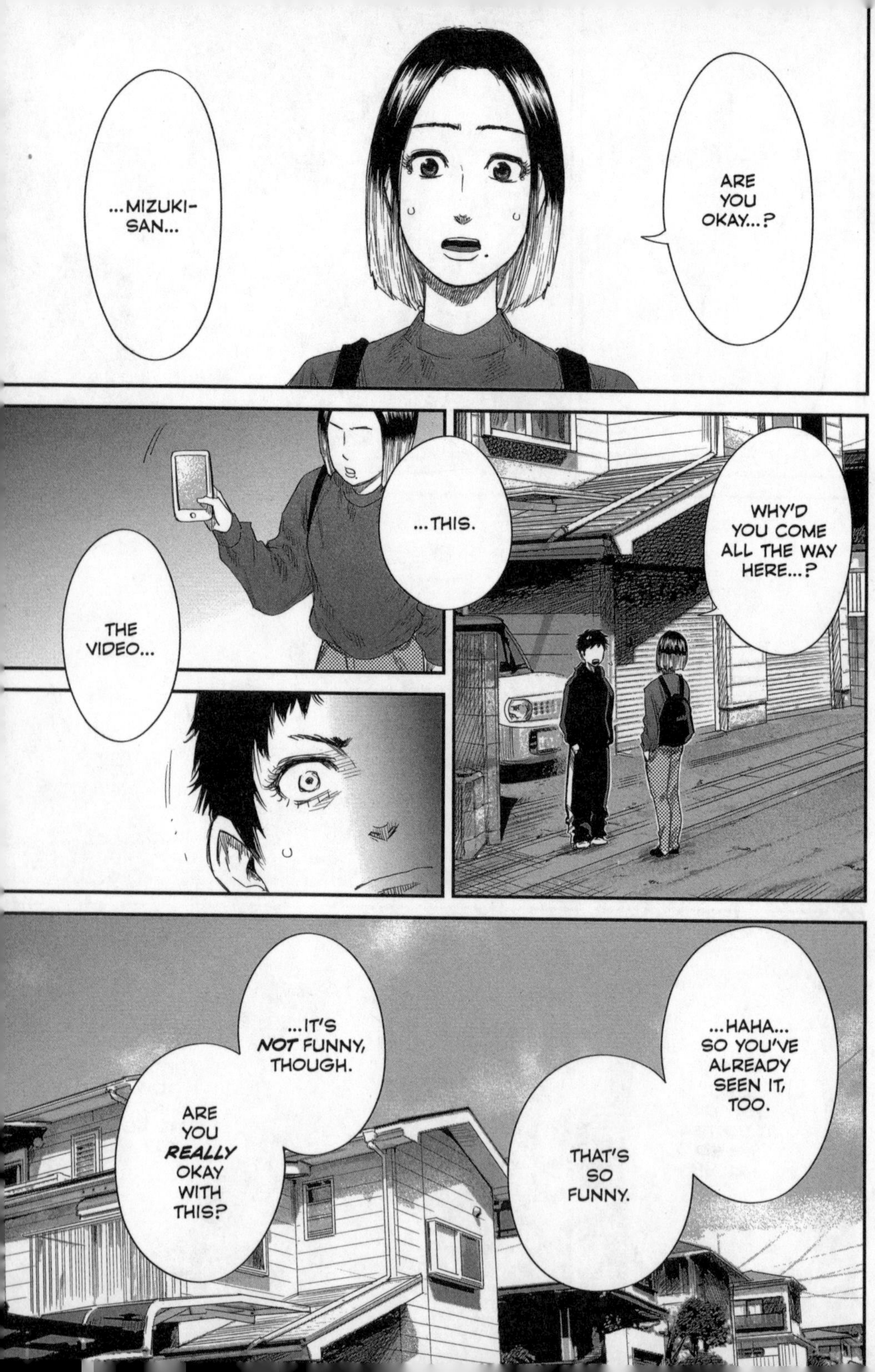
ARE YOU OKAY...?
...MIZUKI-SAN...
WHY'D YOU COME ALL THE WAY HERE...?
...THIS.
THE VIDEO...
...HAHA... SO YOU'VE ALREADY SEEN IT, TOO.
THAT'S SO FUNNY.
...IT'S NOT FUNNY, THOUGH.
ARE YOU REALLY OKAY WITH THIS?

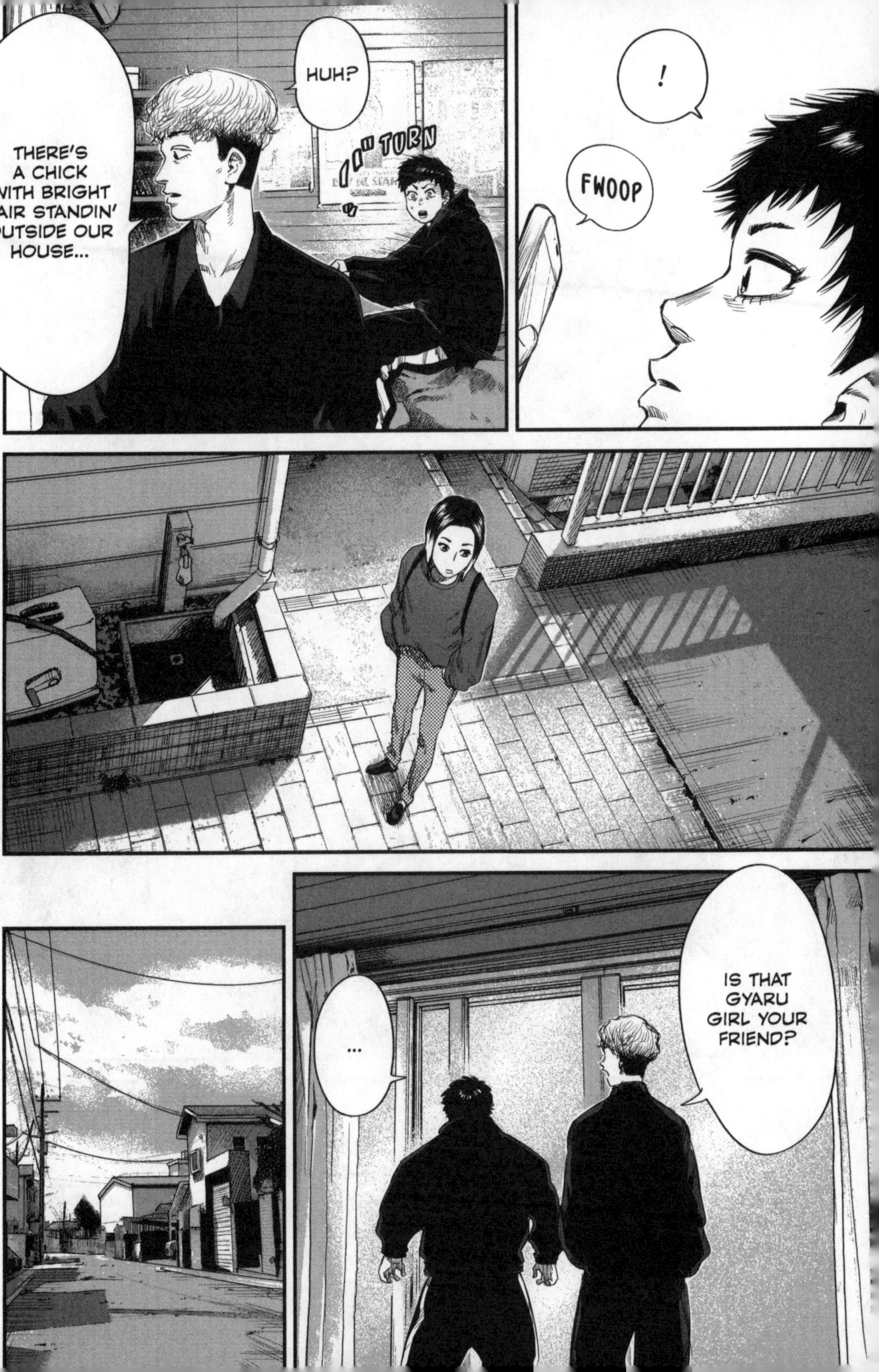
!
FWOOP
HUH?
TURN
THERE'S A CHICK WITH BRIGHT HAIR STANDIN' OUTSIDE OUR HOUSE...
IS THAT GYARU GIRL YOUR FRIEND?
...

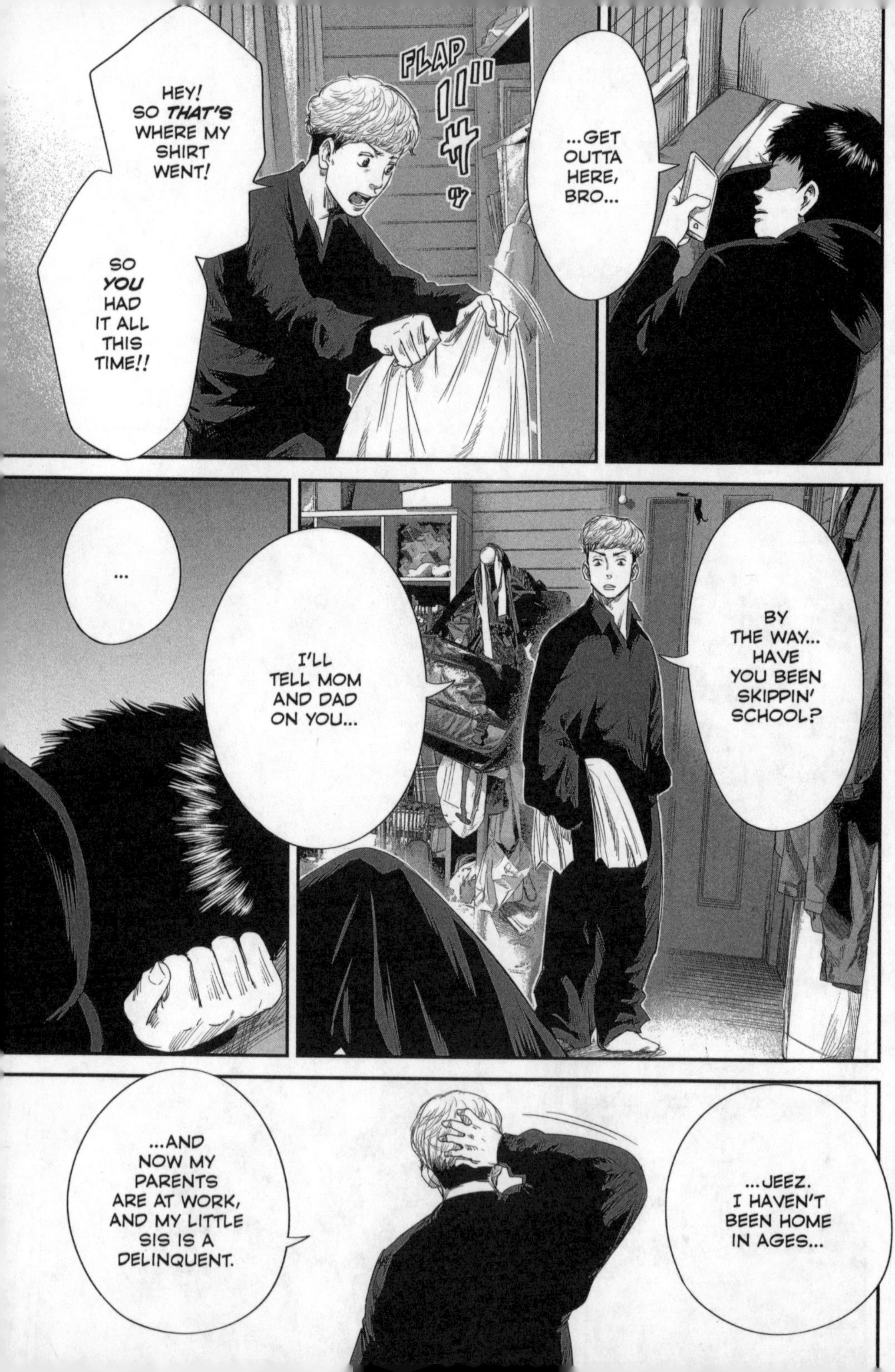
...GET OUTTA HERE, BRO...
FLAP
ガッ
HEY! SO *THAT'S* WHERE MY SHIRT WENT!
SO *YOU* HAD IT ALL THIS TIME!!
BY THE WAY... HAVE YOU BEEN SKIPPIN' SCHOOL?
I'LL TELL MOM AND DAD ON YOU...
...
...JEEZ. I HAVEN'T BEEN HOME IN AGES...
...AND NOW MY PARENTS ARE AT WORK, AND MY LITTLE SIS IS A DELINQUENT.

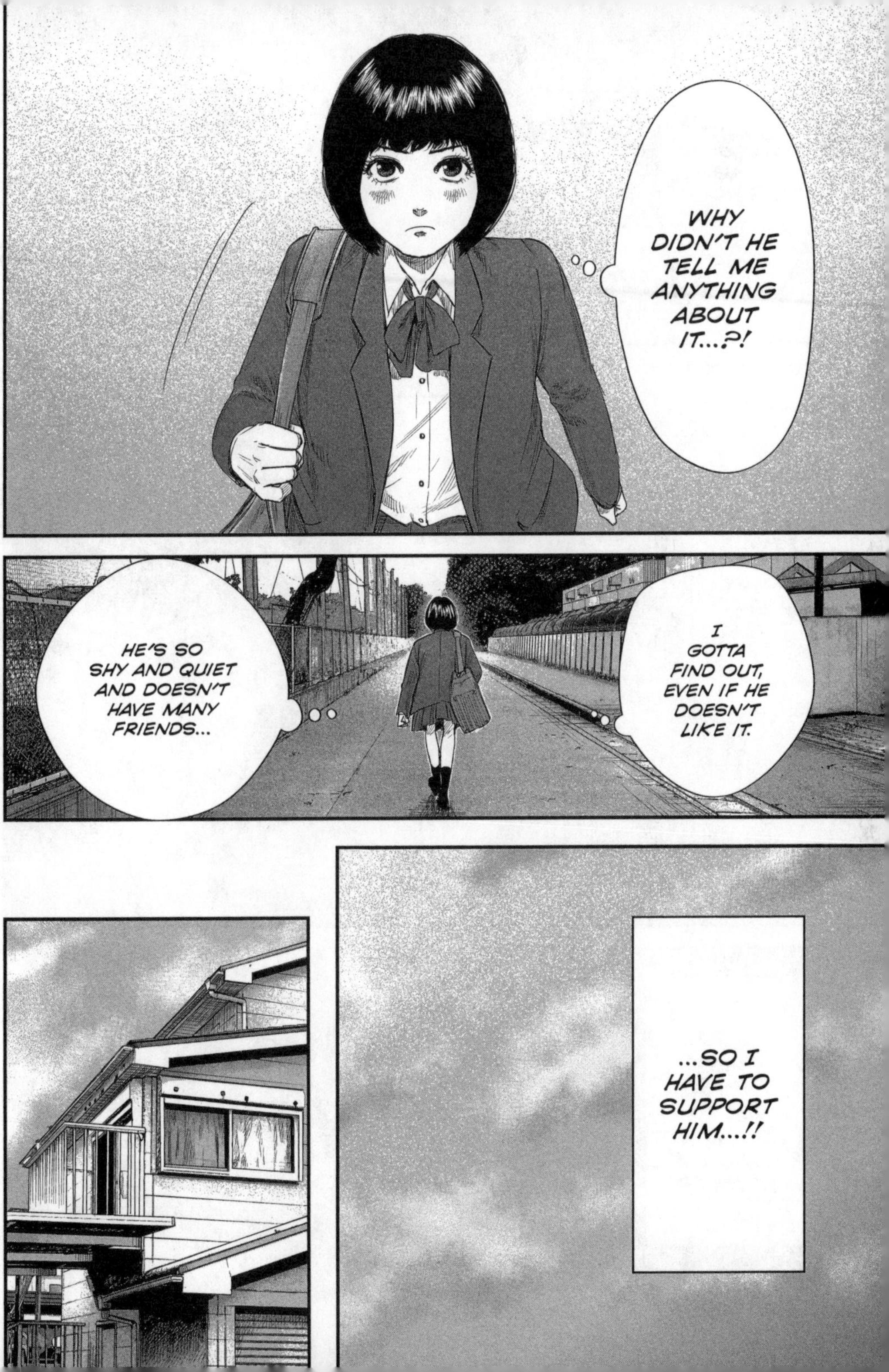
WHY DIDN'T HE TELL ME ANYTHING ABOUT IT...?!
I GOTTA FIND OUT, EVEN IF HE DOESN'T LIKE IT.
HE'S SO SHY AND QUIET AND DOESN'T HAVE MANY FRIENDS...
...SO I HAVE TO SUPPORT HIM...!!

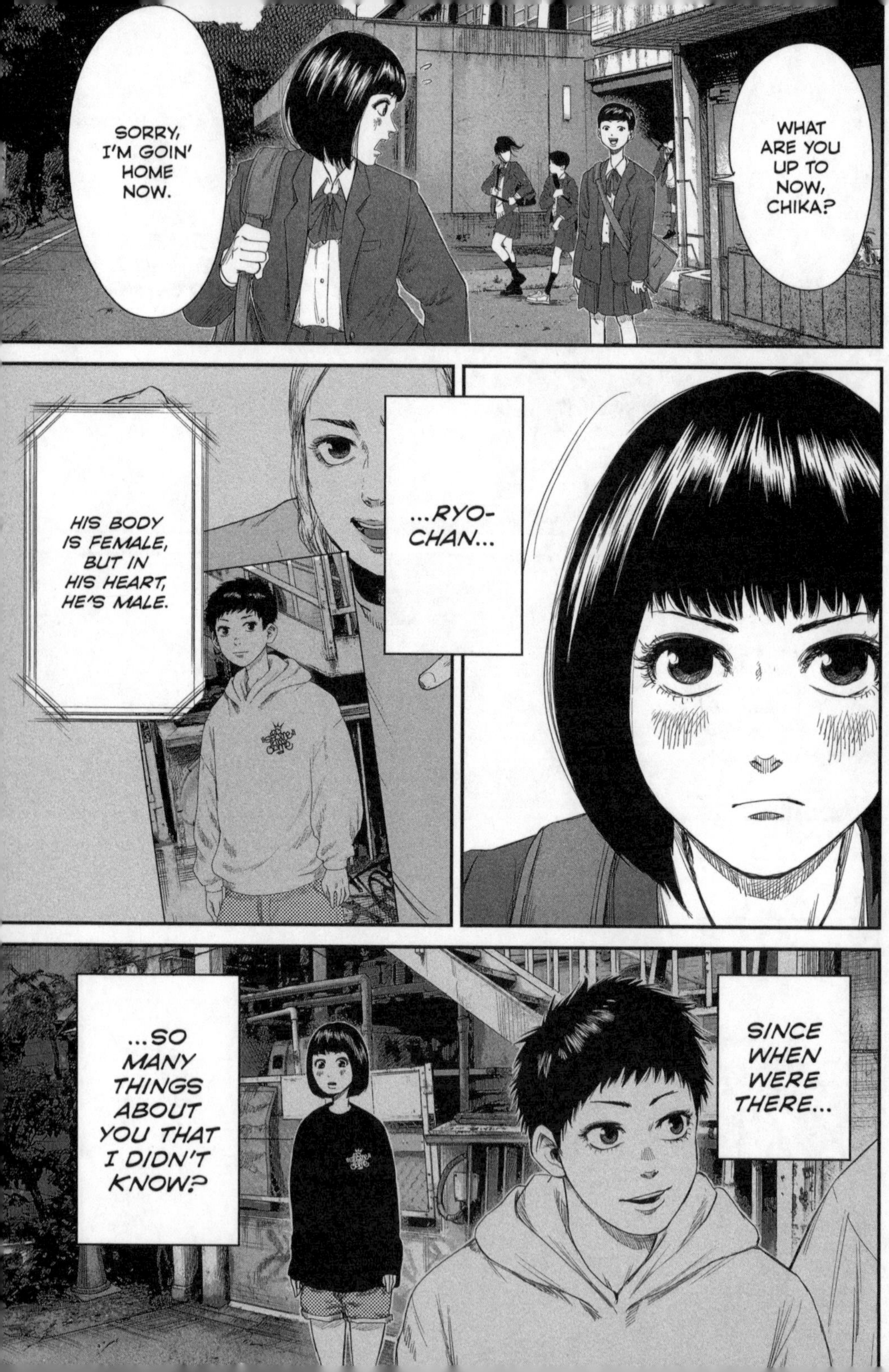
WHAT ARE YOU UP TO NOW, CHIKA?
SORRY, I'M GOIN' HOME NOW.
...RYO-CHAN...
HIS BODY IS FEMALE, BUT IN HIS HEART, HE'S MALE.
SINCE WHEN WERE THERE...
...SO MANY THINGS ABOUT YOU THAT I DIDN'T KNOW?

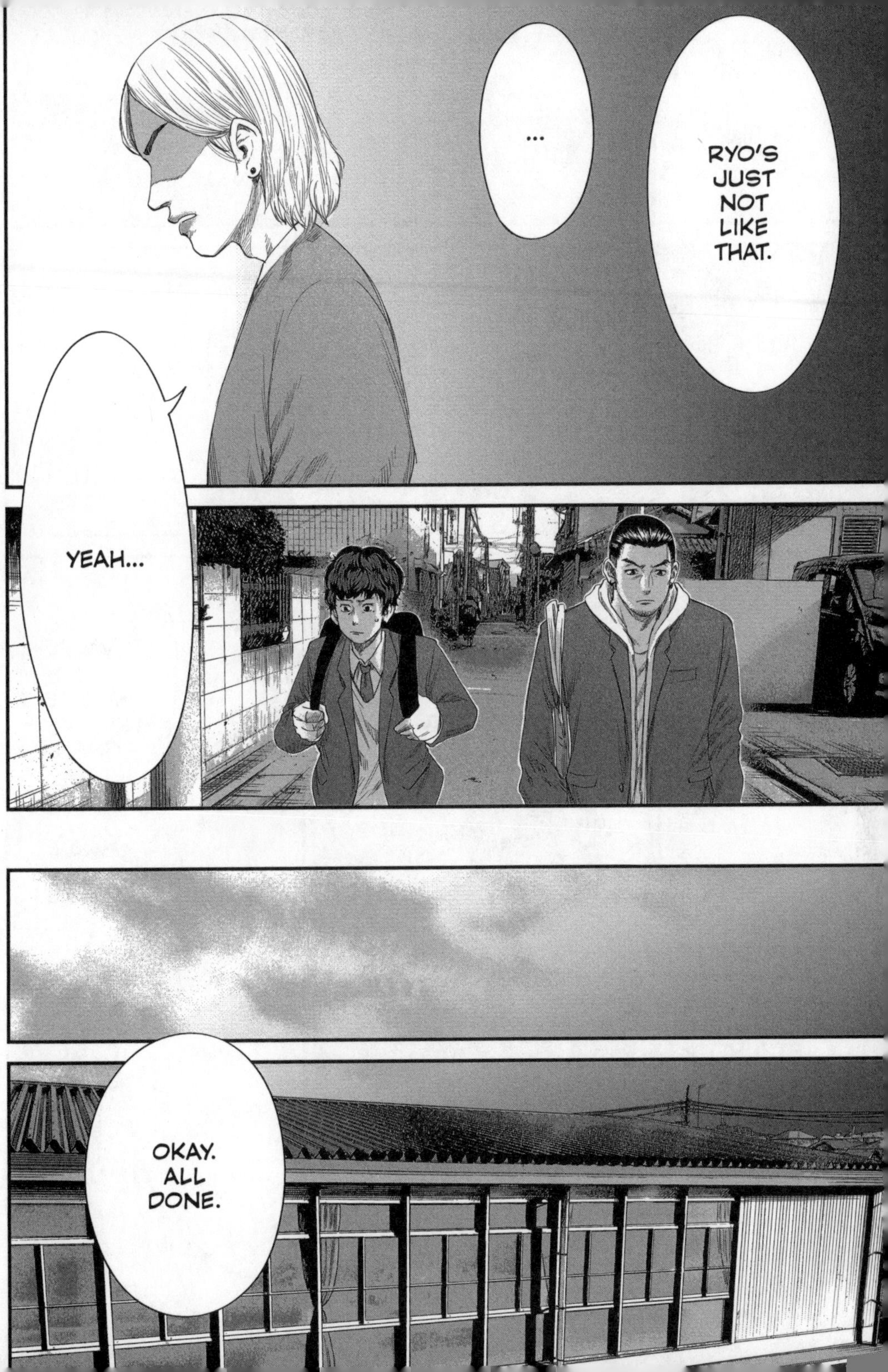
RYO'S JUST NOT LIKE THAT.
...
YEAH...
OKAY. ALL DONE.

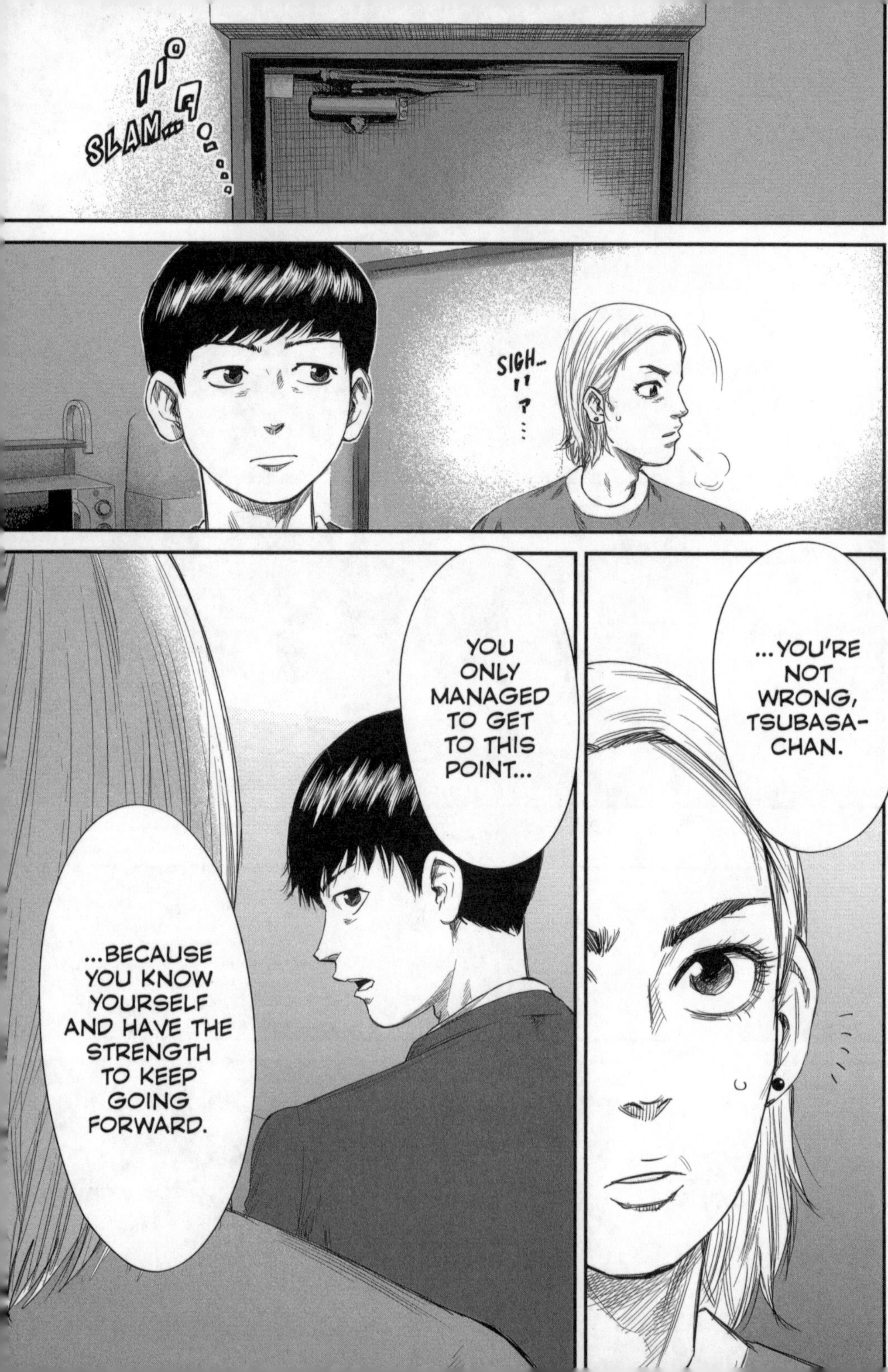
SLAM...
SIGH...
...YOU'RE NOT WRONG, TSUBASA-CHAN.
YOU ONLY MANAGED TO GET TO THIS POINT...
...BECAUSE YOU KNOW YOURSELF AND HAVE THE STRENGTH TO KEEP GOING FORWARD.

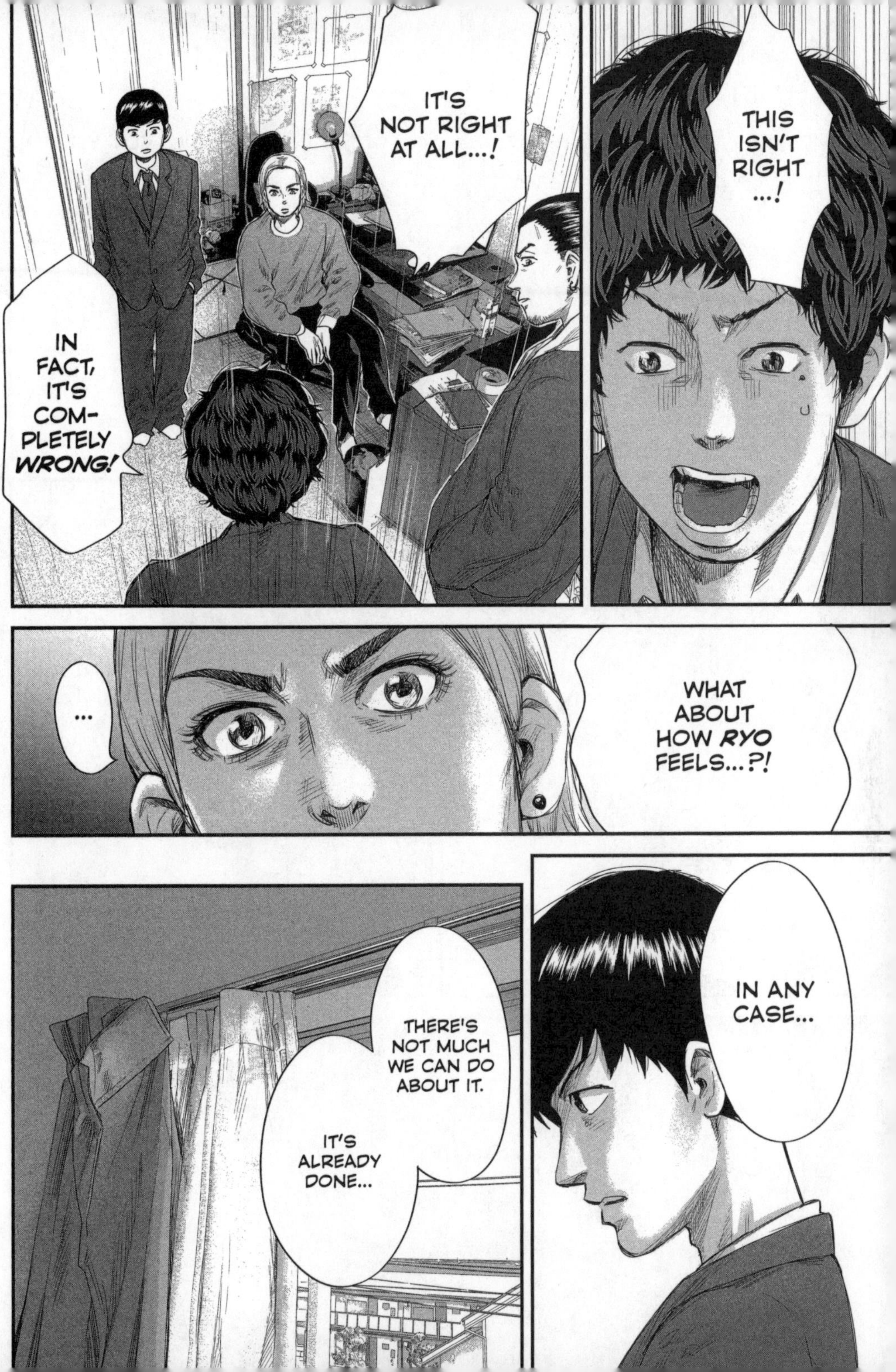
THIS ISN'T RIGHT ...!
IT'S NOT RIGHT AT ALL...!
IN FACT, IT'S COM- PLETELY **WRONG!**
WHAT ABOUT HOW **RYO** FEELS...?!
...
IN ANY CASE...
THERE'S NOT MUCH WE CAN DO ABOUT IT.
IT'S ALREADY DONE...

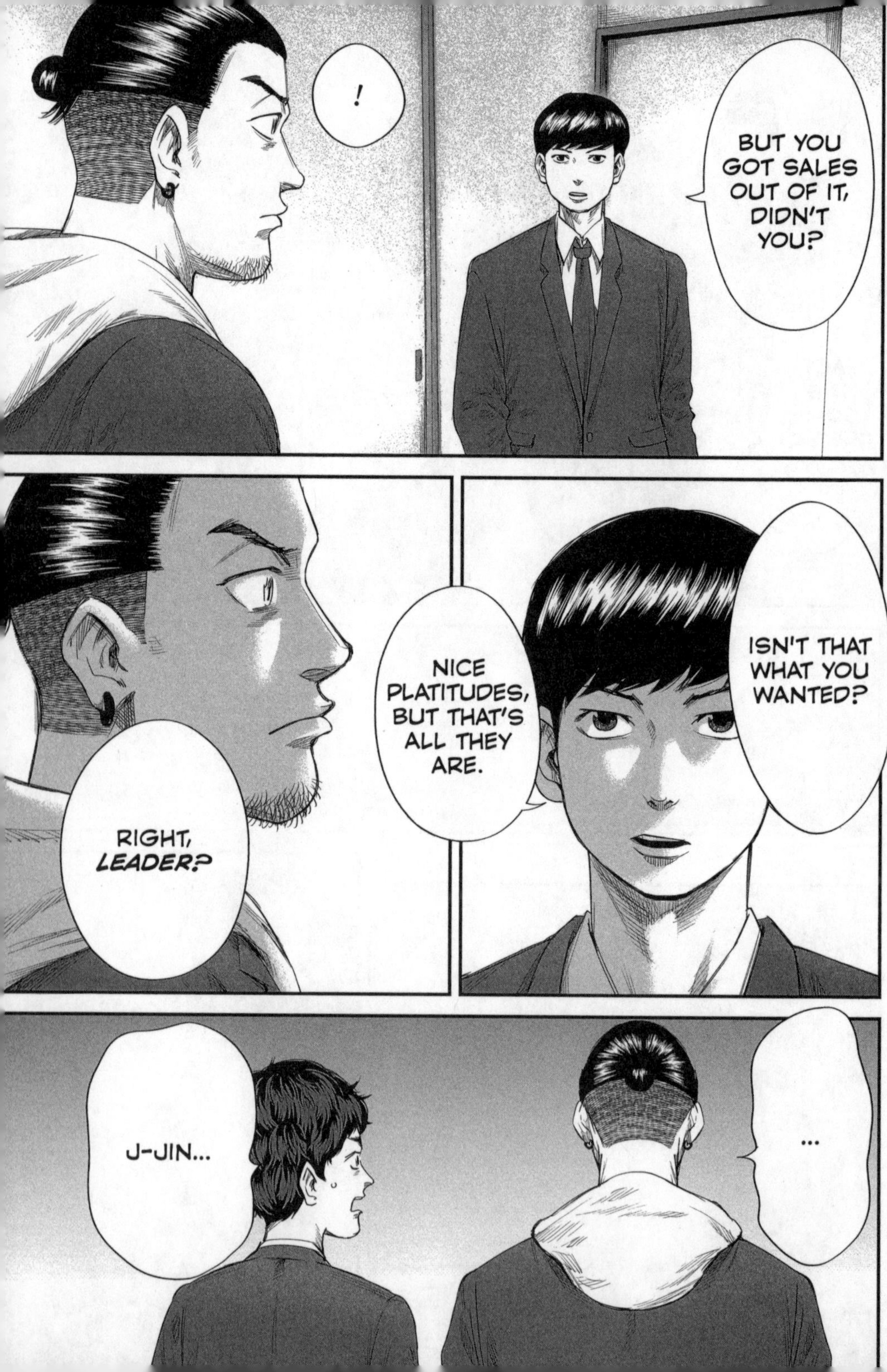

BUT YOU GOT SALES OUT OF IT, DIDN'T YOU?
!
ISN'T THAT WHAT YOU WANTED?
NICE PLATITUDES, BUT THAT'S ALL THEY ARE.
RIGHT, *LEADER?*
...
J-JIN...

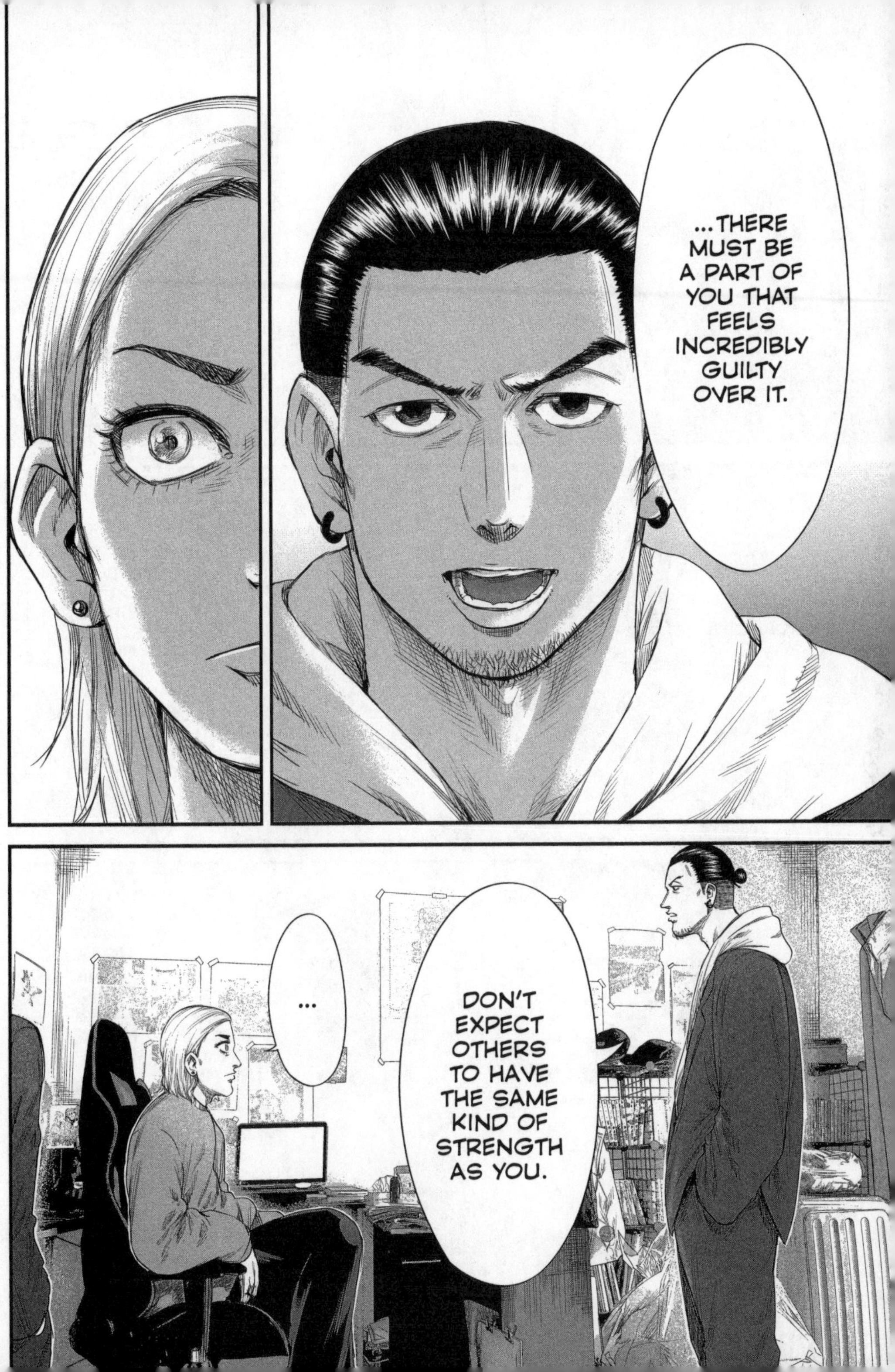
...THERE MUST BE A PART OF YOU THAT FEELS INCREDIBLY GUILTY OVER IT.
DON'T EXPECT OTHERS TO HAVE THE SAME KIND OF STRENGTH AS YOU.
...

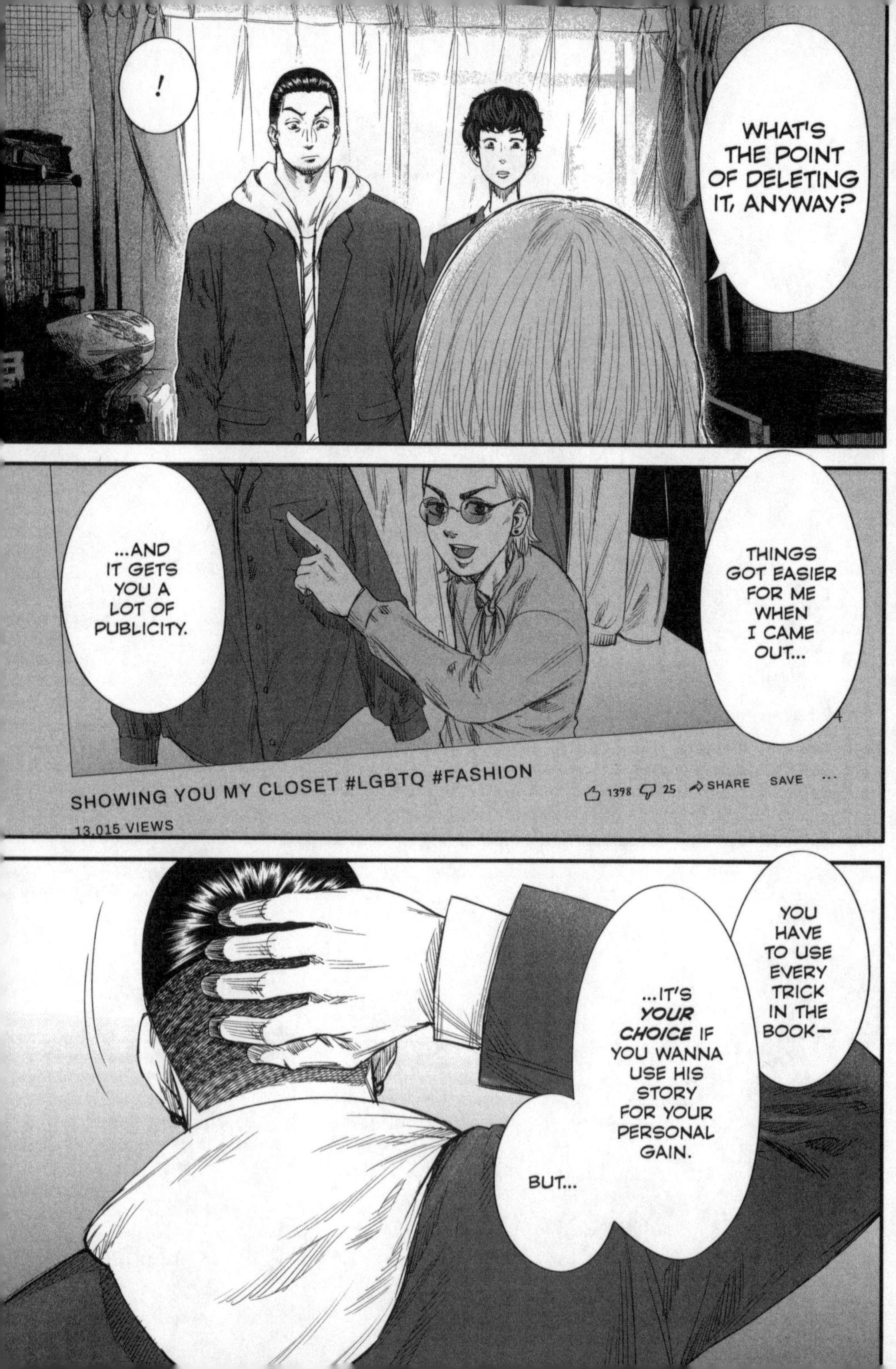
WHAT'S THE POINT OF DELETING IT, ANYWAY?
!
THINGS GOT EASIER FOR ME WHEN I CAME OUT...
...AND IT GETS YOU A LOT OF PUBLICITY.
SHOWING YOU MY CLOSET #LGBTQ #FASHION
1398 25 SHARE SAVE ...
13,015 VIEWS
YOU HAVE TO USE EVERY TRICK IN THE BOOK—
...IT'S YOUR CHOICE IF YOU WANNA USE HIS STORY FOR YOUR PERSONAL GAIN.
BUT...

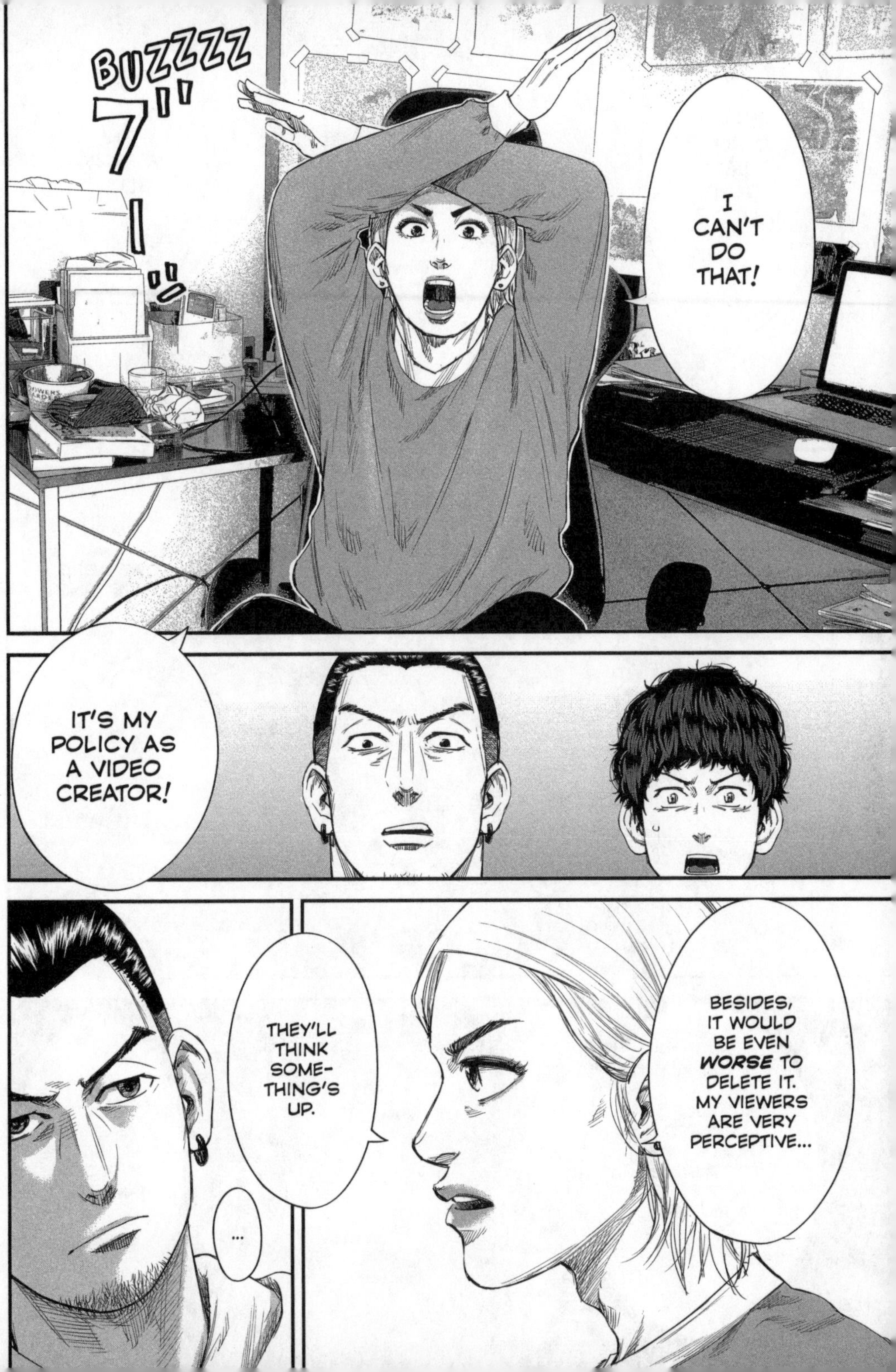
I CAN'T DO THAT!
BUZZZZ
IT'S MY POLICY AS A VIDEO CREATOR!
BESIDES, IT WOULD BE EVEN ***WORSE*** TO DELETE IT. MY VIEWERS ARE VERY PERCEPTIVE...
THEY'LL THINK SOME-THING'S UP.
...

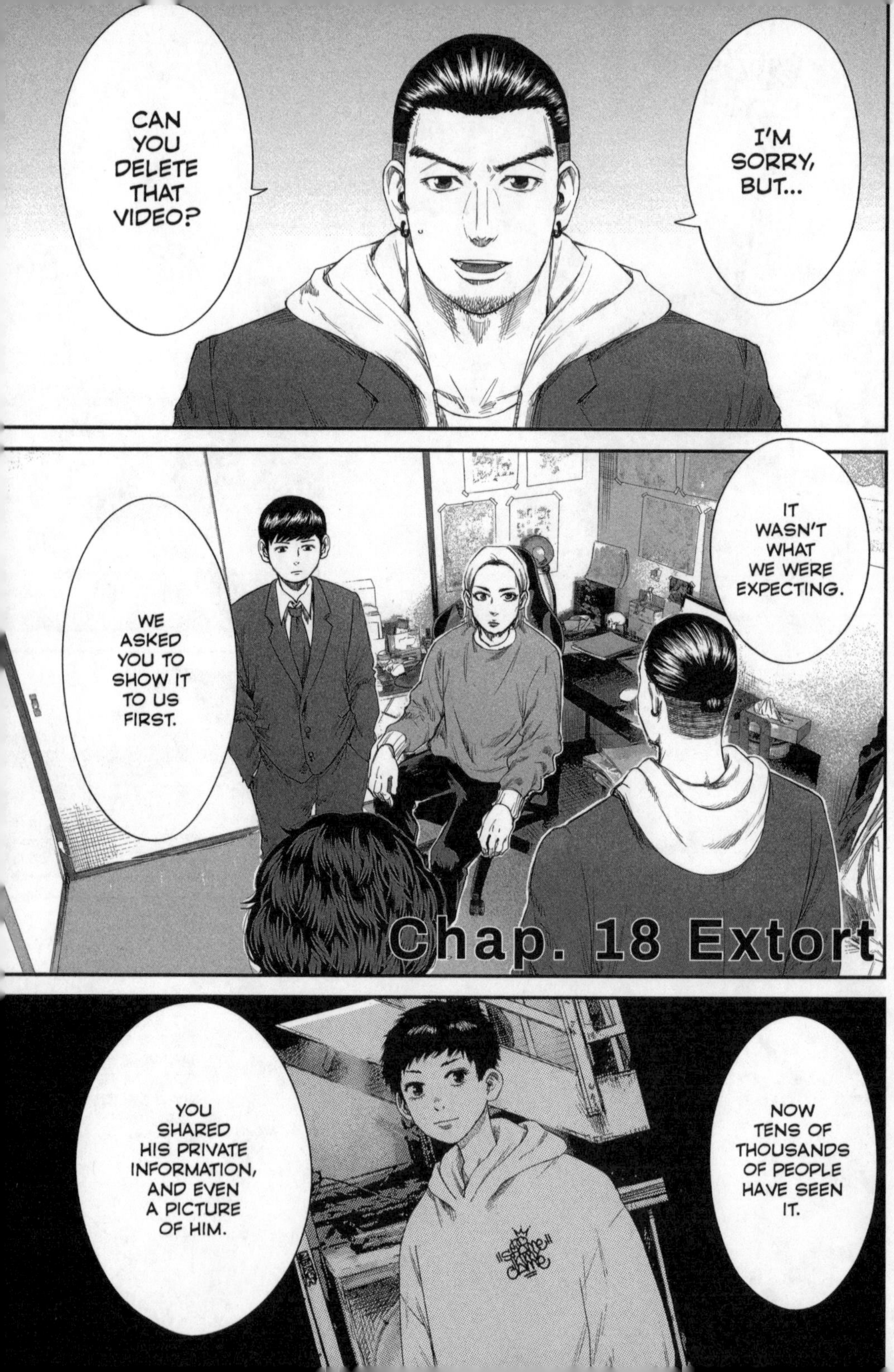
I'M SORRY, BUT...
CAN YOU DELETE THAT VIDEO?
IT WASN'T WHAT WE WERE EXPECTING.
WE ASKED YOU TO SHOW IT TO US FIRST.
Chap. 18 Extort
NOW TENS OF THOUSANDS OF PEOPLE HAVE SEEN IT.
YOU SHARED HIS PRIVATE INFORMATION, AND EVEN A PICTURE OF HIM.

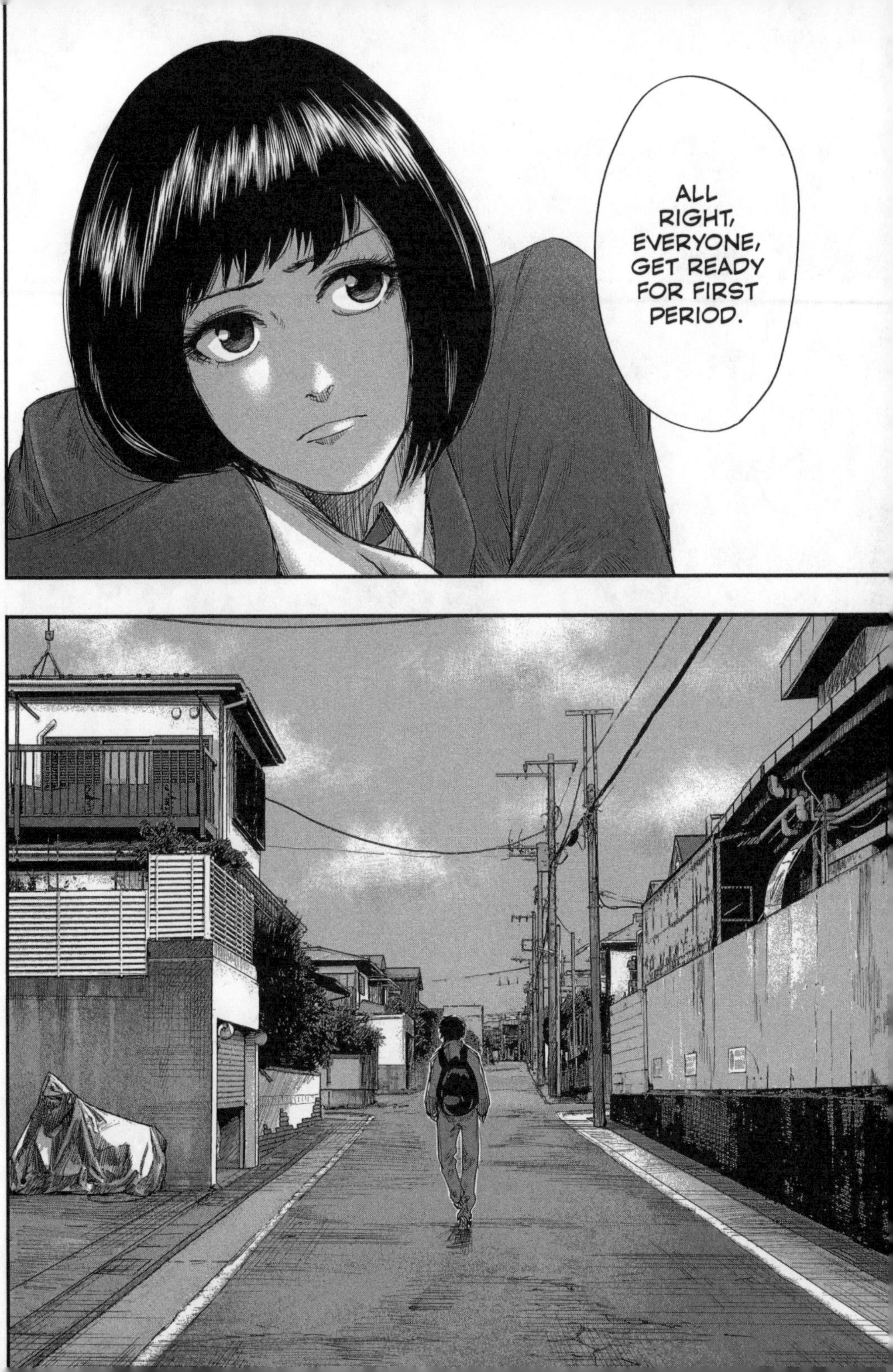
ALL RIGHT, EVERYONE, GET READY FOR FIRST PERIOD.

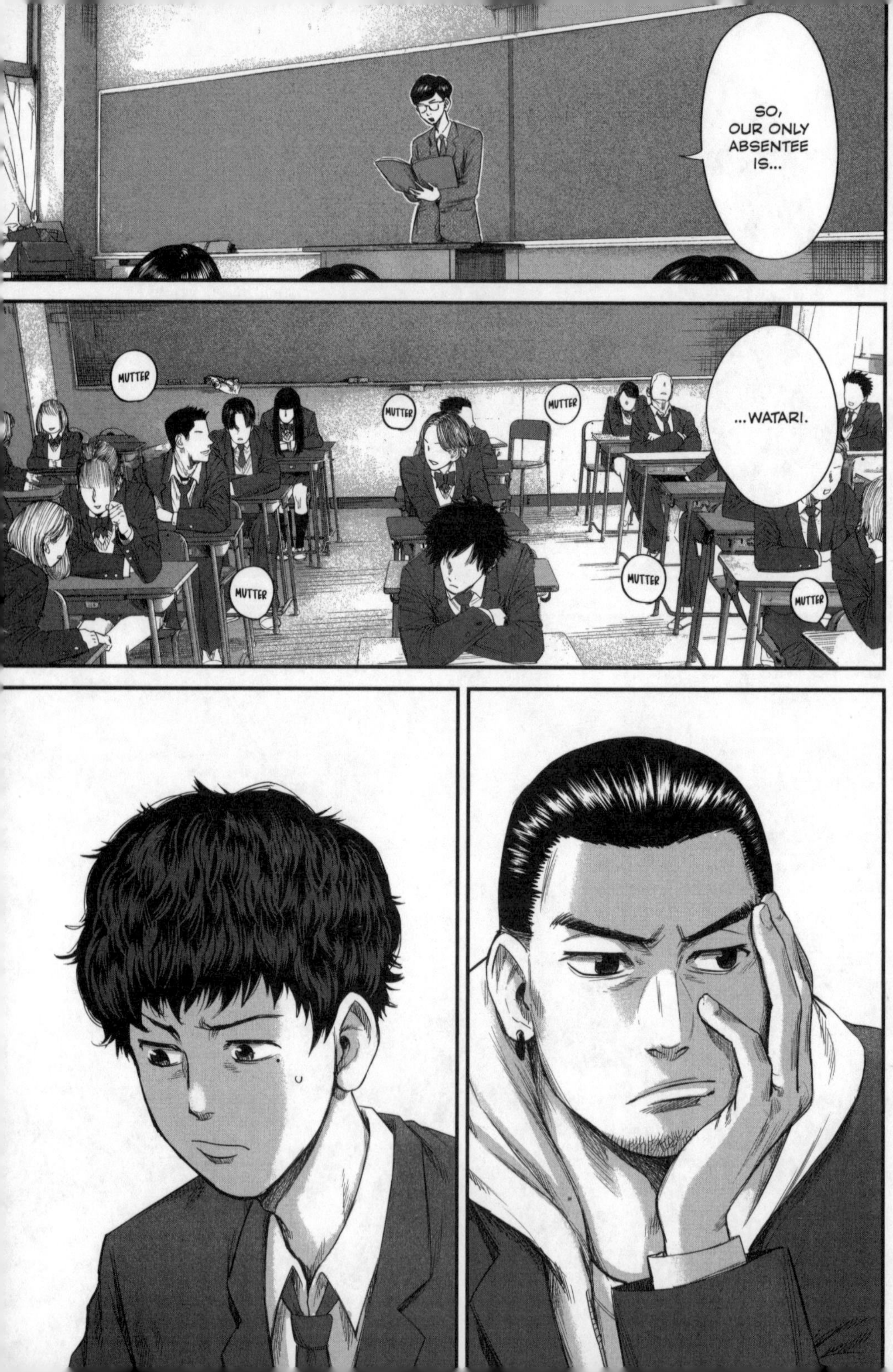
SO, OUR ONLY ABSENTEE IS...
...WATARI.
MUTTER
MUTTER
MUTTER
MUTTER
MUTTER
MUTTER

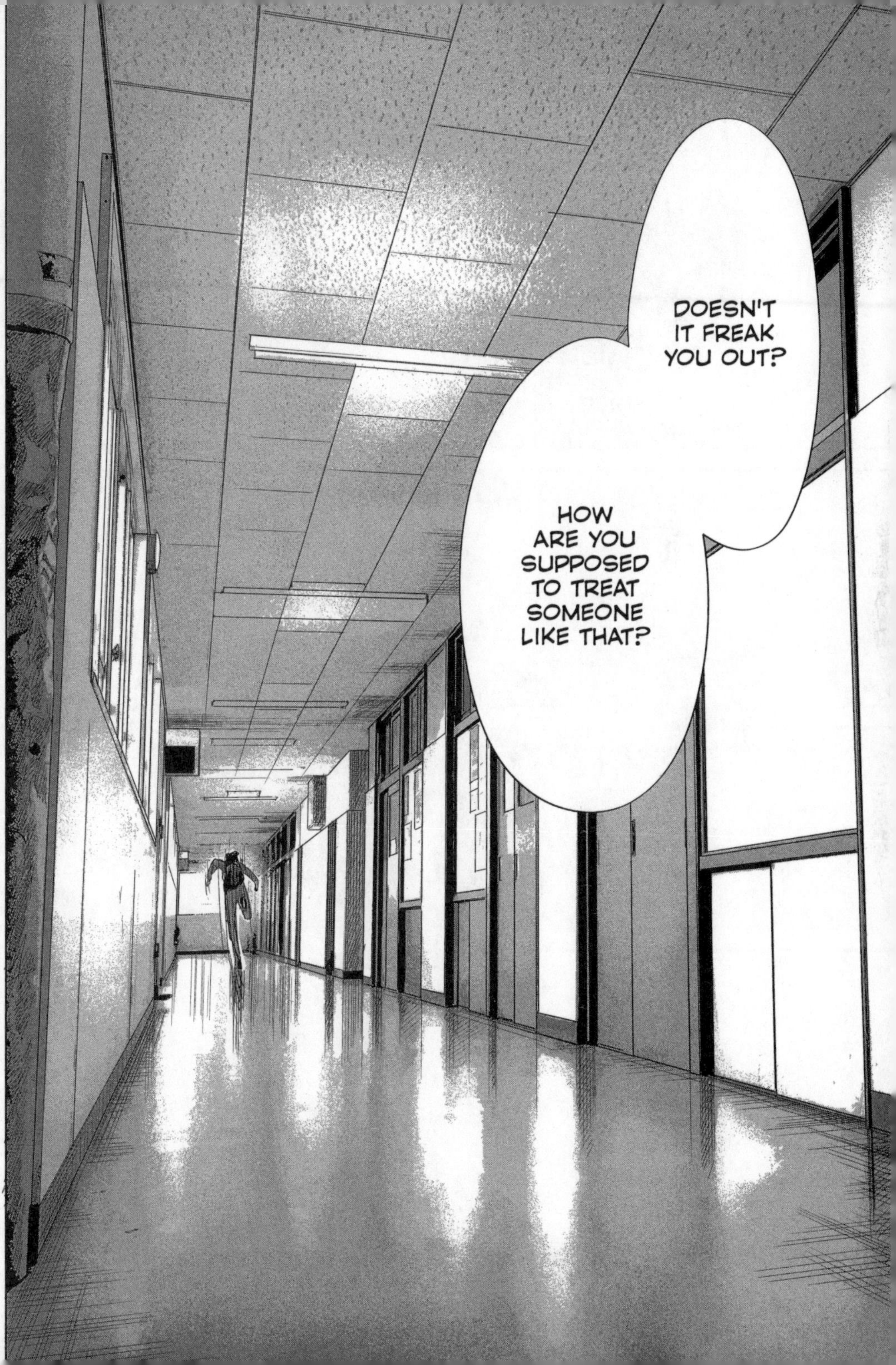
DOESN'T IT FREAK YOU OUT?
HOW ARE YOU SUPPOSED TO TREAT SOMEONE LIKE THAT?

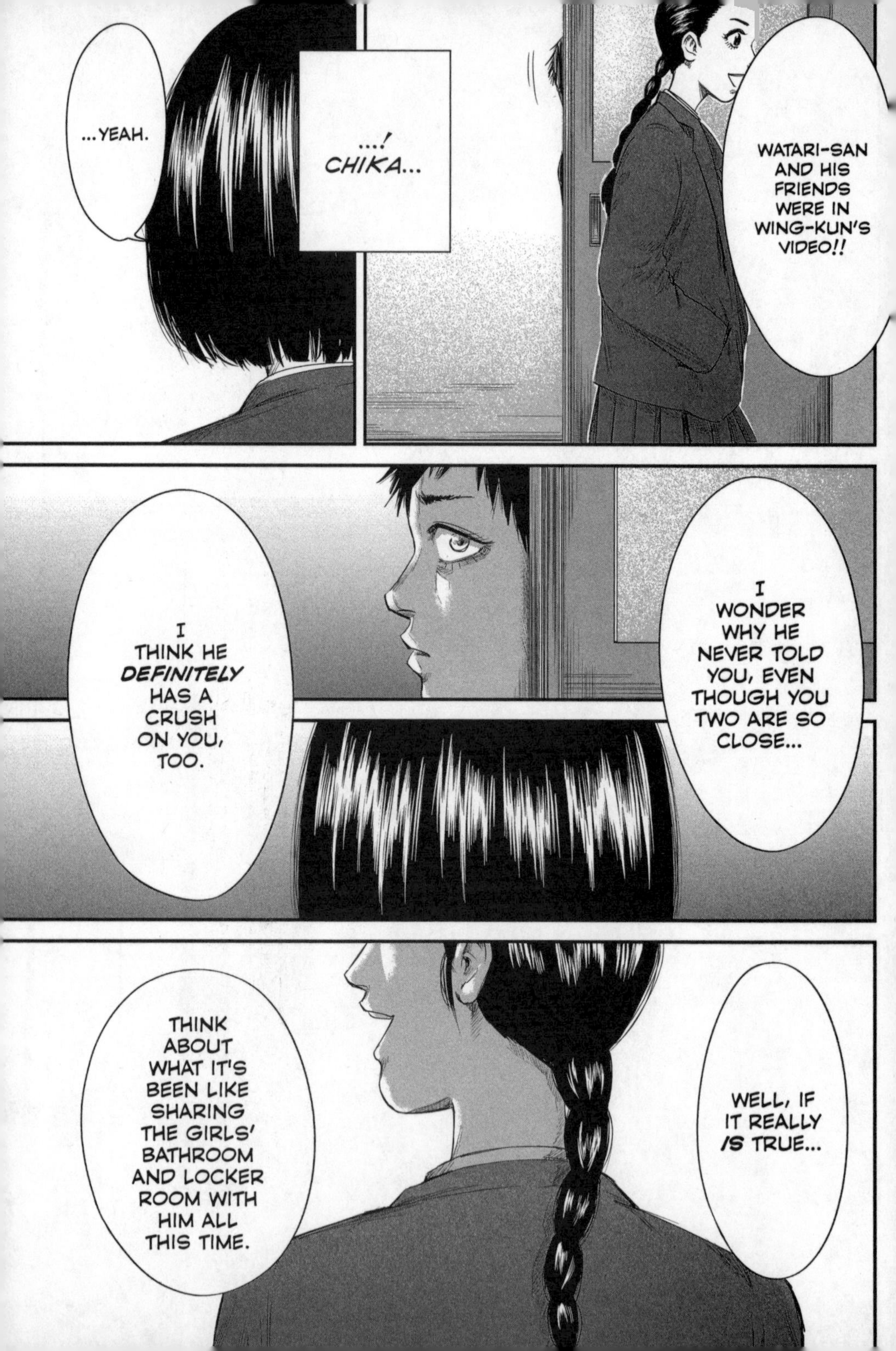
WATARI-SAN AND HIS FRIENDS WERE IN WING-KUN'S VIDEO!!
...! CHIKA...
...YEAH.
I WONDER WHY HE NEVER TOLD YOU, EVEN THOUGH YOU TWO ARE SO CLOSE...
I THINK HE *DEFINITELY* HAS A CRUSH ON YOU, TOO.
WELL, IF IT REALLY *IS* TRUE...
THINK ABOUT WHAT IT'S BEEN LIKE SHARING THE GIRLS' BATHROOM AND LOCKER ROOM WITH HIM ALL THIS TIME.

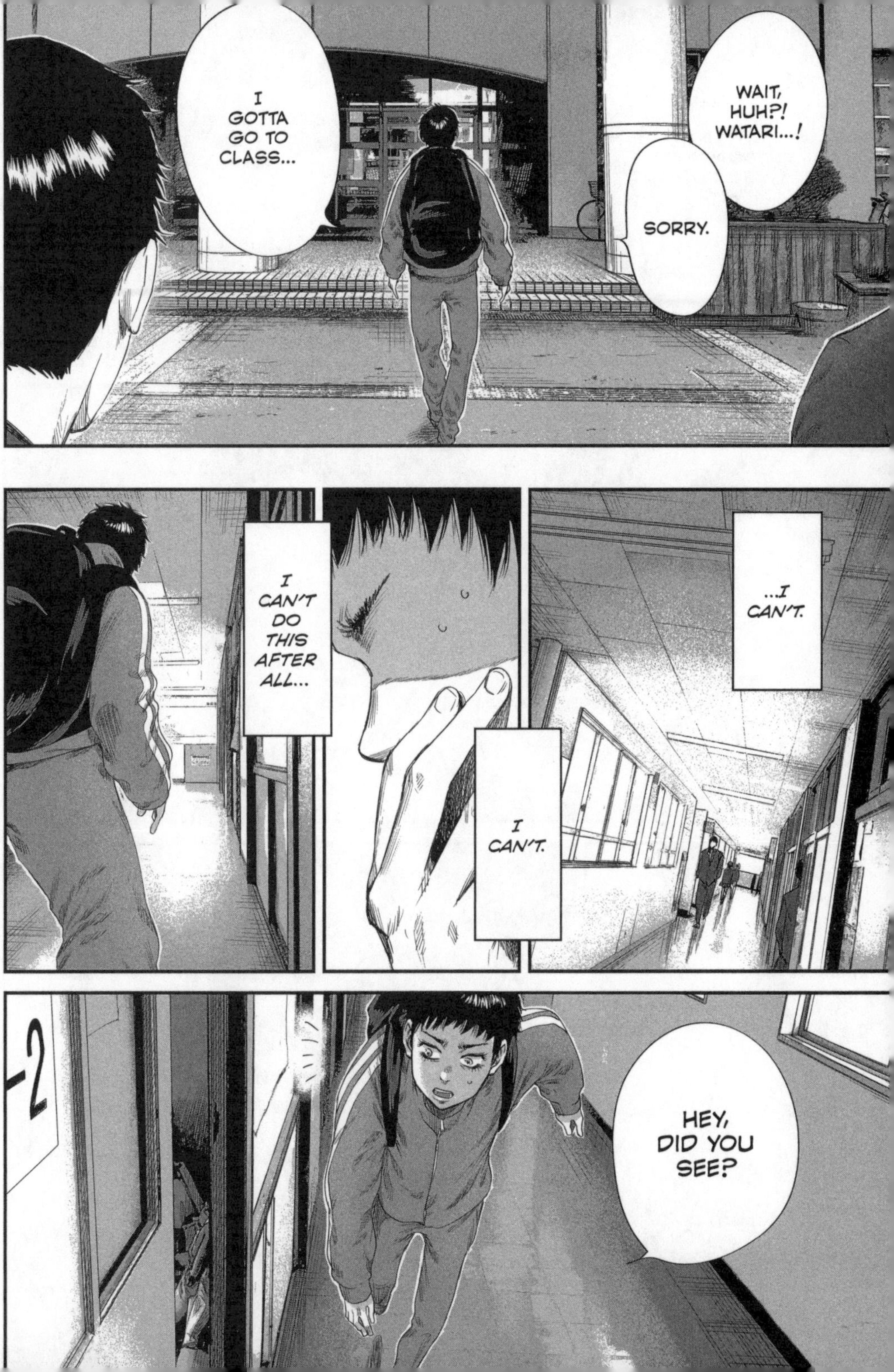
WAIT, HUH?! WATARI...!
SORRY.
I GOTTA GO TO CLASS...
...I CAN'T.
I CAN'T.
I CAN'T DO THIS AFTER ALL...
HEY, DID YOU SEE?

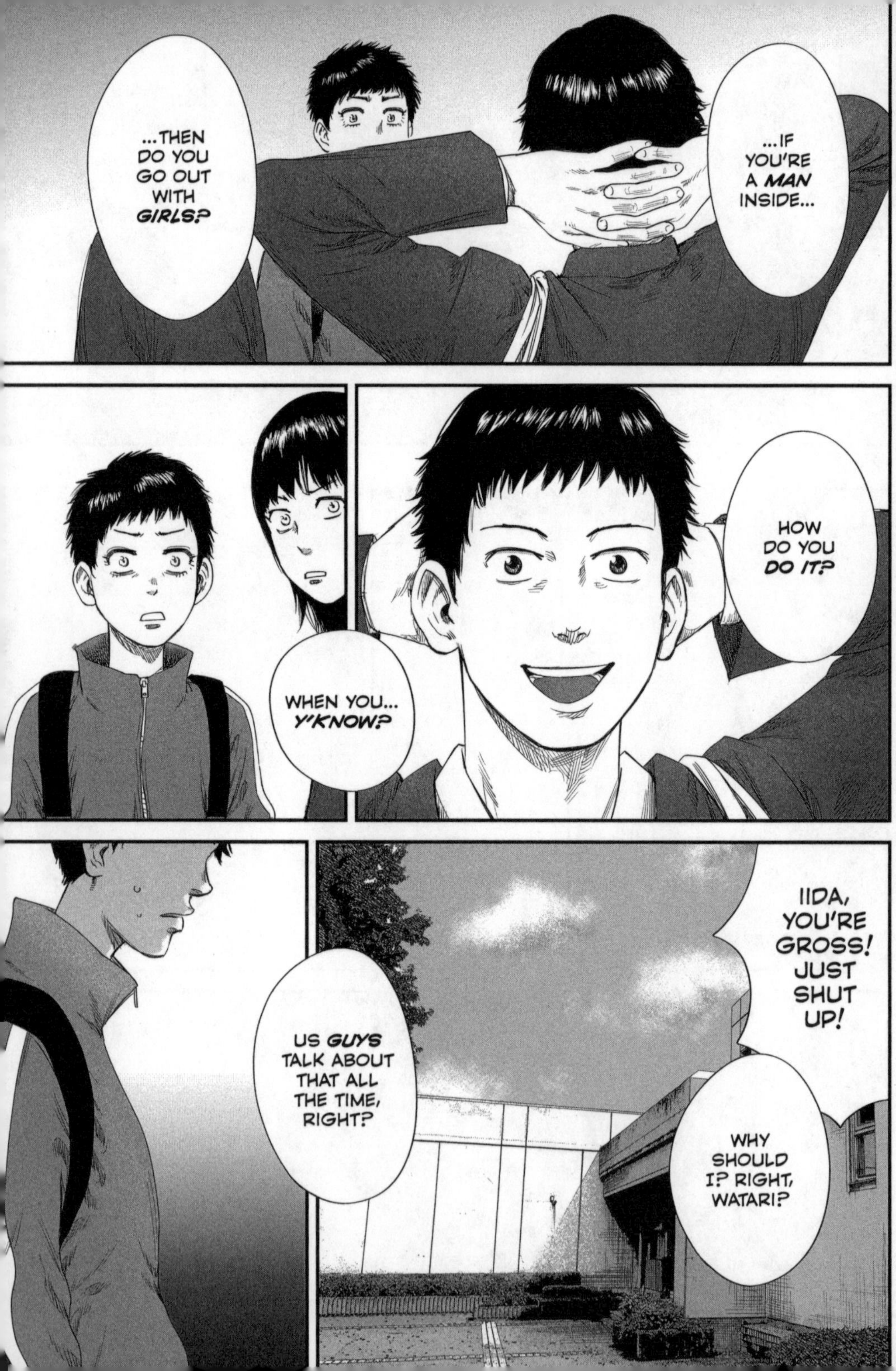
...IF YOU'RE A *MAN* INSIDE...
...THEN DO YOU GO OUT WITH *GIRLS?*
HOW DO YOU *DO IT?*
WHEN YOU... *Y'KNOW?*
IIDA, YOU'RE GROSS! JUST SHUT UP!
WHY SHOULD I? RIGHT, WATARI?
US *GUYS* TALK ABOUT THAT ALL THE TIME, RIGHT?

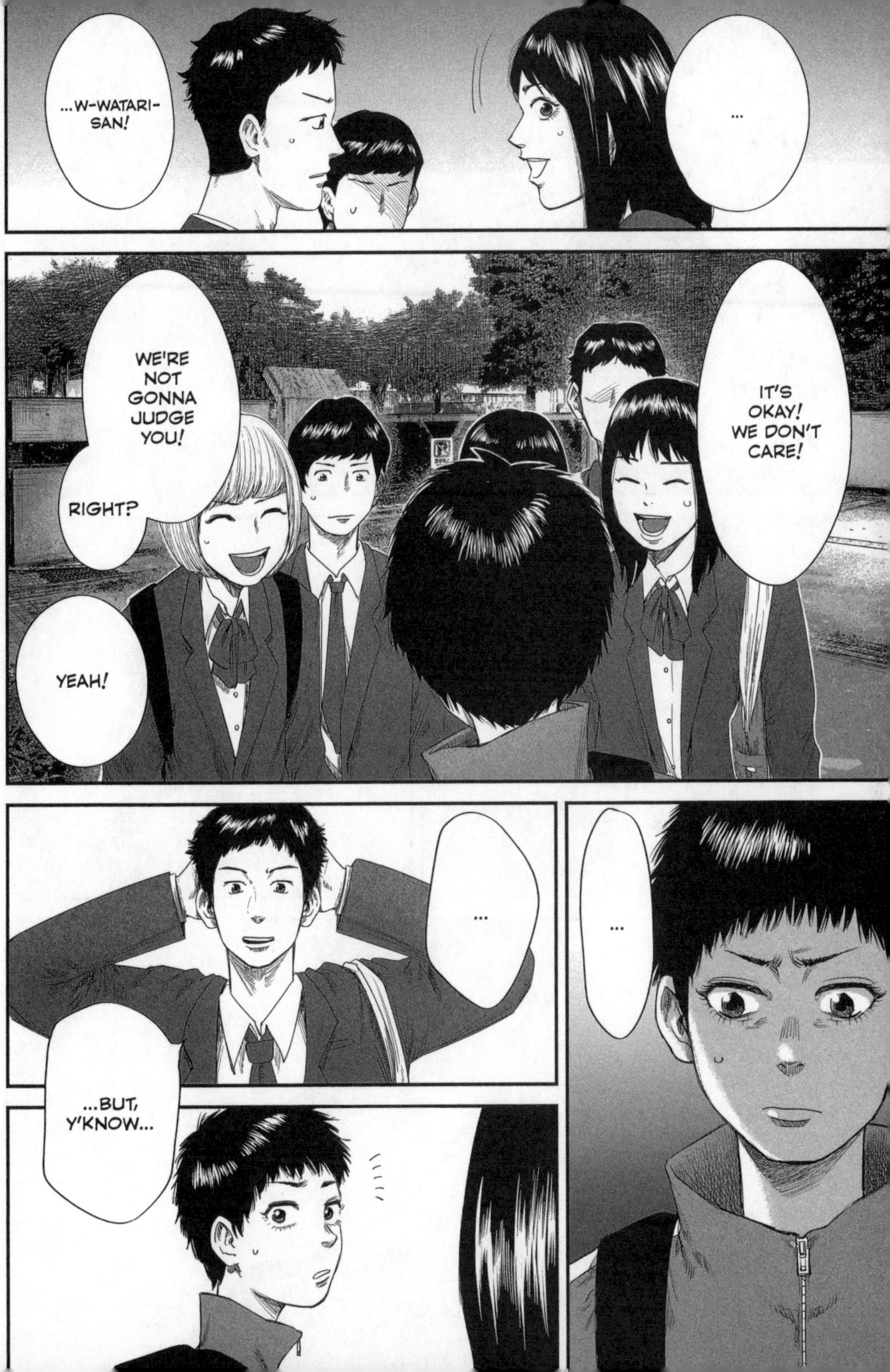
...
...W-WATARI-SAN!
IT'S OKAY! WE DON'T CARE!
WE'RE NOT GONNA JUDGE YOU!
RIGHT?
YEAH!
...
...
...BUT, Y'KNOW...

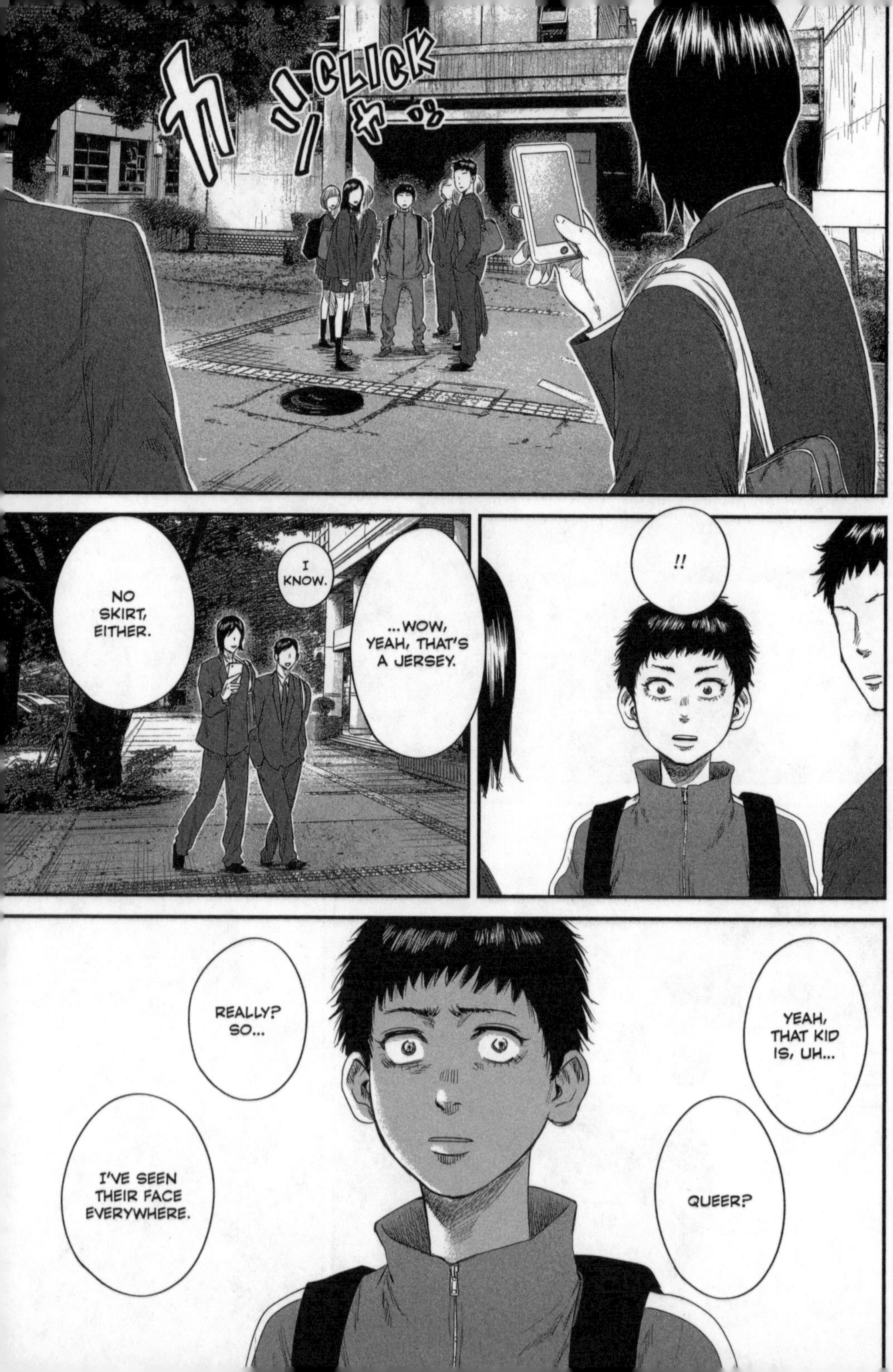
CLICK
!!
...WOW, YEAH, THAT'S A JERSEY.
I KNOW.
NO SKIRT, EITHER.
YEAH, THAT KID IS, UH...
QUEER?
REALLY? SO...
I'VE SEEN THEIR FACE EVERYWHERE.

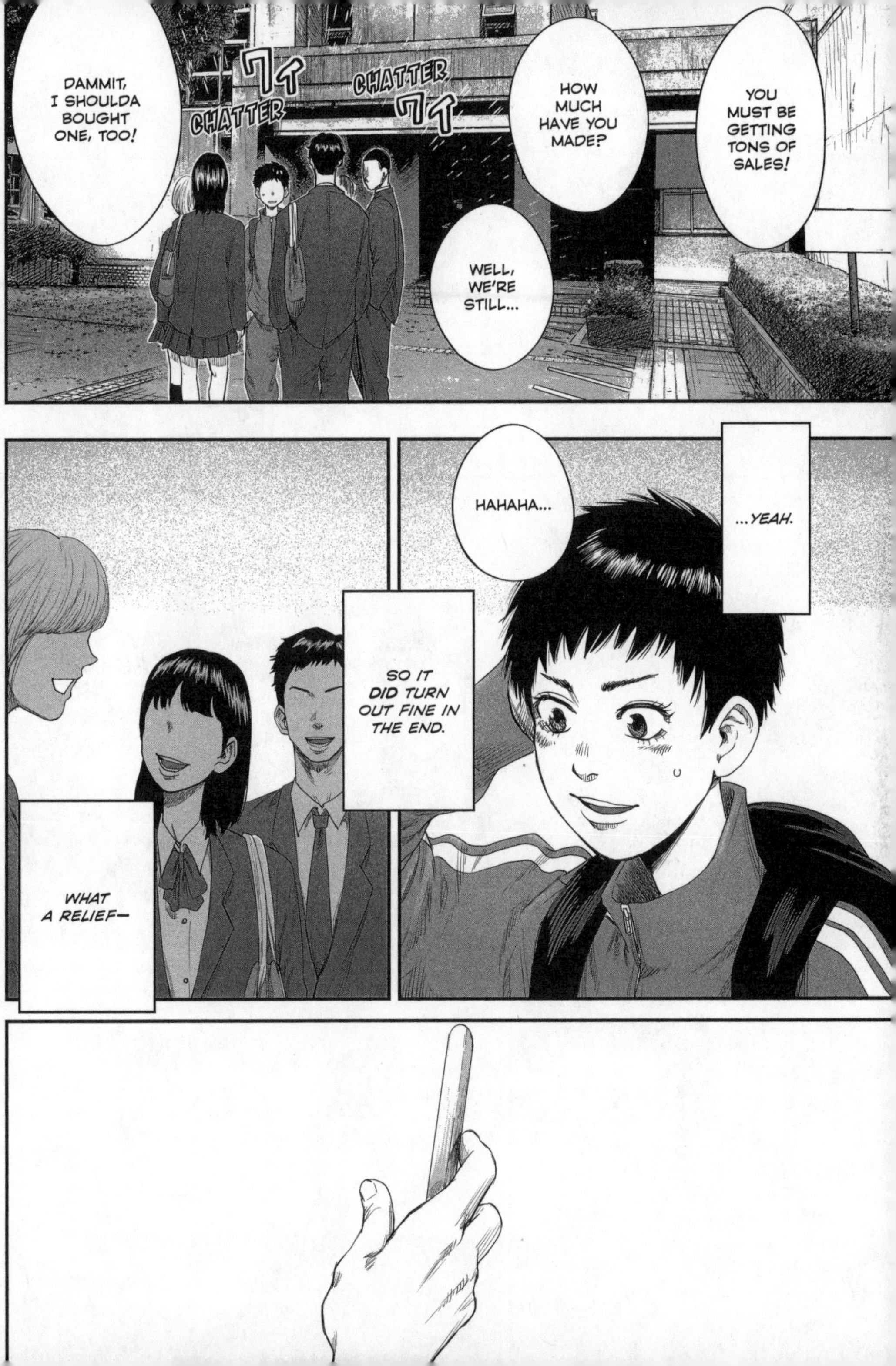
YOU MUST BE GETTING TONS OF SALES!
HOW MUCH HAVE YOU MADE?
WELL, WE'RE STILL...
ワイ CHATTER
ワイ CHATTER
DAMMIT, I SHOULDA BOUGHT ONE, TOO!
...YEAH.
HAHAHA...
SO IT DID TURN OUT FINE IN THE END.
WHAT A RELIEF—

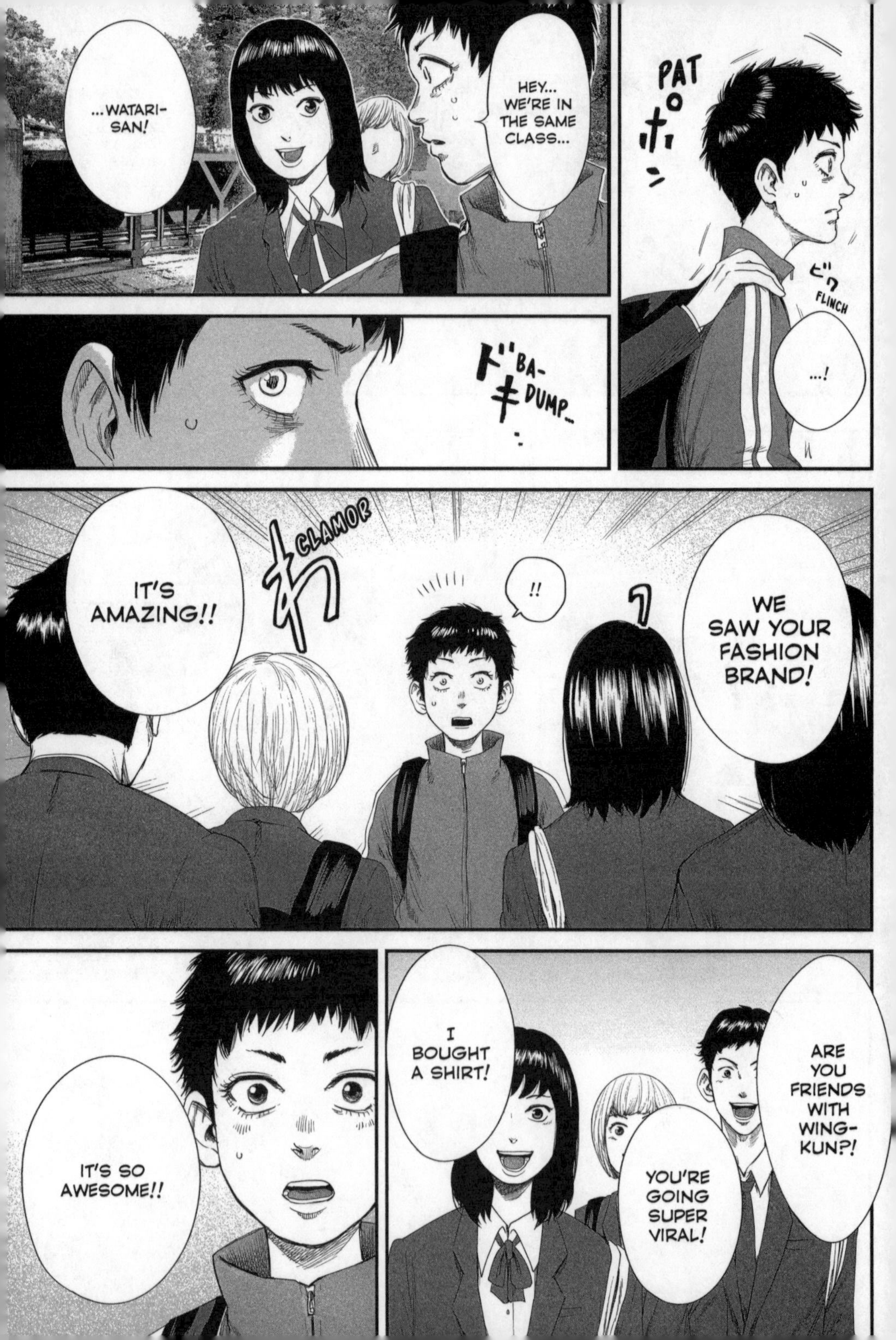
PAT
FLINCH
...!
HEY... WE'RE IN THE SAME CLASS...
...WATARI-SAN!
BA-DUMP...
WE SAW YOUR FASHION BRAND!
!!
CLAMOR
IT'S AMAZING!!
ARE YOU FRIENDS WITH WING-KUN?!
YOU'RE GOING SUPER VIRAL!
I BOUGHT A SHIRT!
IT'S SO AWESOME!!

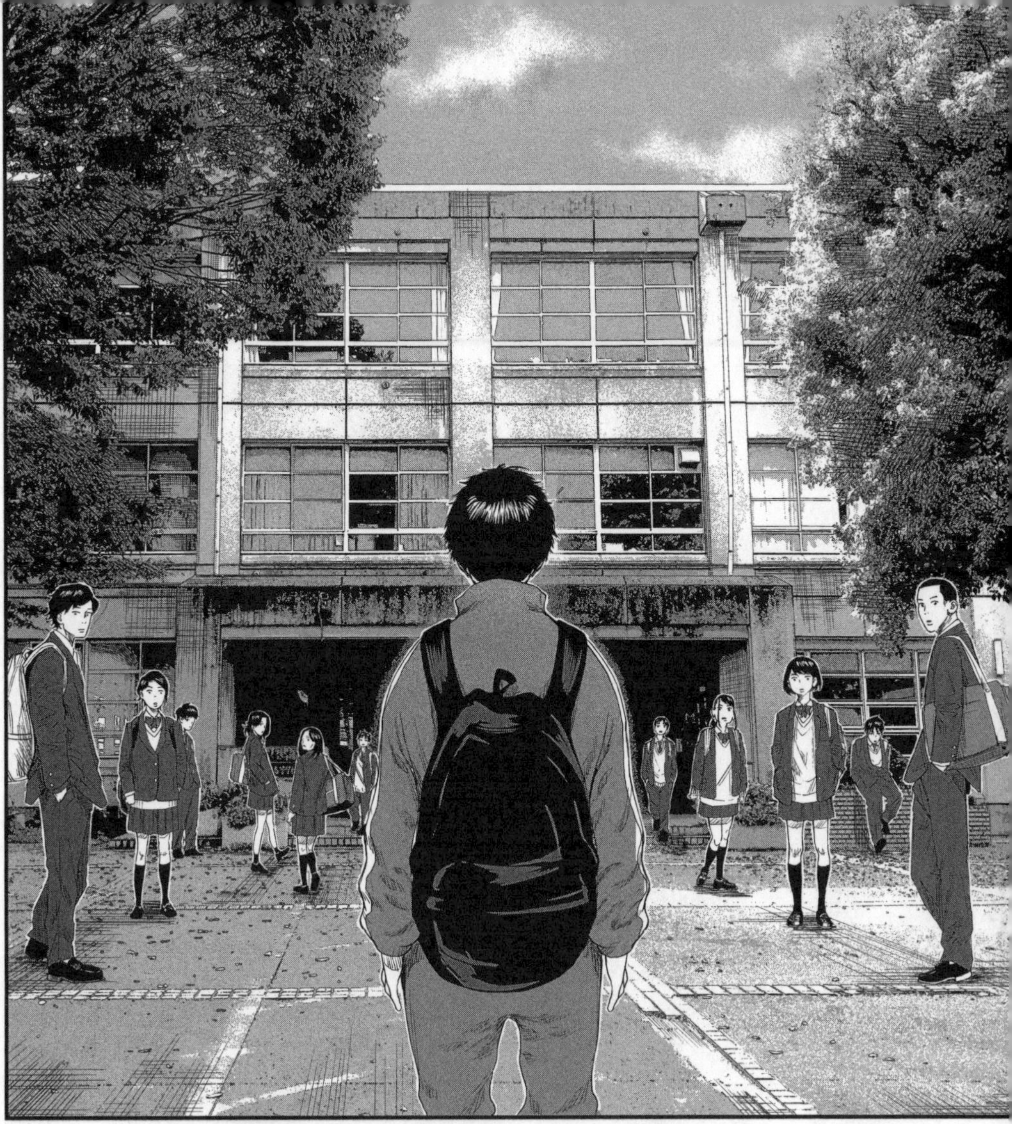

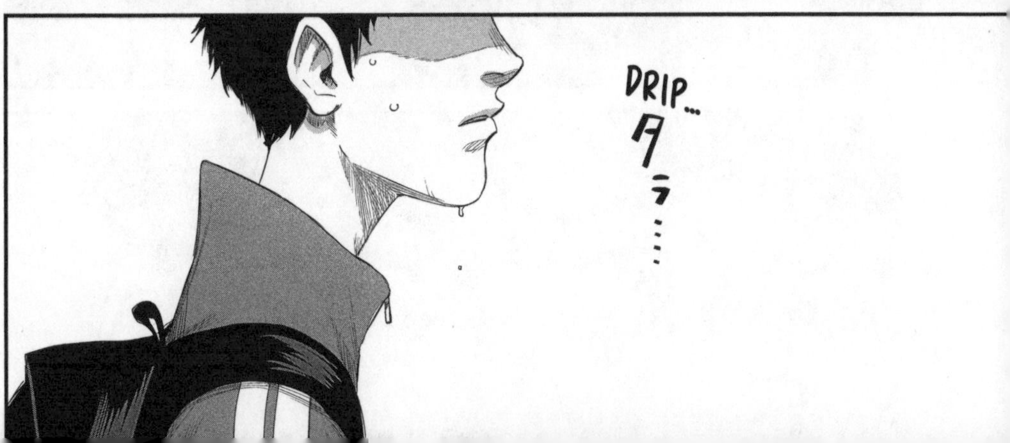
DRIP...
タラ……

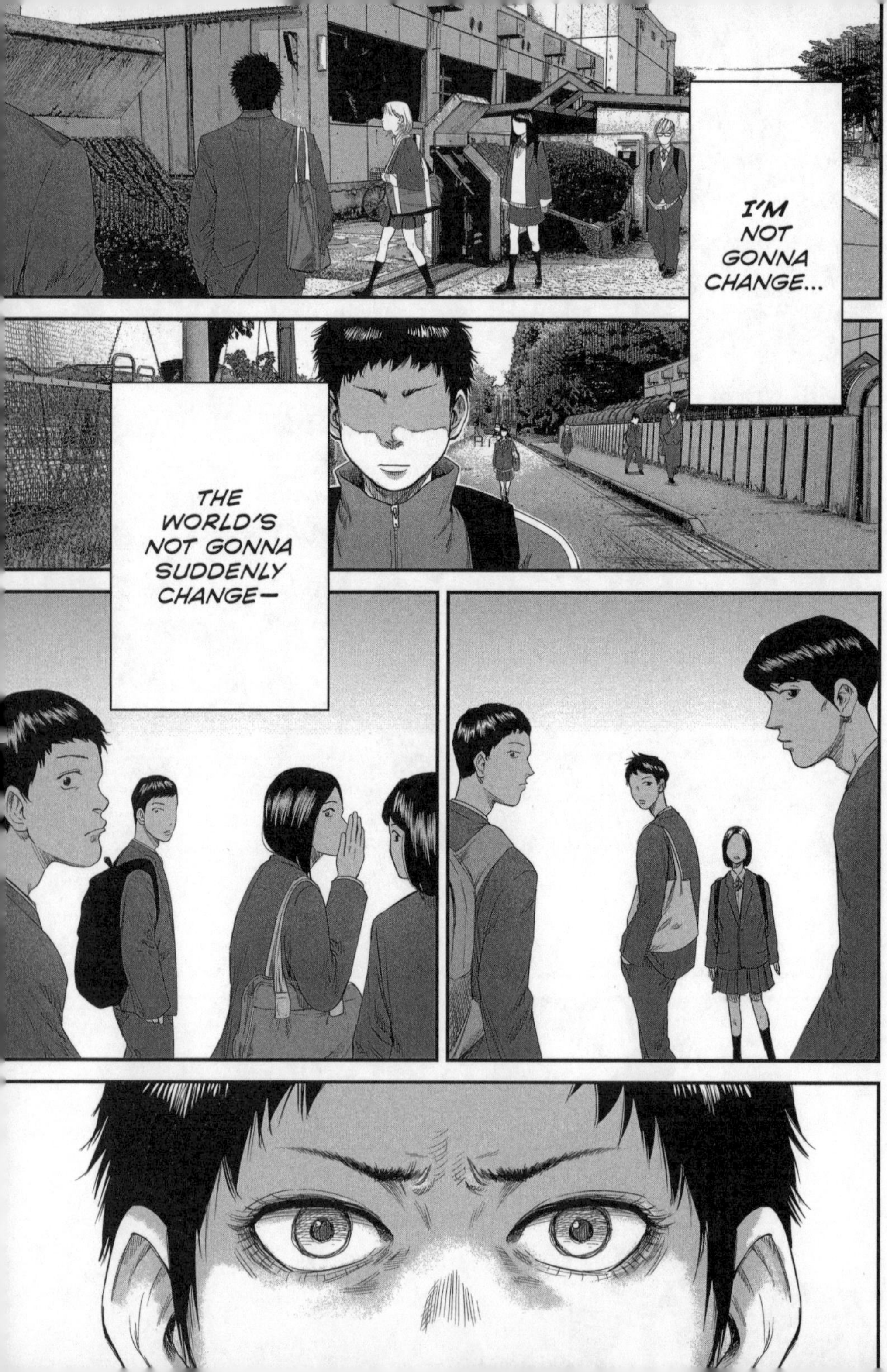
I'M NOT GONNA CHANGE...
THE WORLD'S NOT GONNA SUDDENLY CHANGE—

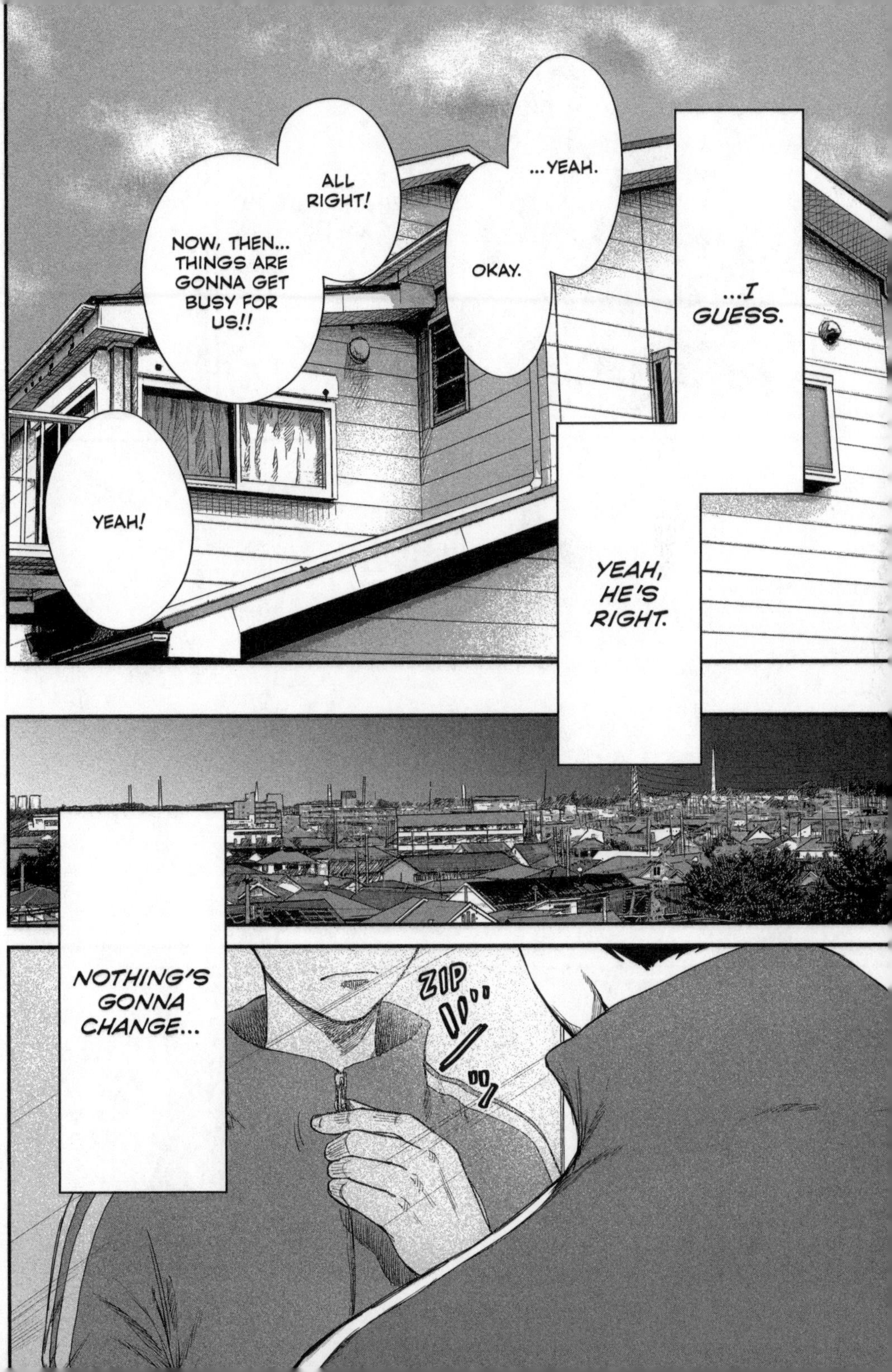
...I GUESS.
...YEAH. OKAY.
ALL RIGHT! NOW, THEN... THINGS ARE GONNA GET BUSY FOR US!!
YEAH!
YEAH, HE'S RIGHT.
NOTHING'S GONNA CHANGE...
ZIP

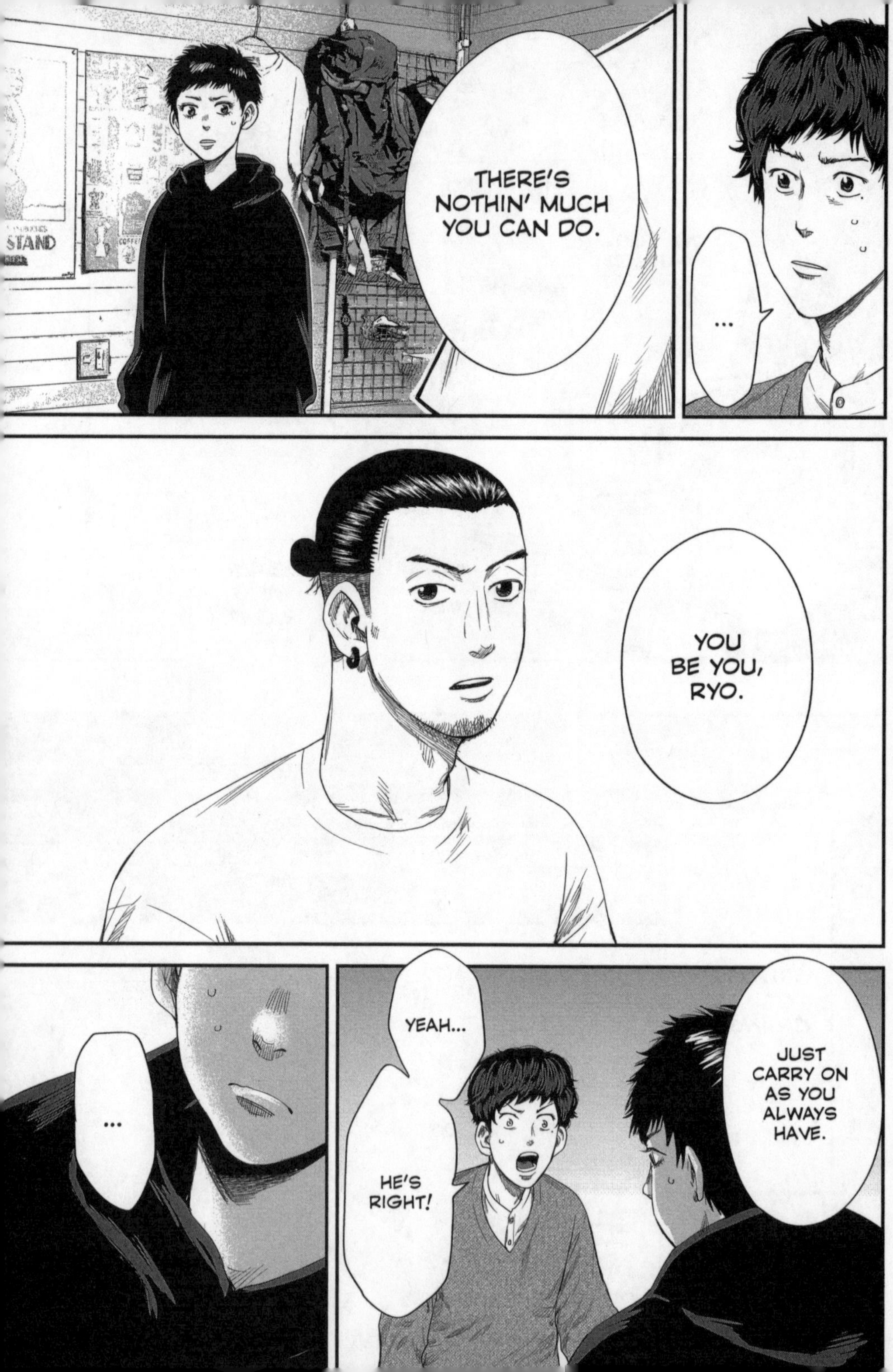
...
THERE'S NOTHIN' MUCH YOU CAN DO.
YOU BE YOU, RYO.
JUST CARRY ON AS YOU ALWAYS HAVE.
YEAH...
HE'S RIGHT!
...

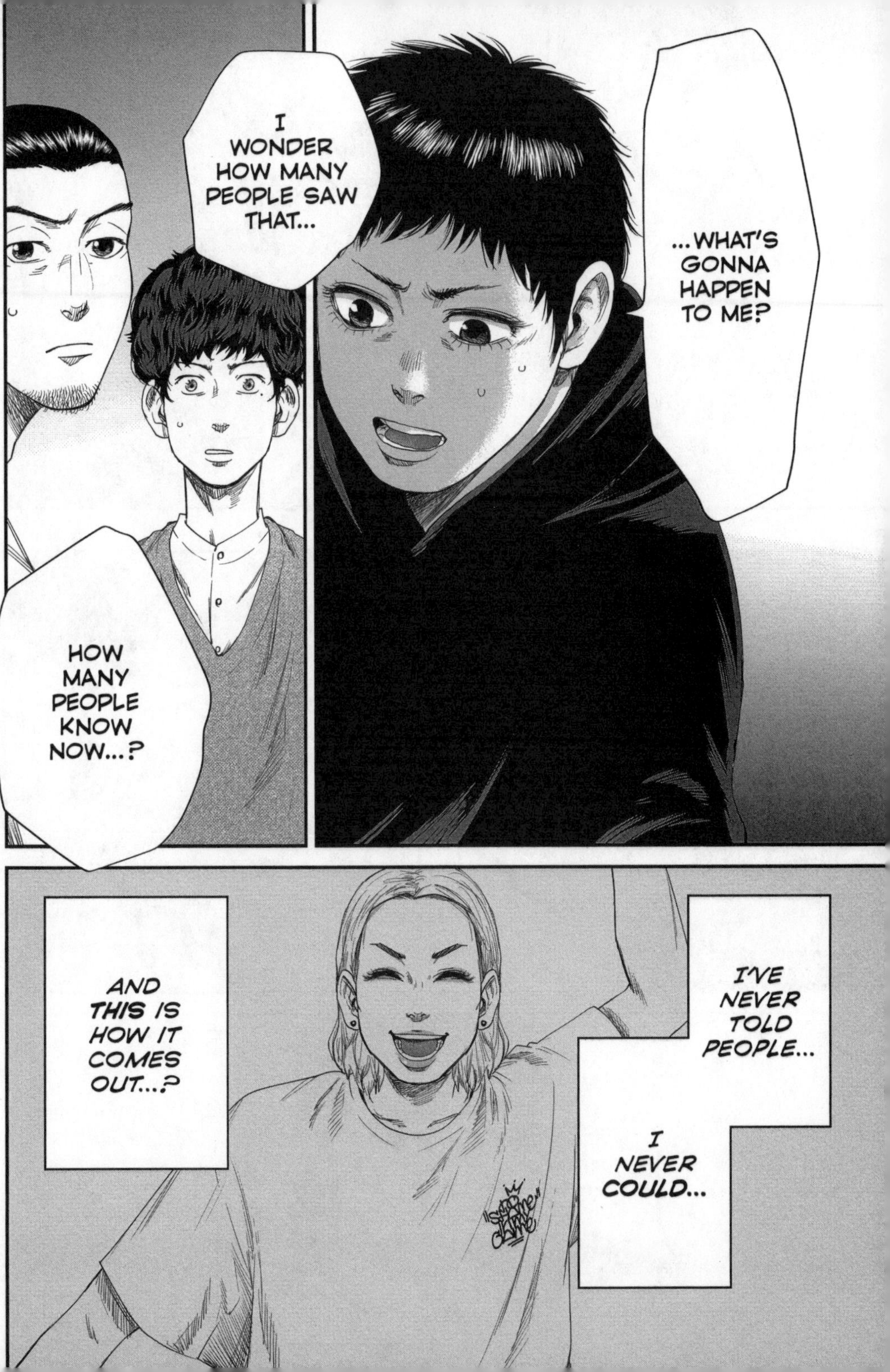
...WHAT'S GONNA HAPPEN TO ME?
I WONDER HOW MANY PEOPLE SAW THAT...
HOW MANY PEOPLE KNOW NOW...?
I'VE NEVER TOLD PEOPLE...
I NEVER COULD...
AND THIS IS HOW IT COMES OUT...?

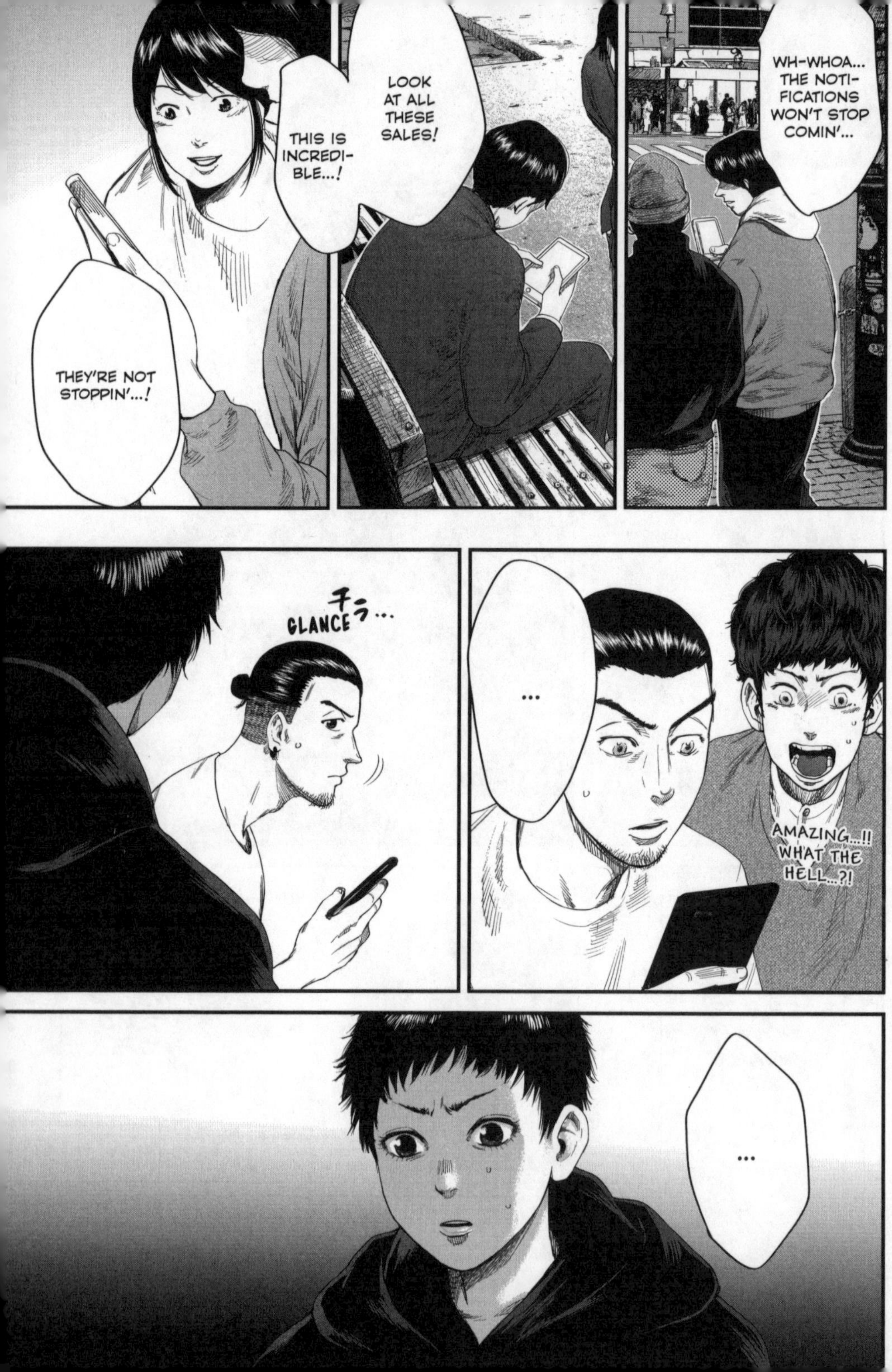
WH-WHOA... THE NOTI-FICATIONS WON'T STOP COMIN'...
LOOK AT ALL THESE SALES!
THIS IS INCREDI-BLE...!
THEY'RE NOT STOPPIN'...!
...
AMAZING...!! WHAT THE HELL...?!
チラ
GLANCE...
...

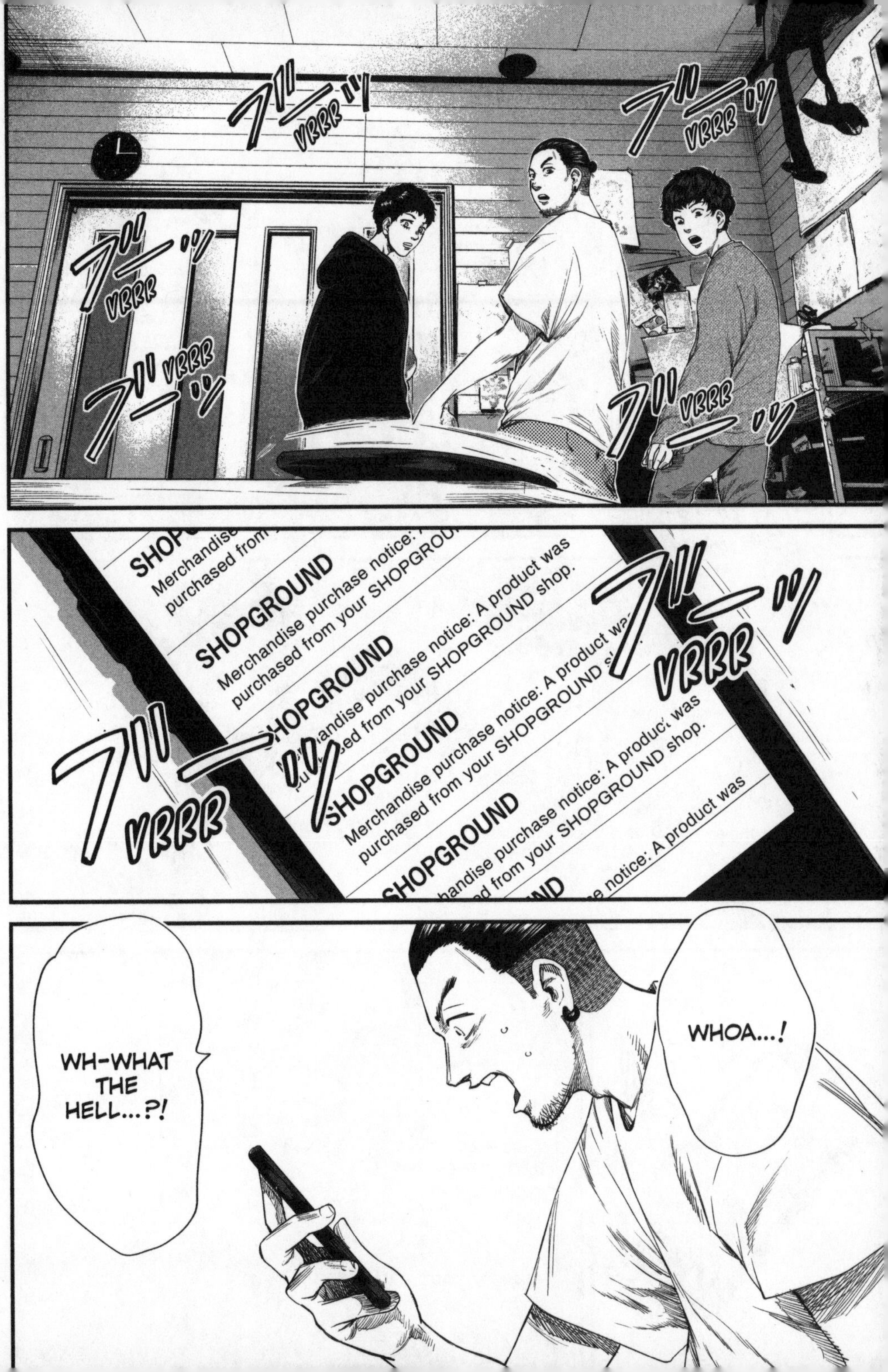
VRRR
VRRR
VRRR
VRRR
VRRR
VRRR
VRRR
SHOPGROUND
Merchandise purchase notice: A product was purchased from your SHOPGROUND shop.
SHOPGROUND
Merchandise purchase notice: A product was purchased from your SHOPGROUND shop.
SHOPGROUND
Merchandise purchase notice: A product was purchased from your SHOPGROUND shop.
SHOPGROUND
Merchandise purchase notice: A product was
VRRR
WHOA...!
WH-WHAT THE HELL...?!

Chap. 17 Stare

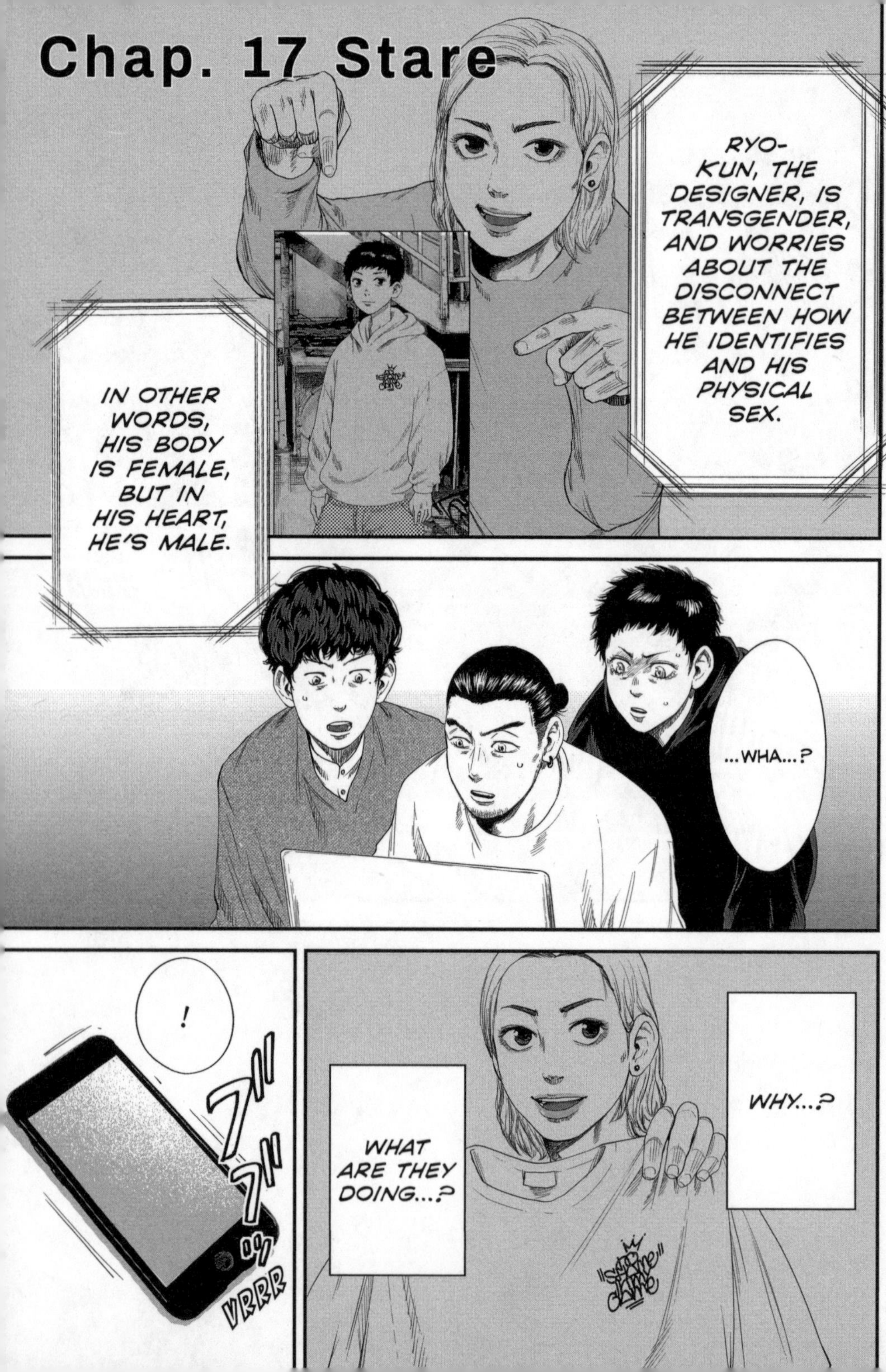
RYO-KUN, THE DESIGNER, IS TRANSGENDER, AND WORRIES ABOUT THE DISCONNECT BETWEEN HOW HE IDENTIFIES AND HIS PHYSICAL SEX.
IN OTHER WORDS, HIS BODY IS FEMALE, BUT IN HIS HEART, HE'S MALE.
...WHA...?
WHY...?
WHAT ARE THEY DOING...?
!
VRRR